CANADIAN COUNSELLING AND COUNSELLING PSYCHOLOGY IN THE 21ST CENTURY

Canadian Counselling and Counselling Psychology in the 21st Century

Edited by

ADA L. SINACORE AND FREDA GINSBERG

McGill-Queen's University Press

Montreal & Kingston • London • Ithaca

ISBN 978-0-7735-4456-7 (cloth)
ISBN 978-0-7735-4457-4 (paper)
ISBN 978-0-7735-9691-7 (ePDF)
ISBN 978-0-7735-9692-4 (ePUB)

Legal deposit first quarter 2015
Bibliothèque nationale du Québec

Printed in Canada on acid-free paper that is 100% ancient forest free
(100% post-consumer recycled), processed chlorine free

McGill-Queen's University Press acknowledges the support of the
Canada Council for the Arts for our publishing program. We also
acknowledge the financial support of the Government of Canada
through the Canada Book Fund for our publishing activities.

Library and Archives Canada Cataloguing in Publication

Canadian counselling and counselling psychology in the
21st century/edited by Ada L. Sinacore and Freda Ginsberg.

Includes bibliographical references and index.
Issued in print and electronic formats.
ISBN 978-0-7735-4456-7 (bound). – ISBN 978-0-7735-4457-4 (pbk.). –
ISBN 978-0-7735-9691-7 (ePDF). – ISBN 978-0-7735-9692-4 (ePUB)

1. Counseling – Canada. 2. Counseling psychology – Canada.
I. Sinacore, Ada L., author, editor II. Ginsberg, Freda, author, editor

BF636.6.C35 2015   158.30971   C 2014-906234-6
                                             C 2014-906235-4

This book was typeset by Interscript in 10.5/13 Sabon.

Contents

Handwritten annotations:
GCAP 633 lesson 1
GCAP 633 lesson 6
GCAP 633 Lesson 4
p.122 list of notable researchers
p. 130 generation immigrant def.

BCAP 633
lesson 12

We dedicate this book to the foremothers and forefathers
of Canadian counselling psychology, whose leadership,
dedication, and vision made this book possible.

Foreword

This foreword comes from two long-time counselling psychologists, Vivian Lalande and George Hurley, who have followed somewhat different paths in Canadian counselling psychology that now interface yet again as we write this joint foreword. George has served primarily in a training, service, and administrative capacity while Vivian has served primarily within a teaching, research, and practice capacity. Both of us, however, have been involved in Canadian counselling psychology from the point of witnessing the incubation, birth, and growth of our specialty area to its current youthful and increasingly robust status. Like proud parents, each of us has stories to tell about this grand enterprise called Canadian counselling psychology, and each of us can now reflect on those who carry our specialty area forward so ably as exemplified within the bounds of this text.

George came to the scene in the very early 80s when the Counselling Psychology Section of the CPA was only a glint in the eyes of a few dreamers. A young whippersnapper then, he noticed in filling out his annual CPA dues statement that there was no Section on counselling psychology. After he remarked on this briefly to his colleague Mark Schoenberg, Mark was on the phone not ten minutes later calling the then–CPA president, asking how many CPA members we needed to form a new section. Back then five was the magic number. As we reached out to colleagues across the country, we found very quickly that many were eager to sign the petition and launch this new enterprise. With some adroit planning and legwork we were able to launch a new CPA Section on Counselling Psychology in 1986. Through further work with the CPA accreditation committee, and some sometimes tough negotiating, we were able to get counselling psychology deemed an accredited CPA specialty.

Those early days were heady and fruitful and the Section quickly prospered in terms of membership from across the country, thanks in part to the Section volunteers who gladly undertook the tasks to create the Section bylaws and develop a Section newsletter. Many committed counselling psychologists from across Canada put their shoulders to the wheel in those early days to create a home for counselling psychology in the Canadian Psychological Association.

However, much remained to be done after the baby was birthed, named, and walking. As late as 2004, Vivian notes, a real surprise arose when she was asked to write an article that described the then-current status of counselling psychology in Canada. This article was to be for a special issue about the profession of counselling psychology in Western countries, and Vivian agreed, thinking it would be an easy task. Surely, Vivian thought, it would be a relatively simple matter to define and provide an overview of the history and current status of the counselling psychology profession in our Canadian culture. After all, she mused, she had practiced counselling psychology for over thirty years, taught at the University of Calgary, held leadership positions in both the C PA and the C C PA, served as editor of the *Canadian Journal of Counselling*, and was familiar with most of the current research and writing produced by Canadian experts in the field. Certainly this task should be straightforward. As the story goes, for the most part, the article came together by her reviewing the published literature on this subject, hearing the stories of people who had been involved in the profession for many years, and reading archived documents, such as newsletters and Annual General Meeting minutes from the Canadian Psychological Association Section of Counselling Psychology. However, it surprised Vivian that she could not find a formal Canadian definition of counselling psychology anywhere.

What Vivian recalls as most interesting was that she was not alone in this struggle to define and characterize counselling psychology in the context of her culture. The other authors in this special issue from various countries had difficulty differentiating their profession from other psychology professions and explicating how their area was unique from other cultures (Pelling, 2004). The reactions from readers of her article were also interesting but not so surprising. During the Canadian Psychological Association conventions following the article's publication, Vivian heard from students, academics, and other professionals who agreed that we indeed wanted and needed a formal definition of our Canadian specialty area. Although many had a solid understanding of what makes counselling psychology in Canada unique, it had not been fully captured at any one point in time. Students in particular spoke about an ongoing curiosity about how the profession differed from other psychology professions, and a frustration that this had not succinctly been provided. It was exciting to see this renewed interest in counselling psychology, followed by the adoption of an official definition and, now, the publication of this text.

Although Ada Sinacore, co-editor of this text, provided in 2011 a detailed history of the work leading to the publication of this book, what is less obvious are the initiative and collaborative processes undertaken over nine years contributing to the many other signature accomplishments along the way. Many individuals again donated hours to committee work, writing, talking, and thinking. Collaboration and input were a top priority, utilizing newsletters, symposia, meetings, and consultation, all of which were time-consuming but essential to ensure that the product represented a consensual perspective. Culminating all of this thoughtful work was the successful Inaugural Canadian Counselling Psychology Conference that was organized by Ada Sinacore and Freda Ginsberg (Sinacore, 2011b), and then this text.

How important is this milestone book? As co-editors of this text, Ada and Freda have brought together a detailed profile of Canadian Counselling Psychology reflecting the work of many individuals working together for many years. It provides us with a better understanding of one of our cultural identities: as a member of the counselling psychology culture in Canada. Vivian reports that she used to joke with colleagues that she could distinguish counselling psychologists from other psychological professionals because of the smile lines on their faces and their openness in social interactions. She knew we were different but was not able to elaborate clearly the uniqueness of this culture. In chapter 3, by Nancy Arthur and Sandra Collins, culture is defined as "shared clusters of worldview, beliefs and values; rituals, practices, customs, or norms; social, religious, or spiritual traditions; language, history, ties to geographic locations; and/or adherence to social, economic, or political structures." This book reminds us of the values, beliefs, and worldviews of counselling psychologists and our common knowledge base, research, and counselling practices. The chapters elaborate how this culture has evolved to be uniquely Canadian, along with some of the socio-political challenges counselling psychologists have encountered while establishing themselves as a distinct entity in the Canadian Psychological Association and as part of the valued health professions nationally and internationally. The book elaborates for us an understanding of this culture beyond the smiles and openness of its members. More importantly, others will be able to better understand their identity as members of the culture of Canadian counselling psychology.

Of course this book provides more than a description of the Canadian counselling culture; it attempts and achieves a snapshot of the current status of the various components of the profession. This is invaluable to students, researchers, practitioners, and others interested in our area. Our recommendation: read, enjoy, and be enlightened by this text as our field moves forward into the twenty-first century. Canadian counselling psychology and counselling are alive and well.

Vivian Lalande and George Hurley

ACKNOWLEDGMENT

This book was funded in part by the Social Sciences and Humanities Research Council.

CANADIAN COUNSELLING AND COUNSELLING
PSYCHOLOGY IN THE 21ST CENTURY

Introduction to Canadian Counselling and Counselling Psychology in the 21st Century

ADA L. SINACORE

The disciplines of counselling and counselling psychology share common roots in educational psychology and a common set of principles (Hurley, 2010). Yet, counselling psychology differs from the discipline of counselling when it comes to professional identity. That is, counselling psychologists' primary identity is within the field of psychology while professional counselling has its roots in counsellor education. Counsellor training programs typically train master's-level practitioners whose primary professional affiliation is with the Canadian Counselling and Psychotherapy Association (CCPA). These programs oftentimes embrace a scholar-practitioner training model whereby master's-level trainees become consumers of research rather than researchers themselves. Alternatively, counselling psychology programs are geared towards training doctoral-level psychologists whose professional affiliation is with the Section on Counselling Psychology of the Canadian Psychological Association (CPA) (Hurley, 2010; Robertson, 2012). As well, counselling psychology programs, which, if accredited, receive this status from the Canadian Psychological Association, typically embrace a scientist-practitioner training model, and have a strong orientation toward developing both researchers and clinicians.

Given the similarities and differences between these two disciplines and the limited number of counselling psychology doctoral programs in Canada, it is not unusual for individuals trained in counselling psychology doctoral programs to become professors in master's-level counselling programs. That is, the entry-level degree needed for teaching at a university is a doctorate. As such, given counselling programs' orientation toward training master's-level prac-titioners, these programs oftentimes hire doctoral-level counselling psychologists due to their historical common values. As a result, there is a great deal of overlap in the professional orientation of coun-sellors and counselling psychologists, with some counselling psy-chologists having a dual identity as both counsellors and counselling psychologists (Robertson, 2012). Further, these identity overlaps result in difficulty distinguishing between the scholarship and research being produced by counsellors versus that of counselling psycholo-gists. Scholars from both disciplines publish in the same journals, participate in similar professional activities, and share a common set of professional values. That is, both disciplines have a wellness and strength-based orientation to clinical practice, focus on prevention, emphasize the importance of career development, highlight multicul-turalism and social justice, and embrace both qualitative and quanti-tative research methods. Given the relationship between these two disciplines, it is difficult to distinguish between the scholarship pro-duced by counsellors and that produced by counselling psychologists. Additionally, training programs in both disciplines use scholarship and research conducted by professors teaching in both counselling and counselling psychology programs. As such, in this book every effort has been made to include the works of both Canadian coun-selling and counselling psychology scholars.

However, a number of scholars have been concerned that the over-laps in these two disciplines may lead to confusion regarding the distinctions between counsellors and counselling psychologists. Spe-cifically, there are important distinctions between psychologists and counsellors when it comes to licensure, mental health service deliv-ery, and the environments in which they work. As such, the orien-tation of this book is one of inclusion of the literature of both counsellors and counselling psychologists due to the aforementioned disciplinary similarities; yet, the impetus for this book emerged out of the historic and current events within the discipline of counselling psychology, and therefore, a brief history of that discipline is high-lighted below.

To begin, in less than three decades, Canadian counselling psy-chology has grown from a grassroots initiative of a few dedicated individuals to the Canadian Psychological Association's (CPA) Section for Counselling Psychology (Hurley, 2010). Over the course of that time, a number of important articles and book chapters (e.g. Beatch et al., 2009; Bedi et al., 2011; Lalande, 2004) have been written documenting the history of Canadian counselling psychology. Most recently, Young and Lalande (2011) highlighted the "defining moments" (p. 248) that have resulted in the ongoing growth and development of the discipline. These seminal moments include: (a) the formation of the Section on Counselling Psychology (SCP) in the Canadian Psychological Association (CPA); (b) the initial accreditation of counselling psychology doctoral training programs and the subsequent revision of the accreditation criteria to be inclusive of the values of counselling psychology; (c) the development and approval of an official definition of counselling psychology; and (d) the Inaugural Canadian Counselling Psychology Conference (ICCPC). Each of these historic moments will be described briefly below, followed by a discussion of the significant outcomes resulting from these events.

First, the seeds for the development of the Section for Counselling Psychology (SCP) were sown in informal discussions held at Memorial University in Newfoundland. These discussions led to the crafting of a petition, and subsequently the securing of forty-six signatures requesting the development of a new section representing counselling psychology in the CPA. In 1986, the CPA approved this request, and the following year, at the CPA Annual Convention, the SCP held its first business meeting, which was attended by twenty-seven individuals. At that meeting, the topics discussed included: naming the section, selecting officers, training students, research, and whether or not to develop a newsletter. From these humble beginnings, the SCP grew from a membership of twenty-seven in 1987, to eighty-eight in 1988 (Hurley, 2010), to three hundred and eighty-three in 2013. Furthermore, that early group of dedicated volunteers launched the first SCP newsletter (*The Matrix*), appointed a student affiliate, formed committees, developed bylaws, reviewed conference programs, and nominated SCP officers. As well, these volunteers started an initiative to address the accreditation procedures for counselling psychology doctoral training programs (Young and Lalande, 2011). This initiative to develop accreditation procedures culminated in 1989, only three short years after the inception of the SCP.

Next, the leadership of the SCP made a request to the CPA to institute an accreditation process for doctoral counselling training programs and internships in Canada (Lalande, 2004). In order to

have this request granted, the s c p was asked to adopt the accreditation criteria and procedures of the Section on Clinical Psychology
(Young and Lalande, 2011). Although these two areas of specialization (counselling and clinical) have common accreditation standards, it was expected that qualified faculty providing the training
within each specialization would ensure that each discipline's unique
features would be highlighted (Beatch et al., 2009). Hence, one strategy that s c p leadership utilized to protect the professional identity
of counselling psychology was to participate in the c p a accreditation processes for professional psychology training programs and
internships, in hopes that counselling psychology professors would
ensure that counselling psychology values were instilled in these
accredited training programs. However, the generalist nature of
accreditation criteria continued to challenge the eventuality of
Canadian counselling psychology values being embedded in those
few accredited counselling psychology doctoral training programs
(Sinacore, 2011a).

To remedy this problem, in 2006 the leadership of the s c p struck
an ad-hoc committee to provide feedback to the c p a with regard to
proposed revisions to the *Accreditation Standards and Procedures
for Doctoral Programs and Internships in Professional Psychology*.
At that time, the members of the s c p executive were concerned that
the existing criteria did not reflect the values, practice, training,
research, and philosophy of counselling psychology, and rather
favoured a more clinical psychology orientation. To be as transpar-
ent as possible, the ad-hoc committee consulted with both the s c p
executive and membership regarding potential revisions. Following
these consultations, proposed changes to the accreditation standards
were then sent to the c p a Committee on Accreditation in 2010. This
feedback compiled by the s c p Ad Hoc Committee on Accreditation
was well received, and though common accreditation criteria remain
in place for clinical, counselling, and school psychology programs,
the 2011 revision of the *Accreditation Standards and Procedures
for Doctoral Programs and Internships in Professional Psychology*
currently reflects the issues and values of Canadian counselling psychology. According to Young and Lalande (2011), these accreditation
standards revisions serve as a significant accomplishment, as they
align the current definition of counselling psychology with the standards of high-quality doctoral training programs in Canada, and, in

so doing, distinguish counselling psychology as a unique discipline in Canada.

In addition to the creation and development of the S C P and the subsequent accreditation of counselling psychology doctoral programs, the creation of the official *Definition of Counselling Psychology* was an important stepping-stone for the discipline. At the forefront of this work was the chair of the S C P, who posited that while a number of definitions of counselling psychology existed, each was specific to the setting in which it was conceived and applied (e.g. educational programs, provincial associations) (Lalande, 2004). Lalande further highlighted that there was no common definition of counselling psychology endorsed by either the C P A or the S C P. As a result, counselling psychologists were implored to commemorate the unique nature of Canadian counselling psychology with an official definition. Beatch et al. (2009) "highlighted the need for a common definition by outlining the reasons for this need as including: (a) reducing the confusion of counselling psychology with other similar professional areas, such as clinical psychology; (b) guiding the information given to clients, before they give consent for counselling; (c) informing the training programs and ultimately the competencies of counselling psychologists; (d) clarifying the limits of practice; and (e) reducing the risk of having other professions erode the professional scope of practice of counselling psychology" (cited in Young and Lalande, 2004, p. 249).

Thus, in January 2007, a committee was struck to develop an official Canadian definition of counselling psychology. This committee was composed of seven volunteers from a cross-section of geographic locations in Canada who worked in a variety of counselling psychology occupations, including practitioners in private practice and public agencies, counsellor educators, and researchers. To achieve its mandate, the committee embarked on a three-year consultation process, conducted extensive literature reviews, and reviewed the documents of local counselling psychology associations and counsellor training programs. In the end, the committee identified positive psychology and the promotion of diversity as key components of the counselling psychology identity. Ultimately, the work of this committee culminated in the development of a Canadian definition of counselling psychology. The S C P finally adopted this definition at their Annual Business Meeting held at the C P A Annual Convention in 2009. That same year, the CPA adopted the definition that reads as follows:

> Counselling psychology is a broad specialization within professional psychology concerned with using psychological principles to enhance and promote the positive growth, well being, and mental health of individuals, families, groups, and the broader community. Counselling psychologists bring a collaborative, developmental, multicultural, and wellness perspective to their research and practice. They work with many types of individuals, including those experiencing distress and difficulties associated with life events and transitions, decision-making, work/career/ education, family and social relationships, and mental health and physical health concerns. In addition to remediation, counselling psychologists engage in prevention, psychoeducation and advocacy. The research and professional domains of counselling psychology overlap with the domains of other professional areas such as clinical psychology, industrial/organizational psychology, and mental health counselling. Counselling psychology adheres to an integrated set of core values: (a) counselling psychologists view individuals as agents of their own change and regard an individual's pre-existing strengths and resourcefulness and the therapeutic relationship as central mechanisms of change; (b) the counselling psychology approach to assessment, diagnosis, and case conceptualization is holistic and client-centered; and it directs attention to social context and culture when considering internal factors, individual differences, and familial/systemic influences; and (c) the counselling process is pursued with sensitivity to diverse sociocultural factors unique to each individual. Counselling psychologists practice in diverse settings and employ a variety of evidence based and theoretical approaches grounded in psychological knowledge. In public agencies, independent practices, schools, universities, health care settings, and corporations, counselling psychologists work in collaboration with individuals to ameliorate distress, facilitate well being, and maximize effective life functioning.

Research and practice are viewed as mutually informative and counselling psychologists conduct research in a wide range of areas, including those of the counselling relationship and other psychotherapeutic processes, the multicultural dimensions of psychology, and the roles of work and mental health in optimal functioning. Canadian counselling psychologists are especially concerned with culturally appropriate methods suitable for investigating both emic and etic perspectives on human behaviour, and promote the use of research methods drawn from diverse epistemological perspectives, including innovative developments in qualitative and quantitative research. (Canadian Psychological Association, 2009b)

Young and Lalande (2011), as well as many others in the discipline, believe that this definition, along with the accompanying committee report (Beatch et al., 2009), signifies a great accomplishment for the discipline of Canadian counselling psychology.

Subsequently in 2011, the members of the definition committee published an article in *Canadian Psychology* based on their important work, entitled "Counselling psychology in a Canadian context: Definition and description" (Bedi et al., 2011). Publishing this article in the leading psychology journal in Canada served to both broadly recognize this new definition and educate the field of professional psychology about the often misunderstood discipline of Canadian counselling psychology (Haverkamp, Robertson, Cairns, & Bedi, 2011). Ultimately, as suggested by Young and Lalande (2011), the publication of the definition of Canadian counselling psychology "provide[s] a basis from which counselling psychology could influence social initiatives such as policies on mental health in Canada and international initiatives in health and education" (p. 3).

Next, in November 2010, with the accreditation process and official definition in place, to commemorate the current state of the discipline and encourage a pan-Canadian dialogue, the Inaugural Canadian Counselling Psychology Conference (ICCPC) was held in Montreal. This conference gathered the leading counselling psychologists, counselling professionals, and students from across Canada, and aimed to document the history of Canadian counselling psychology, identify the current state of the discipline, and conceptualize future directions for growth. Thus, for the first time in the history of Canadian counselling psychology, the ICCPC catalyzed a national discussion between counsellors and counselling psychologists with regard to the discipline of counselling psychology in Canada, its identity, and its future. Additionally, this conference was the first time that counsellors and counselling psychologists formally met separately from the annual C P A and C C P A conferences. Specifically, the I C C P C had student poster presentations, symposia, and focused discussion sessions to consider topics emerging directly from the official definition of Canadian counselling psychology, namely: (a) professional issues and identity; (b) research and scientific issues; (c) career development; (d) multicultural counselling, social justice, and advocacy; (e) counselling, training, and supervision; and (f) health, wellness, and prevention. The focus on these topics allowed conference attendees to review the current state of affairs in the discipline, identify issues and challenges, and discuss implications for future development. Ultimately, the conference opened a dialogue between counsellors and counselling psychologists, strengthened their professional collaborations, and collectively advanced innovative thinking regarding the training, research, and clinical practice of counselling and counselling psychology.

However, this conference not only served to further the dialogue between counsellors and counselling psychologists, it also led to concrete outcomes, one of which was the establishment of an S C P archive. Specifically, after the I C C P C, an S C P Archive Committee was established to compile and document the history and current activities of the S C P. In particular, the goal of creating an S C P archive was both to preserve the historical records of the S C P and to put a system in place for the ongoing preservation of S C P initiatives. These archival materials are now organized, digitized, highlighted with summary documents, and stored on the S C P website for public viewing. Ideally, this archive will serve as an accessible resource for current and future counselling psychologists to become educated about the unique history, development, and achievements of the discipline of counselling psychology in Canada.

A second by-product of the I C C P C emerged from a conference discussion about how the dearth of peer-reviewed Canadian publication outlets specifically dedicated to counsellors and counselling psychologists results in these scholars publishing in the United States or internationally, rendering the work and profiles of Canadian counsellors and counselling psychology scholars invisible. To address this concern, at the conclusion of the conference, the editor of *Canadian Psychology* was approached about devoting part, or a complete issue, of the journal to the discipline of counselling psychology. As a result, for first time in the history of Canadian counselling psychology, *Canadian Psychology* featured a Special Section on Canadian

Counselling Psychology published in November 2011. The articles published in this Special Section highlighted scholarship authored by Canadian counsellors and counselling psychologists and mapped out the history and current state of the discipline of counselling psychology. All articles paid particular attention to the ways in which the unique Canadian context shaped the literature that was reviewed. The topics covered in the Special Section mirrored the themes of the ICCPC, including: history and future directions; professional identity and issues; training and supervision; research and scientific issues; and Canadian counselling psychologists' contributions to applied psychology in the areas of career development, health, wellness, and prevention, and multiculturalism and social justice. Not only did this Special Section further identify the journal of *Canadian Psychology* as a viable outlet for the work of counselling psychologists, it also consolidated, and thereby educated the broader psychological community about, the research and scholarship being produced by Canadian counsellors and counselling psychologists.

Finally, a major outcome following the ICCPC is this book, which, to date, is the first comprehensive compilation and synthesis of Canadian counselling and counselling psychology scholarship, which is often ignored in mainstream psychology literature. As such, this book offers a much-needed and near-exhaustive summative overview of the current state of training, research, and clinical practice in the disciplines of counselling and counselling psychology in Canada, and is designed to lay the path for future development.

To ensure representativeness, all the chapters are co-authored, by scholars who hail from a range of institutions across Canada. To guarantee a high level of quality, those authors who were invited by the co-editors to write chapters were either experts or emerging experts in their field, with some chapters having advanced doctoral students contributing as well. More specifically, chapter authors were given explicit instructions to guide their writing to guarantee that the book reads as a seamless whole and covers the wide array of scholarship being produced by both French and English counsellors and counselling psychologists in Canada. As for the nature of the instructions given to chapter authors, all were asked to: (a) provide a comprehensive review of the relevant Canadian counselling and counselling psychology literature, capturing both well-seasoned researchers' work and that of less known authors; (b) focus primarily on works authored by Canadian counsellors and counselling psychologists, regardless of where this work has been published, and to the greatest extent possible, capture the works written by Francophone counsellors and counselling psychologists; (c) refer to works authored by non-Canadians only if they are foundational to the discussion; (d) utilize a contextual framework that attends to diversity in all its forms, as well as the societal factors and broader issues at play; (e) where appropriate employ a lifespan perspective in the literature review and the discussion of processes by which individuals, families, and communities respond and adapt to challenges they face across the different stages of their development; (f) highlight counselling and counselling psychology's emphasis on strength, resilience, and resourcefulness, as well as prevention and psycho-education; (g) attend to and provide a balanced presentation regarding the diversity of methodological frameworks used by counsellors and counselling psychologists; (h) summarize the strengths and challenges faced by counselling and counselling psychology researchers and educators in their efforts to contribute to the larger field of applied mental health service provision in Canada; and (i) offer an analysis of the strengths, challenges, and future directions for the area under consideration. In the end, this book comprises eleven chapters (including this introduction) that highlight the state-of-the-art in Canadian counselling and counselling psychology. A brief overview of each of the chapters will be provided below.

To begin, the two chapters following this introduction provide a basis for much of the discussion that follows; the first addresses research and scientific issues and the second multicultural counselling. In the research chapter, the authors provide a comprehensive discussion of the current state of research, including methods and dissemination. Next, the multicultural counselling chapter provides a critical analysis of the ways that culture has been defined and informs counselling and counselling psychology; as such, the authors suggest that a conceptualization of multiple cultural identities and culture fluidity across life roles and contexts be considered when applying a multicultural framework. Building upon the discourses framed in the research and multiculturalism chapters, the next three chapters present scholarship relevant to specific populations, including Indigenous peoples of Canada, sexual minorities, and immigrants. In each of these chapters the authors address the historic and socio-political realities of these populations, as well as the resulting mental health issues emanating from these challenges. For example, the chapter on Indigenous people focuses on the definition and practice of Indigenous mental health and healing, and discusses how these practices differ from dominant approaches to counselling and psychotherapy. In a similar vein, the chapter on lesbian, gay, bisexual, transgender, and intersexed populations (L G B T I) elucidates the current concerns and needs of sexual minorities, with a particular emphasis on the myriad of socio-cultural and socio-political challenges that this population and their families are confronted with as a result of living in a heterosexist society. Likewise, the chapter on immigration offers an analysis of Canadian immigration processes, policies, and procedures, as well as the resulting challenges faced by individuals and families who migrate to Canada. These authors provide a comprehensive discussion of the educational, occupational, and familial factors that influence the cultural transitioning of immigrants, as well as the ensuing discrimination that results from being an outsider in Canadian society.

Moving forward, the next four chapters illuminate the overarching areas of scholarship central to the identity of counselling and counselling psychology, namely health, wellness, and prevention, career psychology, and assessment. Accordingly, the chapter on health, wellness, and prevention explores the importance of mental health in the Canadian public health care agenda. In this light, the authors identify significant contributions made by Canadian counselling and counselling psychology scholars to the understanding of those mental health issues identified as high priority by the Mental Health Commission of Canada. Next, the career chapter offers an overview of the changing nature of work and an examination of the broader global and societal forces currently influencing career development and psychology. Similar to previous chapters, these authors offer an analysis of how multiculturalism and social justice relate to Canadian career psychology. Likewise, the authors of the assessment chapter posit that the values of holism and social justice are intrinsic to counselling and counselling psychology in Canada, resulting in a strong emphasis on contextual sensitivity in assessment. These authors therefore provide an analysis of contextual assessment paradigms and their application to the social and cultural diversity in Canadian society. Supplementary to the preceding chapters, the next chapter examines current issues in training and supervision in a Canadian context. As such, the authors identify student funding, gatekeeping, and the movement towards evidence-based practice as key issues in the training of future counsellors and counselling psychologists.

Finally, the book concludes with a consideration of a social justice agenda relevant to the future development of the disciplines of counselling and counselling psychology in Canada. These chapter authors suggest that the current political climate in Canada is ripe for mental health practitioners to engage in social justice work in all areas of the discipline, including research, teaching, and clinical practice. Specifically, these authors advocate that the practice of social justice become more than a theoretical ideal, and implore counsellors and counselling psychologists to become agents of social change at all levels of society, with the ultimate result of better mental health outcomes for all citizens.

2

The Present and Future of Counselling and Counselling Psychology Research in Canada: A Call to Action

JOSÉ F. DOMENE, MARLA J. BUCHANAN,
BRYAN HIEBERT, AND ERIN BUHR

The first decade of the twenty-first century has been a period of expansion and maturation for the related but distinct disciplines of counselling and counselling psychology in Canada. This is evident in refinements to professional identity, broader legislative recognition, increased availability of Canadian training and education programs, and growing membership in discipline-specific professional associations such as the Canadian Counselling and Psychotherapy Association (CCPA) and the Counselling Psychology Section of the Canadian Psychological Association (CPA) (Alves & Gazzola, 2011; Bedi et al., 2011; Domene & Bedi, 2012; Lalande, 2004). Commensurate with the advancement of the two disciplines has been a growth in counselling-related research conducted by scholars and practitioners in Canada, and published in a wide range of Canadian and international venues (Hiebert, Domene, & Buchanan, 2011). In this chapter, we examine the landscape of counselling and counselling psychology research in Canada. In addition to drawing on the small but informative body of existing literature on Canadian counselling and counselling psychology, our conclusions have been supplemented by a survey we conducted in 2011 about research practices in Canada. (A brief description of the survey procedures and respondents can be found in the Appendix section of this chapter).

The central argument underlying our review of counselling and counselling psychology research in Canada is that, to fully realize our distinct identity as presented in the literature (e.g., Bedi et al., 2011; Domene & Bedi, 2012), we need to continue to change and improve our research practices and training; although we have already made strides in creating ways of generating knowledge specific to Canadian counselling and counselling psychology, there is much more to be done. In the first half of this chapter, we lay the groundwork for this argument by describing the current state of Canadian counselling and counselling psychology research, discussing the focus of research, methods used in conducting research, research dissemination practices, and the research-related training provided in our disciplines. We then elaborate on our argument by identifying several strengths, challenges, and key directions for the future of counselling and counselling psychology research in Canada. Finally, we conclude with a call to action, an appeal for researchers and practitioners alike to make the changes necessary for our research practices and training to more fully reflect the visions presented in recent definitions of our disciplines.

FOCUS OF RESEARCH

The content of the various chapters in this volume reveals the breadth of topics in which Canadian counselling and counselling psychology scholars conduct research. Although the focus of research in our disciplines is very broad, and varies widely from one scholar to another (Buhr & Domene, 2012), there are some areas of research in which we have made a substantial contribution to the field at a global level. Specifically, in her seminal review of the disciplines as they exist in the Canadian context, Lalande (2004) identifies three areas of particular expertise for Canadian counselling and counselling psychology research: diversity and multicultural issues, career development / career counselling, and research and evaluation methodology (particularly qualitative research methods).

However, these foci may be only the tip of the iceberg, with the respondents from our survey identifying a vast array of topics in which they conducted research in the past five years. In order, the most frequently endorsed research foci were in the fields of health and health counselling, counselling process research, career counselling and development, stress and related psychological disorders, and qualitative research methods. These areas are addressed in depth in other chapters in this book. Other emergent categories of expertise included: assessment in counselling, ethics, family therapy, grief and loss, hope, immigration, inter-professional practice, professional issues, postmodern psychotherapies, school counselling, stigma in mental health, and the study of the self. Even from only the thirty-nine counsellors and counselling psychologists who responded to our survey, it is evident that Canadian scholars conduct research in a wide range of areas, representing the full breadth of what Bedi et al. (2011) and Domene and Bedi (2012) have described as being within the scope of our disciplines. Although we acknowledge that Canadian researchers are also contributing substantially to knowledge in areas such as health, counselling process research, and stress and related disorders, space limitations require us to elaborate only on the key areas of strength identified by Lalande.

Diversity and Multicultural Issues

One of the defining characteristics of counselling and counselling psychology research in Canada is openness to diversity and multicultural issues in both training and practice (Bedi et al., 2011; Bedi, Klubben, & Barker, 2012; Domene & Bedi, 2012). This defining feature of the disciplines naturally leads to counselling and counselling psychology researchers making substantial contributions at an international level to the literature on multicultural and diversity issues in counselling and psychology (Sinacore et al., 2011; Young & Nichol, 2007). Specifically, Canadian counselling and counselling psychology researchers have contributed to knowledge on (a) attending to culture in counselling (e.g., Collins & Arthur, 2010; Grant, Henly, & Kean, 2001; James & Foster, 2003; Moodley, 2007a; Peavy & Li, 2003; Young, Marshall, & Valach, 2007); (b) models of counselling that originate from outside of Europe / North America (e.g., Grégoire, Baron, & Baron, 2012; Ishiyama, 2003); (c) experiences and counselling needs of immigrants, international students, and Canadians from specific religious and cultural backgrounds (e.g., Cardu & Sanschagrin, 2005; Popadiuk, 2009; Sandhu, 2005; Sinacore, Mikhail, Kassan, & Lerner, 2009; Yohani & Larsen, 2009); and (d) conducting research and counsellor education in culturally appropriate ways (e.g., Chen, 2004; Merali, 2008a; Moodley, 2012; Morrisette, 2003; Stewart, 2011). We have also expanded knowledge on counsellor education and counselling practices for other minority status individuals, including gay, lesbian, bisexual, and transgender populations (e.g., Alderson, 2000, 2004a; Schneider, Brown, & Glassgold, 2002), and people who have a disability (e.g., Iaquinta, Amundson, & Borgen, 2012; Tews & Merali, 2008; Weiss, Lunsky, & Morin, 2010).

Another prominent manifestation of Canadian counselling and counselling psychology researchers' focus on diversity and multicultural issues is the subject of counselling First Nations, Métis, and Inuit clients. In addition to general discussions of issues related to counselling Aboriginal clients (e.g., Nuttgens & Campbell, 2010), this body of scholarship includes exploration of topics such as (a) the incorporation of Aboriginal knowledge and healing practices into counselling (e.g., Heilbron & Guttman, 2000; Oulanova & Moodley, 2010; Wihak & Merali, 2003); (b) the development and evaluation of distinctly Aboriginal models of counselling (e.g., McCormick, 1997; Stewart, 2008; Poonwassie & Charter, 2001); and (c) adapting European / North American counselling approaches for Aboriginal clients (e.g., Löwenborg, 2001; Malone, 2000; Miller et al., 2011; Shepard, O'Neill, & Guenette, 2006). Indeed, Domene and Bedi (2012) have reported that there are more articles in the *Canadian Journal of Counselling and Psychotherapy* related to counselling with Aboriginal Canadian clients than any other ethnic minority group. They further contend that although the body of research is limited, it suggests that incorporating traditional healing practices may be beneficial for Aboriginal clients. However, this research is not without controversy, with some authors arguing for the benefits of adapting standard counselling approaches for Aboriginal clients (e.g., Shepard et al., 2006) while others claim that it is necessary to counsel Aboriginal clients with distinctly Aboriginal approaches to practice (e.g., McCormick, 1998; Poonwassie & Charter, 2001).

There are numerous factors to consider in understanding why diversity and multicultural issues are such an important focus of research in Canadian counselling and counselling psychology. One factor is the practice of recruiting participants representing many different groups within Canadian society, rather than relying primarily on undergraduate student participants (Buhr & Domene, 2012). This aspect of diversity was reflected in the analysis of results from our survey, which revealed that the majority of articles published by survey respondents had non-university samples. This emphasis on researching diversity and multicultural issues may also be linked to counsellors' and counselling psychologists' commitment to social justice and assisting marginalized groups (Arthur, Collins, McMahon, & Marshall, 2009; Beer, Spanierman, Greene, & Todd, 2012; Sinacore et al., 2011). Additionally, diversity and multicultural issues have historically been associated with our disciplines (Domene & Bedi, 2012; Lalande, 2004; Young & Nichol, 2007), and have recently been affirmed as important foci by the definition of counselling psychology adopted by the CPA in 2011, which explicitly identifies "the multicultural dimensions of psychology" as an area of research focus (Bedi et al., 2011, p. 130). In light of this, it is possible that our disciplines attract scholars who are aware that there is a particular openness to researching diversity and multicultural issues.

Career Development and Counselling

A second major focus of research, one that has been present since the inception of counselling and counselling psychology in Canada, is career development and career counselling (Bedi et al., 2011; Domene & Bedi, 2012; Lalande, 2004; Sinacore et al., 2011; Young & Nichol, 2007). Indeed, career-related issues are the primary area of research for most scholars working in Francophone counsellor education programs in this country. Canadian researchers have contributed to this area of focus in many ways and stages of life, including (a) career counselling and development in childhood, adolescence, and emerging adulthood (e.g., Bloxom et al., 2008; Borgen & Hiebert, 2006; Goyer, 2007; Larose, Ratelle, Guay, Senécal, & Harvey, 2006; Morgan & Ness, 2003); (b) issues affecting adults in the workforce, including work-life balance issues, unexpected career change, and work transitions (e.g., Butterfield, Borgen, Amundson, & Erlebach, 2010; Chen, 2006b; Lachance, Brassard, & Tétreau, 2005; LeBreton, 2009; Simard & Chênevert, 2010); and (c) factors that are salient for older workers, including the transition to retirement (e.g., Fournier, Gautier, & Zimmermann, 2011; Osborne, 2012). Canadian scholars have also contributed substantially to the literature on career-related counselling and guidance strategies, tools, and approaches (e.g., Bujold & Gingras, 2010; Niles, Amundson, & Neault, 2011; Savard, Michaud, Bilodeau, & Arseneau, 2007; Shepard, 2005; Stewart, 2003) as well as engaging in the broader, international discourse on the nature of career counselling and career development research (e.g., Boivin & Goyer, 2006; Baudouin et al., 2007; Young & Domene, 2012).

The focus on career-related issues within Canadian counselling and counselling psychology research was evident in the results of the survey we conducted in preparation for writing this chapter, in which eight of the thirty-nine respondents described career-related issues as an area of research expertise (and this proportion would likely have been higher if the survey had also been available in French). There are numerous additional indicators of the strength of career development / counselling as an area of research within Canada. For example, Richard Young from the University of British Columbia was recently cited as the most frequently published author of qualitative research in the field of career development internationally, in a content analysis of twenty years of articles in eleven English-language career-related journals (Stead et al., 2012). Similarly, career development and counselling is one of the few areas of scholarship within counselling and counselling psychology that has a purely research-based doctoral program dedicated specifically to it (Laval University's *doctorat en sciences de l'orientation*). Finally, it is one of the few specializations within Canadian counselling and counselling psychology that has a dedicated publication venue, the *Canadian Journal of Career Development*, separate from more generalist counselling and applied psychology journals such as the *Canadian Journal of Counselling and Psychotherapy* or the *Canadian Journal of Behavioural Sciences*.

Research and Evaluation Methodology

Another prominent focus of Canadian counselling and counselling psychology research is studying, critiquing, and creating ways of conducting counselling and psychotherapy research. This was evident even in the limited sample represented in our survey, where six of the twenty-two respondents who completed the items about their published research over the past five years identified publications where the primary focus was on research or evaluation methodology.

Canadian counselling and counselling psychology researchers have advanced knowledge about a wide range of research methodologies and issues in conducting research (Domene & Bedi, 2012). However, the greatest contributions have been to qualitative methods

(Drapeau, 2004; Haverkamp, 2005), and approaches for conducting evaluations of counselling and psychotherapy services (Young & Nichol, 2007; Hiebert et al., 2011). The former is evident in publications describing how research methods such as the action project method (Young, Valach, & Domene, 2005), community-based research (Harris, 2009), the critical incident technique (Butterfield et al., 2009; Leclerc, Bourassa, & Filteau, 2010), focus group research (Leclerc, Bourassa, Picard, & Courcy, 2011), interpersonal process recall (Larsen, Flesaker, & Stege, 2008), and participatory methods (Martin et al., 2009) can be applied to studying counselling-related phenomena. The latter includes publications describing deficits in existing approaches to program evaluation in counselling and counselling psychology (e.g., Lalande & Magnussen, 2007; Ryan & Smith, 2009) and innovative approaches for gathering evidence about the effectiveness and value of counselling practice, including the use of conversational evidence in treatment evaluation (e.g., Strong, Busch, & Couture, 2008), and the comprehensive approach for assessing the effectiveness of career services proposed by the Canadian Research Working Group for Evidence-Based Practice in Career Development (Baudouin et al., 2007; Slomp, Bernes, & Magnusson, 2011).

It is evident from this description of the focus of research in our disciplines that there is a wide range of scholarship related to counselling and counselling psychology being generated in Canada. What is less clear is what proportion of counsellors and counselling psychologists are actively involved in research, and to what degree the existing research is being incorporated into practice. These are important questions to consider when examining the methods being utilized by Canadian counselling and counselling psychology researchers.

METHODS USED IN CONDUCTING RESEARCH

Developing an understanding of the nature of counselling and counselling psychology research in Canada raises the question of methodology. It is important to know not only what we study, but also how we engage in research, and so in this section of our chapter we discuss issues related to methods within the discipline. First we describe the methodological diversity that characterizes counselling and counselling psychology research in Canada, and then we address the issue of whether current approaches to research within our disciplines allow for sufficient incorporation of research into practice.

Methodological Diversity

The Canadian definition of counselling psychology claims that the discipline is concerned with "appropriate methods suitable for investigating both emic and etic perspectives on human behaviour, and promot[ing] the use of research methods drawn from diverse epistemological perspectives" (Bedi et al., 2011, p. 130). Hiebert and colleagues (2011) provide evidence supporting this claim based on a systematic review of three Canadian journals in which counsellors and counselling psychologists publish. Additionally, even a cursory examination of published research in the field as a whole reveals that scholars in our disciplines utilize a vast array of research methodologies, including quantitative strategies such as cluster analysis (Fournier et al., 2009), confirmatory and exploratory factor analysis (e.g., Daniluk, Koert, & Cheung, 2012; Tellides-Jaffee et al., 2012), modelling of change / growth (e.g., Larose et al., 2006), multivariate concept mapping (e.g., Bedi, 2006), structural equation modelling (Dunn, Whelton, & Sharpe, 2012), and various quasi-experimental and clinical trial research designs (e.g., Russell-Mayhew, Arthur, & Ewashen, 2007; Watson, McMullen, Prosser, & Bedard, 2011). Similarly, researchers in our disciplines employ a wide range of qualitative methods. Aside from the methods identified in the previous section, Canadian counselling and counselling psychology researchers also publish research using methods such as arts-based inquiry (Yohani & Larsen, 2009), consensual qualitative research (e.g., Gazzola, De Stefano, Audet, & Theriault, 2011), conversation analysis / comprehensive process analysis (e.g., Strong & Massfeller, 2010), discourse analysis (e.g., Zverina, Stam, & Babins-Wagner, 2011), grounded theory (e.g., Van Vliet, 2008), ethnography (e.g., LeBreton, 2009), interpretive content analysis (e.g., Fournier et al., 2011), narrative inquiry (e.g., Buchanan-Arvay & Keats, 2004), and phenomenology (e.g., Everall & Paulson, 2002). This diversity is further underscored by the results of our survey, in which the thirty-nine respondents identified thirty-two research methods that they had previously used.

This acceptance of a wide range of methods, particularly qualitative approaches (Bedi et al., 2011; Lalande, 2004), stands in marked contrast to the continued dominance of quantitative methods in other branches of psychology in Canada (Rennie, Watson, & Montiero, 2000, 2002). There are numerous factors that appear to contribute to the acceptance and use of qualitative research methods by counselling and counselling psychology researchers. First, the philosophy and worldview that underlie Canadian counselling and counselling psychology are not only open to diversity, but are a particularly good fit for qualitative research methods (Bedi et al., 2011; Young & Nichol, 2007). Second, the location of Canadian training programs within faculties of education, which have historically been more qualitatively oriented than departments of psychology, facilitates the acceptance of qualitative methods (Domene & Bedi, 2012; Lalande, 2004; Rennie et al., 2002). Finally, the growing emphasis on multidisciplinary research by federal funding agencies, such as the Canadian Institutes of Health Research (C I H R), the Natural Sciences and Engineering Research Council of Canada (N S E R C), and the Social Sciences and Humanities Research Council of Canada (S S H R C), has increased counselling and counselling psychology researchers' involvement in interdisciplinary collaborations, including collaborations with disciplines where qualitative and mixed methods are more widely accepted, such as education, nursing, and social work (Arthur et al., 2004; Hiebert et al., 2011).

The evidence supports the claims of previous authors who have described counselling and counselling psychology as disciplines where a wide range of methodologies are utilized in research (Bedi et al., 2011; Domene & Bedi, 2012; Hiebert et al., 2011; Young & Nichol, 2007). However, many of the methods that emerged from our survey and that were listed in the preceding paragraph were originally designed for knowledge generation rather than for providing evidence of the effectiveness or benefits of counselling and psychotherapy practice. Given that our disciplines claim to be evidence-based (Bedi et al., 2011; Domene & Bedi, 2012), the issue of how well our methods allow research to be incorporated into practice must be considered.

Incorporating Research into Practice

Hiebert and Uhlemann (1993) found that for Canadian counsellors and counselling psychologists in practice, one of the most important guiding questions was "Which kinds of interventions work best with which types of clients?" Clearly, a strong research base is needed to address this question, which is one of the foundational reasons for the creation of task forces on evidence-based practice by both the American Psychological Association and the CPA (Dozois, 2011a; Levant, 2005). The work of these task forces has the potential to demonstrate the value of the services provided by counsellors and counselling psychologists, provide assistance to practitioners in selecting the "best" treatment combinations, and provide greater assurance to clients regarding the outcomes they can reasonably expect from the interventions they receive.

Another reason for placing greater emphasis on incorporating research into practice relates to job security. In times of budgetary restraint, it is particularly important for counselling agencies to be able to demonstrate that the money invested in their services is having an impact on the lives of the clients seeking those services (e.g., HRSDC, 2011). Agencies that are not able to provide evidence attesting to the success of their interventions are vulnerable. Paradoxically, many employers actively discourage their clinical staff from doing research because it is time-consuming and does not generate fees. Thus, subversively embedding research and evidence-gathering into clinicians' regular daily practices (Hiebert & Magnusson, in press) is one way to ensure that there are data to support intervention efficacy. Incorporating research into practice is one way of expanding the evidence base supporting the interventions used in an agency, thereby increasing the likelihood of continued funding.

Currently, randomized controlled trials (RCTs) are most often used as the basis for making judgments about the effectiveness of counselling and counselling psychology services. However, there are problems with using RCTs as the sole basis for incorporating research into practice (e.g., Hiebert et al., 2011; Horan, 1980). To begin with, in journal articles reporting the results of RCTs, the intervention is often not described in sufficient detail to permit replication. In these cases, it becomes difficult for practitioners to incorporate research findings into their daily practices. Furthermore, in many research publications, there is little attention paid to intervention compliance by either the experimenters or the participants; that is, few data are provided to indicate how closely an intervention guide was followed by either experimenters or research participants. Thus, for many (perhaps most) studies, the articles become reports of what happens when participants are assigned to a research condition or intervention, and not evidence for the effectiveness of an intervention per se.

For many practitioners, the process of random assignment creates a problem. In clinical settings, clients are virtually never assigned randomly to an intervention condition. Instead, a counsellor or psychologist conducts a detailed assessment of a client's needs and goals, and then the client and practitioner together decide on the intervention plan that is most appropriate for meeting the client's goals. Random assignment creates a disconnect between research and practice because a fundamental requirement when providing psychotherapeutic services is that the service needs to match the needs for which a client is seeking assistance. The determination of which intervention condition a client will receive is a purposeful enterprise, not random, and this disconnect contributes to the reluctance of many practitioners to trust the applicability of an RCT study to clients with whom they are working.

Given these limitations, non-RCT approaches to gathering evidence about effectiveness hold greater potential for demonstrating the probable predictability of treatment outcome. In other words, RCTs are only one approach among many for establishing a causal link between intervention and outcome. For example, in the field of Applied Behaviour Analysis, a treatment withdrawal condition (often referred to as an A-B-A or an A-B-A-B design) is often used to demonstrate cause and effect with a single case (see Sulzer-Azaroff & Mayer, 1991). When this process is replicated in different settings with different clients and different practitioners, it is possible to establish the existence of similar outcome expectations associated with a particular intervention for similar clients, in different settings, working with different practitioners.

Another relevant procedure drawn from Applied Behaviour Analysis is the use of multiple baselines across clients, settings, or time. In this method, a similar intervention process is used, beginning with establishing a baseline and then implementing an intervention. Typically, the start times for clients are different so that the baseline period serves as a no-treatment condition for clients who already have begun the intervention and also controls for time-dependent effects. A causal link between intervention and outcome is established if the pattern of change is similar for all clients, regardless of the time they began the intervention (see Hersen & Barlow, 1976).

To the extent that the purpose of applied research is to increase confidence in the predictability of outcomes resulting from an intervention, perhaps the strongest evidence comes from traditional Chinese medicine. In China, replication utilizing a large number of clients to demonstrate consistent patterns for connecting interventions and outcomes is commonly accepted as sufficient evidence for that intervention. Adopting a similar approach in counselling and counselling psychology practice could be accomplished by having careful recordings of client symptoms, detailed descriptions of intervention procedures, and careful documentation of outcomes. Many people would view such replications as providing evidence of a causal link between intervention and outcome and forming a suitable basis for predicting treatment outcome, especially when they have occurred across several years of practice with multiple clients. These approaches have been in operation for several decades, continue to be used in other disciplines (see Harvey, May, & Kennedy, 2004), and have amassed a consistent track record for being able to demonstrate the effectiveness of interventions (Christ, 2007).

Another promising approach for integrating research and practice is the "local clinical scientist" approach (Hiebert, Domene, & Buchanan, 2011; Stricker & Trierweiler, 1995; Trierweiler & Stricker, 1998; Trierweiler, Stricker, & Peterson, 2010). Local clinical scientists approach their practice in a scientific manner, documenting what they do, recording the corresponding effects on clients, and identifying patterns that link counsellor actions with client outcomes. Each client becomes an $n = 1$ experiment and, over time, sufficient evidence is amassed to permit reasonable predictability around the goal of determining what interventions, with what particular clients, produce what kinds of outcomes. We suggest that in order to more completely integrate research and practice in counselling and counselling psychology, more local research is needed, using local research participants, situated in local settings (see also Hiebert et al., 2011; Manthei, 2006). A local clinical scientist approach will help to address that situation.

We describe these various methodologies to illustrate that there are many ways to demonstrate treatment effectiveness, and many ways to approach the integration of research and practice. We suggest that RCTs are not the only acceptable way of conclusively demonstrating treatment effectiveness: RCTs can contribute to the literature base, but so too can other practice-oriented research methods. There are advantages and problems associated with using each of these procedures. Our purpose in raising this matter is not to convince readers that any specific procedure should be adopted as the "gold standard" for practice-oriented research. Instead, it is to emphasize that there are many acceptable approaches, each with substantial support, and the literature base in counselling and counselling psychology may best be served by examining the issue of effectiveness through multiple lenses.

In summary, any discussion of connecting research more closely with counselling and counselling psychology practice must address two questions: (a) "What constitutes acceptable evidence of client change?" and (b) "What constitutes acceptable research?" On this topic we propose broadening the scope of acceptable evidence in Canadian counselling and counselling psychology research to include informal data, observational data, behaviour checklists, and self-assessments, in addition to standardized assessments. We also argue for the usefulness of qualitative research and mixed methods research, in addition to RCTs. Finally, we propose that individualized indicators of success can increase the relevance of the data for both counsellor and client (Hiebert et al., 2012) in the day-by-day professional work of practitioners.

RESEARCH DISSEMINATION PRACTICES

In addition to knowing what we study and the common methodologies we use, to better develop an understanding of the landscape of Canadian counselling and counselling psychology research, it is important to examine how we disseminate research. There has been limited previous examination of where Canadian researchers choose to publish their research. Gazzola, Smith, King-Andrews, and Kearney (2010) also report that professional texts, including journal articles, are only one of many sources of professional information for practitioners in Canada. There are some indicators that researchers in our disciplines are recognizing this situation and using alternative venues to disseminate their work, including websites designed for the general public (e.g., http://myfertilitychoices.com/), websites designed to provide practitioners with resources (e.g., http://www.crwg-gdrc.ca/crwg/index.php/resources), websites designed to inform students (e.g., http://www.usherbrooke.ca/education/recherche/regroupements/crcdc/), YouTube and other repositories of video-recorded information (e.g., http://www.youtube.com/playlist?list=PL65EB530408A867AB&feature=plcp), and more traditional methods of disseminating knowledge such as public lectures (e.g., Domene, 2011). The tendency of researchers in our disciplines to disseminate knowledge widely and to multiple stakeholders will only increase, given the recent emphasis that has been made by federal agencies such as the CIHR and the SSHRC to fund grant applications that attend fully to knowledge translation and create an impact beyond the research community.

Nonetheless, Canadian counselling and counselling psychology researchers continue to view academic journals as an important source of knowledge dissemination. Hiebert and colleagues (2011) identified three primary Canadian journals for counselling psychology publication, all of which publish material in both French and English: *Canadian Psychology*, the *Canadian Journal of Behavioural Sciences*, and the *Canadian Journal of Counselling and Psychotherapy (CJCP)*. Domene and Bedi (2012) identified four additional Canadian venues in which counsellors and counselling psychologists publish: the *Canadian Journal of Career Development*, the *Canadian Journal of Community Mental Health*, the *Canadian Journal of Psychiatry*, and the *Canadian Journal of Psychoanalysis*. Hiebert and colleagues stated that the CJCP appeared to be the Canadian journal that is the most accepting of counselling psychology research. This argument is partially supported by Buhr and Domene's (2012) systematic review of recent peer-reviewed journal articles published by faculty in counselling and counselling psychology graduate programs in British Columbia. Their analyses revealed that, although only eighteen percent of researchers' articles were published in Canadian venues, seventy-five percent of those articles were published in the CJCP. Additional information about publication practices is provided by the results of the survey conducted for this book chapter, where the eighteen respondents who provided information about their publications identified seventy-two different journals in which they had published over the past five years. If eighteen researchers, all of them Anglophone, choose to publish in that many different journals, how many more publication venues would be represented if it were possible to comprehensively survey the publications of all counselling and counselling psychology researchers in Canada?

In summary, counselling and counselling psychology researchers in Canada are actively involved in disseminating knowledge, and do so using a variety of media and publication venues. The breadth of knowledge dissemination suggests that Canadian research is reaching a wide audience. At the same time, the practice of disseminating knowledge so widely can lead to challenges, which will be discussed in the second half of this chapter.

RESEARCH-RELATED TRAINING

There is a small but substantive body of literature that has commented on the research-related training and development of counsellors and counselling psychologists in Canada. Education programs in our disciplines provide at least some training in research for all students, although the nature of that training can vary widely from program to program, and from student to student within any given program. In terms of what models of research training have been adopted by Canadian education programs, all CPA-accredited doctoral programs in counselling psychology follow a scientist-practitioner, rather than a practitioner-scholar model (Bedi et al., 2011, 2012). It is less clear the degree to which master's-level programs adopt a scientist-practitioner versus a practitioner-scholar model, at least in part because there is substantial variation in the research training provided by different Canadian counsellor education programs (Beatch et al., 2009).

A major contributor to this variability is that some counselling associations and regulatory bodies (e.g., the Ordre des Conseillers et Conseillères d'Orientation du Québec [OCCOQ]) require training in research methods, while others, including the CCPA, do not mandate coursework in research methods as part of their certification procedures. In contrast, coursework in statistics and research methods is a requirement for licensure to practice as a psychologist in Canada. Given this situation, it is possible that master's-level counselling and counselling psychology programs designed to prepare students for doctoral studies tend to retain a scientist-practitioner model, while programs designed to prepare students to enter practice at the master's level may choose to adopt a practitioner-scholar approach. Supporting this possibility are Bedi and colleagues' (2011) claim that research training at the master's level is more focused on critical and integrative consumption of research than on research production, and Alves and Gazzola's (2011) failure to find research as a salient theme in their study of professional identity in a sample of master's-level practitioners. Regardless of whether a training program adopts a scientist-practitioner or practitioner-scholar approach, how well they succeed in preparing students to fully integrate research into practice remains in question: the discussion presented in the "Incorporating Research into Practice" section suggests that there is room for improvement.

In terms of preparing students to be producers of research, Hiebert and colleagues (2011) report that programs offering doctoral degrees in counselling and counselling psychology offer courses in program evaluation, qualitative research, and statistics. Apart from statistics, however, these courses tend to be electives, so there is no guarantee that a student will be exposed to the full range of research methods that are used in our disciplines. Furthermore, results from our survey revealed that across the fourteen counselling and counselling psychology programs represented by the respondents, numerous research methods courses were taught by faculty from other disciplines (e.g., education), which poses a question about how well those courses reflect research practices and research issues that are specific to counselling and/or counselling psychology (e.g., counselling process research; the empirically supported treatment debate).

Instead, the primary mechanism to train students to conduct research in counselling and counselling psychology in Canada appears to be the completion of a master's or doctoral thesis under the supervision of a faculty member. However, what tends to occur in thesis and dissertation work is the development of an in-depth understanding of one or two particular ways of conducting research, rather than the development of equivalent expertise across different research methods. Furthermore, this model of training in research production is highly dependent on the quality of the supervision that is provided, which can vary substantially from supervisor to supervisor. This variability is exacerbated by the fact that many faculty members lack any formal training in research supervision and some feel external pressures that may cloud their judgment on issues related to working together with students on research (Arthur et al., 2004).

In summary, an understanding of research is vital for disciplines that claim to be evidence-based in their practice. Furthermore, research-related training and supervision/mentoring have been found to be conducive to the development of professional identity for at least some individuals in our disciplines (Gazzola et al., 2012). Counsellor and counselling psychologist education programs appear to be meeting the challenge of training students in research by providing various opportunities for them to become reflective consumers and producers of research, through coursework and research supervision.

Despite this, there are indicators that counselling and counselling psychology students will not all receive equivalent research training experiences, through their own choices (e.g., choosing to complete a course-based master's degree) or through the nature of the opportunities offered to them (e.g., advanced research methods courses may only be offered infrequently or may be taught by instructors from other areas of academia). These challenges to the state of research in our disciplines will be addressed more fully in the final portion of this chapter, addressing strengths, challenges, and future directions for Canadian counselling and counselling psychology.

STRENGTHS, CHALLENGES, AND FUTURE DIRECTIONS

Strengths

It should be evident from the preceding discussion that the disciplines of counselling and counselling psychology in Canada have many areas of strength and contribute much to research and practice on a global level. Due to space limitations, only two of our strengths will be elaborated in this section. First, not only is the work of Canadian researchers accepted and published more internationally than in Canadian publication venues, but working in Canadian counselling and counselling psychology programs are numerous world-renowned researchers whose contributions have shaped the field on a global level. To name only a few, these scholars include Jacques Limoges at the Université de Sherbrooke, Roy Moodley at the University of Toronto – Ontario Institute for Studies in Education, Jeff Sugarman of Simon Fraser University, and Richard Young of the University of British Columbia. Jacques Limoges is an internationally recognized expert in factors affecting integration into the workforce and a recipient of the Stu Conger Award for Leadership in Career Development in Canada. Roy Moodley was a driving force behind the recently published edited volume, the *Handbook of Counseling and Psychotherapy in an International Context* (Moodley, Gielen, & Wu, 2012), which summarizes the current state of counselling and psychotherapy in thirty-five countries and regions around the globe, and his Centre for Diversity in Counselling and Psychotherapy has generated numerous international research collaborations on multicultural and diversity-related issues in counselling.

Richard Young is an established leader in career development research, whose contextual action theory of career is routinely cited in career development and counselling textbooks around the world, and who has been acknowledged a world leader in conducting qualitative research on career development (Stead et al., 2012). Jeff Sugarman has contributed in several substantive ways to the advancement of theoretical/philosophical psychology around the world, particularly to conceptualizations of self and human agency. He has been recognized for the excellence of his work by the APA and the American Educational Research Association.

Another clear area of strength is the breadth of research being conducted in Canada. Although previous authors have argued that we are best known for contributions to knowledge in the areas of diversity, career, and qualitative methodology (Lalande, 2004), Canadian researchers generate knowledge across the full scope of counselling and counselling psychology practice, and sometimes make contributions to other fields as well, through interdisciplinary collaborations or by studying phenomena that are multidisciplinary in nature. The breadth of our research is also evident in the approaches that we use to generate knowledge, which span the full range of methods for social inquiry. Finally, this breadth is apparent in where and how we choose to disseminate our knowledge, which goes well beyond publishing in Canadian academic journals. However, the very nature of this strength also creates challenges that need to be recognized.

Challenges

FOCUS OF RESEARCH   One of the challenges that arises from the breadth of subject areas in which Canadian counselling and counselling psychology programs conduct research is that individual researchers may feel more closely connected to and have more in common with colleagues from other disciplines who focus on the same area of research than with other researchers from our own disciplines. For example, a counsellor or counselling psychologist who studies trauma may be more likely to attend interdisciplinary trauma conferences and read research that is published by scholars from clinical psychology, nursing, social work, and psychiatry on the topic of trauma, than to follow the conferences and publications of other counsellors and counselling psychologists whose research focus is career development and career guidance. This lack of connection with other researchers from within our own disciplines is problematic when counselling and counselling psychology are still establishing their identities within Canada. It has also been found to be distressing for at least some students within our programs (Gazzola, 2012). What remains to be seen in the future is whether the disciplines can find some way to address this identity diffusion and lack of connection within our professions without losing the strengths inherent in being disciplines that contribute to knowledge in many different areas of health and development.

METHODS USED IN CONDUCTING RESEARCH   Despite recent evidence suggesting that adopting a scientist-practitioner approach where research and practice are mutually informative is one factor that fosters professional identity in Canadian counselling psychologists (Gazzola et al., 2012), one of the challenges currently facing Canadian research practice pertains to the relative lack of emphasis given by counsellors and counselling psychologists to research-related activities. For example, Hiebert, Uhlemann, and Simpson (1992) and Hiebert and Uhlemann (1993) found that the publication rates of counsellors and counselling psychologists are exceedingly low, with the modal rate being less than one article per year, even amongst those in academia. In disciplines that profess to embrace an evidence-based orientation, it seems that there is a conceptual gap between saying and doing in research (Dozois, 2011b), and that this gap has existed for some time in Canada (Hiebert et al., 1992; Hunsley, 2007). Additionally, researchers in other countries (e.g., Methei, 2006; Sexton & Whiston, 1996) have found that research findings are not widely incorporated into the day-by-day functioning of practitioners, likely because practitioners do not find the experimental methodology to be useful or applicable (Sexton, 1996). Although we are not aware of any similar studies conducted in Canada, we believe that the situation is quite similar, for as Young and Domene (2012) have explained, even to the present day we are struggling with the question of how to reduce the gap between the evidence-based approach that has been an integral part of our disciplines (Baudouin et al., 2006; Young & Nichol, 2007) and the daily work of counselling and counselling psychology practitioners. We frame this challenge as one relating to the methods that are used in conducting research in our disciplines because part of the problem is that researchers in our disciplines have been reluctant to adopt research methodologies that more closely match the way that practice is normally conducted in the field.

From our perspective, continuing allegiance to an evidence-based approach to counselling and counselling psychology practice is important for the legitimacy of our disciplines. However, it is important to avoid setting unnecessarily narrow boundaries around that approach. The concept of evidence-based practice is theoretically neutral and can easily encompass a wide variety of research methodologies and methods that can be adapted from other health disciplines, some of which were described in the "Incorporating Research into Practice" section. Grounding our practice in evidence is as well suited to action research approaches as it is to RCTs (Whiston, 1996). It easily embraces a local clinical scientist approach, as well as other methods for demonstrating the predictability of interventions for facilitating client change. However, it appears that many who espouse the evidence-based practice approach have an unnecessarily narrow interpretation of what methods can legitimately generate evidence, assuming that RCTs are some kind of "gold standard" for establishing evidence of treatment effectiveness. We propose that the challenge of how to better connect research and practice is not to promote RCTs as the primary way of conducting research in our discipline but, instead, to embrace the methodological diversity that characterizes Canadian counselling and counselling psychology research by adopting a broad definition of research evidence. We agree with Young and Domene's (2012) assertion that it is important for the future of both practice and research within our disciplines to more closely connect these historically separate endeavours. Expanding the evidence base by using a range of research methods to generate knowledge, including methods that better match actual counselling practice, may be the best way to meet the challenge of practitioners not incorporating research into their work. After all, as Dozois (2011a, 2011b) reminds us, if we want more evidence-based practice we need more practice-based evidence.

RESEARCH DISSEMINATION PRACTICES It is evident from our discussion of research dissemination activities that counselling and counselling psychology researchers in Canada are actively involved in sharing the knowledge that they are generating. Many of these efforts appear to be targeted to an international rather than a

Canadian audience and spread across many different formal and informal venues. Although this has the advantage of increasing the potential audience for Canadian counselling and counselling psychology research, it also creates a challenge for our disciplines, by increasing practitioners' difficulty in obtaining practice-oriented research evidence that attends specifically to the Canadian social context. If practitioners primarily read material in the C J C P or other Canadian venues, they will only be exposed to a small fraction of the literature being generated by Canadian counselling and counselling psychology researchers.

Separate from but related to this challenge is the problem imposed by the language divisions that exist in Canadian counselling and counselling psychology (Bedi et al., 2012; Domene & Bedi, 2012), which impede the dissemination of knowledge generated by Francophone counselling and counselling psychology researchers to an English-speaking audience, and, to a lesser extent, vice versa. Not only does this challenge mean that many of us are failing to utilize all the available evidence to inform our practice, but it may also contribute to divisions in our disciplines, where Francophone practitioners identify themselves primarily as *conseillers/conseillères en orientation* (career and guidance counsellors), while Anglophone practitioners may identify themselves more generally as counsellors or counselling psychologists (Young & Nicol, 2007). This difficulty is partially remedied by the combination of Canadian journals' practice of publishing abstracts (and in some cases, entire articles) in both languages and the increasing accessibility of convenient, though sometimes inaccurate, software for automated language translation (e.g., Google Translate). Nonetheless, there are many unilingual counselling and counselling psychology practitioners and researchers in Canada, which makes dissemination of research findings to their full potential audience somewhat more difficult.

RESEARCH-RELATED TRAINING Given the elective nature of many research-related courses in Canadian counselling and counselling psychology education programs, and the variability that exists in the research supervision they receive, it is likely that some students do not avail themselves of all the opportunities offered to them, and may even perceive the mandatory aspects of their research training as an irrelevant nuisance to suffer through on their way to becoming practitioners. No matter how many opportunities exist in training programs to develop sophisticated research-related skills, it is a problem if students do not perceive these skills as relevant to their future professional life. Part of the solution to this problem is to increase students' understanding that being an informed consumer of research is a core part of working in a discipline that claims to be evidence-based. Another piece of the puzzle may be for educators to adapt their research-related training so that it becomes more practitioner-oriented. This could, for example, involve providing more courses devoted specifically to program evaluation and counselling process research methods, integrating a "researching your own practice" component into counselling skills courses and practica, or providing explicit training in how to disseminate knowledge in ways that are more accessible to practitioners, consumers, and policy-makers.

Future Directions

In addition to taking steps to address the challenges that were described in the preceding section, we propose several future directions that should be prioritized by counselling and counselling psychology researchers in Canada. These future directions relate to promoting better integration of research and practice in our training and knowledge-dissemination activities.

It is generally accepted that learning is greatest when there is congruence between what instructors say and what they do. This underscores the importance of ensuring that our training programs provide good examples of the type of learning that we want our students to demonstrate. Perhaps the most obvious way to model the integration of research and practice is for educators of counsellors and counselling psychologists to ensure that research findings are prominent in the courses that students take, especially in courses related to the development of skills and the application of interventions. This integration is lacking in textbooks dealing with psychotherapeutic interventions (Howarth, 1989), and omitting discussions of research from skills courses may unintentionally communicate the message that research is separate from practice.

Another way to promote the integration of research and practice is to use our courses as both a research source and an opportunity for students to participate in counselling process research. This proposed future direction for our disciplines would demonstrate that practice-based research is not only about outcomes, but also about identifying the optimal ways to engage with clients. Many of the activities in counselling skills courses involve students reflecting on their performance in practice sessions. Adding an explicit research component to these kinds of course activities has been successfully achieved in some contexts (Hiebert & Johnson, 1994; Uhlemann, Lee, & Hiebert, 1988), and provides an example of how research can improve practice and emphasizes the interdependence of theory, research, and practice (Meara et al., 1988).

As we explained in the first half of our chapter, Canadian scholars of counselling and counselling psychology pursue research on a wide range of different topics, including some that are only tangentially related to working with clients. To better promote involvement in applied research and incorporation of research into practice, it may be necessary to pursue multiple programs of research that encompass both our personal areas of interest and topics related to working with clients. It is interesting to note that Galassi, Stoltz, Brooks, and Trexier (1987) found that, in American counsellor educators' experience, providing students with early hands-on research and opportunities to participate in research teams was the most effective way to raise the profile of research in their programs. If we generalize those findings to Canadian counselling and counselling psychology training programs, it may be that letting students interact with productive faculty members and become actively engaged in research activities could be an important way to promote the importance of connecting research and practice. Such practices would provide more opportunities to involve students in meaningful research activities (i.e., more than simply transcribing interviews or entering data), in addition to demonstrating that research is important for improving practice. The results of the survey conducted for this chapter suggest that professors in Canadian counsellor / counselling psychologist education programs are already engaged in these activities with at least some of their students. What we are highlighting here is the potential benefit of involving even those students who have no aspirations for entering academia, with firsthand experience pertaining to the value of research for improving practice.

A theme running through this chapter is the importance of developing a literature base that delineates the effectiveness of counselling psychology interventions for creating a positive impact on the lives of clients. However, it is important to realize that even the most effective intervention or program is useless if no one knows about it.

As Ronson and Suprenant (2012) point out, all too often the results of our research do not influence practice because researchers often do not have the time, the expertise, or the inclination to describe their findings in language that is comprehensible to people outside of academia. To counteract this problem, it is important for Canadian counselling and counselling psychology researchers as a group to adopt some variant of the adage "Tell the people who need to know, in language that they can understand, what we are doing and the difference it is making in the lives of clients." Consequently, we need to publish in sources that practitioners are likely to read and to use language that practitioners can relate to. If we want the public to be more aware of the services that are available and the types of personal changes that counsellors and counselling psychologists can provide, we need to reach out to public forums in order to make the message heard. If we want to reach policy-makers, then we need to disseminate our findings in sound-bites that policy-makers will attend to, and place them in forums that are frequented by policy-makers. If we want funding agencies to give greater priority to applied research in counselling and counselling psychology, then we need to become members of the review boards of those funding agencies so that we have a voice at the table where funding decisions are made. No one person will be able to do all of that, but it is possible to achieve these goals collectively, especially if our efforts could be coordinated by professional associations that undertake the task as part of their mandate, such as the CCPA, the OCCOQ, and the Counselling Psychology Section of the CPA. Adopting these future directions will help to ensure the relevance and benefits of research being conducted in our disciplines.

A CONCLUSION AND CALL TO ACTION

In this chapter, we have described the accomplishments of the disciplines of counselling and counselling psychology in Canada in relation to conducting, disseminating, and training for research. It is evident from the discussion of the current state of affairs, areas of strengths, challenges that we are facing, and proposals for future directions that, although much has already been achieved, there remain many things to accomplish. A recurring theme in the literature is that counselling and counselling psychology practitioners need to be responsive to the changing contexts that their clients face.

We believe that similar needs for reform exist for researchers and educators in our disciplines. Perhaps the allegory presented below illustrates this point. There is a legend from the United States of Rip Van Winkle, a farmer of Dutch descent, who lived in a village at the foot of a small mountain range. One autumn day he went wandering into the mountains, where he encountered strangely dressed men who he assumed to be ghosts of early explorers who were rumoured to exist there. After drinking some of their liquor, he settled down under a shady tree and fell asleep. When he awoke and returned to his village, he realized that twenty years had passed. He discovered that everyone he knew had died or moved away. He saw that there were strange and noisy vehicles that did not require any horses to make them go, and many other changes that he could barely comprehend.

Suppose that Rip Van Winkle fell asleep twenty years ago and, after waking up today, wandered down the mountain and into a hospital, would he see much difference? Suppose he wandered into a bank; would he see much difference? Now suppose he wandered into a university program for training counsellors and counselling psychologists; how much change would he see? In one class he might see an instructor using PowerPoint slides to support the concepts being discussed, and in another he might be fascinated by the new ways in which students record their practice sessions. However, we think that he would notice that the general approach to counsellor training has remained basically unchanged in the past twenty years, especially in terms of connecting practice and research.

Even twenty years ago, counsellors and counselling psychologists (e.g., French, Hiebert, & Bezanson, 1994; Hiebert, 1984; Hiebert & Uhlemann, 1993) were pointing out that, in our consumer-driven society, it would become increasingly necessary for practitioners to demonstrate tangibly that their interventions make a difference in the lives of clients. This is difficult to accomplish unless practitioners (a) obtain sufficient training in a broad range of research methods to systematically review and critique the full range of literature in our disciplines; (b) are provided with research findings that are disseminated in a way that describes interventions in sufficient detail to permit them to replicate the procedures that demonstrated effectiveness; and (c) have a procedural orientation that fosters placing client intervention within frameworks for practice that are grounded in research evidence.

Underlying the ideas we have presented in this chapter is an agenda for action within our disciplines that parallels the call to social action that is present in counselling and counselling psychology (Bedi et al., 2011; Sinacore et al., 2011). As Baudouin and colleagues (2007) and Hiebert and Magnusson (in press) explain, we need to be able to provide policy-makers, as well as managers, supervisors, and funders, with the evidence they need to provide counselling and counselling psychology practitioners with the type and amount of support we need. We need to find out how to engage our policy-makers and government departments to work together with us to create the infrastructure needed to support life-long and life-wide services for all who need them. This will involve identifying the individuals who are in positions of influence and who can assist us to make changes, then learning how to communicate with these people in a way that provides the information they need to hear, in language they can understand, as well as pointing out to them how it is in their best interest to support counselling and counselling psychology services. The task is larger than any of us could manage individually, so we need to be able to recruit others in the quest to address the whole-person needs of our clients across the lifespan. We also need to expand the focus of our research to better address these issues, and our training programs to include the broad spectrum of competencies that are needed to help future practitioners work effectively with the clients they encounter. This includes competencies related to understanding and reviewing existing research, producing research that is relevant to and useful for practice, and becoming researchers of our own clinical work. Joining together to promote counselling and counselling psychology as disciplines where there is substantial evidence for what we do will accomplish much more than any person could accomplish individually. All of us are more capable than any of us.

APPENDIX

The literature described in this chapter was supplemented by material from an online, self-report survey about respondents' recent (i.e., from 2007 to 2011) research practices. The survey consisted of a demographic questionnaire and twenty-two self-report questions asking about experiences in conducting and publishing research, obtaining research funding, and supervising and educating students

about counselling / counselling psychology research. It was conducted between October and December 2011.

The survey was only available in English and was distributed
electronically to the Counsellor Education chapter of the CCPA
(162 members) and to the Counselling Psychology Section of the
CPA (385 members). However, it is not known how many individuals received and chose not to respond to these invitations: some individuals opt out of or ignore messages from their organization's
listserv, an unknown proportion of the membership of the organizations are not eligible to participate (e.g., international affiliates),
some emails may have been automatically rejected by spam filters,
and some Francophone counsellor educators and counselling psychologists may not have read the invitation.

Forty-four people completed the survey, and after we removed
respondents who were students, the final sample consisted of individuals who identified primarily as practitioners (n = 9), academics
(n = 21) or "other," which included individuals who described themselves as administrators, program directors, psychologists, and counsellor educators (n = 9). Respondents were asked to list their
publications for the past five years. Eighteen respondents did so,
with four additional respondents providing other information in the
response box (e.g., only the journals in which they published; explanations for why they did not have publications in the past five years).
From this information, we obtained 115 articles published in peer-
reviewed journals. These articles were reviewed using content analysis (Braun & Clarke, 2006), and the emerging data were used to
supplement the respondents' self-report data. In terms of demographic characteristics, 58 percent were women and 42 percent were
men, ages ranged from 31 to 67 (mean age = 52 years). In terms of
educational attainment, 78 percent had obtained a doctoral degree,
11 percent held a thesis-based master's degree, and 11 percent held
a course-based master's degree. Fourteen counselling / counselling
psychology graduate programs were represented in the sample,
including programs in public and private educational institutions,
programs located in every region of the country, and programs that
only offer master's degrees as well as those that offer both master's
and doctoral degrees. Information was from survey respondents
whose claims, for the most part, were consistent with those made in
the literature about Canadian counselling and counselling psychology research.

3

Multicultural Counselling, Education, and Supervision

NANCY ARTHUR AND SANDRA COLLINS

The definition of counselling psychology in Canada incorporates cultural diversity as a core value (Bedi et al., 2011). Canadian counselling psychologists are going beyond the challenge to respond to diversity in all its complexity, to lead the field in inclusive professional practices that contribute to the health and well-being of all Canadians. In the past several decades, Canadian researchers and theorists have increasingly recognized the importance of cultural diversity, as well as the broader systemic factors that influence health and well-being. They have begun to look beyond the individual to the contexts and relationships that shape worldview, self-perception, and behaviour, as well as social, economic, and political privilege. Critical analysis of cultural identities provides a lens through which individual and group experiences are positioned and integrated into practice (Collins & Arthur, 2010c).

The purpose of this chapter is to highlight the contributions of Canadian counselling psychologists in the areas of multicultural counselling, education, and supervision. We begin with an overview of demographic changes in Canadian society. The concepts of culture, cultural identity, multiculturalism, and diversity are then discussed as a foundation for considering who has been and should be represented in multicultural counselling. Background information about the multicultural counselling movement provides context for an examination of contemporary issues, including development of multicultural counselling competency frameworks and connections to social justice. The implications for education, supervision, and research are then highlighted. Our basic premise is that responsiveness to cultural diversity forms an essential foundation for competent professional practice as a counselling psychologist, and that this is only truly possible when the broader community, organizational, and social systems are taken into account in both understanding and addressing client concerns.

CULTURAL DIVERSITY
IN THE CANADIAN CONTEXT

The dominant image of Canada as a multicultural mosaic (Bowman, 2000) places primacy on cultural diversity as a national value. People of all cultural backgrounds have a right to equitable treatment and participation in society, and individuals and groups are encouraged to maintain their cultural identities. Canada is known worldwide for its foundational policies on multiculturalism, which emphasize cultural pluralism, and for its designation of two official languages, English and French (Arthur & Collins, 2010c). However, Canadians in the field of counselling psychology recognize the gap between aspired-to values and lived experiences. For example, although Canada is officially a bicultural nation, in its recognition of two official languages, many services and systems appear to be designed around separate usage by regionally clustered English- and French-language speakers (Sinacore, Borgen, et al., 2011; Young & Nicol, 2007). The official bilingualism policies are also not consistently promoted within the profession of counselling psychology (Young & Nicol, 2007). In this section, we will situate the ensuing discussion of culture and multicultural counselling within the experience of cultural diversity in Canada, drawing on selected expressions of cultural identity: Aboriginal peoples, immigration and ethnic diversity, religious diversity, sexual orientation, and social class. We intend these examples only as illustrative of the vast cultural diversity of the more than thirty-four million people who call Canada home (Statistics Canada, 2011a).

Honouring First Nations

When the first European colonialists arrived in Canada, there were more than fifty-six indigenous nations who spoke more than thirty languages, with diverse social, economic, and spiritual norms that had existed for hundreds of years. In spite of the strong cultural heritage and established communities of these First Nations, the foreign settlers dominated social, political, and economic structures and attempted to eradicate the pre-existing systems of First Nations people (Poonwassie & Charter, 2001).

The colonization of First Nations people in Canada has left a legacy of health, social, economic, and cultural challenges (Goodwill & McCormick, 2011). Attempts at cultural genocide, through purging children of their traditional language, values, and beliefs by isolating them from their family and community structures, created long-term health effects, now termed the residential school syndrome (Robertson, 2006). Canadian counselling psychologists recognize not only the need for national accountability for historical oppression, but also the ongoing threats to the cultural heritage of First Nations people within dominant Canadian society. Blue, Darou, and Ruano (2010) emphasize the adverse effects on individual and collective health and the stereotypes of First Nations people based on inequities in health status. First Nations people are often depicted in negative ways based on skewed analysis of drug and alcohol addiction and suicide rates. Blue et al. advocate for a strength-based approach in counselling practices through honouring core values, rules of behaviour, and demonstrations of resiliency.

The imposition of counselling psychology theories and models, which reflect the hierarchical and individualistic Western/European worldview and values, is unethical, offensive, and culturally oppressive to those who adhere to traditional First Nations values (Blue et al., 2010; Wihak & Merali, 2005). Counselling psychologists who work with First Nations people need to be knowledgeable about the ways in which a person's worldview impacts belief systems (White, 2007). There is debate about whether existing theories can be adapted for First Nations clients and whether new culturally grounded models need to be developed (Nuttgens & Campbell, 2010). For example, Miller et al. (2011) provided an example of how an anxiety-reduction program for adolescents, based on cognitive-behavioural therapy, was culturally enriched with specific content for Aboriginal students. Wihak and Merali (2003, 2005) provided suggestions for adapting Western counselling practices, as well as integrating traditional healing models, based on Inuit traditional knowledge and a spiritual worldview. Carr-Stewart (2006) and McCormick and Gerlitz (2009) argued, however, that counselling interventions should be designed principally from foundational values and strengths of the target populations. For example, Heilbron and Guttman (2000) offered an example of group counselling with First Nations women using traditional healing methods. Offet- *look this up* Gartner's (2011) research detailed how First Nations women overcame challenges to access post-secondary education and how they connected their academic success to future options for their families and communities. Wyrostok and Paulson's (2000) study reinforced First Nations post-secondary students' valuing of traditional Native healing practices; however, these authors cautioned against non-Aboriginal counsellors integrating these practices, advocating instead for consultation, referral, and collaboration with traditional healers. Selected theories and models must connect meaningfully to cultural values, particularly related to family, spirituality, and cultural identity (McCormick, 2000a).

Immigration and Ethnic Diversity

Immigration continues to contribute significantly to the diversity of the Canadian population. Canada received more than 280,000 immigrants in 2010 (Statistics Canada, 2011b). Within the next decade, it is estimated that one in five Canadians will be a member of a visible minority group (Statistics Canada, 2007a). Immigration is inextricably linked to Canada's economic policies related to population growth and skilled labour (Arthur & Flynn, 2011). The source countries of immigrants have shifted during the past thirty years, and depending on the degree of voluntariness associated with immigration, pre-migration circumstances can impact longer-term psychological health (Arthur, Merali, & Djuraskovic, 2010). There are also growing numbers of temporary foreign workers and international students who attempt to integrate into Canadian society, but who are positioned on the margins for employment, health care, and social integration services (Arthur, in press; Chen, 2008; Popadiuk, 2009; Sinacore, Park-Saltzman, Mikhail, & Wada, 2011).

Despite inclusive multiculturalism policies, some immigrants to Canada live biculturally, others hold to their original cultural identities, and many feel marginalized in society (Berry, 2005, 2008). Although the role of receiving countries in the acculturation process has been acknowledged (Berry, 2008), the onus continues to be placed on immigrants to fit into existing Canadian systems (Chirkov,

2009). Early counselling psychology research tended to focus on immigrant adjustment (Lee & Westwood, 1996; Westwood & Ishiyama, 1991); more recently, both the barriers and facilitators to successful integration have been emphasized (Amundson, Yeung, Sun, Chan, & Cheng, 2011; Chen, 2008).

Integration success appears to pivot around gainful employment. However, oppression, discrimination, and inequitable access to education, employment, and related economic systems position many immigrants on the margins of Canadian society (Chen, 2008). The acculturation experience is an ongoing process; immigrants live within multiple contexts, and their cultural identities are negotiated across situations (Djuraskovic & Arthur, 2009; Justin, 2010). Counselling psychologists recognize that the responsibility for the successful integration of immigrants, temporary foreign workers, and international students largely rests with members of the dominant population and the health care, educational, and other systems designed to foster integration. As previously noted, the theories and models of counselling psychology cannot be applied without taking into account diverse client worldviews (Costigan, Su, & Hua, 2009; Shariff, 2009). The general principles of cultural formulation may be used as a framework for counselling immigrants who hold more collectivistic worldviews (Arthur & Popadiuk, 2010). Honouring between and within group differences in language, religion, customs, and beliefs is essential to avoid stereotyping (Sinacore, Mikhail, Kassan, & Lerner, 2009). Categorizing people as immigrants assumes a uniform pathway of entering Canadian society and a fixed cultural identity. Counselling psychologists recognize that diversity within countries and cultures and the varying circumstances that lead to immigration can impact mental health and well-being in the settlement process.

Religious Diversity

With a wider range of source countries for Canada's population, new customs and practices are introduced, including growing religious diversity. Although the majority of Canadians identify as Christian, their numbers are declining, while other faith traditions (predominantly Muslim, Hindu, and Sikh) have doubled (Citizenship and Immigration Canada, 2009; Fadden & Townsend, 2009). Religion and spirituality are clearly connected to health, illness, and models of healing. However, the relationship between religion, spirituality, and multicultural counselling continues to be an uneasy one. Faith-based practices may raise values conflicts, and many counselling psychologists are ill-prepared for and/or uncomfortable with the role of religion and spirituality in counselling (McLennan, Rochow, & Arthur, 2001; Plumb, 2011).

which is my gift ... in a path leading to and practice of integrating both

Lesbian, Gay, Bisexual, Transgendered, Transsexual (LGBTT) Populations

We do not have the same hard data on Canadian demographics for members of non-dominant sexual orientations. Alderson (2010) suggests that the percentage is likely between three and ten percent of the adolescent and adult population. Even less information is available on gender identity diversity. Canada is a country where same-sex common-law unions and marriages are legally endorsed (Alderson, 2004b). However, LGBTT and two-spirited populations remain largely invisible, and many individuals do not feel comfortable or safe expressing their sexual/gender identities publically in employment and social contexts.

Canadian counselling psychologists are required to develop competence in working with LGBTT populations, on issues of both sexual orientation and gender identity. Counselling psychologists are expected to attend to their own beliefs and attitudes and to translate cultural awareness into practices that affirm the cultural identities of LGBTT clients. The absence of LGBTT content in counsellor education curricula is a barrier for future service provision (Alderson, 2004a). Negative stereotypes must be replaced by recognition of the resiliency, loving relationships, and cultural strengths of these populations (Alderson, 2010; Collins & Oxenbury, 2010).

← show Sandra the article in the lit review.

Poverty and Social Class

Diversity of socio-economic status and class (SESC) has received insufficient attention in Canadian multicultural counselling literature. Yet SESC is central to the management of everyday life and to overall health and well-being. Canada has relatively high rates of poverty and poverty persistence (Valetta, 2006). Not surprisingly, socio-economic status is inversely related to health status: lower SESC is associated with greater mental health concerns (Pope &

Arthur, 2009) and negative clinical outcomes (Leschied, Chiodo, Whitehead, & Hurley, 2006). Many rural Canadians face poorer socio-economic conditions due to limited educational and employment opportunities, and disparities in resource allocation to rural communities (Malone, 2011). Economic disadvantage intersects with other socially defined aspects of identity, as people with non-dominant identities, including gender, disability, and race, are amongst the poorest of all Canadians (Campaign 2000, 2011; Finn, 2011).

A major barrier in service delivery is treating everyone as if they were classless and failing to recognize the impact of economic power within society. Counselling psychologists are called upon to address negative stereotypes associated with people from lower SESC and to advocate for resources so that individuals, families, and communities are not underserved.

CONCEPTUALIZATION OF CULTURE AND MULTICULTURAL COUNSELLING IN CANADA

One of the biggest challenges in writing about multicultural counselling is to define what is meant by the terms *culture, cultural identity, diversity,* and *multiculturalism.* The perspectives of Canadian counselling psychologists on these important constructs are described in this section, as well as the implications for positioning these constructs within theory and practice.

Making Meaning of Culture

Culture is most often defined by shared clusters of worldview, beliefs, and values; rituals, practices, customs, or norms; social, religious, or spiritual traditions; language, history, and ties to geographic locations; and/or adherence to social, economic, or political structures. There are three guiding assumptions about culture that have implications for understanding cultural identity and for multicultural counselling practice: (a) each individual is a cultural being; (b) culture is learned and is transmitted through social interactions and from generation to generation; and (c) culture is dynamic and mutable (Arthur & Collins, 2010c).

There is general consensus that culture is not a static, essential characteristic of individuals; rather, both individuals and groups may hold multiple, complex, and sometimes conflicting *cultural identities,* either simultaneously or evolving and shifting over time as they navigate diverse social structures and interactions. Paré (2008) noted that discourse about culture has tended to emphasize distinctions between people and cautioned against viewing our clients as "rooted in particular cultures" (p. 138). He argued against positioning people based on group designation in favour of recognizing the fluidity of people's culture as constructed across time and across contexts of interaction. Kassan and Sinacore (as cited in Sinacore, Borgen, et al., 2011) highlighted a ubiquitous approach in which culture is defined broadly and through which multiple and client-defined cultural identities are explored in the counselling process. In assessing the salience of a client's cultural identity, it is important to go beyond only visible characteristics of difference, to incorporate variables such as demographics (e.g., age, gender), status (e.g., social, educational), affiliations (both formal and informal), and ethnography (e.g., nationality, ethnicity) (Enns et al., 2004). The ubiquitous approach is consistent with a broader view of culture and the premise that all counsellor-client interactions are, to some extent, multicultural in nature (Pedersen, 1999). No two clients are alike, and the unique interactions of counsellor and client identities come together in the counselling relationship. The salience of cultural identity may change over time and across contexts. Collins (2010a, 2010b) elaborated on the notion of multiple cultural identities, emphasizing the complexity of understanding and navigating cultural influences for individuals who identify with multiple non-dominant cultures. She used the metaphor of a kaleidoscope: the images alter through both the internal movement of the elements of colour and the background against which the image is viewed.

There has been a tendency to view culture as something located within the individual that influences perceptions and behaviours, rather than viewing culture as shaped and made meaningful through interaction (Knapik & Miloti, 2006). Canadian counselling psychologists agree that both practitioners and clients bring their cultural backgrounds and contexts into the counselling process. Counsellors' self-awareness affects the cultural lens through which they view clients presenting concerns, case conceptualization, and the range of potential outcomes and processes for counselling, as well as client cultural factors, contexts, and socio-economic and political implications of cultural identification. However, less attention has been paid to the complexity of the cultural interface between counsellor and client. Cultural identities emerge, are defined, and gain saliency as components of the relationship between counsellor and client. This postmodern view of culture requires attention to the interaction and meaning-making constructed between counsellor and client (Young & Lalande, 2011). It is within the context of counselling and the conversation that transpires between counsellor and client that the meanings of culture emerge (Strong, 2002).

Ascribing cultural identity through external labelling is overtly or covertly related to people's social, economic, or political power. Individuals are often socially positioned due to one or more aspects of their cultural identities, affording them more or less privilege in Canadian society. Counselling psychologists must, therefore, grapple with not only how culture is defined, but also how difference is perceived and acted on. Moodley (2007b) argued that the multi-cultural movement has focused on the differences between ethnic minority groups at the expense of attending to these disparities in power and to the common experiences of oppression across groups. A similar argument is presented by Canadian authors in bridging feminist and multicultural perspectives (Collins, 2010b; Lalande & Laverty, 2010; Sinacore & Enns, 2005a). These authors challenge us to look beyond group differences to consider what it is about society that positions people as more or less dominant, as more or less val-ued, and as having more or less access to resources. Power differ-ences between individuals and groups lead to social inequities and contribute to mental health issues. In a critical review of the litera-ture, Sinacore and Enns (2005a) identified four central commonali-ties between the multicultural and feminist literatures that are instructive for the education, supervision, and practice of counsel-ling psychologists. These common foundations are (a) individual empowerment and social change, (b) knowledge and the knower, (c) single or multiple oppressions and privileges, and (d) reflexivity and self-awareness.

In summary, culture and cultural identities are both self-defined and socially constructed; they are fluid, contextualized, and made meaningful in relationship; they are imbued with personal, interper-sonal, and systemic meaning; and they are directly related to social positioning in terms of power and privilege. Counselling psycholo-gists are cautioned against defining or confining clients by visible differences. Instead, they are encouraged to invite and facilitate inclusive and open cultural conversations. They are also implored to attend to the socio-political forces that lead to differential power and access to services and resources in Canadian society.

Conceptualizing Diversity and Multiculturalism

The term *multicultural* is often used interchangeably with the terms *diverse* or *diversity*. This is one area where Canadian counselling psychology diverges most consistently from American perspectives. In the United States, culture has been narrowly defined and primacy has been placed on non-dominant ethnic and racial groups in defining the term *multicultural*, and consequently defining multicultural counselling competencies, standards, and practices. The term *diversity* has been used for other aspects of cultural identity, often relegating them to a less central position. Canadian counselling psychologists more often embrace a broader definition of *multicultural*, referring to "a wide range of identity factors, most commonly: ethnicity, gender, sexual orientation, mental and physical ability, socio-economic status, religion, and age" (Arthur & Collins, 2010c, p. 15).

This more inclusive definition of *multicultural* is consistent with the understanding of culture in the previous section. It is important, however, to not limit cultural inquiry to any pre-defined list of cultural factors, recalling the personal, interpersonal, and systemic influences on cultural identity. For example, Malone (2011) argues that rural contexts need to be factored into our understanding of Canadian cultural experiences. Living in rural Canada not only represents living particular lifestyles, but, in many geographical areas within Canada, there are inequities in terms of access to facilities and resources in local communities. Again, readers are reminded that there is cultural diversity within any population, and people's experience of rural living in Canada may be profoundly impacted by the social acceptability of other aspects of their identities, such as ethnicity, religion, and sexual orientation. Individuals may position themselves on the basis of one or more multicultural dimensions, may redefine their cultural identities across contexts, and may find that particular dimensions of their cultural identity are emphasized more or less by other people.

Implications for Theory and Practice

The discussion of cultural diversity in Canada at the outset of this chapter highlighted one of the ongoing debates in counselling psychology. Many authors focused on a particular non-dominant population, contributing substantively to our understanding of the specific cultural worldviews, strengths and challenges, and social positioning of that group. This culture-specific emic approach (Daya, 2001) honours the uniqueness of each cultural group, while adapting theoretical models and strategies to be sensitive to cultural identities and experiences. Other authors adopt a more universalistic etic approach (Daya, 2001), focusing on the commonalities across groups, arguing that all encounters involve cultural differences, and identifying theoretical constructs and counselling processes that can be generalized across populations. Moodley (2007b), for example, argued that ethnicity has been emphasized at the expense of attending to commonalities across experiences of cultural oppression, such as racism, ageism, sexism, homophobia, ableism, or classism. The latter approach may support an understanding of the complex and idiosyncratic nature of cultural identities and also encourage counselling psychologists to examine social inequities on a broader level.

THE MULTICULTURAL COUNSELLING MOVEMENT IN CANADA

The field of counselling psychology in Canada, including multicultural counselling, has been strongly influenced by developments in other countries, primarily the US (Young & Nicol, 2007). For detailed accounts about the historical development of multicultural counselling in the US, readers are referred to Arredondo and Perez (2006) and Arredondo, Tovar-Blank, and Parham (2008). Our focus will be on examining the Canadian multicultural counselling movement against the backdrop of these international foundations.

The multicultural counselling movement stemmed from the Division of Counseling Psychology (Division 17) of the American Psychological Association (APA), which formed a committee for the purpose of developing culturally relevant counselling competencies. An initial framework of multicultural competencies was published in 1982 (Sue et al.), which identified eleven competencies, organized according to beliefs and attitudes, knowledge, and skills. The revised framework published ten years later (Sue, Arredondo, & McDavis, 1992) contained thirty-one multicultural competencies within three core characteristics: (a) "counsellor awareness of own assumptions, values, and biases"; (b) "understanding the worldview of the culturally different client"; and (c) "developing appropriate intervention strategies and techniques" (p. 481). Each of the three characteristics was expanded along the three dimensions of beliefs and attitudes, knowledge, and skills. The multicultural counselling competencies published by Arredondo and colleagues (1996) maintained the same structure, while elaborating on each of the competencies. Although the focus of the competency frameworks has been primarily placed on individual change, Sue et al. (1998) added organizational development as a fourth domain to their competency framework in recognition that counselling occurs in a cultural context. The tripartite competencies model has been the primary reference in the field, from which future iterations and practice documents were developed; for example, the APA *Guidelines on Multicultural Education, Training, Research, Practice and Organizational Change for Psychologists.*

Social and Political Contexts of Multicultural Counselling

It is important to recognize the cultural contexts that prompted the multicultural counselling movement and the development of the competencies in the US context, particularly historical racial tensions (Arredondo & Perez, 2003). One of the main criticisms of the multicultural movement has been the primacy and exclusivity surrounding issues of race and ethnicity. Similarly, the emergence of feminist psychology, as a direct reflection of the social, economic, and political emancipation of women, resulted in a movement that, at least initially, was not considered inclusive of other individuals or groups not well represented in the dominant socio-political or theoretical discourse, including women of colour (Collins, 2010b).

In more recent years, and particularly within the Canadian counselling psychology context, both movements have embraced the broader definition of culture reflected in this chapter and have begun to examine the intersections of identity, such as gender and ethnicity, heterosexism and racism, ability and socio-economic dis-privilege (Collins, 2010b). In addition, the multicultural movement has begun to expand both the understanding of the etiology of client concerns and the target of change to the broader social, economic, and political systems (Arthur & Collins, 2010d). These shifts, however, have not been fully reflected in the evolution of the multicultural counselling competencies, particularly in the US. In addition, much of the multicultural counselling literature is still based within European and North American societies and is grounded in those cultural values (Pettifor, 2010).

Pettifor (2010) encouraged the profession to draw from resources developed at the international level, such as the *Universal Declaration of Ethical Principles for Psychologists* (Gauthier, Pettifor, & Ferrero, 2010), which proposed four overriding principles: (a) respect for the dignity of persons and peoples; (b) competent caring for the well-being of persons and peoples; (c) integrity; and (d) professional and scientific responsibility to society. Pettifor also noted that if we extend the concept of culture to all counselling interactions, the need for specialist guidelines for specific populations would decrease: "However, as long as non-dominant groups of people are treated unequally and marginalized there will be a need and a demand for special training and guidelines" (p. 187). In Canada, these include the following Canadian Psychological Association (CPA) publications: *Guidelines for Ethical Psychological Practice with Women* and *Guidelines for Non-Discriminatory Practice*. However, counselling psychologists continue to highlight the disparities across cultural groups in Canadian society and the connections between experiences of privilege/dis-privilege and cultural oppression.

Critique of the Multicultural Counselling Competencies

There has been little evolution in the competencies in the last several decades. The focus and language of multicultural competencies continue to carry an implicit assumption that culture is defined in terms of *otherness* (Collins, 2010a), which sets up the norm for who is in the position of professional (e.g., White, middle-class) and who is in the position of client (e.g., non-dominant ethnicity, religion, ability, sexual orientation, etc.).

The assumption that the competencies would be transferable across nations ignores contextual differences between the US and Canada, including important historical and contemporary nuances of Canadian society, demographics, and political influences that are relevant for the practice of multicultural counselling (Arthur & Stewart, 2001; Lalande, 2004). Multiculturalism in Canada begins from a very different set of national philosophies and assumptions (Bowman, 2000), which emphasize cultural pluralism, respect for and maintenance of cultural diversity, and expression of multilingual and multicultural identities. Collins and Arthur (2010b) offer both a detailed critique of the competencies movement and a revision of the competencies framework to address the need for a more inclusive definition of culture; stronger emphasis on the relational, interpersonal, and contextual aspect of cultural identities and multicultural counselling practice; and recognition of the importance of addressing systemic injustices through broader systems change.

Positioning Multicultural Counselling within Counselling Psychology

In spite of the recognition of cross-national differences, we face similar challenges in defining and positioning multicultural counselling within the counselling psychology profession in Canada. As noted earlier in the chapter, the tension remains between culture-specific and universal approaches to counselling practice; there is a tendency to stereotype individuals/groups; and we sometimes fail to appreciate the complexity, multiplicity, and construction of cultural identities.

One of the additional challenges in Canada, as in the US, is the lack of clarity or consensus in the positioning of multicultural counselling relative to the practice of counselling psychology generally. Pedersen (1999) claimed that multicultural counselling was the fourth force paradigm shift, necessitating the integration of culture into the theory and practice of counselling psychology. Concerns have been raised that many theories and practices in counselling psychology are based on Western values and worldview and have been applied in a way that is exclusive and ethnocentric (Young & Lalande, 2011). Nuttgens (2009) described an approach to teaching counselling theories that positioned both feminist therapy and multicultural counselling as meta-theoretical lenses through which all counselling psychology theory and practice should be critiqued. The multicultural counselling competencies provided a starting place for identifying the critical points of intersection of cultural awareness and counselling practice. However, there remains a dearth of inclusive conceptual or theoretical models to enable counselling psychologists to embrace this important agenda both in Canada and the US.

MULTICULTURAL COUNSELLING THEORY, MODELS, AND PROCESSES

In the US, the multicultural counselling competencies were transformed into a series of meta-theoretical principles (Sue, Ivey, & Pedersen, 1996), providing a conceptual lens for viewing both theory and practice. Fuertes and Gretchen (2001) reviewed other emergent theoretical models, noting the multiplicity in approach, the emphasis on idiosyncratic client cultural identities, and the supplementary nature of these models relative to traditional counselling theories and practices. Many existing models are defined against the backdrop of mainstream theoretical models in counselling psychology, and practitioners are left to either adapt the theoretical conceptualization and practices to be more culturally inclusive or embrace or develop culture-specific interventions.

There is also no consensus in Canada on an inclusive or comprehensive model of multicultural counselling theory and practice. Counselling psychologists in Canada have focused their research and theoretical writing in several areas: (a) guidelines and principles for increasing cultural awareness of either/both of counsellor cultural identities and client cultural identities (e.g., Collins & Arthur, 2007; Nuttgens & Campbell, 2010); (b) assessment and identification of multicultural counselling competencies, often in reference to specific populations (e.g., Arthur, Collins, Marshall, & McMahon, 2009; Kassan & Sinacore, 2011); (c) strategies and principles for working with particular non-dominant populations (e.g., Fowler, Glenwright, Bhatia, & Drapeau, 2011; McCormick, 2000b; Yohani & Larsen, 2009), including the need for or design of culture-specific assessment or intervention approaches and the integration of traditional healing methods and healers (e.g., Goodwill & McCormick, 2011; Oulanova & Moodley, 2010; Wihak & Merali, 2003, 2005); (d) application of non-Western models of counselling (e.g., Daya, 2000; Ishiyama, 2003); and (e) elucidation of population-specific needs and challenges (e.g., Beharry & Crozier, 2008; Malone, 2011; Sinacore et al., 2009; Weiss, 2012), including acculturation and cultural identity issues (e.g., Costigan et al., 2009; Djuraskovic & Arthur, 2009; Petersen & Park-Saltzman, 2010; Shariff, 2009). Where Canadian counselling psychologists are also making a mark on models of multicultural counselling is in the emphasis placed on the co-construction of cultural awareness in and through the counselling relationship and the positioning of the client and the counselling process within broader familial, social, economic, and political contexts. Two more comprehensive models of counselling share these important foci.

Peavy's (2001) *sociodynamic counselling* model provides a constructivist philosophical lens for the counselling process and offers both a collaborative and co-constructive model for the counselling process and a set of cultural tools (rather than psychological techniques) to support client goal attainment. "Intercultural counselling is concerned at once with 'communication practices' and 'cultural meanings' and is an interactional achievement, based largely on negotiation of meanings" (Peavy & Li, 2003, p. 190). The emancipatory focus of this model engages clients in both "internal unfreedoms such as low esteem and undeveloped capacity, and external unfreedoms such as prejudice, poverty, and oppressive relationships" (p. 189). Peavy's work comes closer to a *separate* model of counselling, and he strongly cautioned against adapting traditional theoretical models (Peavy, 2001; Peavy & Li, 2003).

Arthur and Collins' (2010a, 2012) *culture-infused counselling* model emphasizes four domains of multicultural competency: (a) counsellor self-awareness of cultural identities; (b) awareness of client cultural identities and contexts; (c) an active integration of this awareness within the context of a culturally sensitive working alliance; and (d) engagement in social justice action to directly influence systems that negatively impact clients' lives. They outlined competencies in the foundational domains to support a collaborative relational process in which cultural meanings are co-constructed and the goals, targets of change, and processes of counselling are actively negotiated within the cultural context of the client. Using the *culture-infused* model offers the possibilities of both adapting existing counselling psychology models and generating culture-specific approaches, as part of the client-centred, collaborative negotiation of goals and tasks that characterizes a culturally sensitive working alliance (Collins & Arthur, 2010a, 2010b). They have developed a cultural auditing tool to support reflexive, culture-infused counselling practice (Collins, Arthur, & Wong-Wylie, 2010).

There continue to be insufficient ties between feminist, queer, multicultural, and other bodies of literature, theory, and applied practice principles with counselling psychology in Canada (Enns, Sinacore, & Ancis, 2004; Sinacore & Enns, 2005b). Facilitating this integration is essential if the profession is to fully honour the complexity, multiplicity, and intersection of cultural identities in the design and delivery of responsive models and approaches (Collins, 2010a, 2010b). Future developments of the theory and practice of multicultural counselling must be inclusive of foundational principles emergent from theoretical streams that share the common goal of promoting inclusivity and responsiveness to the diversity of human experience.

THE INSEPARABILITY OF MULTICULTURAL COUNSELLING AND SOCIAL JUSTICE

One of the concerns of the multicultural counselling movement in Canada is the tendency to treat culture as an attribute of individuals or groups, rather than positioning culture as a highly politicized ideological construct (Gustafson, 2007). There is growing recognition in Canada that culture is not a neutral concept; neither are the cultural dimensions used to position people as *others* (e.g., gender, race, religion, sexual orientation, ability, age, ethnicity, etc.), nor the attempts to define culture *essentially* through group membership (Collins, 2010a). In the absence of critical reflection on issues of power and oppression (Moodley, 2007a), psychological issues or mental health concerns may be ascribed on the basis of externally ascribed cultural identity, instead of examining the impact of *otherness* and cultural oppression on individual and collective well-being. The locus of both etiology and change may be misplaced without careful attention to the person-environment interaction. Exclusion of the socio-political influences on clients' concerns may unintentionally support the very structures and systems that adversely impact people's health and well-being.

The growing recognition of the impact of broader systems of power and privilege shifts the focus within counselling psychology, from recognizing diversity and being culturally responsive in practice, to a call for active engagement to address the connections between cultural diversity and social justice (Arthur & Collins, 2010d). Social justice may have been central to the development of Canadian counselling psychology (Palmer & Parish, 2008), but the profession lacks a contemporary vision of what social justice really means in practice. More theoretical and applied practice principles and models are needed to articulate what it means to incorporate social justice into the roles and responsibilities of counselling psychologists in Canada.

The definition of *counselling psychology* (Bedi et al., 2011), endorsed by the CPA, uses the term *advocacy* and highlights the importance of attending to the social and cultural contexts of counselling and of clients' lived experiences. However, it does not explicitly include *social justice* as a guiding value. Not only do we still debate what constitute culturally responsive practices, but "counselling psychology in Canada has to find the conceptual and methodological grounding for the principles of liberty and equality that undergird social justice" (Young & Lalande, p. 252). Unless we resolve these questions, the profession falls prey to the very systems that cause distress for our clients. The social justice lens mandates us to move beyond remedial interventions that support clients to adapt to contextual barriers, to direct action within the systems that adversely impact clients. The discussion in this chapter is intended to introduce the connections between cultural diversity and social justice, which are more fully explored in chapter 11. Although we have emphasized the importance of assessing individual cultural identities and life contexts, we also want to emphasize the importance of building on the strengths, common experiences, and resiliency of individuals from non-dominant groups and addressing the social conditions that adversely impact their mental health.

IMPLICATIONS FOR PROFESSIONAL EDUCATION

There is little agreement about how multicultural counselling should be taught. Some graduate programs incorporate a specialist course on multicultural counselling, while others use a more integrated approach (Arthur & Collins, 2005). There is no evidence to suggest that either model is superior. Multicultural competencies are not only difficult to operationalize and measure, but they are also difficult to teach (Knapik & Miloti, 2006). Enns and colleagues (2004) reviewed key approaches and noted that the lack of a unifying framework has resulted in a "hodgepodge" (p. 423) approach to enhancing students' multicultural counselling competence. They add that the lack of structure is accompanied by a lack of research to inform pedagogy. It appears that there is more written about the concepts of cultural diversity and social justice for professional education than about how to impact students' competence. Nonetheless, some key directions may be gleaned from available literature.

Curriculum must be considered within the umbrella structures of counsellor education programs so that the missions, mandates, and operational policies also reflect a commitment to cultural diversity and social justice, e.g., hiring policies and faculty and staff composition representative of diverse cultural worldviews. The overall message is weakened if one faculty member, either by virtue of token representation or research interests, is left to champion the multicultural counselling agenda. In designing a counselling psychology curriculum, it is also critical to consider who speaks for multicultural counselling and social justice. Which perspectives are privileged and which ones are sidelined? Arthur and Collins (2005) demonstrated how to apply their cultural auditing model to both micro- and macro-level critiques of counsellor education programs and curricula.

The teaching of counselling psychology is not neutral; educators must critically analyze assumptions and values (e.g., individualism) that may be positioned as universal truths (Christopher & Hickinbottom, 2008). Examples were provided earlier in the chapter of both culture-specific and more universal multicultural counselling models, which challenge these (sometimes covert) assumptions. The conceptualization of culture and cultural diversity also determines approaches to counsellor education curriculum. Alderson (2004a) noted the relative absence of curricula addressing the needs of LGBTT clients. Malone (2000) highlighted how a curriculum devoted to counselling Aboriginal people fails to adequately address gender issues. Sinacore-Guinn (1995b) developed a diagnostic protocol that can be used to educate students about the influence of culture and gender diversity on clients' presenting issues and their coping resources. The diagnostic process emphasizes four domains:(a) cultural systems and structures, (b) cultural values, (c) gender socialization, and (d) the effect of trauma. Counsellor educators are urged to move beyond designing a curriculum that reifies notions of race, gender, social class, ability, religion, and sexual orientation, toward one that emphasizes how people's lives are constructed through the intersections of cultural identities. Exposing students to international perspectives on multicultural counselling will also broaden their appreciation of diverse worldviews (e.g., Arthur & Pedersen, 2008; Gerstein, Heppner, Ægisdóttir, Leung, & Norsworthy, 2009; Launikari & Puukari, 2005).

It is also important to consider "how we teach as well as what we teach" (Enns et al., 2004, p. 420). Attention needs to be paid to bridging the gaps between awareness, knowledge, and skills competencies. Counsellor education has tended to focus on the awareness and knowledge domains and may not provide sufficient opportunities for students to improve their skills. Teaching and learning strategies are required that involve students in the community, engage them in service, and provide other forms of active integration of knowledge.

Sinacore and Enns (2005a) proposed an Integrated Social Justice (ISJ) pedagogy based on the four common dimensions found between multicultural and feminist pedagogies, noted earlier. Their model integrated knowledge acquisition and experiential learning; matched concepts of empowerment and social change with learning experiences that help students link individual and societal levels; encouraged self-awareness and recognition of privilege; and included knowledge sources not typically included in curricula to facilitate awareness of diverse worldviews and experiences. The model emphasized the importance of exploring personal biases, assumptions, and attitudes as an essential component of learning reflexive practices. Sinacore and Kassan (2011) detail how ISJ pedagogy was integrated into a graduate course on multicultural psychology through the use of community-based portfolios.

Both openness to new learning and effective integration of that learning may also require students to develop what Wong-Wylie (2007) terms *reflection-on-self-in/on-action*. The cultural auditing model is another example of how such reflection practices can be facilitated in pedagogy for multicultural counselling (Collins et al., 2010). More research is necessary to identify appropriate models of experiential learning and to identify the mechanisms through which such learning enhances students' multicultural and social justice competencies. Instructors also require the skills to facilitate and debrief learning activities in ways that help students to make connections with multicultural counselling competencies (Arthur & Achenbach, 2002).

IMPLICATIONS FOR SUPERVISION

Supervision is central to competency development, reflective practice, and the application of multicultural counselling concepts in practice. The supervision experience typically begins with practicum or internship experiences, but ideally extends to a life-long process of learning and enhancement of multicultural counselling competence. A central goal of supervision is to improve the quality of counselling offered to clients; therefore, the supervision process itself must support culturally sensitive and relevant counselling practices. Supervision is increasingly recognized as an area that requires both specific competencies and particular attention to ethical standards (Pettifor, McCarron, Schoepp, Stark, & Stewart, 2011); this is even more critical in the context of multicultural counselling.

In keeping with the focus of this chapter, *multicultural supervision* is defined by differences in cultural identities among supervisor, supervisee, and/or client, rather than by race or ethnicity alone (Schroeder, Andrews, & Hindes, 2009). There are three basic perspectives on multicultural supervision (Arthur & Collins, 2005, 2010b). The first view emphasizes the dynamics of culture that transpire between the counsellor/supervisee and client dyad, attending to both counsellor and client cultural identities in the working alliance and therapeutic processes. The second view emphasizes the cultural identities of supervisees and supervisors, the interpersonal process of supervision, and the facilitation of learning about cultural influences within and through the supervisory relationship. A more integrated approach examines the influences of culture on the professional relationships in the triad of counsellor, client, and supervisor. Ideally, what transpires between the supervisor and supervisee strengthens multicultural counselling with clients. In multicultural, as well as cross-racial, supervision the strengths of the working alliances in the counsellor-client-supervisor triad are critical (Schroeder et al., 2009).

There are a number of barriers to effective multicultural counselling supervision. Supervisors may not have formal training in supervisory practices, in multicultural counselling, or in multicultural counselling supervision. Mismatches between the needs of supervisees and the capacity of supervisors may interfere with learning about multicultural counselling. Supervisees may assess the attitudes of their supervisors as making it unsafe to explore personal competencies related to multicultural counselling. Some supervisees may feel silenced; other supervisees may be more informed than their supervisors and may perceive supervisors as uninformed or uninterested in multicultural counselling (Arthur & Collins, 2010b; Schroeder et al., 2009). Culturally competent and ethical supervision requires collaboration and minimization of power differentials that may undergird some of these perceived barriers (Pettifor et al., 2011; Reynolds, 2010).

When supervisees view their supervisors as culturally aware and receptive to alternate points of view, the supervisory relationship can be strengthened. Supervisors who are open to learning with and from their trainees facilitate discussions that lead to fruitful exploration and reflection about cultural identities. Supervisees can also be supported to explore potential influences of culture in case conceptualization and intervention planning.

There is a lack of research about multicultural counselling supervision in the Canadian context; however, some suggestions for enhancing multicultural counselling through supervision are available (Arthur & Collins, 2005, 2010b; Schroeder et al., 2009). Ideally, the negotiation of cultural differences and similarities between counsellors/supervisees and their supervisors strengthens their working relationship. When supervisors share personal reflections, including disclosing struggles and challenges related to multicultural counselling, they model the ongoing process of reflective practice and open the door for supervisees to take risks with their own competency development. The establishment of trust is essential for counsellors/supervisees to engage in discussion about cultural identities. A lack of attention to cultural dynamics in supervision or a difference in levels of acculturation between supervisor and supervisee, on the other hand, may foster defensiveness, misunderstandings, and invisible or unspoken barriers and power differences in supervisory relationships. Power differences make it difficult for supervisees to challenge their supervisors' views of multicultural counselling, which in turn can compromise multicultural case conceptualization. If unaware of their personal cultural biases and assumptions, supervisors may inadvertently impose their worldview on both supervisees and clients, without considering the cultural strengths found in different points of view. The key issue is how power may be used, overtly or covertly, within the supervisory relationship in a way that is detrimental to the development of supervisees and/or to enhancing practices with clients.

Supervisors are encouraged to centralize cultural conversations about the supervisor-supervisee-client triad as part of their normal supervision practice with all supervisees and in relation to all clients. It is the responsibility of supervisors to initiate and facilitate practices with supervisees in a learning process that supports multicultural counselling. A collaborative approach to exploring cultural identities can ultimately strengthen the supervisory working alliance and the transfer of learning to enhance multicultural counselling competence.

Shared reflection on the systemic influences on client well-being can also facilitate examination of the broader role of counselling and counsellors in supporting a just society (Pettifor et al., 2011). Reynolds (2010) introduced a *supervision of solidarity* approach aimed specifically at facilitating social justice activism through counsellor engagement in peer supervision "solidarity" groups. The six core principles: "(a) centring ethics, (b) doing solidarity, (c) addressing power, (d) fostering collective sustainability, (e) critically engaging with language, and (f) structuring safety" (para. 14) offer promise in collective consciousness-raising and resistance of systemic injustices.

IMPLICATIONS FOR RESEARCH

In this chapter, we have attempted to overview the state of the art in terms of multicultural counselling within Canadian counselling psychology. In the process, we have highlighted a number of central debates about the role of culture in counselling psychology; the philosophical, theoretical, and applied practice foundations of multicultural and social justice practice; and the implications for education and supervision. These debates are critical to charting future directions and standards of practice (Arthur & Stewart, 2001). However, there is an imbalance in the amount of conceptual literature informing these professional dialogues in comparison to research studies. There is also a lack of dialogue about the very nature of multicultural research and critical reflection on the implications of cultural diversity for research processes (Offet-Gartner, 2010; Stewart, 2011). For example, are participants expected to follow the protocols of researchers when the topics and methods are not consistent with their personal priorities? How might knowledge of Indigenous values strengthen the utility of research conducted within Indigenous communities and also inform ethical practices using other approaches? Additional conceptual challenges and potential directions for future research are highlighted in this section of the chapter.

The boundaries of multicultural counselling research are unclear and reflect the debates about how culture and multicultural counselling are defined. If all counsellors and all clients are approached as cultural beings and all interactions are considered cultural encounters, at least to some degree, then what counts as multicultural counselling research? Is it the topic addressed or the lens through which the research is constructed that defines it as multicultural? It becomes difficult to discern what research on counselling processes is explicitly directed towards multicultural counselling. On the other hand, if multicultural counselling research is relegated to population-specific studies, there is a risk that these groups become further marginalized through the resultant specialist approach to multicultural counselling. This direction seems counterintuitive to an aspiration of integrating cultural competence into ethical practice for all counselling psychologists (Pettifor, 2010).

The development of instruments on multicultural counselling competencies has primarily focused on the original competency frameworks. As new developments and revisions to competency frameworks occur, there is also a need for corresponding assessment instruments to support students and experienced professionals in identifying both strengths and areas to enhance their continuing professional development. The field of multicultural counselling is also expanding to include social justice competency and action. However, there is no consensual conceptualization of what social justice means, with many authors using the term indiscriminately and multiple, multidimensional definitions emerging. Further research is needed to illuminate how counselling psychologists view their roles and responsibilities related to social justice.

More than a decade ago, many graduates reported not feeling adequately prepared to work with the diversity of their clientele (Arthur & Januszkowski, 2001). With an increasing emphasis on multicultural counselling integrated into the curriculum and emphasized in specialist courses, it is timely to consider whether or not progress has been made. There is also surprisingly little research available with experienced practitioners regarding their perspectives on, and enactment of, multicultural counselling in Canada. Practice examples could provide important models to bridge the gap between conceptualization of multicultural counselling and effective practices. Such research would inform professional education aimed at enhancing the preparation of counselling psychologists.

There is also a dearth of research on client perspectives, which may reduce the applicability of research and practice to the lived experiences of clients with non-dominant cultural identities. As previously noted, increasing inclusiveness with non-dominant populations requires researchers to adopt research philosophies and methods that are congruent with the values of the research participants (Archibald, Jovel, McCormick, Vedan, & Thira, 2006; Offet-Gartner, 2011; Stewart, 2011). Unfortunately, there is a legacy of research that expropriates the perspectives of persons in vulnerable positions. Researchers are challenged to demonstrate how multicultural counselling research can be transformative, reflecting an ethical mandate to do more than *no harm*, through making positive contributions to the lives of research participants (Pettifor, 2010).

Finally, more research on multicultural counselling needs to be conducted within the Canadian context. Although we have benefited from the many contributions of our international colleagues, there is also a danger in making assumptions about the cultural validity of research. The Canadian context is not homogeneous; we need to generalize existing research with caution and identify new research initiatives to inform the practice of counselling psychology in Canada.

CONCLUDING COMMENTS

The multicultural counselling movement has emerged in response to dynamic forces within society and within the profession of counselling psychology. The shifting demographics within Canadian society suggest that the clientele of the past will not be the same as the clientele of the future. There have been many positive advances in the integration of cultural diversity as a foundational construct for the practice of counselling psychology in Canada; however, professionals cannot afford to become complacent.

There is growing evidence that existing services do not fully address the needs of culturally diverse clients and that many Canadians do not access these services. Common barriers include knowledge about psychological services, help-seeking behaviours, cultural norms about consulting outside of the family or community, language barriers, lack of financial resources, and degree of acculturation to traditional healing methods (Kuo, Kwantes, Towson, & Nanson, 2006; Sinacore et al., 2011). The ways that services are funded may also influence how services are organized, what kinds of treatments are delivered, and what count as effective interventions (Arthur & Lalande, 2009). The empirically validated treatment movement within counselling psychology in Canada, for example, assumes, by its very nature, homogeneity of target groups and standardization of treatment, in ways that may threaten the ability of counselling psychologists to be culturally inclusive. The primacy placed on standardized design and delivery of services may not take into account the needs of clients with different worldviews and cultural identities, particularly when success and/or failure rates are measured against dominant social norms and populations. Moodley (2009) made the further point that the traditional masculine structures, language, and processes of counselling psychology are organized in ways that marginalize and exclude members of many non-dominant groups.

It is important to challenge both cultural and professional norms about who is served, by whom, and whose voices are present in or absent from our systems of governance and service delivery. It is critical also to consider who speaks for whom and how we might make the experiences and voices of individuals and groups who have been positioned on the margins of our society more central to the discussion of what it means to offer inclusive services. These issues are essential to our credibility as a profession in the eyes of an increasingly diverse consumer population.

As multicultural counselling and social justice become increasingly intertwined, in both theory and practice, clearer statements are needed about where the profession of counselling psychology stands on both the value of social justice and its application to practice. Both proactive and preventative approaches must be positioned at the core of professional services to address the systemic bases of cultural oppression. Assessment and intervention must expand to include individuals, institutions, and broader social systems. What are currently more peripheral roles for counselling psychologists, such as advocacy, public policy, community outreach, or facilitating indigenous support systems, may need to form the heart of service delivery.

Embracing a multicultural and social justice agenda may also require acknowledgment that the theories and practices of counselling psychologists are not apolitical. We make choices, consciously or not, about how we leverage our roles and professional power to either change or, by default, support structural and social norms. We end this chapter with a call to action for counselling psychologists to see their roles as broader agents of change and to use their expertise and social power to influence systems in ways that support the health and well-being of all people who live in Canada.

4

Counselling Indigenous People in Canada

SUZANNE L. STEWART AND
ANNE MARSHALL

INTRODUCTION

Indigenous peoples are defined by the Assembly of First Nations (2002) as comprising three distinct cultural groups: First Nations (status and non-status Indians), Métis, and Inuit. The term *Indigenous* is often used interchangeably with *Aboriginal, Native,* and *Indian.* Among the many cultural minority groups within Canada, Indigenous peoples are among the fastest-growing populations. Indigenous peoples represent approximately 3.9 percent of Canada's total population or about a total of 1,172,785 people (Statistics Canada, 2003a). Over 50 percent of the Indigenous population is under the age of 24 and 40 percent is under the age of 16. Thus the population is a growing one with a high concentration of youth. Since the 1970s, there has been a large migration of Indigenous people from rural areas and First Nation reserves to cities. Currently, over 600,000 self-identified Indigenous people live in cities – 54 percent of the total Aboriginal population – and the numbers are expected to grow according to demographic trends. The Indigenous population is becoming increasingly urban; in 2006, 54 percent lived in an urban centre, an increase from 50 percent in 1996. From 2001 to 2006, the Indigenous population in Canada increased by 196,475; this is an increase of 20.1 percent, a rate five times that of the non-Indigenous population.

Mental health is a vital aspect of overall health for Canadian Indigenous people. However, Indigenous cultural understandings of mental health and healing are distinctly different from the understandings that have prevailed in most North American mental health provider settings, including in counselling contexts. With few exceptions, counsellor training in Canada is based almost exclusively on a Western paradigm of health that differs from an Indigenous world-view (Gone, 2004; Stewart, 2008). These differences in paradigmatic worldviews can form a barrier to effective helping for Native people who seek counselling services from formally trained counsellors, including those who may be trained in cross-cultural or multicul-tural approaches. Further, Duran (2006) suggests that counselling Indigenous individuals from a non-Indigenous perspective (i.e., a Western perspective) is a form of continued oppression and colo-nization, as it does not legitimize the Indigenous cultural view of mental health and healing. "A postcolonial paradigm would accept knowledge from differing cosmologies as valid in their own right, without their having to adhere to a separate cultural body for legiti-macy" (Duran & Duran, 1995, p. 6).

Most mental health services are based on non-Indigenous concep-tions of health and healing (Government of Canada, 1991; Health Canada, 2003; Waldram, 2004). The impact of colonization prac-tices on Indigenous health across Canada has been summed up as the destruction and discontinuity of the structure of community, and of the transmission of traditional knowledge and values, such as an Indigenous paradigm of health and wellness (Kirmayer et al., 2000). Mental health is viewed as a critical component of overall health and well-being. Health professionals, counsellors, and community leaders are increasingly concerned regarding the mental health of Indigenous people and how to address this problem today. Research demonstrates that culture provides a resource for positive mental health and fulfills a person's need for identity (Mussell, 2005; Stewart, 2008). Traditional cultural practices, such as living within a Native worldview of a holistic approach, which means balance within and between the four sacred aspects of the self (emotional, physical, spir-itual, and intellectual), are what define mental health for Native groups according to current counselling literature (Blue & Darou, 2005; Mussell, 2005; Mussell, Cardiff, & White, 2004; Stewart, 2008). As suggested above, the health indicators suggest a pessimis-tic view of conditions in Canadian Aboriginal communities in terms of high rates (compared to non-Aboriginal populations) of mental health problems. However, there also exist many positive and empow-ering initiatives and health indicators for Indigenous peoples, which are currently taking shape, such as the Aboriginal healing movement. Prior to 1980, when the Indian Act of 1876 began to undergo some reform, Indigenous communities suffered severely in terms of freedom, autonomy, and cultural identification. Subsequent to 1980, and particularly in the 1990s, there has been a renewed awareness of spirituality, Native identity, and healing in many Aboriginal communities across Canada, known collectively as the Aboriginal healing movement (Aboriginal Healing Foundation, 2002; Kirmayer et al., 2000; Medicine-Eagle, 1989). Thus there are tremendous resources and strengths within Native communities that are working to rebuild social support systems to improve individual, family, and community well-being. Identity and community have also been identified within the literature as cornerstones to healthy mental functioning in a variety of ways, such as by providing a sense of belonging, bolstering self-esteem and self-efficacy, and promoting healing through interdependence; these concepts are especially vital for Native mental health and healing because identity and community were part of what was taken away through the legislated acts of colonialism, such as forced land relocation, residential schooling, and more (McCormick, 1997, 2000b; Stewart, 2008, 2009a).

Counselling professionals are increasingly recognizing the inseparability of cultural foundations and mental health needs and are attempting to undertake more effort to explore traditional cultural conceptions of mental health and healing. For example, Indigenous mental health and healing training, education, and practice have been incorporated into many post-secondary training programs across the country (see Coverdale et al., 2013; Stewart, 2009b). In order to address more culturally relevant knowledge regarding mental health and healing, this chapter begins with a brief history of Indigenous peoples and the implications for mental health, followed by an overview of key issues, challenges for counselling, and principles and models for Indigenous counselling. We conclude with several implications and suggestions for future directions.

A BRIEF HISTORY OF INDIGENOUS MENTAL HEALTH IN CANADA

According to oral tradition, prior to first contact with Europeans in the sixteenth century, the incidence of health problems among Indigenous peoples in what is now called Canada was low (Waldram,

2004). However, contact brought a dramatic increase in physical and mental illness to Aboriginals (Kirmayer et al., 2000). Over seven million Indigenous people are estimated to have inhabited North America prior to contact in 1492, with almost ninety percent of these people dying as a result of indirect and direct effects of European settlement by 1600. Infectious disease brought from Europe was the major killer, followed by a change from a traditional diet to one of European foodstuffs (Young, 1988). Today there continue to be health problems in Native communities related to diet and epidemiology, such as diabetes and obesity (Kirmayer et al., 2000).

Implementation of federal government policy has destroyed Indigenous cultures through the creation of land reserves, residential schools, and bureaucratic control. Indigenous settlements were chosen by non-Native governments, who forced Indigenous groups off of their traditional lands and onto other territories, often grouping bands together that had previously had no history of living together (Dickason, 1997). These groupings were forced to make new social structures and sustainable ways of life. Indigenous groups were also relegated to lands with few or no natural resources, i.e., lands not deemed livable for settlers (Royal Commission on Aboriginal Peoples, 1994). Referring to a damaging example of this relocation for the Inuit peoples, Kirmayer et al. (2000) write: "The disastrous 'experiment' of relocating Inuit to the Far North to protect Canadian sovereignty – a late chapter in this process of forced culture change – revealed the government's continuing lack of awareness of cultural and ecological realities" (p. 609).

Prior to contact with European explorers, North American Indigenous communities had effective methods for preventing and treating illness and injury (Young, 1988). For example, Bopp and Lane (2000) have recorded how the Nuxalk people of British Columbia effectively survived the smallpox epidemic by creating and following a plan to "avoid complete annihilation": community members were ordered by leaders to scatter from villages in pairs and to remain "in shouting distance" apart, and if one partner died, the other was to bury him or her (p. 7). If the remaining person then became ill, he or she was to bury him- or herself in a shallow grave until dead. After one year of this separation, surviving members were to return to their villages. All the Nuxalk then gathered near the river, and it was estimated that of the thirty thousand people who were alive before the epidemic, two hundred and forty-seven remained. Thus the Nuxalk survived and treated a major illness.

Through the colonization, bureaucratization, missionization, and education processes of the Canadian colonial governments, the control of healing and other health practices was largely transferred from Indigenous peoples to programs and institutions sponsored by the Canadian government (Waldram, 2004). According to Waldram, while this new system helped to mitigate some of the devastating health problems brought from Europe (such as influenza, tuberculosis, and smallpox, which developed through the early contact period), it failed to protect the health and well-being of Indigenous people in the following ways.

First, the health care services provided by the Canadian federal government had no foundation in the traditional knowledge and cultural values and practices of Indigenous peoples. The government's health care practices were unfamiliar and frightening for many Indigenous people and further undermined their trust in and identification with their own practices and resources; this undermining was also supported by the assimilationist education provided through residential schools. These health care services also took some Indigenous individuals away from their communities, sometimes for extended periods, when they required certain types of medical treatment, such as for tuberculosis or pneumonia. Second, traditional healers were ridiculed and persecuted by the dominant culture and by governmental legislation; in reaction, traditional healers were forced to practice their traditions such as potlatch ceremonies, sundance, sweatlodge ceremonies, and traditional healing in secret. As a result, many Indigenous people no longer accessed the benefits of their traditional healers' skills and knowledge, either because they did not know how to access these services or because they had been taught to mistrust, fear, or condemn their own healing traditions. Through this process of eliminating the practice of traditional healers, a great deal of very valuable cultural knowledge has been mitigated or lost. Third, the Western perspectives that dominate mental health interventions have roots in modernism, a worldview that values objective truth, rational thinking, and the constancy of measurement (Sue & Sue, 1990). This focus on Western perspectives on mental health means that Aboriginal communities have only had access to certain Western types of treatment and prevention programs, mostly those that focus on individuals and diagnostic labels rather than on the type of traditional healing, human and community development, and interdependence that are needed to restore Indigenous individuals, families, and communities to a level of health and wellness (Smith, 1999). Last, Indigenous people lost control over the institutions and processes that were supposed to protect their health (Alfred, 1999; Waldram, 2004). Indigenous people were taught, through missionization and residential schools, that the dominant society knew best which services and programs they needed. Even now, as many Indigenous communities are negotiating with the Canadian government for the transfer of health programs to their control, they are often being given administrative responsibility for existing mental health programs but very little real power to actually recreate culturally based health and social service programming in order to move toward maximum health and well-being (Waldram, 2004).

CURRENT MENTAL HEALTH ISSUES

Kirmayer, Brass, and Tait (2000) explain that cultural discontinuity and oppression are linked to high rates of alcoholism, suicide, depression, and violence for many Indigenous groups today, particularly youth, yet that many communities continue to grow and even thrive despite such challenges. The history of health and colonization, beginning in the 1500s and continuing into current times, shows a clear connection between mental health and colonization; Kirmayer et al. (2000) link specific health problems, such as obesity, diabetes, low self-esteem, depression, and suicide, to this colonial history and oppression; there are social origins for the mental health distress currently being experienced in Native Canadian communities. These social origins include the government policy that created residential schools, and poverty and economic marginalization. These authors write that residential schools are a major source of cultural extermination for Aboriginal peoples; from 1879 to 1973, the Canadian government mandated church-run boarding schools to provide education for all Native children. Aboriginal children were forcibly removed from homes and relocated to residential schools, often geographically far from their families, with siblings usually sent to separate schools, in order to fulfill the policy goal of systematically breaking down Aboriginal culture and family. In residential schools Aboriginal children were denied all ties to their cultures, including language and customs. In short, their identity as Aboriginal was completely taken away. Physical and sexual abuse by teachers and clergy was rampant in residential school life, and these atrocities have only recently been acknowledged by the government and churches.

Poverty and economic marginalization, as part of Aboriginal colonial history, contribute to the current legacy of mental health problems. The effects of poverty include third-world living conditions, especially on many reserves, and the high rates of chronic health problems that exist in today's communities. Kirmayer et al. (2000) state:

> The effects of poverty are seen in the poor living conditions on many reserves and remote settlements that lead to chronic respiratory diseases, recurrent otitis media with hearing loss, and tuberculosis; in the past, these necessitated prolonged hospitalizations that further subverted the integrity of families and communities. (p. 610)

This economic marginalization is seen as a creation of the social order in which Native peoples are embedded within Canadian society. Further, it is suggested by Kirmayer et al. that the presence of the mass media in such communities today makes the values of consumer capitalism central and creates feelings of deprivation for those community members where none previously existed. Kirmayer et al. note that health research in Indigenous communities does not always allow for differences in the incidence and prevalence of specific mental health problems among and between communities, but rather tends to generalize information to all Native communities. Kirmayer et al. suggest that in Indigenous contexts today, there are constant transformations of forms of community, and that this sort of evolution is at the root of recovery, or "revitalization and renewal." Further, it is the "mediating mechanics," or what are described as individual and self-perceptions, contributing to social and mental health problems that are closely related to issues of individual identity and self-esteem (p. 611). These factors are influenced by the collectives of communities. For example, the wide variation of suicide rates across Native communities indicates that it is important to consider the nature and health of the overall communities and how these communities respond to the ongoing stresses of colonization and governmental control, including socio-political marginalization.

The mental health implications of this colonial history are significant for Indigenous communities and individuals (Duran, 2006; Kirmayer et al., 2000; Waldram, 2004). These implications include high rates (compared to non-Indigenous populations) of grief and loss, depression, family violence, sexual abuse, substance abuse, addictions, trauma, and suicide. Of these issues, trauma and suicide will be discussed in detail because of their saliency within communities and because of their prevalence as presenting problems when counselling Indigenous clients (Duran, 2006).

Trauma has been documented in the literature as a major healing issue in many Indigenous communities across Canada (see Bopp & Lane, 2000; Caron, 2012, 2004; Menzies, 2009; Wilson, 2004). Bopp and Lane (2000) write that trauma for Native individuals and communities is a complex and intergenerational phenomenon that has its roots in the colonial history that has taken away and destroyed many traditional Native cultural practices. Bopp and Lane define trauma as "the psychological, physical, and mental effects associated with a painful experience or shock" (p. 25). Experiencing trauma events puts an individual or community in a position of being overwhelmed emotionally with the traumatic experience. This overwhelm is dealt with in many different ways by different people and communities. People often turn to substance abuse, violence toward others or the self, suicide, and many other forms of self-destructive behaviour; these effects are often described as indicators or consequences of psychological trauma (Tedeschi & Calhoun, 1996).

In a report based on a health study with the Nuxalk Nation of British Columbia, Bopp and Lane (2000) write that psychological trauma can occur from a single event or a series of prolonged events, and that trauma can strike individuals as well as communities. Regardless of the specifics of the traumatic events, the trauma itself creates certain characteristic effects on individuals and the way that they understand their environments and relationships. "Trauma affects whole communities by undermining social, cultural, economic, and political structures and relationships as well as the capacity of that community to interact in a healthy balanced way with the society around it" (Bopp & Lane, 2000, p. 26). When trauma is ongoing, or occurs more than once, a sense of helplessness and hopelessness often sets in for the individual or the community. Bopp and Lane conclude that healing support for Indigenous communities and individuals dealing with psychological trauma must address these core aspects of trauma.

Karmali et al. (2005) conducted a population-based observational study that describes the epidemiological characteristics of severe psychological trauma among status Indians in the Calgary health region. They discovered that in their sample, severe trauma – such as suicide or accidental death – occurred about four times more among status Indians than among non-Indigenous groups. Further, a large difference in rates was present for specific causes, such as suicide, assault, and car accident.

In addition to understanding rates and epidemiological characteristics of trauma in Indigenous communities, issues of morbidity and accurate depictions of the real effects of trauma must be documented and understood in qualitative and quantitative terms, and must include all Aboriginal peoples – not only status Indians (Caron, 2004). This need for qualitative information is because there exists ample evidence to suggest that suicide is a problem, but not enough data to describe what this means to the individuals and communities involved. Also, health care services, including mental health services, must be more accessible and more culturally appropriate for Native communities dealing with psychological trauma, and such qualitative data could be used to improve these services. Caron (2004) suggests that traumatic injury and death are easily preventable health problems, but that it would take the support of the health care community and greater society to work collaboratively with Indigenous groups to deal with the psychological effects of trauma.

Substantial research on Indigenous suicide shows high levels of suicide in some, but not all, communities. As discussed above, Indigenous people in general do not have the same health status as non-Natives in Canada; however, when it comes to suicide, the difference is especially dramatic. The overall First Nations death rate for injuries, including suicide, is 2.9 times higher than for non-Natives. The 1999 crude death rate for First Nations males overall was 30 percent higher than for First Nations females overall, largely due to injury. One of the leading causes of death by injury among males overall was suicide.

Studies by Bagley, Wood, and Khumar (1990) and Bohn (2003) identified regional variations in Indigenous community suicides, indicating that Health Canada's generalized statistics may not fit specific communities. Chandler and Lalonde's (1998) early research further elaborates on this within-group difference as linked to Aboriginal self-government and cultural identification and practices. In the 1980s, the federal government initiated a process meant to transfer health care responsibility to First Nations and Inuit governments. The rationale for this decision by the government was that Indigenous people best understood their communities' health care and service delivery needs and thus should be in control of these services (Health Canada, 2003). In 1994, Health Canada conducted a study on the success of this transfer of health care services program and found that transferring management control had led to a decrease in health problems and issues within communities and more culturally sensitive health care delivery (Health Canada, 2006). In addition, health care, including dealing with suicide, became a priority that could be acted upon. Seminal research by Chandler and Lalonde (1998) examined suicide in the context of self-government and local control of health care, education, and other infrastructure. In studying suicide among British Columbia's nearly two hundred Aboriginal communities, they found that while some communities had suicide rates eight hundred times greater than the national average, in other communities, suicide was practically non-existent. Chandler and Lalonde further identified six protective factors that help make sense of the differing suicide rates across some Native communities. These factors are discussed as *cultural continuity*, and could be considered an index of community-level success in renewing or reclaiming cultural tradition: (1) land claims, (2) self-government, (3) education services, (4) police and fire services, (5) health services, and (6) cultural facilities. More specifically, Chandler and Lalonde found that communities with some form of self-government had the lowest rate of youth suicide. Land claims was the second and education the third most important factors in predicting a low suicide rate in the communities studied. Communities possessing three or more cultural continuity factors experienced substantially fewer suicides than communities without such factors present. Thus these factors are important to consider when regarding the mental health of communities in terms of suicide rates. Further study is currently needed to examine other correlates of mental health such as depression, self-esteem, addictions, and family violence with such factors of cultural continuity.

CHALLENGES FOR CURRENT COUNSELLING SERVICES

Mental health treatment in Canada has been predominately viewed in non-Indigenous ways that disregard ideas such as holistic health and healing. Mental health interventions typically utilize a range of Western-based perspectives, from the DSM-IV's pathological model to person-centred therapy, where the focus is on the individual and not on interdependence with others, as it would be in an Indigenous model. Duran (2006) writes that much of the Western paradigm of mental health is marked by beliefs in logical positivism, linear thinking, and individualism that promote illness instead of Indigenous wellness; "Western trained therapists are trained to think within a prescribed paradigm that targets pathology" (p. 19).

Specific challenges arise when Western mental health care concepts and systems are imposed on Indigenous people and communities. First, Western and Indigenous notions of mental health are different; second, counsellors trained in Western notions of mental health do not effectively service Indigenous mental health populations; and third, using a Western paradigm of mental health in an Indigenous context is a form of continued oppression of Indigenous people.

Related to the first point, counselling that is based on Western notions of health and healing does not match Indigenous conceptions of well-being. Western-based counselling approaches are culturally inappropriate in Indigenous contexts because the many values and ways of being and doing are different (Duran, 2006). Any Western approach will not be effective with Indigenous clients if it does not take into account the context of the client's life. Often, health policies and programs designed by non-Indigenous individuals or institutions have been inappropriate for dealing with Indigenous problems because the philosophies and ways of living that underpin each approach are very different (Gone, 2004; Kirmayer, Brass, & Valaskakis, 2009; Vicary & Bishop, 2005). Indigenous healing is different because it employs a holistic approach to well-being, which is defined as a whole person that includes mind, body, and spirit (Waldram, 2008, 2004). Western approaches to counselling such as constructivism and family systems are often considered more culturally appropriate in Indigenous contexts because they consider the contexts of the individual; however, they are not based on Indigenous worldviews or paradigms that reflect notions of interconnectedness, spirituality, and Native rules of behaviour (Blue & Darou, 2005; Stewart, 2009b). Western culture in Canada emphasizes a hierarchical and individualist worldview, which is in opposition to Indigenous beliefs. Western approaches to counselling are largely based on individualism, such as the person-centred approach (Duran, 2006). McCormick (2000b) maintains that the European-Western paradigm is built on a model of creation containing a hierarchy of God, humans, and nature, including concepts of domination of humans by God, of animals by humans, and of humans exploiting the land. An Indigenous counselling model, according to McCormick (2000a), would be based on connectedness, equality, and harmony between people and nature.

King (1999) conducted a survey with an urban Indigenous adult population in Denver, Colorado, to identify their mental health needs. This study is cited due to a lack of related Canadian data; however, due to similarities in the cultural themes and colonial histories of different North American Indigenous peoples, King's study is relevant to Canadian populations. King concluded that mental health provider agencies are not meeting the current needs of urban Native adults, who stated a preference for Native health service providers or at least providers who are sensitive to cultural community needs. Over ninety percent of the adult respondents said they would use mental health services if they were made available by Native persons trained in mental health services or non-Natives who had training in Native sensitivity as well as mental health services. Community health was also a theme in King's data. The study's authors' recommendations were that all levels of Indigenous community mental health are in dire need of mental health services that are grounded in an Indigenous paradigm. Mental health is underpinned by community health, according to King, and community-level interventions that fit the Indigenous culture of the community, such as prevention and education, are needed to address the mental health of individuals sampled in this community. Blue (1977), Blue and Darou (2005), and McCormick (1997) have also studied and written about how and why Indigenous people utilize services only when these services are grounded in a First Nations helping model. These researchers have worked in Canadian contexts and conducted interviews with Native clients in counselling.

Research (McCormick & Gerlitz, 2009; Oulanov, 2009; Stewart, 2009a) suggests that mental health approaches in general could benefit from the worldviews of Indigenous healing methods. These are usually informal and naturally existing help-giving methods present in all traditional Indigenous cultures that focus on interdependence or connectedness in healing. For example, in traditional Dene communities in Canada's north, grandparents not only took care of grandchildren so that parents could do valuable work for the community such as hunting and craft-making, but these grandparents also passed on cultural knowledge that was vital for individual and group survival as a distinct people. In counselling relationships, interdependence can be understood as helping clients to create healthy relationships within the therapeutic alliance, within their identity as a cultural person, and with ceremony and traditional spiritual practices (Stewart, 2008).

With regard to the second point, counsellors who receive training only in Western approaches to mental health and healing are not meeting the needs of Native clients seeking counselling services; but at the same time, there is currently an under-use of mental health services such as counselling by ethnic minority groups, including Indigenous peoples (Stewart, 2008). Some researchers have suggested that this under-use stems from the fact that counselling approaches are not culturally sensitive to the Indigenous clients' values, beliefs, or worldviews: "Counselors may lack basic knowledge about the client's ethnic and historical backgrounds; the client may be driven away by the professional's counseling style; the client may sense that his or her worldview is not valued" (Trimble & Thurman, 2002, p. 61).

Recently, there has been an increase in post-secondary training programs focused on counselling with Indigenous clients. Some concentrate on traditional concepts and healing methods (McCormick, 2009; Medicine-Eagle, 1989); others promote a blended or "hybrid" (Duran, 2006) approach that integrates traditional and Western counselling (Guenette & Marshall, 2008; Marshall et al., 2014). A new graduate program in counselling at the University of Victoria emphasizes the community context that is central to Indigenous notions of health and healing (Marshall et al., 2014). These counsellor training courses and programs include a curriculum that addresses historical trauma, effects of colonization, Indigenous worldviews, acculturation, and appropriate healing methods in an effort to better meet the diverse needs and experiences of Aboriginal clients and communities.

To address the third point, a Western perspective on mental health continues the oppression of Indigenous peoples because it delegitimizes an Indigenous view of health and healing. According to the Aboriginal Healing Foundation (2002), conceptions of traditional health and healing are integral to current efforts by Canadian Indigenous peoples to face the legacy of suffering and dislocation brought on by the history of colonialism. For example, in 2000, the Champlain District Mental Health Implementation Task Force, in Ontario, began the implementation of mental health reform in two specific First Nations communities (Akwesasne and Golden Lake). This reform is marked by recognizing the need to support First Nations' capacity to design, deliver, and control their own mental health services, and to respect traditional contemporary Indigenous approaches to healing and wellness (Poushinsky & Taillion-Wasmund, 2002). Further, the reform recommends that within First Nations communities, there must be at least one of, or a combination of, three streams of available mental health services: traditional mental health services provided by traditional healers and healers through ceremonies; Indigenized mental health services (Western mental health paradigms that have been converted and delivered by Natives); and Western mental health services delivery to Natives by non-Natives.

The intent and results that have underpinned much mental health research have been a tool of power and control over First Nations groups in Canada (Hudson & Taylor-Henley, 2002). Many mental health treatment applications have been designed to dominate and control people with mental illness. This process of social control was first explored in the literature by Foucault (1971), who wrote that when the church lost control of much of the general Western population in the 1800s, the medical profession seized the opportunity to control the masses. The movement of the medical profession at the time evolved into the present-day mental health care system in the Western world, including Canada. In this perspective, mental health care practitioners can be seen as possessing and exerting social control through the process of labelling in diagnosis and the sometimes subsequent taking away of a person's rights when they are deemed not of sound mind. In Indigenous contexts, colonial mental health care systems continue this oppressive practice when they provide only Western counselling services to Indigenous individuals, thus providing Eurocentric models of mental health and counselling that do not take into account Indigenous cultural norms or healing practices (Gone, 2011; McCormick & Gerlitz, 2009).

INDIGENOUS MENTAL HEALTH AND HEALING

In 1991, the Government of Canada published its "Agenda for First Nations and Inuit Mental Health." It includes a description of mental health within a framework of holism and positive psychology as they are embedded in community and cultural identity:

> Among the First Nations and Inuit communities, the term mental health is used in a broad sense, describing behaviours which make for a harmonious and cohesive community and the relative absence of multiple problem behaviours in the community, such as family violence, substance abuse, juvenile delinquency and self-destructive behaviour. It is more than the absence of illness, disease or dysfunction – it is the presence of a holistic, psychological wellness which is part of the full circle of mind, body, emotions and spirit, with respect for tradition, culture and language. This gives rise to creativity, imagination and growth, and enhances the capacity of the community, family group or individual identities to interact harmoniously and respond to illness and adversity in healing ways. (p. 6)

This holistic description of mental health makes an important point about the interrelatedness of spiritual, mental, social, and community aspects of health. Health viewed as possessing an interrelated quality along with notions such as community and identity allows for an examination of mental health through a systemic lens that is grounded in an Indigenous paradigm.

Mussell (2005) writes that mental health in the context of Indigenous counsellors and policy-makers is about focusing on the mental health issues that exist as the most serious detriments to the survival and well-being of Native peoples. Part of an Indigenous worldview is the notion of holistic health, which marks how people view themselves, their families, and their communities in a forward-thinking manner. "Holistic health is the vision most First Nations peoples articulate as they reflect upon their future. At the personal level this means each member enjoys health and wellness in body, mind, heart, and spirit. Within the family context, this means mutual support of each other ... From a community perspective it means leadership committed to whole health, empowerment, sensitivity to interrelatedness of past, present, and future possibilities, and connected between cultures" (p. 26). An integral concept to the notion of holistic health is the concept of interdependence, as pointed out by Mussell. For Indigenous people, mental health problems result from lack of balance and interdependence among the four aspects of human nature, identified above. When balance, or harmony through interconnectedness, is restored through paying attention to the needs of the four aspects of the self, the family, or the community, health is achieved in Indigenous worldviews.

The medicine wheel model is a conceptual and practical framework for the holistic philosophy of mental health. Absolon (1994) defines the medicine wheel as "a paradigm that is relevant to the needs for assessment purposes in healing work, an expression of a First Nations Worldview, that views healing as a process that achieves a balanced relationship with the self, Mother earth, and the natural world" (p. 25). Originating with the Plains Natives, the medicine wheel is an ancient and widely used concept in Indigenous North American cultures that models health and wellness for multiple aspects of a person or community (Mussell, 2005). When considering the medicine wheel, it is important to note that the term *medicine* as it is used by many First Nations people does not refer to drugs or herbal remedies (Thunderbird, 2005). Storm (1972) explains that medicine in Plains culture refers to the personal characteristics and strengths of individuals that come to them through a particular animal reflection that occurs though the wheel. The characteristics of this reflection on an individual are determined by the nature of the animal itself (e.g., bear, eagle, wolf, pheasant), and also by the location of the individual him/herself.

Storm, a Plains Native and teacher of the lessons of the medicine wheel, explains the philosophies of the circle. The medicine wheel is seen as demonstrating that we need multiple perspectives through its construction of the circle as a non-linear structure (Storm, 1972). She writes that the medicine wheel, as a circle, can be best understood in terms of a mirror that reflects all aspects of life and world.

"Any idea, person, or object can be a Medicine Wheel, a Mirror, for man" (p. 5).

Teachings in contemporary Indigenous communities based on the medicine wheel create an epistemological paradigm that employs a holistic foundation for human behaviour and interaction; it informs a framework for mental health through a discussion of its four quadrants, each one a separate representation of North, South, East, and West (Thunderbird, 2005). For example, in the Sault. Nation the construction of the wheel is meant to help people seek strong, healthy bodies (represented by the North-facing quadrant), strong inner spirits (represented by the South-facing quadrant), healthy minds (East quadrant), and inner peace (West quadrant) (Four Directions, 2005).

The medicine wheel embodies how Indigenous mental health can be conceptualized in a theoretical and pragmatic model for health care delivery (Poushinsky & Tallion-Wasmund, 2002). The Dze L K'ant Native Friendship Centre Society (2006) in Smithers, British Columbia, employs a holistic healing model based on the medicine wheel in their counselling programs. The medicine wheel model is described as one of the Centre's tools for reaching the goal for mental health counselling, which is to "help Aboriginal and non-Aboriginal clients with serious forms of mental illness by supporting their ability to function in social relations and manage their daily lives" (p. 1). The Centre's model embeds practices of "mental health support" and "being in sound mind" through the acknowledgement of the four aspects of each person's personal "will" as depicted by the medicine wheel (Dze L K'ant Friendship Centre Society, 2006, p. 2). Mussell et al. (1993) have also created a medicine wheel as a working tool for mental health practitioners that depicts the same four components of mental health. Each component is linked to specific needs that individuals must meet in order to achieve balance, or health, in all parts of self, with a person's will in the centre, which represents the power to make decisions and act upon them. The needs of the intellectual aspect of self consist of concepts, ideas, thoughts, habits, and discipline. The needs of the spiritual aspect of self involve a sense of connectedness with others, and with creations of the Great Spirit. The emotional aspect's needs include love, discipline, recognition, acceptance, understanding, privacy, and limits, while the physical aspect's needs consist of air, exercise, water, sex, food, clothing, and shelter. The ability of a person to meet these needs is through their own personal power, throughout their sense of will.

France and McCormick (1997) developed a healing circle based on medicine wheel teachings. They call this healing circle a helping circle, and it models a training program of a peer counselling service for First Nations university students. France and McCormick's First Nations Peer Support Network was created because they saw a need to make counselling services more accessible and culturally appropriate for First Nations students. The program is based on local Indigenous philosophies and practices and employs several traditional cultural tools, including the medicine wheel, along with contemporary counselling approaches.

The purpose of the First Nations Peer Support Network is to provide an informal helping and support service using volunteers from the First Nations community to work with other First Nations people. "What we hope will make the support network effective, is to combine both established helping practices with the traditional 'spirit' that makes First Nations people unique" (p. 27). The program is implemented through a training model that is based on the circle of the medicine wheel, which is called the Helping Circle. The students training to become peer supports sit in a circle, which is opened with a prayer or excerpt of Native philosophy. A stone is passed to each person in the circle as a symbol of their opportunity to speak and share their story. In the Helping Circle the facilitator should model the target skill and provide the participants an opportunity to practice the skill. The facilitator may choose to let all of the participants use the skill as a group or allow individuals to volunteer to use the skill (p. 28). The authors explain that the First Nations helping approach must be based on the four principles as depicted in the medicine wheel. In the phases of the training for their program, the four dimensions of the self are explored or employed. Further, the circle, as a model, which embodies a non-linear perspective, represents the cultural view of helping as counselling and teaches this to the students by use of the metaphor of the wheel with its emphasis on holism. "Helping generally does not move in a direct line. In this sense, helping is cyclical as compared to a linear line or moving direct from a statement of the issue to a solution" (p. 31).

Stewart (2008) also developed a medicine wheel model of counselling based on research with First Nations counsellors in a community social service setting. This model places concepts of community, holism, identity, and interdependence within each of the four quadrants of the wheel to represent the elements of counselling that support a culturally based conception of mental health. In other words, when counselling actively integrates these four aspects into the counselling process and relationships, culturally based cross-cultural interactions may occur between counsellor and client (Stewart, 2009b). Holistic counselling from this perspective entails paying attention to the spiritual, as the missing piece in standard Western counselling practices.

Spirituality is an integral aspect of healing for Indigenous people, and without attention to this, counsellors may be lacking an integral part of the healing process for clients (McCormick, 2009; Stewart, 2009b). In practice this may mean praying or smudging with traditional medicines such as sage or sweetgrass in counselling sessions, and working in collaboration with Elders and traditional healers (Stewart, 2008). Community elements to counselling with Indigenous clients takes this notion of collaboration one step further by integrating community-based interventions with individual clients; for instance, this includes involving traditional ceremonies conducted by Elders and traditional healers in the overall treatment plan of the client. It can also include inviting immediate and extended family to be part of the counselling process both within sessions and as part of the client's treatment plan in activities in daily life.

Mental health issues related to work and employment within Aboriginal populations are an area that needs more investigation. Compared to non-Indigenous groups, Indigenous men and women experience significantly higher rates of unemployment, which is often linked to higher rates of depression, substance use, and family violence (Marshall et al., 2013). McCormick, Amundson, and Poehnell (2002) developed the *Guiding Circles* program, a group approach that focuses on strengths and self-esteem as it guides Aboriginal participants through the process of self-reflection, exploration, and decision-making in the context of career. Recent research with Indigenous youth and young adults indicates that educational gaps, training access, and racism are work-related problems that counsellors need to address (Marshall et al., 2013).

There is little information in the current literature regarding counselling approaches for specific Indigenous population groups, such as youth, women, men, and children. There are two possible explanations for this. On the one hand, there is a lack of research data in these areas. More studies and practice-oriented literature focused on Indigenous clients and groups would be very helpful for counsellors and for counsellor training programs. Although the Indigenous population is extremely diverse, there are a number of common principles and concepts that have relevance across a broad range of contexts. For example, the patriarchal influences and regulations that were part of colonization have particularly impacted Aboriginal women in Canada – loss of First Nations status, hereditary rights, and property limitations represent cultural losses that have only recently been reversed (Shepard, O'Neill, & Guenette, 2006). Women's roles and responsibilities within the family and community have also been significantly affected by poverty and marginalization. It is critical that counsellors working with Indigenous women and children understand these historical and present-day inequities.

Another possible explanation for the dearth of specialized research and practice literature relates to the lack of emphasis on individual experiences. From traditional knowledge perspectives, there is often not a separation of care and treatment for individuals – a collectivist orientation prevails and works toward healing for individuals from interdependent and community-based modalities. A typical Western counselling focus on individual needs can be uncomfortable for Indigenous clients.

IMPLICATIONS AND FUTURE DIRECTIONS

From the above discussion, there are a number of implications related to enhancing the practice of counselling psychology with Indigenous groups. It is abundantly clear that more research and practice evidence is needed, involving both broad samples in a wide variety of contexts and specialized populations such as women and youth. At the same time, it is vital that counsellors pay close attention to the particular contexts of their clients and avoid making generalizations.

All counsellors need an understanding of the historical and political events that have impacted the lives of Indigenous people in Canada and of the relationship of these events to present-day mental health problems as well as strengths. Stories of resistance and resilience can be found in even the most dire situations, as evidenced by the recent Truth and Reconciliation hearings held across the country.

Counselling should include community-based counselling inter-ventions that are founded on cultural models of health and healing. Counsellors should explore health and healing from an Indigenous paradigm and how this can better serve Indigenous clients and non-Indigenous clients whose needs are not being met by the current Western system of counselling and psychotherapy. Working in col-laborative ways with both Indigenous communities and non-Native communities is one way to begin integrating multiple worldviews and practices. It is necessary to pay closer attention to the ethics of cross-cultural interactions in counselling and to how Western approaches can be used to empower, rather than oppress, Indigenous clients and communities (Marshall et al., 2014).

Stewart (2008) conducted a study that identified a culturally based conception of Indigenous mental health and healing and presented a culturally based model for counselling practice with Indigenous cli-ents as described by Indigenous counsellors. A major implication from the results of the study suggested the development of culturally based training models that incorporate traditional healing practices and Western counselling approaches. Embedded in the narratives of the participants was the reality that Indigenous people's stories of healing and health promotion are still evolving within the current social context, which includes involvement with Western health care practices. This blended approach can be found in many recent train-ing initiatives and programs, which is encouraging.

The picture of mental health and healing services from Indigenous perspectives is not well defined in the current literature (Caron, 2004; Karmali et al., 2005; Stewart, 2009a). There are at least two challenges inherent to delivery of Indigenous and Western models of mental health care to Indigenous populations: (1) there is little sys-tematic research that informs counselling education and practice from an Indigenous paradigm of health (Duran, 2006; Kirmayer et al., 2000; Mussell, 2005; Stewart, 2009a); and (2) before counsellors and counsellor educators can address the largely unmet mental health needs of Native peoples, we require more information from Indigenous counsellors and clients about the experiences and poten-tial effects/successes of a hybrid of Western and Indigenous holis-tic-based mental health services and interventions (Caron, 2004; Stewart, 2009b). Thus, conducting community-based studies from Indigenous and blended paradigms will better inform culturally based counselling with Indigenous people.

CONCLUSION

It is important to have awareness of the mental health problems currently facing Indigenous communities; it is from this point of understanding that the profession of counselling can shift its focus from problems and dysfunctions to identifying strengths and healing solutions within the counselling context. Culturally based mental health and healing is a major issue for Indigenous peoples in Canada, as there is currently a health crisis in some communities. Applying a community-based cultural lens to counselling services represents a process that honours both Western and Indigenous notions and practices of healing. Working together collaboratively allows both counsellors and clients to share their healing resources to respectfully and effectively address the needs of both the people and the profession.

5

Lesbian, Gay, Bisexual, Transgender, and Intersex Individuals

KEVIN G. ALDERSON WITH
JANE M. OXENBURY

Many acronyms are in usage today, reflecting writers' attempts to be inclusive of the various segments comprising the nondominant sexual and gender community. What began as a "gay community" later became known as two communities: gay and lesbian. As the definition expanded, bisexual individuals were added, thereby creating a gay, lesbian, and bisexual (L G B) community. Over time, individuals with varying gender expressions (i.e., transgender) and gender identities (i.e., transgender or transsexual) were included, creating the L G B T acronym. One can also add a "Q" for those who are questioning either their sexuality or their gender, another "Q" for those who call themselves "queer," and an "I" for those who are intersex (referred to in the D S M as disorders of sexual development).

This chapter adopts L G B T I as the acronym of choice. The rationale is that those who are questioning can be viewed as "visitors," individuals who are exploring without commitment to what may or may not become an enduring aspect of identity. The research that has been conducted on L G B T I individuals includes primarily those who have already achieved an identity that they are willing to disclose. The label of "queer" is not included as some people continue to view this word as derogatory, but also because, as Savin-Williams (2005) has indicated, the identifier has not been adopted by members of the community to any appreciable extent. As writers often adopt different definitions for the terms that comprise the L G B T I community, we encourage readers to refer to the glossary (see Appendix).

As sexuality is, for the most part, unrelated to gender expression and gender identity, these two groups are discussed in separate sections. We begin with those who have differing sexual identities and affectional orientations.

OVERVIEW OF CANADIAN LGBTI PEOPLE, HISTORY, AND POLICIES

LGB People in Canada

The history of LGBTI individuals has been rife with conflict, prejudice, discrimination, oppression, subjugation, condemnation, persecution, and violence. Unlike racial/ethnic minority groups, however, LGBTI individuals have lived mostly invisible lives and/or they have been rendered invisible by the dominant culture. Consequently, much of the history of LGBTI individuals remains lost: unheard, unwritten, and uncelebrated.

The history of LGB individuals here provides only a few recent highlights. A book that provides a comprehensive history is Warner's (2002) *Never Going Back: A History of Queer Activism in Canada.*

If you had asked college or university students in 1970 if they knew any gay individuals, particularly as friends, the majority would have replied "No." Today's reality is that most post-secondary students know at least one gay and/or lesbian person.

What happened? While a gay culture existed before 1969, it was underground and largely secretive. Grube (1990) noted a study by Maurice Leznoff that revealed that gay individuals in Montreal, Quebec, in the early 1950s felt a strong pressure to "pass" as heterosexual. While some were openly gay, they worked in stereotypically gay occupations such as artist, hairstylist, or interior decorator, or in low-status occupations such as bellhop.

Bill C-150, introduced by Prime Minister Pierre Trudeau, passed in the Upper House on 26 August 1969, legalizing private homosexual behaviour between consenting adults. The decriminalization of homosexuality in Canada, however, was only the beginning of the fight for equal rights.

On 5 February 1981, more than three hundred men were arrested in bathhouse raids in Toronto, Ontario (CBC News, 2007), an event to be repeated in Calgary, Alberta, in December 2002 when seventeen men were similarly charged (CBC News, 2002). Police raids of gay establishments were not uncommon in Canada, occurring in the 1950s (Paré, 2009), the 1970s (Pride Library at the University of Western Ontario, n.d.), and even as late as 1990 in Montreal (Burnett, 2009).

The Canadian Charter of Rights and Freedoms was later introduced by Pierre Trudeau, becoming law in 1982. Section 15, which dealt with minority rights, did not become effective until 1985, however. Court decisions concerning LGBTI rights have been won ultimately through reference to this Charter (Lahey & Alderson, 2004).

In 1996, the federal government added "sexual orientation" to the Canadian Human Rights Act. In 2002, Marc Hall, an Ontario teen, was denied permission to take his boyfriend to a Catholic high school prom, and after a short court battle, he won: but perhaps only for himself. For several reasons, Marc dropped the court case on 28 June 2005 (Grace & Wells, 2005). One of the most seminal events in Canadian gay and lesbian history occurred on 20 July 2005 when Bill C-38, the Canadian Civil Marriage Act (Hurley, 2005), received royal assent, making same-sex marriage legal throughout the country (CBC News, 2007).

Our discussion of LGB subgroups focuses almost entirely on research that has been done in Canada with application to counselling practice. Consequently, the research will appear lacking in certain areas. There is a vast American literature in the area of LGBTI studies, and few studies have revealed differences between the subgroups in the two countries (Alderson, 2013).

Counsellors would do well to remember that our discussion is primarily focused on *identities*. Identities are as unique for LGBTI individuals as they are for those belonging only to the dominant culture. Our goal as counsellors is to help individuals live productive, healthy lives, and to feel good about themselves during the process. We will only succeed in that if we successfully surrender the stereotypes that even research can create and focus instead on the individual sitting before us. Nonetheless, there are some commonalities that, if nothing else, help lead us to formulate appropriate questions in the counselling session that tell the person before us that we are informed and open to this form of diversity.

LESBIAN WOMEN   There are multiple meanings (i.e., identities) to the word *lesbian* (McDonald, 2006), just as the lesbian client today may be the heterosexual or bisexual client tomorrow, and vice versa.

Several studies highlight the fluidity of female sexuality (Diamond, 2008; McElwain, Grimes, & McVicker, 2009; Ravel & Rail, 2008). Nonetheless, many women will maintain a lesbian identity indefinitely. Every identity brings with it advantages and disadvantages. Lesbian women are likely to develop relationships based on equality (Schneider, 1986) together with strong emotional bonds (Ackbar & Senn, 2010). While this degree of relationship closeness has sometimes been seen as excessive or "fusion" (Igartua, 1998), one must be careful to not view a same-sex relationship through a heterosexist lens. Strong emotional bonds between a female couple are often healthy and functional (Ackbar & Senn, 2010). Another potential relationship outcome is "bed death," where lesbian women will frequently stop being sexual with each other after some time in their relationship. However, research has also shown that many lesbian couples enjoy very positive and fulfilling sex lives together (Cohen, 2011), and that sexual satisfaction is "an extremely strong predictor of relational well-being" (Holmberg, Blair, & Phillips, 2010, p. 1). Furthermore, lesbian women who are in relationships are less likely to experience depression (Ayala & Coleman, 2000).

Lesbian women are often more androgynous than heterosexual women (LaTorre & Wendenburg, 1983), and they often subscribe to feminist ideals (Ellis & Peel, 2011; Sinacore & Enns, 2005b). Subscribing to a feminist ideology often helps lesbian women develop healthier body images compared to heterosexual women (Bergeron & Senn, 1998). While they are more likely to become overweight and physically inactive (Brittain, Baillargeon, McElroy, Aaron, & Gyurcsik, 2006), such outcomes, when they occur, may result from their response to discrimination, their choice of maintaining androgynous gender expression, and/or their rejection of heterosexual expectations that they remain slim to satisfy male sexual fantasies, sexual pleasures, or both.

In general, compared to their heterosexual counterparts, lesbian women experience more stress-related problems including substance abuse disorders, mood disorders, suicidality (Daley, 2008), smoking, and excessive drinking (Steele, Ross, Dobinson, Veldhuizen, & Tinmouth, 2009), yet they are less likely to seek medical help (Mathieson, Bailey, & Gurevich, 2002; Steele, Tinmouth, & Lu, 2006). While lesbian women are often resistant to disclosing their identity to others (Barbara, Quandt, & Anderson, 2001; Daley, 2010), lesbian feminists generally experience less internalized homophobia and are more likely to disclose their identities (Bergeron & Senn, 2003). While this helps some receive regular health care as a result (Steele et al., 2006), there is a long history in Canada of health care discrimination against lesbian women (Polonijo & Hollister, 2011; Ross, 1995; Sinding, Barnoff, & Grassau, 2004). For instance, artificial insemination for lesbian women was illegal and many had to access secret support groups to obtain sperm for self-insemination (Ross, 1995). When trying to adopt, same-sex couples are held to a higher standard compared with opposite-sex couples (Ross et al., 2008) and are often denied the option to adopt or even to become foster parents. (To read about additional challenges regarding donor insemination, see Kranz & Daniluk, 2006, and Leblond de Brumath & Julien, 2007.)

Individuals with marginalized identities have a need for community, and those who receive it are generally psychologically healthier. Unfortunately, every time a lesbian woman moves, she needs to re-establish herself in a community that may be difficult to find or enter (Liddle, 2007).

Schneider (1989) interviewed twenty-five young lesbian women (ages 15–20) in Toronto. Their "plea" included a "need and desire for acceptance" (p. 129). While we may think that young women's experience of same-sex desire is substantially different today from yesteryear, Logan and Buchanan (2008) found in their qualitative study of seven women, ages 19–25, that they continued to report the effect of growing up in a homophobic and heterosexist environment. These women repressed and denied their same-sex desire in adolescence, leaving them feeling unfulfilled. Secrecy and silencing themselves remained the norm, and only later could they become accepting of themselves. However, some may have same-sex relationships but never define themselves as lesbian, or never act on their same-sex attractions (Reynolds, 2003).

Every study on the topic of same-sex parenting has found that lesbian couples make excellent parents. Nelson (1999) found that of those female same-sex couples who are raising children, there are differences between their experiences of family building and family life, depending on whether the children were conceived within a prior heterosexual relationship or during the lesbian relationship, generally through donor insemination. Sexual minority women may be more likely to experience perinatal depression (Ross, Steele, Goldfinger, & Strike, 2007), perhaps because they are more likely to lack social support, particularly from their families of origin, and they may experience increased stress due to homophobic attitudes and discrimination from others (Ross, 2005). This may be overcome to a large degree by the friendship network that is seen as an extended family (Nelson, 1996). A study from Quebec found that mothers with same-sex partners had lower levels of social support, and higher levels of substance abuse, suicidal thoughts, and psychological distress (Julien, Jouvin, Jodoin, l'Archeveque, & Chartrand, 2008).

Furthermore, Nelson (1996) notes there are fewer role models and access to the experience of others, an assumption of heterosexuality in public, and multiple myths about children in lesbian-led families. However, while these families may have lower socio-economic levels, they often have higher levels of education (Nelson, 1996), and their children are equally well-adjusted in their family relationships, peer relationships, psychological adjustment, and psychosexual development (Lerner & Sinacore, in press). Lerner and Sinacore feel that generally these homophobic beliefs about lesbian-led families are continued because there is still the assumption the heterosexuality is the healthy and normal alternative when research between these groups is conducted.

Some lesbian clients will prefer to work with lesbian counsellors (Quartaro & Spier, 2002), and some have suggested that lesbian clients' transferences will be affected by their perception of their counsellor's affectional orientation (Igartua & Des Rosier, 2004). Igartua (1998) offered seven recommendations when counselling lesbian couples: (a) same-sex affectional orientation might not be experienced as a choice; (b) heterosexual counsellors should not look at lesbian women through a heterosexist lens; (c) counsellors must ascertain where the clients are at in their coming-out process; (d) some lesbian women may have concerns that the counsellor will try to convert them; (e) counsellors should learn about their clients' social support and degree to which they disclose their identities to others; (f) lesbian women may need help in creating some interpersonal distance from their partner; and (g) counsellors must not assume that sexual and physical abuse cannot occur between lesbian partners.

There are three books that may be of interest to students wanting to read more about the lesbian experience in Canada. These are *The Romance of Transgression in Canada* (Waugh, 2006); *The House That Jill Built: A Lesbian Nation in Formation* (Ross, 1995); and *Lesbians in Canada* (Stone, 1990).

GAY MEN   While Canadians, particularly the younger generation, are more accepting of homosexuality compared with Americans generally (Andersen & Fetner, 2008), studies indicate that gay male students continue to experience varying degrees of homophobia and discrimination in Canada (Jewell & Morrison, 2010; Taylor et al., 2011). The underlying ethos that not all people are equal extends itself into the gay community itself. Several studies have shown that there is a hierarchical structure within gay culture. Asian (Poon, 2006; Poon & Ho, 2008) and Muslim (Rahman, 2010) gay men are perceived as lower in status compared to their White counterparts, and White gay men create further statuses among themselves, with younger better than older (Green, 2008), muscular better than overweight (Boisvert & Harrell, 2009), richer better than poorer (Green, 2008), and so forth. Gay men are certainly not immune to internalized homophobia either (Dupras, 1994), and as speculated in Alderson (2012), perhaps the hierarchies are another way that individuals project deep-rooted self-loathing. Teaching people about sexual and gender minorities has resulted in greater tolerance toward the LGBTI community (Alderson, Orzeck, & McEwen, 2009; Summers, 1991).

Research has revealed some group differences between heterosexual and gay men, and it is important to know these if one is to provide competent multicultural counselling to this group. For example, a higher percentage of gay men report experiences of childhood sexual abuse compared to straight men (Ratner et al., 2003; Stanley, Bartholomew, & Oram, 2004). Adam (2006) found that many gay men develop non-monogamous relationships over time, for example, which is uncommon for opposite-sex and lesbian couples. Green (2006) studied a sample of heterosexual and gay men in New York City between 2000 and 2003 (i.e., before same-sex marriage became legal in Canada). He concluded that having access to marriage was related to his finding that heterosexual men seek fewer sexual adventures over time and become more vested in monogamy, while gay men, who could not marry, became more interested in sexual exploration and non-monogamous relationships. Now that gay men (and lesbian women) can marry, an area for future research is comparing people in an opposite-sex marriage with those in a same-sex marriage.

A common stereotype of gay men is that they are effeminate, and gender nonconformity *is* more prevalent with gay men compared to heterosexual men (Landolt, Bartholomew, Saffrey, Oram, & Perlman, 2004). Nonetheless, this is a large group difference, similar to the finding that women have better verbal skills compared with men. While these differences occur statistically when comparing large groups to one another, there are so many exceptions that one has to look at each person individually. Plenty of effeminate men are either heterosexual or bisexual, and many gay men present as highly masculine.

Drug use is considered prevalent in some segments of gay culture (Otis et al., 2006), and this is particularly common at circuit parties (these are all-night "raves" frequented primarily by gay men; O'Byrne & Holmes, 2011), in nightclubs, and perhaps in gay bathhouses as well (these are rental quarters where sex between men occurs). The bodily ideal of having a thin muscular body is common among gay men, and consequently, body dissatisfaction and eating disorders are more prevalent than they are with heterosexual men (Brennan, Crath, Hart, Gadalla, & Gillis, 2011). This may become a focus for counselling. Other foci found in the Canadian counselling literature include increasing feelings of self-acceptance (Smith, 1985), drug reduction strategies (Greenspan et al., 2011), working with those living with HIV/AIDS (Burgoyne, 1994; Vasconcellos, 2003), group counselling (Conlin & Smith, 1981–82), couples counselling (Sanders, 2000), and offering support groups (Frank, 1999).

BISEXUAL INDIVIDUALS Berenson (2002) found that bisexual women defined themselves as being in a category that removed rules and boundaries when it came to membership; they were no longer restricted by the rules of either homosexuality or heterosexuality. Bower, Gurevich, and Mathieson's (2002) subjects resisted adopting the bisexual label while simultaneously working for bisexual visibility. However, they often ended up caught between being ostracized in both the straight and lesbian communities.

That is also true of bisexual men. Most cities do not have a substantive bisexual community, and heterosexual, gay, and lesbian individuals tend not to trust them, believing they are fence-sitters who are unwilling to commit to an "either-or" identity (Mohr & Rochlen, 1999). The minimization of bisexual individuals and the suspicion they arouse from others may be one reason why many men who engage in sexual relations with other men define as heterosexual and consequently choose to never adopt a bisexual identity.

Many bisexual individuals live polyamorous lifestyles (i.e., engagement in multiple and simultaneous sexual or romantic relationships with the consent of all people involved). In one American study, thirty-three percent of bisexual individuals were in this kind of relationship while fifty-four percent believed it was the ideal (Page, 2004). Rambukkana (2004) wrote about the pressures that those living polyamorous lifestyles may face in defining as bisexual, similar to what feminists in the 1970s felt in defining as lesbian. According to Udis-Kessler (as cited in Rambukkana, 2004), the intersection between radical feminism and lesbian culture in the 1970s led activists to question whether heterosexual women could be viewed as "good" feminists. This created pressure for some to define as lesbian, even if this were not the case. Others simply remained silent regarding their affectional orientation and/or their sexual identity.

Self-identifying as bisexual is associated with minority stress and social isolation (Eady, Dobinson, & Ross, 2011). The resulting stigmatization is likely linked to the higher rates of "psychological distress, anxiety, depression, suicidality, alcohol misuse, and self-harming behaviour among bisexual populations" (Eady et al., 2011, p. 378). Compared to heterosexual and lesbian women, bisexual women are the most likely to report poor or fair mental and physical health, anxiety or mood disorders, and lifetime suicidality (Steele et al., 2009).

Rieger, Chivers, and Bailey (2005) found in their study of thirty heterosexual, thirty-three bisexual, and thirty-eight homosexual men that bisexual men did not demonstrate strong genital arousal to both male and female sexual stimuli. Instead, most bisexual men appeared homosexual in their genital arousal, while some appeared heterosexual. Nonetheless, they self-reported that they were sexually aroused by both sexes.

LGBT INDIVIDUALS   The research reported so far focused on only lesbian women, gay men, or bisexual individuals, but often researchers are interested in work that compares one or more of the above groups. These studies often have a sizeable number of gay and lesbian participants, few numbers of bisexual persons, and still fewer transgender people, often to the point that they appear as "token" participants. The amount of Canadian research combining two or more groups is sizeable, so all that will be included here are studies of seminal import.

Affectional orientation and gender identity impact the career choices that many LGBT individuals make, and discrimination remains a reality for many in the community. Transgender individuals likely are the most vulnerable group of all (Schneider & Dimito, 2010).

Igartua, Gill, and Montoro (2003) established a link between internalized homophobia and both anxiety and depression in a sample of 220 participants. They also found that the greatest risk for suicidality was during times when a lesbian or gay person was disclosing to family. A study by Homma, Chen, Poon, and Saewyc (2012) established that East and Southeast Asian LGB adolescents in British Columbia are more likely to use alcohol, marijuana, and other illicit drugs compared to heterosexual teenagers (weighted $N = 51,349$). Overall, "sexual orientation minorities are vulnerable to poor mental health outcomes, including suicide attempts" (Bolton & Sareen, 2011).

An insulating factor from such outcomes is having a supportive relationship and receiving social support from others (Blair & Holmberg, 2008). The Internet and other social media are providing opportunities for LGBT individuals to connect with others, which can have a positive impact on their mental health and development (McIntosh, 2011). Most LGB adolescents successfully deal with their issues and attain the same level of health and well-being as their heterosexual peers (Saewyc, 2011).

Research has repeatedly shown that same-sex couples enjoy as much relationship quality as opposite-sex couples. They demonstrate good sexual communication and satisfaction in their relationships (Holmberg & Blair, 2009). They also derive many positive effects within their sexual relationships, but report negative effects that pertain to the negative social and cultural attitudes held toward them (Cohen, Byers, & Walsh, 2008). Gay and lesbian individuals who have married have reported overwhelmingly positive effects from having their commitments sanctified in this way (MacIntosh, Reissing, & Andruff, 2010).

Interestingly, there is some validity to the concept of "gaydar," which is the ability to distinguish someone with a gay or lesbian identity from someone who defines as heterosexual by using nonverbal cues (Rule, 2011; Rule, Ishii, Ambady, Rosen, & Hallett, 2011). Both gay men and lesbians seem to be able to pick out, with fairly good accuracy, others who are of the same affectional orientation.

TTI People in Canada

Some historians and researchers have written that people have cross-dressed and displayed cross-gender behaviour since the beginning of recorded history (Bullough & Bullough, 1993; Docter, 1988; Steiner, 1982). The terms *transvestite* and *transsexual*, however, did not get coined until 1910 and 1923, respectively, by Magnus Hirschfeld (Buhrich & McConaghy, 1977). Today, most individuals who cross-dress find the term *transvestite* offensive due to its association with pathology and sexual arousal.

Transsexual studies did not flourish until several years after the media sensationalized the case of George Jorgensen, who became Christine Jorgensen, in 1952 (Docter, 1988). In 1979, the Harry Benjamin International Gender Dysphoria Association (now called the World Professional Association for Transgender Health) developed the International Standards of Care, outlining a treatment protocol that is still used today (Fontaine, 2002). A sister organization, called the Canadian Professional Association for Transgender Health (CPATH; http://cpath.ca), is the world's largest professional national organization dedicated to transgender health.

Intersex activism has a more recent history, beginning after the Intersex Society of North America was founded in 1993. A case involving a Canadian received a great deal of media attention (J. Alderson, 2004). Bruce Reimer was surgically assigned to the female gender at eight months of age. He later identified as male, however, and changed his female name of Brenda to David. For reasons perhaps only tangentially related to his gender, David committed suicide at age thirty-eight. The current consensus among experts is that gender should be assigned to newborn infants, regardless of whether surgical interventions are to be postponed (Pasterski, 2008).

Bill C-279, a private member's bill that would add gender identity and gender expression both into the Canadian Human Rights Act and into the criminal code under hate crimes, is currently before Parliament. If passed, it will help protect transgender people from discrimination (Tieman, 2012).

While some have debated whether transgender individuals ought to be included as part of the LGB community, Devor (2002) argued that they have in fact been the most visible group of those involved in same-sex sexual practices. They are also a symbol of what many people envision when they think about gay and lesbian people.

This section begins with transgender individuals who do not identify as transsexual, although many do experience some degree of gender dysphoria. We then focus on transsexual individuals (sometimes referred to as *trans-identified*) before moving onto intersex persons.

TRANSGENDER INDIVIDUALS   Here the focus will be first on two-spirit people and second on fetishistic cross-dressing individuals. Two-spirit individuals do not fit neatly into any of the identities included in this chapter as they reside along the entire LGBTI spectrum. The term *two-spirit* is often used by individuals of Aboriginal descent who in Western culture would be called gay, lesbian, bisexual, or transgender (Meyer-Cook & Labelle, 2004). Usage of the term *two-spirit* by some is more restrictive, pertaining only to those who embrace masculine and feminine qualities and who dress accordingly (i.e., more typical of what many Western people would call *transgender*). However, some gay and lesbian Aboriginals prefer the term *two-spirited*, while others do not embrace it at all, preferring to be defined as gay, lesbian, bisexual, or transgendered. In the past, these individuals were often revered and considered medicine men or women by their bands, called *berdache*. Unfortunately, today most bands are very homophobic and do not honour this population. Many two-spirit individuals face marginization and exclusion from their Aboriginal community (because they define as LGBTI), from the LGBTI community (because they are Native), and from the dominant culture (because of their dual minority status; Brotman, Ryan, Jalbert, & Rowe, 2002).

Fetishistic cross-dressing (FC) individuals often face huge oppression themselves as their behaviour is often poorly understood. Often their girlfriends or wives are unaware of their cross-dressing. When they find out, they are usually anything but pleased. A common reaction by women is to question their FC partner's sexuality or gender, believing the FC means either that they are gay or that they actually want to become women (Alderson, 2013). In actuality, FC generally begins in adolescence and as cross-dressing becomes associated with sexual fantasies and accompanying masturbation, a fetish is born (Zucker & Blanchard, 1997). The cross-dressing, which begins as a fetish, often continues through the lifespan but its motive will likely sway away from sexual release to instead creating a feeling of comfort while cross-dressed. The behaviour is viewed as harmless by most mental health professionals. Furthermore, there are no controlled outcome studies that have demonstrated the behaviour can be eradicated (Newring, Wheeler, & Draper, 2008). Nonetheless, a diagnosis for FC is found in the DSM-IV, and in the DSM-V, released in 2013, it is called Transvestic Disorder (American Psychiatric Association).

TRANSSEXUAL INDIVIDUALS   Canadian researchers – especially those working at the Centre for Addiction and Mental Health in Toronto (CAMH) – have done a great deal to expand our knowledge of transsexual individuals. Ray Blanchard and Ken Zucker are considered world experts in the field. Through mostly Blanchard's research endeavours with contributions earlier by Kurt Freund, a popular classification scheme has emerged that suggests two types of male-to-female (MTF) and two types of female-to-male (FTM) developmental pathways. A major distinguishing feature concerns their affectional orientation.

The homosexual MTF person is only attracted to men. They present as typically very feminine from a young age and in many respects fit the stereotype laypersons have of MTF individuals. In consequence of their early awareness of gender dysphoria, many who physically transition do so while in their late teens or early twenties. They typically have the best psychological outcome post-transition.

The non-homosexual MTF individual is attracted primarily to women and perhaps secondarily to men. They tend to present as typically masculine through both childhood and adulthood. Due to their interest in women, it is not uncommon for them to marry and have children. Blanchard (1994) found that those who are married with children are likely to be older when they first request help for gender dysphoria. Blanchard (1989) also suggested that their gender dysphoria results from autogynephilia, which he defined as "a male's propensity to be sexually aroused by the thought of himself as a female" (p. 616). His theory has both supporters and others who are vehemently opposed to it. Perhaps non-homosexual MTF persons experience greater degrees of denial, given that they can "pass" readily as cisgendered men. Furthermore, one would expect that most transsexual individuals would sexually fantasize themselves being the gender to which they belong. Their psychological adjustment is generally not as favourable compared to homosexual MTF persons.

According to this classification scheme, there are also homosexual and non-homosexual FTM persons. The homosexual FTM individuals are usually overtly masculine in childhood. Their erotic interests are exclusively toward women. They typically have the best psychological outcome post-transition.

The non-homosexual FTM individual is attracted primarily to men and perhaps secondarily to women. They rarely appear as masculine in childhood and instead impress as more typically feminine. Their psychological adjustment is generally not as favourable compared to homosexual FTM persons. Both groups typically transition while in their twenties.

It is important to note that most children, male and female, with gender dysphoria will outgrow it without any intervention. However, the majority will later define as gay or bisexual.

Many transsexual individuals will seek counselling as one of the requirements for beginning the physical transition process. The typical protocol for working with those who want to physically transition is, first, that they meet the diagnosis of Gender Identity Disorder (GID) in the DSM, and second, that the clinician and others involved in care follow the World Professional Association for Transgender Health Standards of Care for the Health of Transsexual, Transgender, and Gender Nonconforming People. Another excellent resource is an article by Bockting, Knudson, and Goldberg (2006). The name for GID has changed in the DSM-V to simply Gender Dysphoria (American Psychiatric Association, 2013). The name has also been revised in the SOC.

Transsexual or trans-identified individuals deal with particular discriminations in economic areas. Many of the sex reassignment surgeries they need to undergo have been cut from coverage in various provinces at one time or another, and other treatments, such as hair removal or voice lessons, are not covered at all. This often places an undue financial pressure on the transition process, adding to the already increasing emotional cost for the individual.

INTERSEX INDIVIDUALS While most counsellors will likely never have a client who is open about having a disorder of sexual development, it is important to be aware of the ongoing controversy regarding their treatment. Should surgeons and/or parents have the right to decide on the gender of their child at or near birth if he or she has ambiguous genitalia? Holmes (2008) argued that intersex individuals ought to have the right to their bodies and to decide for themselves what happens to them. The Intersex Society of North America supports the position that surgery be avoided unless it is medically required (which usually it is not) until the individual becomes capable of making their own choice concerning these surgeries. Others disagree, however, arguing that children with ambiguous genitalia will not develop a clear gender identity, and they may be stigmatized by others who are aware of their condition (Slijper, Drop, Molenaar, & de Muinck Keizer-Schrama, 2000). The current consensus among experts is that gender should be assigned to newborn infants, regardless of whether surgical interventions are to be postponed (Pasterski, 2008). Counsellors wanting to learn more about intersex conditions are referred to both Alderson (2013) and Pasterski (2008).

Socio-Political Realities of LGBTI People

A major socio-political reality that still exists is homo-bi-transphobia, heterosexism, and violence toward LGBTI individuals. Janoff (2005), for example, reported on an approximate number of alleged hate crimes (assaults = 335; murders = 100) targeted at LGBTI individuals in Canada between 1990 and 2005. Taylor et al. (2011) conducted a national survey of Canadian high school students (N = 3,700) between December 2007 and June 2009. Nearly half of the sample (48 percent) reported hearing homophobic epithets every day in school: the percentage of trans students (74 percent) and LGB students (55 percent) who heard these remarks was higher. One in five (20 percent) of the LGBTQ sample ("Q" representing students identifying as either questioning or queer) and 10 percent of non-LGBTQ students reported being physically harassed or assaulted because of their perceived affectional orientation or gender identity. In addition, when the LGBTI individual believes the stereotypes, myths, and fears of the homophobic world, the resulting internalized homophobia can be devastating (Szymanski, 2005). It can complicate the process of coming out and lead to psychological issues that threaten the psychic stability of the individual (Fassinger, 1991; Reynolds, 2003).

Same-sex domestic violence (SSDV) also occurs in between 25 and 33 percent of lesbian and gay relationships. These statistics are similar to that which occurs in heterosexual relationships. While the rates of

SSDV are similar when comparing gay men and lesbian women, gay male SSDV generally involves more physical abuse while emotional and verbal abuse is more characteristic in lesbian relationships.

Although survey studies report widely varying rates of lesbian SSDV (Ristock, 2002), lesbian couples are not immune from domestic violence, including physical, emotional, psychological, sexual, economic, and spiritual abuse. The root of such violence, as in heterosexual relationships, is the need for power and control; however, the secrecy and isolation are greater for victims and perpetrators of same-sex violence, even within the lesbian community itself. The myth that women don't abuse women reinforces the silence (Ristock, 2002). Homophobia prevents women and men from talking about the issue out of fear that they will not be believed or supported, or that they will be discriminated against. They often find themselves blamed by medical, police, and legal personnel for an assault because of their affectional orientation. They also face the risks of public exposure if they report the assault (Fassinger, 1991; Herek, 1996).

In addition, the perpetrator may use homophobia as a means of control. Threats of outing the victim to children, work or school colleagues, friends, or family can keep the cycle going and increase the sense of entrapment (Rohrbaugh, 2006). There can also be a threat to take stepchildren away from the relationship, and the victim may have no legal recourse (Rohrbaugh, 2006).

Last, when domestic violence occurs, it often takes place after a sexual encounter. This may be a reaction to the level of vulnerability involved. Rates of domestic violence are directly related to experiences of internalized homophobia (Balsam & Szymanski, 2005). If one partner is struggling with her own internalized homophobia, she/he may find it more difficult to maintain her/his own level of denial when she/he has just been sexual with another person of the same gender. This insecurity, self-doubt, and fear may lead to violent acts designed to reestablish control.

Counsellors should always screen for domestic violence with their clients, as it is often overlooked. We are fortunate in Canada that there is some legal protection and service available for same-sex couples; this is not the case in many other countries (Rohrbaugh, 2006).

However, research across cultures reveals that people who do not conform to hegemonic forms of sexuality and gender are punished in some way (Alderson, 2013). Despite the legal gains made by the LGBTI community in Canada over the past forty years, LGBTI individuals face barriers to accessing the health care system because of the "ideology of heterosexuality" (Daley, 2006, p. 794). While same-sex couples are approved for adoptions in Canada, they are less likely to actually be matched to children than their heterosexual counterparts (Sullivan & Harrington, 2009). An analysis of findings regarding refugee claims on grounds of bisexuality were shown to be less successful in Canada compared to the claims of lesbian and gay individuals (Rehaag, 2010). Grant (2000) suggested that Canadian lesbian women face both obvious and less obvious consequences. Some examples include "material and ideological disciplining and punishment, including loss of friends, family, credibility, employment, and housing and/or threats, harassment, ridicule, and violence." Grant goes on to suggest that lesbian and feminist activists are identified as "unfeminine, loud, brash, unwomanly, angry, unladylike, unsatisfied, frigid, manhaters and dykes" (p. 65). To break the mould of femininity is to risk losing even the subjugated status that comes with being a woman.

Bisexual individuals often choose and/or are relegated to an invisible status compared to gay and lesbian individuals. Bisexual people can often pass if they want, as they tend to present as more typically heterosexual (Matteson, 1996). Unfortunately, such invisibility has not helped them to form a bisexual community, and one does not exist in most places (Matteson, 1995). Heterosexual and gay/lesbian individuals are often judgmental toward those who identify as bisexual, believing that they should choose between one group or the other (Mohr & Rochlen, 1999).

A socio-political reality is that people are expected to live with the binary of "either or," whether the subject is affectional orientation (opposite-sex or same-sex) or gender (male or female). Consequently, bisexual individuals and transgender individuals become a challenge to the binary hegemony firmly planted not only in the minds of the dominant culture, but also in the minds of many members of the LGBTI community.

Aging LGBTI individuals also face many struggles, often compounded by their ethos of secrecy, a carryover from their earlier years. Nonetheless, they were often very resilient and creative in living their dual lives and connecting to "community" (Anderson, 2001). Their affectional orientations and/or gender expressions/identities, even when they are out about these, may be minimized and denied to them by health care professionals and other caregivers.

In particular, those in nursing homes may be the most silenced or feel they must be secretive about their orientation or relationships.

Disclosing one's gay identity to others, "coming out," carries both advantages and disadvantages. While increased self-disclosure is generally related to self-acceptance (Cain, 1991), a greater sense of congruence in one's identity (Barret & Logan, 2002) and increased social support (Fergus, Lewis, Darbes, & Kral, 2009), disclosing is a complex matter. Disclosing can also lead to estrangement from one's family and job consequences, such as being overlooked for promotion (Alderson, 2012), as well as increased homophobia, issues of personal safety, and loss of child custody (Barret & Logan, 2002).

OVERVIEW OF CURRENT ISSUES AND NEEDS

Several thousand references were reviewed and read during the preparation of *Counseling* LGBTI *Clients* (Alderson, 2013), which itself contains nearly 1,400 references. Alderson (2013) identified thirty problems and issues that LGBTI clients bring to counsellors:

1 Internalized homophobia
2 Affectional orientation confusion
3 Fragmentation of identity
4 Religious conflicts
5 HIV/AIDS
6 Relationship issues/Marital discord
7 Disclosing to others
8 Managing the consequences of external homophobia (e.g., harassment, homophobia, violence)
9 Career concerns
10 Major depression, poor mental health, and suicide risk
11 Weight problems
12 Substance abuse problems (drug and alcohol)
13 Parenthood issues
14 Identity confusion and labelling issues
15 Internalized biphobia
16 Need for family and social support
17 Invisibility and its sequelae
18 Lack of community, secrecy, and feeling isolated
19 *Ego-dystonic cross-dressing and/or compulsiveness
20 *Mild-to-severe gender dysphoria

21 Child and adolescent challenges
22 *Wanting to transition
23 *Transitioning at work
24 *Uncertainty about sex reassignment surgery
25 *Learning new gender scripts
26 Bereavement
27 Post-traumatic reactions
28 Shame and guilt
29 Problems accessing psychological and/or medical services
30 Struggles with self-esteem and self-concept

* These issues pertain almost exclusively to TTI individuals.

The Canadian researchers who have contributed work that led to the development of this list are too numerous to mention here. Nevertheless, a perusal of the list should bring to light something that becomes quickly apparent to counsellors who work with LGBTI clients: most of these problems and issues are the result of internalized and externalized homo-bi-transphobia, heterosexism, gender role expectations, harassment, and prejudice; and the oppression, marginalization, and discrimination that result from these. While LGBTI individuals struggle with higher rates of substance abuse disorders, anxiety disorders, and mood disorders (including suicidality) compared to members of the dominant culture (Alderson, 2013), the reasons underlying this dysfunction are similar to what our First Nations people have experienced. Lack of deeply rooted acceptance and pride in the diversity that our cultures bring to the Canadian mosaic affects the minority groups themselves, and ultimately, everyone involved with them. No one is safe while one group is made to be the "other."

TRAINING AND COMPETENCY ISSUES IN CANADA

Ethics in Counselling LGBTI Clients

The most controversial area in ethics surrounds attempts that some laypeople, paraprofessionals, and professionals have made to change either affectional orientation or gender identity. Such attempts have given rise to many names, but the label chosen here will be *conversion therapy*. While every code of ethics urges counsellors not to offer conversion therapy, most have not taken a definitive stance.

Two reasons are likely at play: (a) some researchers and clinicians have claimed that conversion therapy works, and in turn have had published unsubstantiated studies that support this claim with some individuals; and (b) psychology has not wanted to take a stand against religious doctrines or beliefs that view LGBTI people as abominations.

Grace (2008) from the University of Alberta wrote about many of the problems inherent in conversion therapy. As Grace noted, much of the interest in this area surged after Robert Spitzer (2003) published his study that suggested some very highly motivated gay men could become heterosexual. Recently, Spitzer apologized to the gay community for making these unsubstantiated claims, and for the pain and suffering they have caused (Becker, 2012).

There have also been many attempts made to change gender identity. Severe gender dysphoria experienced by adults does not remit, and psychological treatments aimed at changing it have been unsuccessful. Research identifies sex reassignment surgery as the treatment of choice for transsexual individuals who experience severe gender dysphoria and who want to transition (Lawrence, 2008).

As mentioned earlier, most children outgrow gender dysphoria, although the majority later define as gay or bisexual. Some experts believe it is appropriate to treat gender atypicality in children by focusing on gender roles, attempting to make boys more "masculine" and girls more "feminine" (Zucker & Bradley, 1999), while others are strong opponents (Hill, Rozanski, Carfagnini, & Willoughby, 2007). Currently there is no conclusive evidence to suggest that treating gender atypicality reduces the likelihood that an individual will later define as gay, lesbian, or transsexual.

Other Canadian researchers have focused on the multiple relationships that can develop when an LGBTI counsellor works with LGBTI clients. While ethics codes provide exceptions for counsellors who are themselves part of a small minority group, multiple relationships can still create unforeseen difficulties (Graham & Liddle, 2009). For example, if there is sexual attraction felt by one or both individuals, special precautions may need to be implemented.

Competencies and Training in Counselling LGBTI Clients

Despite the requirement of ethics codes that counsellors be competent in the areas in which they work, counselling psychology graduate students receive little training in gay and lesbian psychology and counselling – a modal response from fourteen Canadian universities of three hours total (Alderson, 2004a). Training to work with TTI clients is likely not included at all in most counselling programs. The culture-infused counselling model of Arthur and Collins (2010) requires competent multicultural counsellors to (a) develop cultural self-awareness, (b) gain awareness of client cultural identities, (c) foster a culturally sensitive working alliance, and (d) embrace a social justice agenda. Clearly, three hours of training is insufficient to accomplish these tasks.

To practice competent multicultural counselling, it is essential that mental health professionals develop affirmative attitudes and beliefs, knowledge, and skills to work with the various factions of the LGBTI community (Alderson, 2013). While one might become competent to work with LGB clients, working with TTI clients requires its own set of specific skills.

As a starting place, ask yourself a few questions. What is your current attitude toward those who have differing affectional orientations, gender expressions, and gender identities? Do you hold a favourable attitude toward each subgroup and maintain a strong belief regarding equality? Do you have sufficient knowledge regarding each subgroup? If not, where can you secure this knowledge? Now take a second look at the list of problems and issues in the previous section. How many in this list do you feel well equipped to handle in a counselling session? While gaining supervision to work with LGBTI clients may not be possible for you, availing yourself of readings in the area and taking professional development sessions will provide a good starting place.

LGBTI-Friendly Services

Finding community support is helpful to LGBTI individuals, many of whom experience varying degrees of isolation and negativity in their environments. Counsellors would do well to learn about resources and services that are affirming of LGBTI people. Liddle (2005), for example, wrote about how feminist bookstores serve an important function for lesbian individuals. In cities, there is often a gay information service or centre that can be found in the phone book. Alternatively, affirming websites and online support groups are plentiful today.

RESEARCH AND COUNSELLING MODELS

Research Contributions in Canada

The contribution of Canadian researchers to the field of LGBTI studies has been substantial. The list of references would be longer than this entire chapter if all of these were acknowledged. Instead, the focus here will be on where the major strengths lie in Canadian contributions, and where these remain minimal. Keep in mind that most of the research on LGBTI individuals has *not* been conducted by counselling psychologists.

As is typical of the entire research base in this field, the amount of research devoted to each subgroup, in descending order, is as follows: gay men, lesbian women, MTF individuals, FTM individuals, other transgender individuals, bisexual people, and intersex persons. There is a large research literature related to health concerns of the various segments of the LGBTI community in Canada. This is especially true concerning lesbian/bisexual women and HIV transmission reduction in men who have sex with men, regardless of their sexual identity labels. There is also a significant focus in Canadian research on biological correlates regarding those with LGBTI identities. Thanks largely to the prolific researchers at CAMH in Toronto and the gender clinic in Utrecht, Canada and the Netherlands are world-renowned for enhancing our theoretical and empirical understanding of TTI individuals. A growing concern for, and a research base focused on, LGBTI youth issues in Canada have also emerged.

As is true of the entire field of LGBTI studies, identity theories have given way to postmodern understandings that purport that identities are social constructions that would be better off having no label. While this has opened an exciting new way to look at individuals, most people continue to give themselves identity labels, perhaps as one way of managing the complexity of living in a postmodern world. It would seem surprising to us if gay men in their thirties today become heterosexual men in their forties a decade from now.

Canadian research remains minimal when we consider most LGBTI ethnic/racial minorities. There is more work focused on Asian gay men than on Aboriginal or Black LGBTI individuals, for example. Frankly, Canadian research has been focused mostly on the weaknesses (i.e., problems, issues) than on the strengths of LGBTI individuals (see Savin-Williams, 2005, for a resilient perspective).

Indeed, with the ever-growing number of immigrants and refugees coming to Canada, there is a great need for further research about LGBTI people in these communities. Usually the issues of discrimination and homophobia in many minority cultural communities are very prominent. For instance, lesbian women of colour or Aboriginal lesbian women will likely experience several complications as they deal with coming out and cultural expectations as they go through their developmental processes (Bridges, Selvidge, & Matthews, 2003; Collins, 2010; Davidson & Huenefeld, 2002; Garrett & Barret, 2003). Many other cultural issues are extensively covered in the chapters on Indigenous and immigrant communities in other sections of this book.

We would be remiss to not mention that Canada remains a foremost world leader in providing legal equality to LGBTI people. This really strikes home when we compare Canada, where legal same-sex marriage with all its privileges is now taken for granted, with Iran, where two men caught engaging in same-sex sexual behaviour will be given a death sentence and publicly hanged. As we ponder ethical directives from our counselling associations to promote social justice and advocacy, we need to remain conscious that the work we do is not only personal: it is also political. Our field has the potential to influence an unjust world.

Selected Canadian Contributions to Counselling LGBTI Clients

Canadian researchers have made a substantial contribution to counselling LGBTI individuals. This area represents the hallmark of our profession.

- Counselling youth (Lemoire & Chen, 2005; Safren, Hollander, Hart, & Heimberg, 2001; Sanders & Kroll, 2000).
- Counselling same-sex couples (MacDonald, 1998; Sanders, 2000; Zuccarini & Karos, 2011).
- Counselling partners of cross-dressing men (Cairns, 1997).
- Leisure counselling with LGB persons (Iwasaki, Mactavish, & Mackay, 2005).
- Counselling bisexual individuals (Butt & Guldner, 1993).
- Counselling for HIV-infected men (Burgoyne, 1994; Myers, 1991).

- Group counselling for gay men (Conlin & Smith, 1981–82; Frank, 1999).
- Lesbian clients (Igartua & Des Rosier, 2004; Quartaro & Spier, 2002).
- Abuse in lesbian relationships (Ristock, 2001).
- Sexual/affectional orientation (Schneider, Brown, & Glassgold, 2002).
- Postmodern counselling (Strong & Zeman, 2005).
- Counselling with depressed LGBTI clients (Ross, Doctor, Dimito, Kuehl, & Armstrong, 2007).
- Advocacy and activism when counselling trans clients (Holman & Goldberg, 2007; Raj, 2007).
- Counselling trans clients (Bockting, Knudson, & Goldberg, 2006).
- Caring for trans clients undergoing sex reassignment surgery (Bowman & Goldberg, 2007).
- Generic guides to counselling LGBTI clients (Alderson, 2012, 2013).

SUMMARY

This chapter has provided a look into the contributions that Canadian researchers have made in LGBTI studies. Where possible, the work of counselling psychologists has been highlighted. Nonetheless, the number of researchers working in non-counselling-related areas far surpasses that of counselling researchers. Perhaps for this reason, the deficiencies of LGBTI individuals have received much greater research focus than have their strengths. As resiliency-based approaches and positive psychology are foundational to the discipline of counselling psychology, a great deal needs to be done that highlights the strengths and contributions of LGBTI individuals in Canada. Most LGBTI individuals are successful in navigating themselves through a social landscape that perpetuates varying degrees of marginalization, oppression, and discrimination. Their coping ability, given what so many have endured, is admirable. When cracks in their shell occur, however, counsellors are there to help mend the damage that for most has been caused by external forces. For this challenge, and despite the little training provided to counselling professionals, LGBTI clients deserve the best help that we are capable of providing them.

APPENDIX: GLOSSARY

AFFECTIONAL ORIENTATION   This term is used instead of the older term *sexual orientation* throughout this chapter as it better reflects "the fact that a person's orientation goes beyond sexuality" (Pedersen, Crethar, & Carlson, 2008, p. 136). *Affectional orientation* refers to the attraction, erotic desire, and philia for members of the opposite gender, the same gender, or both (Alderson, 2010). *Philia* is the propensity to fall in love romantically with members of a particular sex or gender (or both, as in the case of biphilia). The three affectional orientations include opposite-sex, same-sex, and bidirectional. It is debatable whether asexuality should be considered an affectional orientation. Furthermore, the same applies to two new identity terms that mean essentially the same thing: pomosexual and pansexual. Currently these are defined as sexual identity terms that are intended to be more inclusive of transgender individuals than is the term bisexual (Elizabeth, 2013).

ASEXUAL INDIVIDUALS   Refers to those who experience little to no sexual desire. Some such individuals still pursue romantic relationships, presumably because of their capacity to fall in love romantically with members of the opposite sex, same sex, or both (Brotto, Knudson, Inskip, Rhodes, & Erskine, 2010).

BISEXUAL INDIVIDUALS   Individuals who self-identify as having primarily bisexual cognition, affect, and/or behaviour. In effect, bisexual persons acknowledge some degree of affectional interest in both sexes. Bisexual individuals have not established a substantive bisexual community (McKirnan, Stokes, Doll, & Burzette, 1995), so many define themselves as gay, lesbian, or heterosexual (McKirnan et al., 1995).

CISGENDERED INDIVIDUALS   Refers to people who experience their gender as being consistent with their biological sex, regardless of whether they define as heterosexual, gay, lesbian, or bisexual.

CORE GENDER IDENTITY   This is the knowledge one has and the label one uses for defining whether one is biologically male, female, or intersex. It is usually established between ages 18–30 months (Lawrence, 2008).

DRAG KINGS   Women who cross-dress for fun and/or money. A key element of drag is "performance and parody" (Lorber, 2004, p. xxv).

DRAG QUEENS   Gay men who cross-dress for fun and/or money. A key element of drag is "performance and parody" (Lorber, 2004, p. xxv).

FETISHISTIC CROSS-DRESSING INDIVIDUALS   Men who cross-dress, at least during adolescence, because of the sexual arousal it provides, usually accompanied by masturbation and orgasm. Over time, the fetish component generally diminishes or ends entirely, replaced instead by feelings of comfort while cross-dressed. Most of these men define as heterosexual.

GAY MEN   Men who self-identify as experiencing primarily homosexual cognition, affect, and/or behaviour, and who have adopted the construct of "gay" as having personal significance to them.

GENDER BENDERS   A colloquial term used by some people who intentionally "bend," or transgress, traditional gender roles.

GENDER DYSPHORIA   Refers to feeling varying degrees of discomfort with one's biological sex and/or one's expression of gender roles. Most children with gender dysphoria will outgrow it without any intervention. However, the majority will later define as gay or bisexual.

GENDER IDENTITY   This can refer to one's core gender identity in the case of cisgendered individuals (see definition), but it can also refer to one's current sense of gender (Lawrence, 2008).

INTERSEX INDIVIDUALS   People with "congenital conditions in which development of chromosomal, gonadal, or anatomical sex is atypical" (Vilain, 2008, p. 330).

LESBIAN WOMEN   Women who self-identify as having homosexual cognition, affect, and/or behaviour, *and/or* who have adopted the construct of "lesbian" as having personal significance to them (Alderson, 2010). The "and/or" is italicized in the previous sentence to acknowledge that some teenagers and adults identify as lesbian primarily because of their allegiance to a feminist or lesbian ideology and not because of their affectional orientation (Ellis & Peel, 2011).

LGB   An acronym referring to lesbian, gay, and bisexual individuals only (i.e., those who differ according to affectional orientation).

LGBTI   An acronym referring to lesbian, gay, bisexual, transgender (including transsexual), and intersex individuals.

SEXUAL IDENTITY   Refers to the label people use to define their sexuality (Alderson, 2013). The most common sexual identities include heterosexual or straight, gay, lesbian, bisexual, and queer.

Some also identify as asexual, pomosexual, or pansexual (Brotto et al., 2010; DeLuzio Chasin, 2011; Elizabeth, 2013).

SHE-MALES   She-males are "men who have achieved a female chest contour with breast implants or hormonal medication but still retain their male genitals" (Blanchard & Collins, 1993, p. 570).

TRANSGENDER INDIVIDUALS   Individuals who present unconventional gender expressions (e.g., fetishistic cross-dresser, transgenderist, transsexual) and/or those who present unconventional gender identities (e.g., transsexual, transwoman, transman). Transgenderism of all kinds is unrelated to affectional orientation. Note that many transsexual individuals only refer to themselves as transgender, while some do not publicly disclose any label at all. Some go *stealth*, meaning they live fully in accord with their chosen gender and refrain from disclosing to others anything about their lives before transitioning.

TRANSGENDERIST INDIVIDUAL   A male or female who cross-dresses most if not all of the time and who may or may not experience gender dysphoria (Brown et al., 1996; Docter, 1988). Transgenderist individuals with gender dysphoria usually experience it in a less severe form and have resolved (or have had it decided for them) not to proceed with sex reassignment surgery.

TRANSSEXUAL INDIVIDUALS   People who believe their gender is dissonant with their morphology. A post-operative transsexual male-to-female person is often referred to as a *transwoman*, while a post-operative transsexual female-to-male individual is a *transman*. Note that not all transpeople will use the terms of transman or transwoman to define themselves. Some may also refer to themselves as *trans-identified*.

TTI   An acronym referring to transgender, transsexual, and intersex individuals only (i.e., those who express non-dominant gender expressions and gender identities).

6

The Changing Canadian Landscape: Immigration in Canada

ADA L. SINACORE, ANUSHA KASSAN, AND
ALEXANDRA (SASHA) LERNER[1]

Canada has consistently maintained an active immigration program
(Kelley & Trebilock, 2010; Reitz, 2007), which has led it to become
one of the most ethnically diverse countries in the world (Statistics
Canada, 2007b). Currently, immigration continues to play an important role in Canada, as evidenced by the 2006 Canadian Census
which revealed that nearly twenty percent of the Canadian population was foreign-born (Statistics Canada, 2007b). More recently, in
2010, the country welcomed 280,681 new immigrants, the highest
number accepted in fifty years (Citizenship and Immigration Canada,
2011). Further, these 280,681 immigrants constituted almost one
percent of the Canadian population (Citizenship and Immigration
Canada, 2011). In light of the growing number of immigrants settling in Canada, immigration undoubtedly represents an important
topic of consideration for Canadians in general and for counsellors
and counselling psychologists in particular. That is, the increasing
diversity of the population of Canada has influenced, and will inev-
itably continue to influence, the ways in which counselling psychologists and counsellors work in their various roles as clinicians,
researchers, teachers, consultants, and advocates.

Yet, in order to fully grasp the myriad issues surrounding immigration in Canada, an overview of the government's immigration
policies and procedures is necessary. Although Canada's immigration policies have been modified substantially over time, one relatively constant aspect is the fact that immigration is considered a

concurrent power (Knowles, 2007). In other words, authority over immigration-related issues is shared between the Canadian federal government and the Canadian provinces/territories. The extent of each province/territory's jurisdiction over immigration is dependent upon the negotiations that have occurred between the federal government and the specific province/territory. For example, through the Canada-Quebec Accord Relating to Immigration and Temporary Admission of Aliens, Quebec maintains its own immigrant recruitment offices abroad, controls the selection of immigrants, and has authority over immigrant-related services (Reitz, 2007). Although to a lesser extent than Quebec, other provinces such as British Columbia and Manitoba have also been granted a great deal of responsibility over the management and administration of immigration programs.

Beyond the shared influence of the provinces/territories and the federal government on Canada's immigration program, the current state of Canada's immigration procedures developed largely in response to important policy reforms that were enacted in the 1960s (Reitz, 2001a). These policy changes eradicated discriminatory practices including preferential selection of European immigrants, as well as implementing a point system (to be addressed later in this discussion) through which to evaluate the eligibility of immigrants applying as skilled workers (Reitz, 2001a). Such changes resulted in an increasing number of people admitted from Asia, the Caribbean, Africa, and Latin America, as well as an upsurge in the selection of highly educated immigrants (Reitz, 2007). Therefore, the past fifty years have seen a dramatic transformation in the social composition of Canadian society.

OBJECTIVES OF CANADA'S IMMIGRATION PROGRAM

Although the Canadian immigration program serves the essential humanitarian purposes of providing asylum to refugees and reuniting families, it has primarily been propelled by two overarching objectives: national and economic development (Reitz, 2007). Immigrants have played a substantial role in meeting the government's goal of national development, mainly through increasing the number of Canada's inhabitants. In recent years, due to the combination of low birth rates and an aging population, immigrants have accounted for a significant portion of the country's population expansion (Statistics Canada, 2011b). Immigration has also positively contributed to national development by increasing the diversity of Canadian society in an age when multicultural values are considered the hallmark of Canada's identity (Reitz, 2007).

In addition to promoting national development, immigrants have been integral to advancing Canada's economy. Historically, as Canada transitioned from an agricultural to an industrial economy, immigration served to increase the number of farmers, and later, low-skilled labourers in manufacturing and construction (Esses, Deaux, LaLonde, & Brown, 2010; Reitz, 2007). In contrast to previous periods where natural resources were the main path to wealth, today's economy is based on the creation and utilization of knowledge. Consequently, in this current knowledge-driven economy, education has become essential to occupational and financial mobility (Lee & Westwood, 1996; Reitz, 2001a).

In response to the mounting focus on knowledge as a commodity, the Canadian government has tailored its immigration program to attract skilled workers: that is, highly educated individuals with relevant work experience in their chosen field of study (Knowles, 2007). By selectively admitting skilled workers to Canada, the aim has been to increase the employability of immigrants in the existing knowledge economy, thereby reducing their integration-related challenges and creating a larger source of human capital to promote the nation's economic growth (Reitz, 2007).

Consistent with the stated government goals of immigration, individuals who are interested in immigrating can apply under one of the following broad categories: (1) reunification of families, (2) protecting refugees, and (3) contributing to Canada's economic development (Citizenship and Immigration Canada, 2011). The reunification of families category allows Canadian citizens and permanent residents to sponsor a spouse, common-law partner, dependent child, parent, or grandparent to become a permanent resident of Canada. The second category under which individuals can apply for immigration is refugee protection. This category includes people who have experienced or are at risk of danger or persecution in their country of origin (Citizenship and Immigration Canada, 2011). Falling under the third category, economic immigrants are individuals who are selected based on their ability to enhance Canada's economy. Several sub-classes of immigrants fall under the economic immigrant category, such as skilled workers, business immigrants, provincial and territorial nominees, live-in caregivers, and temporary foreign residents with Canadian work or educational experience (Citizenship and Immigration Canada, 2011). Although all of these sub-classes fall under the economic immigrant category, their requirements differ significantly, thereby leading to divergent immigration experiences. In order to shed light on the various modes through which economic immigrants come to Canada, an explanation of these various sub-classes is warranted.

To begin, as previously mentioned, skilled workers are evaluated on a point system wherein they are given points toward acceptance into Canada based on their education, work experience, English and/or French language skills, and other factors that increase their ability to sustain themselves in Canada (Reitz, 2001b). Next, business immigrants comprise people who intend to open their own business or invest money in a Canadian business enterprise. Regarding provincial and territorial nominees, these are individuals who have been selected by provincial/territorial governments because they have skills that meet the specific economic needs of the region. As another sub-class of economic immigrants, live-in care-givers are individuals who, as part of the Canadian Live-in Care-Giver Program, are qualified to live in private homes to care for children, elderly persons, or people with disabilities. Last, temporary foreign workers and international students who have graduated are eligible to apply for permanent residence in Canada (Citizenship and Immigration Canada, 2011).

In light of the different immigration categories, it is interesting to note that 69.3 percent of people who immigrated in 2010 did so under the economic immigrant category, an increase from 54 percent in 2006 (Citizenship and Immigration Canada, 2011; Statistics Canada, 2008). Also in 2010, 18.2 percent of immigrants were admitted under the family reunification category, and 9.2 percent of immigrants came to Canada as refugees (Citizenship and Immigration Canada, 2011).

Demographics of Immigrants to Canada

As this discussion has shown, people immigrate to Canada through a variety of channels and for diverse reasons. Yet questions remain: what are the demographic characteristics of those coming to Canada and from which countries are they arriving? The 2006 Canadian census revealed that recent immigrants were predominantly arriving from China, followed by India, the Philippines, Pakistan, the United States, South Korea, Romania, Iran, the United Kingdom, and Colombia (Statistics Canada, 2007b). Additionally, of the 280,681 immigrants admitted to Canada in 2010, 137,000 were male and 143,681 were female. In terms of age, individuals immigrating to Canada are generally between the ages of twenty-five and forty-four years old (Statistics Canada, 2008). Upon arrival in Canada, new immigrants are predominantly settling in Canada's major metropolitan centres, Toronto, Vancouver, and Montreal (Citizenship and Immigration Canada, 2011). In fact, 45.7 percent of the population of Toronto, 39.6 percent of the population of Vancouver, and 20.6 percent of the population of Montreal are foreign-born (Statistics Canada, 2007b).

IMMIGRATION RESEARCH

Over the past decades, the phenomenon of immigration has transformed the face of Canadian society. The successful adjustment and integration of immigrants into Canada is crucial to the country's continued development and prosperity, and counselling psychologists and counsellors have an important role to play in this regard. As such, Canadian counselling psychologists have made a significant contribution to the extant body of research on immigration, publishing over forty articles on the topic since the late 1980s. In order to elucidate the distinct landscape of Canadian-based counselling and counselling psychology, the following section will discuss the nature and scope of immigration research conducted by these scholars.

In terms of the location of the immigration literature, Canadian counselling psychologists and counsellors have disseminated their immigration-related work in several different journals; however, they have most frequently published in journals within the discipline of counselling. Some of the journals that have often featured the immigration scholarship of Canadian counselling psychologists include the *Canadian Journal of Counselling and Psychotherapy*, the *International Journal for the Advancement of Counselling*, the *Journal of Employment Counselling*, and the *Canadian Journal of Counselling*. Additionally, although to a lesser extent, articles on immigration by Canadian counselling psychologists are found in journals from the domains of career development and vocational guidance, education, international and cross-cultural studies, women's issues, and child and youth studies.

Within the Canadian context, certain counselling psychologists have been particularly committed to investigating immigration-related issues. Canadian counselling psychologists who have produced a notable amount of scholarship on immigration and related topics include Noorfarah Merali, Sophie C. Yohani, Marvin J. Westwood, Ishu Ishiyama, Norman Amundson, Susan James, Charles Chen, Lana Stermac, and Ada L. Sinacore. Since these counselling psychologists have played such a pivotal role in expanding the immigration literature, a brief discussion of these professors' immigration-related research interests is warranted.

From the University of Alberta, Noorfarah Merali's research interests surround family class immigration, acculturation patterns, the influence of cultural transitioning on immigrant and refugee families, immigrant and refugee mental health, and multicultural counselling competence. Also at the University of Alberta, Sophie C. Yohani's research interests similarly encompass refugee mental health, but also include experiences of trauma and resiliency, program and policy development in educational and community settings, and helping professionals who work with under-represented populations. At the University of British Columbia (UBC), Marvin J. Westwood and Norman Amundson's research interests both surround career issues faced by various populations including immigrants, with Dr Westwood additionally investigating individual and group counselling methods with immigrants, older adults, and veterans. In frequent collaboration with Dr Westwood, Ishu Ishiyama has applied his interest in multicultural counselling, anti-discrimination, social-cultural competency training, self-validation issues, and cross-cultural transition to immigrant populations. Next, Susan James has focused her research program at UBC on cultural psychology and anthropology, immigration and acculturation, culture-bound disorders, and psychotherapy. Next, at the University of Toronto, Charles Chen's research interests broadly surround career theories, counselling, and development, as well as counsellor education. Also at the University of Toronto, Lana Stermac's research on immigration has focused on refugees, trauma and learning, and post-traumatic mental health. Finally, at McGill University, Ada L. Sinacore's research interests include career psychology, consultation, social justice theory and pedagogy, feminist/multicultural counselling psychology, and international psychology, and applying these interests to the examination of immigration, among other topics.

In addition to Canadian counselling psychologists, French Canadian scholars in psychology and counselling, as well as Canadian psychologists in domains of psychology other than counselling psychology, have also added to the current knowledge base on immigration. For example, Dr Hélène Cardu, a professor in the faculty of education at the University of Laval, has conducted a substantial amount of research on the identity development and social integration of professional women who immigrate to Canada (more specifically to the province of Quebec). French Canadian psychologists and counsellors have predominantly published their work in journals of cross-cultural psychology and international issues, as well as in journals focusing on psychology and counselling in Canada (e.g., *Canadian Psychology*) and Quebec (e.g., *Revue Québécoise de Psychologie*). The work of French Canadian scholars can also be found in other types of psychology journals (e.g., social psychology, behavioural science), in addition to feminist journals and journals of social issues and urban studies. Similarly, Canadian scholars in domains of psychology outside of counselling psychology have published a great deal in journals of cross-cultural and international psychology, as well as in journals related to social issues, and journals focusing on various other specialty areas of psychology (e.g., applied psychology, behavioural science).

An extensive review of the above-mentioned immigration literature revealed the following major topic areas: acculturation and cultural transitioning; employment and occupational concerns; educational attainment; family challenges; mental health and well-being; and implications for counselling. Within these general areas, scholars have explored discrimination, language barriers, generational challenges, women's issues, ethnic identity, and challenges faced by particular refugees. While there is a great deal of overlap among the topics studied in the broader disciplines of psychology, counselling psychology, and counselling, how these topics are approached varies based on discipline. That is, within the discipline of Canadian counselling psychology, these topic areas have been examined predominantly, though not exclusively, with qualitative methods, while the immigration literature published by French Canadian scholars and Canadian psychologists outside of counselling psychology has mainly employed quantitative methods. Thus, through their utilization of qualitative methods, their focus on the topics of counselling with immigrants and cultural transitioning, and the dissemination of their research in counselling-specific journals, Canadian counselling psychologists and counsellors have created a distinctive niche within the broader discipline of psychology in Canada.

ACCULTURATION AND CULTURAL TRANSITIONING

As previously discussed, much of the literature on immigration has focused on acculturation. Acculturation is said to result when individuals are able to achieve linguistic, sociocultural, and psychological adjustment within the new culture (Olmedo, 1979; Searle & Ward, 1990). Linguistic adjustment refers to host language proficiency and use; socio-cultural adjustment refers to the ability to effectively interact with members of the new cultural environment and is partly based on educational-occupational status and mobility; while psychological adjustment encompasses general well-being or satisfaction in the new cultural environment and is related to cultural values, attitudes, and behaviours. While this research has laid an important foundation in immigration research, counselling psychology research has moved away from the notion of immigrant adjustment and acculturation (Lee & Westwood, 1996; Westwood & Ishiyama, 1991) to a focus on cultural transitioning, which can be defined as the situation where immigrants are able to find occupational, economic, educational, and social security within the new culture (Chen, 2008; Berry, 1997, 2001; Lee & Westwood, 1996). This focus on cultural transitioning is consistent with counselling psychologists' orientation towards career development and life transitions. Attending to contextual factors, such as the immigrant community, combined with supporting transitions related to school and work, is central to the counselling psychology framework. Therefore, moving away from examining immigrant adjustment to the study of cultural transitioning offers an optimistic and strength-based approach to understanding the resiliency of, and challenges faced by, immigrant populations.

Research examining cultural transitioning indicates that the immigrant's community (e.g, ethnic, religious), education, and employment play an important role in successful cultural transitioning and integration (Sinacore et al., 2009). Moreover, successful integration results when the immigrant has been able to maintain aspects of his or her own culture of origin while developing skills and knowledge about the new culture relative to successful transitioning (e.g. Westwood & Ishiyama, 1991). Cultural transitioning is complex because the needs of immigrant groups vary based on country of origin, ethnicity, and religious and cultural norms (e.g. Sinacore et al., 2009). Additionally, younger immigrants may have a different orientation to immigration than older immigrants, which may affect the factors that influence their transition (Sinacore & Lerner, 2013). Thus, the research on factors that contribute to the successful transition of immigrants to Canada will be discussed in detail below.

Employment

Although Canada's immigration program is well established, Canada is not immune to the challenges that accompany the admittance and integration of several thousands of immigrants each year. One of the most pressing issues facing immigrants is in the area of employment, with occupational stress being cited in several studies as a pre-eminent concern when working with immigrants (e.g., Lee & Westwood, 1996; Westwood & Ishiyama, 1991). International research indicates that immigrants have an extremely high work ethic and that the importance of work is capital and immediate (Krau, 1984). Further, in Canada successful occupational integration is essential to the successful cultural transitioning of immigrants (e.g., Lee & Westwood, 1996; Westwood & Ishiyama, 1991). Despite the existence of the aforementioned point system for the selection of skilled workers, and the fact that immigrants tend to be more educated on average than native-born Canadians (Becklumb & Elgersma, 2008; Oreopoulos, 2009; Reitz, 2007), research shows that many immigrants are unemployed or underemployed (Reitz, 2007). As of 2011, the unemployment rate among recent immigrants aged 25–54 was 13.6 percent, over twice the rate of unemployment in the broader Canadian population (Statistics Canada, 2011a). Of those immigrants who are employed, many are working below their skill level as janitors, restaurant servers, cashiers, factory workers, building guards, truck drivers, call centre operators, etc. (Galarneau & Morisette, 2008; Reitz, 2011). For example, as of 2006, 28 percent of recently immigrated men and 40 percent of women were underemployed, whereas among native Canadian men and women, these rates were 10 percent and 12 percent respectively (Galarneau & Morisette, 2008). Even after residing in Canada for fifteen years, university-educated immigrants are still more likely than native Canadians to be underemployed (Statistics Canada, 2008, as cited in Haq & Ng, 2010). Moreover, immigrants earn significantly less than their Canadian counterparts and this wage gap has remained relatively constant in recent years (Frinette & Morisette, 2005).

The occupational difficulties faced by immigrants in Canada have been attributed to a host of factors including negative attitudes towards immigrants, skill discounting, and language difficulties. That is, attitudes of people within the host society can hinder successful cultural transitioning (Berry, 2003; Phinney, Horenczyk, Liebkind, & Vedder, 2001). Esses, Dovidio, Jackson, and Armstrong (2001) argued that perceived competition for resources is the primary source of negative attitudes toward immigrants. These attitudes toward immigrants result in a "fundamental dilemma" (Esses et al., 2001, p. 391) where immigrants are viewed as straining social systems regardless of the accuracy of this view.

One way in which these negative attitudes toward immigrants are expressed is through a type of discrimination called skill discounting, defined as the discounting of foreign-acquired education and work experiences relative to those that are locally attained (Esses, Dietz, & Bhardwaj, 2006). Due to Canada's method of immigrant selection, immigrants come to Canada with high levels of education and work skills acquired in their home countries, yet immigrants often face a lack of recognition or devaluing of their foreign credentials and work experience by Canadian employers (Oreopoulos, 2009; Reitz, 2007). For example, in the Canadian context, education obtained abroad is estimated to have only two-thirds of the value of Canadian degrees (Reitz, 2007). Further, many employers require applicants to have Canadian work experience (Sinacore, Park-Saltzman, Mikhail, & Wada, 2011), rendering it virtually impossible for newcomers to penetrate the Canadian job market in their chosen fields. As a result, many educated and skilled immigrants are not able to practice their chosen occupations in Canada. Because occupation is central to one's self-worth and identity, this loss of occupational status can cause tremendous psychological distress to immigrants. Unfortunately for Canadian immigrants, they are often misinformed that their professional credentials will be valued in

Canada, which exacerbates their feelings of disappointment and frustration (Neault, 2005; Sinacore et al., 2011).

Further complicating the situation, immigrants often do not have knowledge of or connections within the Canadian job market; this lack of job contacts is especially problematic since evidence suggests that eighty percent of jobs in Canada are secured through the hidden job market (McGill University Career & Placement Services, 2004, as cited in Sinacore et al., 2009). Finally, research has shown that discriminatory practices are occurring among employers. For instance, Oreopoulos (2009) conducted a study wherein thousands of job applications were created and submitted in response to on-line job postings, including the resumes of recent immigrants. Results of the study revealed that employers discriminated against applicants with foreign-sounding names and foreign experience by offering them fewer interviews (Oreopoulos, 2009). Correspondingly, the fact that the majority of newcomers to Canada are visible minorities raises the question of whether racial and ethnic prejudice is also a salient factor in the current employment dilemma (Haq & Ng, 2010). In light of the systemic barriers facing immigrants in the Canadian job market and the vital importance of occupational attainment for successful integration, employment is likely to remain an issue of concern in the years to come.

Furthermore, language proficiency greatly impacts immigrants' ability to integrate into the workforce. Even when an individual can demonstrate linguistic fluency in social settings, this ability does not necessarily translate into language mastery specific to their occupation (Sakamoto, Ku, & Wei, 2009; Suto, 2009). That is, technical, professional, and managerial positions often require higher levels of language proficiency, making the attainment of top positions in these occupations out of reach for most immigrants (Neault, 2005). Moreover, even when immigrants have high levels of language fluency, oftentimes they are discriminated against due to their accent. This discrimination is further complicated in Quebec, where bilingualism in English and French is often a workplace requirement and typically immigrants will be more fluent in one of these languages (Sinacore et al., 2011; Sinacore, Mikhail, Kassan, & Lerner, 2009). As such, perceived and real language competence can contribute to immigrants having difficulty securing a job and integrating into the Canadian workforce.

WOMEN'S OCCUPATIONAL TRANSITION   Within the immigration literature, there is a discussion that exclusively focuses on the
occupational transitioning of women. This body of research examines the occupational transitioning of women who have immigrated
to Canada from specific regions, for example, South Asia (e.g. Khan
& Watson, 2005), as well as that of immigrant women as a group
who share a common experience (e.g. Koert, Borgen, & Amundson,
2011). In addition to the employment barriers cited by immigrants
in general (e.g. discrimination, language barriers, deskilling) (Chen
& Asamoah, 2007), these studies have identified the specific occupational challenges faced by immigrant women, including: (a) issues
related to professional identity and social integration (Cardu &
Bouchamma, 2000); (b) loss of extended family (Cardu & Sanschagrin, 2002; Sinacore, Titus, & Hofman, in press); and (c) priori-
tizing family needs and husbands' careers (Cardu & Sanschagrin,
2002). For example, Cardu (2007) has also documented the relationship between what she calls career nomadism and professional
identity. That is, as a result of deskilling, women in her study settled
for temporary, contractual employment below their qualifications
that negatively affected their professional identities. Further, Koert
et al. (2011) conducted a qualitative study where they interviewed
educated women who immigrated to Canada. They used a critical
incident technique (Flanagan, 1954; Woolsey, 1986) to identify factors that either facilitated or hindered women's occupational transitioning. More specifically, they stated that the factors that helped
them pursue their career goals included both internal and external
factors. Internal factors included their personal beliefs and values,
their ability to take action, and their attention to self-care, while
external factors included supportive relationships, networks, and
work environments. Further, factors that hindered their occupational
transition were being deskilled, having unsatisfactory relationships,
facing unhelpful immigration services, and juggling multiple roles.

Education

In addition to occupational attainment, education is an essential
factor in the successful transitioning of immigrants. As previously
mentioned, immigrants whose educational background was deemed
equivalent or transferable to their new society find it easier to secure
employment and, in turn, economic security. In order to establish

education equivalency, immigrants are often forced to undergo a lengthy and costly process, which may include taking exams, completing an internship, and doing additional coursework. This process leads to delayed entrance into the work force and strains families' already limited resources (Aycan & Berry, 1996). As a result of the difficulty in achieving educational equivalency, some immigrants return to school in order to meet Canadian requirements, oftentimes redoing the same degree that they received in their country of origin (Lee & Westwood, 1996; Sinacore et al., 2011). In fact, evidence suggests that a significant portion of immigrants seek post-secondary education, which has been identified as an effective pathway to improve post-immigration occupational outcomes (Anisef, Sweet, & Adamuti-Trache, 2010). In North America's knowledge economy, post-secondary education is of vital importance to occupational mobility and financial well-being for all citizens. Further, the number of Canadians completing college and university has been increasing, resulting in a progressively more competitive job market (Abada & Tenkorang, 2009). As a result, the pursuit of post-secondary education may be crucial to the economic welfare of immigrants.

Yet, returning to school for the purposes of re-careering is not without its challenges. In addition to the financial hardship that may result from returning to school, re-careering immigrants face specific challenges at university. That is, in addition to cultural shock, loss of social status, language difficulties, discrimination, and isolation (Sinacore et al., 2009), re-careering immigrants who return to university oftentimes experience isolation and discrimination within the university environment. That is, research indicates that campus services do not necessarily attend to the needs of re-careering immigrant graduate students and that there are several areas in which these students are particularly challenged at university including: social isolation; ageism, as they tend to be older than their fellow students; difficulty in securing a mentor; lack of academic advisement; lack of appropriate campus services; and discrimination on the part of university personnel (Sinacore et al., 2011). Moreover, even though immigrants return to school in order to be able to secure employment, there is no evidence to suggest that they actually achieve this outcome. Therefore, it may be important to develop specific career services on university campuses to address the needs of re-careering immigrant students. Yet, re-careering immigrants are not the only immigrants who face academic challenges. In addition to this population of students, the research on educational attainment also examines the challenges faced by school- and university-age immigrants.

SCHOOL-AGE IMMIGRANTS   Similar to the factors that influence employability, factors affecting the educational achievement of immigrant students include acculturation, socio-economic status, language proficiency, social support, and parental expectations. With regard to elementary- and high school–age immigrant children, those whose parents are university-educated (Abada & Tenkorang, 2009) and those with higher socio-economic status (SES) are more likely to obtain a university degree (Aydemir, Chen, & Corek, 2005, as cited in Abada & Tenkoreng, 2009). Researchers posit that parents with higher levels of education have the knowledge and experience necessary to prepare and guide their children through post-secondary studies (Perreira, Harris, & Lee, 2006; Suarez-Orozco, Pimentel, & Martin, 2009), while immigrant families with higher SES can afford to provide youth with the resources they need to succeed academically (e.g. computers, books, extra tutoring).

Additionally, proficiency in the language of instruction leads to educational success (Perreira et al., 2006; Suarez-Orozco et al., 2009), while competence in one's native language facilitates the forging of connections and support within one's ethnic community, a resource that has been found to encourage educational persistence (Abada & Tenkorang, 2009). Further, American researchers Suarez-Orozco et al. (2009) found that greater levels of academic engagement among immigrant high school students were associated with school-based support from peers and adults. As well, Abada and Tenkoreng (2009) reported that for immigrant youth, having close, intact families was related to the pursuit of post-secondary education.

Further, generational status and the length of residence in the host country have been found to influence the educational attainment of immigrant youth in Canada. Abada and Tenkorang (2009) define generational status as follows: first-generation immigrants are individuals who immigrated after the age of fifteen; second-generation immigrants include children born of one or both parents from another country; and third-generation immigrants include individuals born to parents who were also born in the host country. Using these generational definitions, researchers have found that earlier generations obtain better grades and achieve higher levels of education than later ones (Keller & Tillman, 2008; Pong, Hao, & Gardner, 2004). The extent of this educational decline has been found to vary by ethnic group (Pong et al., 2004; Suarez-Orozco et al., 2009), indicating that immigrant groups often take divergent educational trajectories.

UNDERGRADUATE STUDENTS   Studies of immigrant undergraduate students indicate that students who immigrate to Canada and attend post-secondary institutions often experience unique challenges (Sinacore & Lerner, 2013) and distinctive familial expectations and pressures (Kwak & Berry, 2001; Li, 2001). Immigrant students may feel pressure to succeed academically in order to show gratitude to their parents for the sacrifices they made in order to immigrate (Maramba, 2008; Suarez-Orozco et al., 2009). They also may experience conflicts between the values of their native culture and the host country, the educational institution, or the discipline in which they study (Calderwood, Harper, Ball, & Liang, 2009). That is, students may be under pressure to choose a major that is supported by their familial or cultural values versus choosing an area of personal interest (Sinacore & Lerner, 2013).

Further, immigrant students must also negotiate multiple identities (Guo & Jamal, 2007), such as the intersections of their ethnic, student, and gender identities (Maramba, 2008). For example, Sinacore, Titus, and Hofman (2013) found that women students were often caught between the conservative gender expectations of their culture of origin and the more liberal expectations of women in Canada. This conflict often resulted in these students feeling like outsiders both in Canadian society and within their cultural community; as a result, these students actively sought out liberal members within their ethnic community.

Further to negotiating multiple identities, immigrant undergraduate students may face discrimination in educational institutions as a function of one or more of those identities (Calderwood et al., 2009) and may have specific academic, cultural, and social needs that go unmet (Kilbride & D'Arcangelo, 2002). Sinacore and Lerner (2013) identified several institutional barriers to immigrant students' educational success; these included challenges transferring credits, unresponsive university staff, and a lack of services specifically geared for immigrant undergraduate students. The results of their study indicated that university staff and academic advisors were found to be unresponsive to the specific needs of immigrant undergraduate students and that few if any services existed at the university to help students navigate the challenges inherent in being an immigrant student.

In addition to institutional barriers, immigrant students face many of the same societal and psycho-social barriers reported by immigrants in general, including discrimination, language barriers, lack of knowledge of the Canadian educational system, lack of social support from members of the host country, and negative attitudes held by Canadians towards immigrants. These barriers may result in immigrant undergraduate students feeling isolated, which may compromise their academic success and result in their not completing their degree (Kilbride & D'Arcangelo, 2002; Sinacore & Lerner, 2013).

Family Issues

Research examining immigration from the perspectives of families has focused on two major areas: intergenerational challenges and transnational immigrant families (Merali, 2008b, 2012; Tardif & Geva, 2006).

INTERGENERATIONAL GAPS   The research carried out to date is focused predominantly on the potentially different experiences that parents and their children face through the immigration process (e.g. Merali, 2002) as well as the possible consequences of these intergenerational gaps (e.g. Rasmi, Chuang, & Safdar, 2012; Shariff, 2009). These generational differences have been found to be related to challenges such as family conflict, parenting stress, confusion around adolescent identity development, and communication issues. Further, much of the research conducted in Canada has focused on particular ethnic groups, such as families who immigrate from Punjab (e.g. Nayar & Sandhu, 2006) or Taiwan (e.g. Petersen & Park-Saltzman, 2010), versus a focus on broader racial or ethnic groups, such as individuals emigrating from Asian or Latin countries.

As previously discussed in this chapter, the process of immigrating to a new country often engenders some degree of acculturation or cultural transitioning. That is, newcomers to Canada must learn to navigate two cultures, that of their original country as well as that of the host country (Kwast-Welfel, Boski, & Rovers, 2004). When considering the acculturation experiences of families as a whole, it is not uncommon for parents and adolescents to disagree on how much they should assimilate into the host society, leading to inter-generational gaps within the family (Merali, 2002, 2004a, 2004b, 2005). For example, Merali (2002, 2004b) found that Central Amer-ican refugee parents and adolescents had a tendency to misjudge the degree of assimilation difference that existed between them, by either overestimating or underestimating the intergenerational gaps and levels of assimilation. The perception of these differences was attrib-uted to internal factors rather than the process of cultural transition-ing as a whole. That is, generally immigrants did not attribute their challenges to the process of cultural transitioning but rather to inter-nal factors (e.g. something is going on with my child) or external factors (e.g. the school system is having an impact on my child) to the problem (Merali, 2004a). Additionally, parents attributed the overestimation of intergenerational gaps to changing family values, stress, and experiences of control within the family, while adoles-cents attributed these gaps to family conflict, dependency, and attach-ment. Alternatively, for parents the underestimation of these gaps was attributed to a respect for family values, positive affect, family harmony, and collaboration around problem-solving, while for ado-lescents the underestimation of these gaps was attributed to respect for their parents, respect for their culture, and openness in family relationships (Merali, 2004b, 2005).

Further, discrepancies in family members' perceptions of assimila-tion were related to level of education and family size. That is, par-ents with higher levels of education appear to be more accepting of their adolescents' assimilative behaviours within the Canadian school system (Merali & Violato, 2002). Consistent with Merali's research, Shariff (2009) found that the discrepancies between par-ents' and adolescents' levels of assimilation are a major source of stress during the process of cultural transitioning.

Along the same lines, Kwast-Welfel et al. (2004), in examining the transmission of values between parents and adolescents from three different groups – Polish immigrants to Canada, Polish non-immigrants in Poland, and Canadian non-immigrants in Canada – found no significant difference in the discrepancy of values across all three groups, suggesting that immigrants' cultural transition to Canada did not lead to value changes between parents and adoles-cents. In a related article, Shariff (2009) addressed adolescents' ethnic identity development and parenting stress within South Asian families who immigrate to Canada. She concluded that it could be quite challenging for second-generation immigrant adolescents to develop a consolidated ethnic identity, as their parents often rejected the bicultural identity that often forms due to interactions with members of both their cultural group and the host society. As such, adolescents' ethnic identity development may become a source of parenting stress and family conflict.

Finally, intergenerational changes in communication styles have been cited as a source of immigration stress in families. For example, in a study of three generations of Punjabi immigrants, Nayar and Sandhu (2006) found generational differences in family members' preferred mode of communication. That is, grandparents, who were born in India and received minimal formal education, preferred an oral model of communication, such as storytelling, narrating traditions, and sharing personal experiences. Parents, who were born in India and received some formal education, preferred a literary mode of communication, such as sharing personal experiences and concrete facts. Children, who were born in Canada and received formal education within this context, expressed an analytic form of communication characterized by exploration, inquisition, and abstraction. Further, it was noted that collectivism dissipated with each generation.

TRANSNATIONAL IMMIGRANT FAMILIES   The phenomenon of transnational living occurs when one family member (or more) moves to another country, while the other family member remains in the country of origin. Studies of transnational families in Canada have focused in two general areas. First, studies have examined transnational living where one parent (typically the mother) moves to another country with his/her children while the other parent (typically the father) remains in the original country in order to work and support the family. The "breadwinner" in this case often travels back and forth between the two countries (e.g. Petersen & Park-Saltzman, 2010). A second area of research is transnational marriage. Transnational marriage occurs either when an international marriage occurs with one spouse immigrating to the other spouse's country, or in the case where both spouses have the same country of origin, one spouse immigrates to the new country, and the second spouse follows at a later date.

With regard to transnational families, Petersen and Park-Saltzman (2010) examined the immigration experiences of transnational Taiwanese youth where youth were living in Canada while their families remained in Taiwan. The youth in this study reported that they developed a heightened sense of independence through their cultural transition to Canada. This independence served them well in navigating between the two cultures and contributing to their changing family system. However, it also caused confusion with respect to their Taiwanese identity development and their future aspirations.

With regard to transnational marriage, Merali (2012) studied the experiences of women who immigrated to Canada following an international marriage. These women immigrated to Canada through family sponsorship policies (Citizenship and Immigration Canada, 2002) as they had a Canadian husband sponsoring them. As a result, in their first three years in Canada, transnational brides do not have access to immigration and social assistance, as the government expects that their needs will be met through their husbands' financial support and other networks. Yet, these women do not automatically receive landed status, as they must independently initiate the process to become a permanent resident of Canada. As such, transnational brides are often unaware of their sponsorship rights, and hence are vulnerable to deportation threats or spousal abuse (Merali, 2008a, 2009). Moreover, fluency in English has been found to be an important factor in mediating this vulnerability and in these women's accessing of services. That is, women who had a minimum level of English proficiency reported being able to access resources regarding the conditions of their sponsorship relationships, which resulted them being knowledgeable about their rights should their husbands withdraw support or abuse them. These women were able to access information about applying for permanent residency and received support from their husbands in this process. To the contrary, those women who did not speak English needed to rely on third-party informants to access information about the conditions of their sponsorship relationships, and were more likely to have miscommunications with their husbands about their legal rights (Merali, 2012).

↑ threat of domestic violence

MENTAL HEALTH ISSUES

In addition to examining the relationship of employment, education, and family to cultural transitioning, researchers have examined the mental health concerns of immigrants to Canada. Research on immigrants' mental health, for the most part, has been conducted by clinical psychologists who employed a medical model (e.g. Kuo, Chong, & Joseph, 2008). Alternatively, scholars within the discipline of counselling psychology have applied a wellness approach to the exploration of the impact of immigration on the mental health of newcomers to Canada (e.g. Stermac, Brazeau, & Kelly, 2008a, 2008b; James, 2001, 2002). For example, in their research examining the mental health of individuals who were exposed to war prior to immigrating to Canada, Stermac et al. (2008a) found that participants experienced negative psychological consequences consistent with symptoms of post-traumatic disorder. These symptoms included re-experiencing the trauma, avoiding and numbing emotions, and hyper-vigilance. However, participants' mental health improved significantly over time outside of the war-zone areas. In a second study examining immigrant students who were exposed to war, the findings of Stermac et al. (2008b) indicated that within four years of immigration, students reported positive mental health and life satisfaction, as well as positive educational experiences such as increased learning, engagement in supportive relationships, and developing a sense of community. The authors suggest that these benefits facilitated development of coping strategies, which assisted these students in their transition to Canada.

Next, with regard to assessment and diagnosis, according to James and Clarke (2001), the definition and treatment of mental illness are culturally embedded. Consequently, when individuals immigrate to a new country, they must navigate different conceptualizations of mental health, which may be in conflict with one another. For example, in a study of immigrant women from the Azores of Portugal, James (2002) gathered verbal and non-verbal descriptions of *agonias*. In Portugal, *agonias* is a mental condition where women report "missing air, burning from within, as well as loss of sight, appetite, and sleep" (p. 168). This condition was related to and expressed within women's social contexts and religious beliefs. That is, participants in the study shared that they engaged in a *powerful* healing through seeking out help in three forms: *redemptive* (through religious figures), *indigenous* (through traditional healers), and *allopathic* (through physicians, mental health practitioners, and psychiatrists) (James, 2012). Thus, it is important when working with immigrants to understand the cultural foundations of symptoms and treatment, as these symptoms and their meaning may not directly translate into the diagnostic categories typically applied in Canada.

SUMMARY AND CONCLUSIONS

The aforementioned research conducted by counselling and counselling psychology scholars has led to some important considerations regarding the cultural transitioning of Canadian immigrants. First, research has indicated that the process of cultural transitioning results in immigrants being confronted with occupational, educational, and familial challenges (e.g. Ishiyama, 1995; Mak, Westwood, Ishiyama, & Barker, 1999; Merali, 2004a; Westwood & Ishiyama, 1991). These challenges are further complicated when immigrants are confronted with negative attitudes from members of Canadian society. Further, the lack of educational equivalence, the lack of Canadian work experience, deskilling, poor language proficiency, and discrimination have been cited as central challenges to immigrants finding employment, resulting in immigrants being either unemployed or underemployed (e.g. Sinacore et al., 2009; Westwood, Ishiyama, & Barker, 1999). As such, researchers have identified securing employment and occupational satisfaction as key factors in immigrants' successful transitioning into Canadian society (e.g. Chen & Asamoah, 2007; Lee & Westwood, 1996; Sinacore et al., 2009).

Additionally, when immigrants are unable to secure employment in Canada they may return to university (re-career) in order to secure a Canadian credential, believing that it will make them more competitive in the Canadian job market (Sinacore et al., 2011). Thus, given the importance placed on educational and occupational transitioning, researchers have made specific recommendations regarding the needs of re-careering immigrants and immigrant university students. To this end, Sinacore et al. (2011) recommend that career services be developed specifically targeting immigrant graduate students, as career centres have been identified as the primary places where immigrant students seek assistance. Likewise, mentoring has been identified as a key factor that may serve to buffer students from culture shock as well as provide them with an avenue where they can find social support, academic advising, and information about the university and the broader community. Similarly, Sinacore and Lerner (2013) reported that university services neither specifically addressed the needs of immigrant students nor facilitated their integrating into university. In addition to creating services geared towards immigrant students, these authors posit that the development of orientation programs specifically targeting immigrant students could provide them with basic information about the university, the local community, and broader Canadian society. In the same light, they noted that university service providers were ill-equipped to work with immigrant students, and thus may need training to be competent in addressing the specific needs of this population (Sinacore & Lerner, 2013). As a result, these researchers and others (e.g. Stearmac et al., 2008b) contend that the university community has the potential to serve as a welcoming place which provides immigrants with the tools, coping strategies, and social support necessary for academic success and social integration.

Moreover, with regard to families, parenting stress and family conflict have been cited as primary concerns for immigrants with young families (Merali, 2004b). These concerns can be understood within the context of cultural transitioning, where parents and adolescents have divergent experiences when it comes to integrating into the broader society. As a result there may be differences in the degree to which each family member has acculturated, which may, in turn, result in stress within the family. Hence, understanding the impact that the process of cultural transitioning has had on both the family as a whole and each individual family member is essential in helping families address the challenges associated with immigration (Merali, 2004a, 2004b).

Finally, it is essential to understand the pathways in which immigrants travelled prior to coming to Canada. That is, the processes that immigrants followed to come to Canada (e.g. transnational families, refugees) and the events that resulted in individuals and families leaving their country of origin may have a significant impact on the cultural transitioning of different groups (Stearmac et al., 2008a, 2008b). Hence, counsellors and counselling psychologists need to be cognizant of the influence that negative pre-immigrant experiences (e.g. war trauma) have had on immigrants and be aware that over time the impact of these experiences may dissipate in a supportive environment. Concomitantly, the prevalence of oppression and discrimination experienced by immigrants once arriving in Canada may serve to exacerbate the negative impact of pre-immigration experiences and inhibit new arrivals' transition into

Canadian society. Therefore, it behooves counsellors and counselling psychologists to develop the requisite knowledge and skills to assist in addressing the complex nature of the concerns and challenges as well as the resiliency of immigrant populations.

NOTE

1 Kassan and Lerner contributed equally to this chapter.

7

Health, Wellness, and Prevention

K. JESSICA VAN VLIET, PATRICE KEATS,
AND AUDREY KINZEL[1]

In Canadian health care services, medical professionals are usually the front line for people experiencing mental health concerns. Psychologists, in contrast, are generally underutilized in Canadian health care, and both physicians and psychologists may lack familiarity with the other group's training and the services they can provide. Despite this disconnect, counselling psychologists have been making important contributions to the management and conceptualization of mental health, particularly by observing a strength-focused rather than a pathology-based orientation to mental health care (Haverkamp, Robertson, Cairns, & Bedi, 2011). A significant aspect of this contribution has consisted of health and wellness studies done by counselling psychology researchers in Canada. This group includes academics in Canadian counselling psychology and counselling programs and practitioners who identify themselves as counselling psychologists or counsellors. Sinacore, Borgen, Daniluk, Kassan, Long, and Nicol (2011), for example, have described a multitude of research areas where Canadian counselling psychologists have been making a positive impact. These have included, under the rubric of health issues, such topics as addictions, post-traumatic stress, interpersonal violence, sexual abuse, vicarious trauma, intergenerational family violence in Indigenous communities, self-harm and suicide risks, chronic illnesses, disordered eating, fetal alcohol spectrum disorder, developmental disabilities, war zone migration, and life stressors; and under the rubric of wellness studies, such topics as prevention, hope, music, spirituality, mindfulness, self-compassion, leisure, self-efficacy, psychological and embodied agency, empowerment, self-care, health literacy, and coping. At an institutional level, counselling psychologists have been working toward building community engagement, creating positive school climates, enhancing systems such as justice, social services, health, and education, and working with culture as a health resource.

In reviewing the literature on these topics, we first set the context for Canadian health research by describing how counselling psychology fits into the Canadian heath care system. We then offer definitions of health, wellness, and prevention. Finally we present an overview of counselling psychology research, highlighting the wellness perspective. The chapter concludes with a discussion of the main challenges for counselling psychology researchers, along with an outline of future directions for research.

HEALTH CARE IN CANADA

Canada has a publicly funded health care system, where universal coverage is available for all Canadians based on their health care needs rather than their ability to pay. *Health Canada* is the federal department responsible for helping Canadians "maintain and improve" their health (Health Canada, 2011a, para. 1). Although equity and fairness are basic values of the system, funding is based on priorities outlined in the *Canada Health Act*, which is designed to deliver the broadest essential services for the greatest number of people with the money that is available (see Department of Justice Canada, 2012). Federal, provincial/territorial, and local or municipal governments are involved in deciding on these health priorities, with the federal and provincial/territorial governments holding the most power in making health care decisions. For example, the federal government is responsible for the health care costs of specific groups of Canadians, such as "First Nations people living on reserves; Inuit; serving members of the Canadian Forces and the Royal Canadian Mounted Police; eligible veterans; inmates in federal penitentiaries; and refugee claimants" (Health Canada, 2011b, para. 21). Provincial/territorial governments, in consultation with physicians' colleges or other groups, each decide on the medically necessary services that public money will finance (e.g., fees for health professionals, public health initiatives, or supplementary benefits for specific groups such as seniors). Local or municipal governments supply resources such as funding for health care facilities or specific local health-related programs.

Health care is divided between primary, secondary, and supplementary services. Primary services consist of comprehensive first-contact care, where patients' needs are assessed and coordinated within a system of more specialized services (e.g., emergency services, maternity care, specialists in specific areas, hospital services, or primary mental health care). There has recently been an increased emphasis on community-based primary health care, with a focus on health promotion, disease or injury prevention, and other programs. Secondary services comprise referrals to specialized care in hospitals, long-term facilities, or communities. For the most part, home- or continuing-care services are not eligible for funding under the Canada Health Act, but some services may be covered for specific groups (e.g., home-care services for veterans, Inuit, or First Nations people on reserves). Finally, supplementary services are those that are not generally funded publically (e.g., dental care, vision care, mobility aids, or prescription medications). The vast majority of mental health care services that are offered by counselling psychologists fall under either secondary or supplemental care.

In this context, health research priorities are defined by Health Canada and funded through its federal agency the Canadian Institutes of Health Research (CIHR). Issues that relate to primary care or that affect the selected groups falling under the federal mandate, as described above, are generally given higher priority. Some of the current CIHR research priorities that are relevant to counselling psychologists and other mental health professionals include the following: population-specific issues, such as women and reproductive health; the mental health and development of children and youth; seniors and aging; equity of access and health outcomes for First Nations and Inuit Canadians; specific mental health issues such as addiction; mental health issues related to HIV; mental health and neurological conditions; autism; and community development.

It is only in the past six years or so that mental health has been incorporated into the national health agenda. In 2007, the federal government created the Mental Health Commission of Canada (MHCC; see Mental Health Commission of Canada, n.d.) in order to recognize and promote improvement in the mental health care system for Canadians. Originating in a national study by a standing Senate committee, the MHCC received a favourable vote by all

four federal parties, and it was endorsed by all provincial and territorial governments (with the exception of Quebec); it developed out
of a recognition that mental health is a factor in all other health-
related issues. The MHCC describes its mission as "improving the
mental health system and changing the attitudes and behaviours of
Canadians around mental health issues" (Mental Health Commission
of Canada, n.d., para. 1). To fulfill this mandate, members of the
MHCC are focused on the following areas: homelessness, peer support, seniors' issues, the mental health of children and youth, and
stigma (including stigmatizing attitudes among medical professionals). Importantly, the MHCC is interested in the well-being of diverse
populations (MHCC, 2009). A prioritization of well-being and prevention was included among the seven goals identified by the MHCC
for improving the state of mental health care in Canada (see MHCC,
2009). For Canadian counselling psychologists and counsellors,
these are important aspects of care, and the MHCC's mission has
mirrored our own priorities for practice and research, in accordance
with our definition of counselling psychology.

WORKING DEFINITIONS OF KEY TERMS

Definitions of the terms *health*, *prevention*, and *wellness* will help to
guide our discussion of the ways that Canadian researchers have
contributed to the knowledge base of counselling psychology. First,
we adopt the World Health Organization (WHO) definition of *health*
as "a state of complete physical, mental, and social wellbeing and
not merely the absence of disease or infirmity" (WHO, 2012a, para.
1). The pursuit of health under this definition promotes the development of partnerships between international agencies, academic institutions, ministries, and citizens, as well as the development of public
health policies that promote health (WHO, 2012b). The WHO
acknowledges that "many of the major health problems" (WHO,
2012c, para. 1) in Canada and other developed and developing
nations are related to the behaviour of individuals; for example,
personal choices may create health problems through inadequate
exercise, dietary choices, smoking, or drug use. The WHO (2012c)
further contends that people need information, life skills, opportunities, and supportive environments to make good health choices.
Second, in light of this definition of health, we see health promotion
as facilitating *prevention*. Prevention is the act of hindering or

stopping negative factors and poor choices in order to reduce disease and nurture good health. Finally, in the context of health and prevention, *wellness* is the ideal end point. Swarbrick (2006) and Swarbrick and Moosvi (2010) speak to wellness as a *process* involving conscious, deliberate choices in order to develop healthy habits, while avoiding self-harming behaviours including toxic relationships and circumstances. Psychological factors impact people's choices and decisions when embarking on the wellness path towards health and disease prevention; for example, self-worth, social connections, school engagement, and nurturance are positively correlated with healthy behaviours and good health (Canadian Institute for Health Information, 2006).

OVERVIEW OF CANADIAN HEALTH RESEARCH

In this section, we outline the types of health research currently being conducted in counselling psychology in Canada. Based on our review of the literature, we have categorized current studies into the following five sections (although some of these areas do overlap): addictions and mental health; chronic illness; traumatic stress; suicide, self-injury, and depression; and women's issues related to reproductive health. The vast majority of these topics are aligned with the Health Canada research priorities for Canadians. In our review of these research areas, we have attempted to include the work of as many Canadian counselling psychology researchers as possible. However, we also acknowledge the contributions of researchers who, due to limitations of space, are not included in this chapter. We also note that this overview does not capture the vast amount of health, wellness, and prevention research being done by researchers outside of counselling psychology (e.g., nursing, medicine, clinical psychology, social work), although there is some overlap in the topics being studied.

Addictions and Mental Health

As noted, addiction and drug abuse constitutes one of the research priorities for Health Canada. Counselling psychology researchers are making a strong contribution in the field. Below we outline some of the key projects.

There are two main types of addiction: substance dependence and behavioural addictions. Substance dependence involves substances such as nicotine, alcohol, cannabis, and opioids, while behavioural addictions involve compulsive behaviours such as gambling, sex, shopping, eating, and computer use. Addictions research by Canadian counselling psychologists is generally concerned with understanding the causes and co-morbidities of substance use, dependency, and behavioural compulsions, and with identifying effective treatments for dependencies and compulsions.

Alcohol and illicit drug use and the relationship to personality, child maltreatment, and deliberate self-harm have been studied (Goldstein & Flett, 2009; Goldstein, Flett, & Wekerle, 2010; Goldstein, Flett, Wekerle, & Wall, 2009; Piran & Robinson, 2011) along with the experiences of female adolescents with addictions to methamphetamines (Newbury & Hoskins, 2010). Goldstein and Flett (2009) investigated the links between personality traits and motivations for alcohol consumption, noting, for example, that individuals who were motivated by coping reported less positive affect, greater anxiety, and greater neuroticism than those motivated by enhancement (i.e., the attempt and desire to enhance mood) or those with no internal motivation. Individuals motivated to consume alcohol for both coping and enhancement tended to consume the most alcohol, whereas those with non-internal motivations consumed the least. In a study investigating child maltreatment and alcohol use, Goldstein, Flett, and Wekerle (2010) focused on understanding the specific motives involved. Results showed that the enhancement motive was common among male problem drinkers who had experienced child maltreatment, whereas for women, a desire to cope with depression was the motive most commonly associated with alcohol misuse. In studying links between substance use, child maltreatment, and personality among university students, Goldstein, Flett, Wekerle, and Wall (2009) also investigated the role of deliberate self-harming behaviour, revealing strong correlations between deliberate self-harm and a history of physical neglect, emotional abuse, and illicit drug use. Piran and Robinson (2011) observed a relationship between substance use and disordered eating patterns in women. Specifically, they found binge drinking, negative consequences of drinking, and cocaine use to be significantly associated with bingeing, purging, and dieting. Additionally, the use of stimulants and amphetamines was found to be associated with dieting and purging. Aston, Comeau, and Ross (2007) studied women living in rural areas of Canada to identify how women respond to their problems with substance abuse. The uniqueness of living in rural Canada with substance abuse problems and strategies for managing were presented. The use of photographs to assist adolescent girls with an addiction to methamphetamines to engage in dialogue and identify strengths was studied by counsellors Newbury and Hoskins in 2010. Together, these findings may assist clinicians and the individuals themselves in understanding substance misuse and in guiding intervention.

Canadian counselling psychology researchers have studied behavioural compulsions including gambling and sexual addiction (Goldstein, Walton, Cunningham, Resko, & Duan, 2009; Kwee, Dominguez, & Ferell, 2007). Goldstein et al. (2009) focused on understanding factors related to youth who had engaged in gambling. Factors associated with gambling for inner-city youth of both genders included alcohol use, cigarette and marijuana use, lower academic achievement, dropping out of school, and violence. Kwee et al. (2007) focused on sexual addiction, and argued that an assessment of sexual addiction that typically assumes sex between partners may inadvertently create difficulties in assessing sexual addiction in unmarried Christian males who engage in solo sexual behaviour such as pornography and masturbation. These researchers emphasize that accurate assessment of sexual addictions must include other contextual factors, rather than just the conventional view of sexual activity between partners.

Treatment research on substance use focuses on Aboriginal traditions (McCormick, 2000b), experiential treatments (Koehn, 2007), and use of the relational approach (Koehn, 2010). McCormick (2000b) has emphasized negative life effects (e.g., substance abuse) that may occur when Aboriginal people are disconnected from their cultural traditions and values. He highlights the importance of strategies to assist people in reconnecting to their Aboriginal culture in the healing process. Similarly Koehn (2010) emphasizes the role of connection and relationship as key concepts in Relational-Cultural Therapy for individuals who misuse alcohol and other substances. The role of relationships is also emphasized in an experiential group technique (i.e., relationship sculpture) for the treatment of alcohol and other substance problems. As demonstrated by these studies, Canadian researchers recognize how the treatment of substance abuse can be facilitated by an emphasis on culture, relationships, and personal connections.

Physical Illness

Counselling psychology research in the broad area of physical illness tends to focus on the psychosocial, behavioural, and developmental components of illnesses such as HIV/AIDS, chronic pain, acquired brain injury, and multiple sclerosis.

In terms of HIV/AIDS, researchers have explored issues related to hope (Harris & Larsen, 2008), empowerment (Harris & Alderson, 2006), and self-efficacy (Harris, Cameron, & Lang, 2011). Harris and Larsen (2008) showed that the use of medication, the acquisition of knowledge about the disease, and the awareness of future possibilities were all sources of hope for individuals diagnosed with HIV/AIDS. Another positive aspect related to feelings of empowerment was found by Harris and Alderson (2006) in a study of different HIV disease trajectories among gay men. Harris, Cameron, and Lang (2011) explored participants' adjustment to living with HIV diagnoses when participants were associated with a community-based HIV agency. Results of the study indicated that association with a community-based agency enhanced the participants' psychological adjustment, including their self-efficacy. The implication of these findings for clinicians assisting individuals with HIV/AIDS is that facilitating hope, empowerment, and self-efficacy as well as connecting these individuals to relevant agencies are important for individuals living with HIV/AIDS.

Another area of physical illness investigated by counselling psychology researchers is chronic pain. For example, research by Schultz et al. (2002) aimed to develop a model that could be used to predict the outcome of occupational low-back disability. Results demonstrated a range of biopsychosocial variables that were significant in predicting disability outcomes, including job threat and recovery expectations. Prkachin, Hughes, Schultz, Joy, and Hunt (2002) investigated the assessment of pain behaviours among participants with low-back pain, finding promising clinical techniques related to sounds and facial expressions exhibited during assessments. Another study inquiring into pain behaviours found that guarding (as a pain behaviour) was linked with disability outcomes (Prkachin, Schultz, & Hughes, 2007). Finally, Kinzel (2011) indicated that acceptance of chronic pain is a construct found to facilitate pain management, and that it helps to enhance quality of life for individuals suffering from chronic pain when existing treatment approaches do not result in adequate pain relief. Future research on pain acceptance may help in the ongoing development of assessment tools and corresponding treatment modules for chronic pain sufferers.

In the area of brain injury, Tasker (2003) conducted a study involving individuals with acquired brain injury that demonstrated the importance of having a future orientation rather than a one-day-at-a-time orientation. She also found that participants had a need to be understood, that they valued the role of spirituality, and that they found significance in caring relationships. It is evident from these findings that therapists, counsellors, and psychologists all have a role in assisting individuals with acquired brain injury in adjusting to their condition.

Canadian counselling research has also investigated psychosocial factors in adjustment and treatment adherence in people with multiple sclerosis. Thannhauser and her colleagues (Thannhauser, Mah, & Metz, 2009) studied the impact of peer relationships and developmental factors on treatment adherence among adolescents living with this chronic illness. The researchers found nonadherence to be related to the adolescents' needs for peer conformity, autonomy (i.e., desire to maintain independence from doctors and caregivers), and the adolescents' "sense of omnipotence, cognitive limitations in assessing risks, and relative inexperience with long-term consequences" (p. 121). Thannhauser (2009) further developed a model to explain experiences of grieving in youth with M S. Central to the model was the role of peer relationships, which either facilitated or hindered adolescents' processes of grieving the many losses that accompanied their illness. The findings of these studies highlight how the developmental and social needs of adolescents with chronic illness need to be considered as part of a holistic treatment approach.

Inroads have also been made into arts-based treatment approaches for chronic illness. For example, Nicol (2010) conducted a phenomenological study on the meaning and experience of listening to music for women with chronic illness. The findings revealed that listening to music altered the women's lived experiences of time, space, and their own bodies in ways that enhanced positive coping. Such research may help stimulate further consideration of arts-based and alternative treatment approaches for chronic illness sufferers.

Traumatic Stress Studies

Traumatic experiences are common occurrences in the lives of many Canadians, and they occur in many different contexts (e.g., home, school, workplace, communities). Health Canada and the Public Health Agency of Canada, which is an agency of Health Canada and the main federal agency responsible for public health, have focused on specific types of trauma, with specific groups of people where trauma is most likely to occur. For example, emphasis is placed on workplace trauma and occupational safety (see Health Canada, 2011c), as well as violence and abuse (see Health Canada, 2011d) with a specific focus on families.

What are Canadian researchers doing in relation to these health research priorities and trauma? Canadian counselling psychology researchers have been addressing these health research priorities in four major areas: violence and abuse, child and youth mental health, military trauma, and drug abuse and alcoholism. First, in terms of violence and abuse, researchers and counselling psychology practitioners have explored a number of areas, including various aspects of how adult survivors of childhood sexual abuse cope in light of childhood trauma (e.g., Hirakata, 2009; Yohani & Hagen, 2010); how family violence issues can be addressed in counselling practice and therapy training (e.g., Martin, 2009; McBride, 2010); and how school violence and bullying can be prevented (Leschied, Chiodo, Whitehead, & Hurley, 2006). Koehn (2007, 2010) has conducted research in the area of counselling treatments for drug abuse and alcoholism among abused women. Her premise is to enhance and develop relational connections as an antidote to the effects of trauma experiences that result in substance abuse as a coping strategy. Finally, from a review of the literature, violence against and abuse of the elderly appear to be absent from counselling psychology research. This is an important area of trauma studies that counselling psychology researchers need to consider.

Second, child and youth mental health and trauma has been researched in a number of different ways. For example, Goldstein and colleagues (Goldstein, Flett, Wekerle, & Wall, 2009) explored how child maltreatment was linked with substance abuse and self-harm behaviours, and how violence and substance use could be used as predictors of depression among adolescents (Goldstein, Walton, Cunningham, Trowbridge, & Maio, 2007). Researchers are also interested in how immigrant youth who have experienced war deal with the Canadian school experience (Stermac, Elgie, Clarke, & Dunlap, 2012; Stermac, Elgie, Dunlap, & Kelly, 2010). Although it is possibly, but not necessarily, related to trauma experiences, counselling psychology researchers have also investigated anxiety in children (e.g., Miller et al., 2011a, 2011b) as it relates to school and parenting issues.

Third, researchers have focused on assisting military members in dealing with traumatic stress; the vast majority of research in this area focuses on male members. For example, trauma interventions that are group-based and that encourage peer support have been explored for counselling military members post-trauma and once traumatized members have returned to civilian life (Armstrong, Westwood, Black, Britt, & Pury, 2008; Westwood, 2009; Westwood, Kuhl, & Shields, 2013; Westwood, McLean, Cave, Borgen, & Slakov, 2010). Keats (2010b) explored how overseas cultural contexts and military culture impacted military members dealing with operational stress injuries. Additionally, Black, Westwood, and Sorsdal (2007) examined how best to assist students who were Canadian veterans in the context of counsellor education programs.

Although not within Health Canada's priorities, counselling psychology researchers have also explored the areas of secondary and vicarious trauma, specific aspects of trauma response, trauma therapy intervention, and educating counselling psychology students in the area of trauma. Of these four areas, secondary and vicarious trauma and trauma intervention have the largest number of reports in the literature. For example, in the area of secondary traumatic stress (STS), Arvay (2001) opened the dialogue about STS for trauma counsellors, with Everall and Paulson (2004) continuing the exploration of the impact of STS on ethical behaviour in counselling, and O'Neill (2010a, 2010b) exploring STS in therapists in northern Canadian communities. STS has also been studied for other frontline Canadian professionals; for example, Keats and Buchanan examined both primary and secondary traumatic stress among journalists and photojournalists reporting trauma, conflict, and disaster news (Buchanan & Keats, 2011; Keats, 2010a; Keats & Buchanan, 2009, 2011). STS has also been examined in relation to interpersonal relationships and illness (Brosseau, McDonald, & Stephen, 2011). Numerous types of trauma therapy intervention have also been explored. For example, group-based interventions have been examined for trauma survivors using therapeutic enactment (Keats & Arvay, 2004; Westwood & Wilensky, 2005) and wilderness therapy (McBride & Korell, 2005). Integration of new approaches has also been studied by a number of researchers; for example, cultivating hope in trauma therapy (Yohani & Larsen, 2012), integrating spiritual beliefs into trauma-focused cognitive behavioural therapy (Merali, 2003), and integrating various techniques, including guided eye movements, balancing, and attunement, that address issues arising in trauma treatment (Bradshaw, Cook, & McDonald, 2011).

Research has also been conducted on specific aspects of the trauma response and counsellor education. Research projects related to the trauma response have included explorations of attachment disruptions (O'Neill, Guenette, & Kitchenham, 2010) as well as shame and avoidance (Van Vliet, 2010). Counsellor education regarding trauma has focused on presenting appropriate educational methods to ensure the safety of the students (Black, 2006, 2008), and teaching interventions that highlight the importance of understanding cultural difference, power, and oppression when working with marginalized populations who have experienced trauma (Shepard, O'Neill, & Guenette, 2006).

Finally, with a specific focus on men struggling with the aftermath of trauma, Foster and Kelly (2012) note the higher rates of trauma experiences and post-traumatic stress for men and a need for interventions that will draw men to seek help when they need it. In terms of counselling intervention, many men suffer "in silence, despite the available counselling and therapeutic services meant to assist them" (Westwood & Black, 2012, p. 286) and do not seek services. Although there are a few Canadian counselling psychology researchers who have noted the importance of peer support and "men helping men" in group-based treatments (e.g., Buitenbos, 2012; Westwood, McLean, et al., 2010), research on gender-sensitive and evidence-based interventions for men is a gap for counselling psychology researchers (see Hoover, Bedi, & Beall, 2012) working in the trauma field.

Suicidality, Self-Injury, and Depression

Research on suicidality, self-injury, and depression has received considerable attention among Canadian counselling psychology researchers. Particularly notable has been the emphasis on emotion regulation, resilience, social interactions, and the complex interplay of related factors. Everall, Bostik, and Paulson (2006) conducted a qualitative study in which forty-one adolescents and young adults were interviewed about their experiences of being suicidal. Participants' difficulties coping with overwhelming feelings of despair, shame, self-hatred, and a sense of social isolation were a salient theme in the interviews. Based on the findings, the researchers pointed to the need for counselling interventions that help suicidal teens strengthen their emotional coping capacities. In a related study, Everall et al. (2006) interviewed thirteen previously suicidal female adolescents about how they overcame suicidality. The findings revealed a number of social, emotional, and cognitive processes that participants found helpful in promoting positive change. In particular, suicidal youth can be perceived as active agents who, through their social interactions, expressions of feelings, shifts in perspective, and purposeful behaviours, created more hopeful futures for themselves.

Factors and strategies that may decrease the risk of suicide among youth have also been studied by Pronovost at the Université de Québec (Dumont, Pronovost, & Leclerc, 2004; Pronovost, 1995, 1998; Pronovost, Rousseau, Simard, & Couture, 1995). Pronovost et al. (1995) compared perceptions of interfamilial communication and parental support among a sample of fifty suicidal and forty-eight non-suicidal adolescents and their parents in Quebec. Significant differences between the groups were found, with communication and parental support being perceived more positively in the families with non-suicidal adolescents. The researchers suggested that a strong parent-child relationship, where adolescents experience active listening, empathy, and space to express their emotions and needs, may help protect youth against suicide. In a sample of 875 French Canadian youth, Dumont, Pronovost, and Leclerc (2004) found that adolescents who utilized a productive coping style (e.g., through focusing on solving the problem, focusing on the positive, seeking social support, and seeking relaxing diversions) demonstrated lower levels of suicidality than adolescents who adopted a non-productive coping style (e.g., worrying, ignoring the problem, self-blame, and keeping to self).

Heath and her colleagues (Heath, Ross, Toste, Charlebois, & Nedecheva, 2009; Heath, Toste, Nedecheva, & Charlebois, 2008) conducted research on the factors related to non-suicidal self-injury (NSSI) among Canadian youth. In addition to providing support for the well-established role of emotion regulation as the primary function of NSSI (Heath et al., 2008), the researchers helped flesh out the social factors influencing this behaviour among youth. For example, one study on undergraduate students suggested that initial attempts at self-injury may follow on the heels of observing or hearing about friends who self-injure (Heath et al., 2009). Moreover, the researchers suggested that the social motivations for NSSI, such as the need for social belonging and support, may be especially strong in the case of youth who struggle with emotion regulation.

In the area of depression, Koszycki was part of an interdisciplinary research team studying the impact of Interpersonal Psychotherapy (IPT) on depression in coronary heart disease patients (Koszycki, Lafontaine, Frasure-Smith, Swenson, & Lespérance, 2004). The importance of this research is highlighted by the high rates of depression that ensue after cardiac arrest, combined with the negative impact of depression on cardiac functioning and mortality (Koszycki, 2006). In a pilot study, Koszycki et al. (2004) found significantly reduced levels of depression among coronary heart patients who participated in twelve weekly sessions of IPT, with benefits appearing to be similar regardless of whether or not participants were also on anti-depressant medication. However, in the subsequent randomized controlled trial, IPT was found to be less effective than anti-depressant medication and no more effective than clinical management in reducing depression in people with cardiac disease (Lespérance, Frasure-Smith, & Koszycki, 2007).

Wong, Bordua, Sandhurst, and Bell (2012) have developed a holistic framework for understanding the etiology of postpartum depression (PPD). The framework takes into account the myriad biological, psychosocial, and sociocultural risk factors associated with PPD and how these factors are interrelated. The researchers pointed to relative neglect of cultural factors and the pathologization of PPD in the North American discourse on PPD. Their framework, which draws in part upon feminist theory, describes how PPD develops in the context of oppressive societal messages about what it means to be a "good mother" or a "good woman." Interventions for PPD, the authors argue, need to debunk these messages. Furthermore, interventions are needed at the level of social policies, through the provision of safe and affordable housing and childcare, for example, or through system-wide changes to help reduce domestic violence.

Some Canadian counselling psychology researchers have also explored the experience of depression and grief/loss among male populations, along with gender-sensitive approaches for working with these issues. Grove (2012) conducted a qualitative hermeneutic inquiry in which she interviewed male participants about their experience of midlife depression. The participants traced their depression back to a history of childhood adversity, combined with their tendency to remain silent about their suffering. At midlife, depression followed on the heels of significant loss, especially losses related to divorce, employment, career, finances, self-esteem, and sense of meaning and purpose. Grove pointed to restrictive gender expectations and roles as contributors to the men's depression. Specifically, she suggested that participants' midlife depression was partly rooted in perceptions of falling short of cultural representations of what it means to be a successful male (e.g., expectations around career and financial success). Grove further suggested that when counselling men with midlife depression, it may be necessary to explore accumulated losses and to consider internalized cultural norms of how grief is expressed.

Hornjatkevyc and Alderson (2011) explored the experience of grief among bereaved gay men who lost their partners to non-AIDS-related causes such as cancer, stroke, or fatal injuries. Phenomenological interviews with participants revealed struggles with isolation, discrimination, and disenfranchised grief following the death of their partners. Although participants sought out resources to assist in the grief process (e.g., bereavement support groups), they found these resources to be either unavailable or inadequately tailored to the unique needs of the bereaved men. Further complicating some men's grief were disputes with members of the deceased partner's family over the partner's estate and last wishes. On the other hand, recognition of the bereaved men's loss and partnership rights helped in the process of bereavement, as did support from other people in the men's social circle. Most participants found support through counselling, with participants experiencing particular benefit from the listening, acceptance, and understanding of the therapist.

Women's Issues Related to Reproductive Health

Following this review of research related to women, we found counselling psychology researchers studying a range of issues involving women and reproductive health. As this is one of the research priorities for Health Canada, counselling psychology researchers have been very influential and productive in this field, studying issues such as infertility and fertility treatment, childlessness and sexuality, and maternity care for Aboriginal women.

In terms of infertility and fertility treatment, Winter and Daniluk (2004) interviewed women who donated eggs to a sister who bore at least one child from them. This research highlights the needed counselling services, support, and emotional impacts of egg donors who might seek out care from professional counsellors or psychologists. Related to fertility, Daniluk and Fluker (1995) explored the physical and psychological consequences of commonly used fertility drugs and the important role of therapists working with women who undergo these treatments. Daniluk (1996) explored the difficulties in transitioning to biological childlessness when fertility treatment was unsuccessful. Looking at more diverse populations, Kranz and Daniluk (2006) studied the experiences of lesbian couples who conceived their child through anonymous donor insemination. Results of the study found that unique family configurations, including families with two female parents, also had particular therapeutic implications specific to the family configuration. McKillo, Martin, Bowen, and Muharjarin (2011) explored emotional responses associated with pregnancy, showing how depression impacts women's pregnancy. Another emotion under study is that of maternal guilt. Seagram and Daniluk (2002) concluded that this type of guilt seemed to be a common emotional experience in mothering for many women.

Topics such as infertility and childlessness are also a focus of research in counselling psychology. Daniluk and Tench (2007) studied adjustment to infertility following medical intervention and explored the impacts on women unable to have children. Other related studies include the experience of infertility treatment (Daniluk, 2001) and the experiences of adoption for infertile couples (Daniluk & Hurtig-Mitchell, 2003).

Finally, counselling psychology researchers have been involved in the study of maternity care for rural Aboriginal women, with the intention of improving safe and accessible care for women living in remote communities (Calam, Varcoe, & Buchanan, in press). This project links with Health Canada's priority of assuring the availability of equitable access to appropriate and effective programs for all.

COUNSELLING PSYCHOLOGY'S EMPHASIS ON A STRENGTH MODEL

Currently, Health Canada is particularly interested in developing mental well-being and promoting preventative activities, with a focus on recognizing and supporting families as a foundation for promoting good mental health and well-being. Below, we look at the types of counselling psychology research that relate to people's strengths and other positive aspects that nurture mental health.

Resilience

Many Canadian counselling psychology researchers have approached their areas of study through a resilience lens, with some researchers conceptualizing resilience as a multi-faceted and dynamic process (e.g., Borgen, Amundson, & Reuter, 2004; Everall, Altrows, & Paulson, 2006; Van Vliet, 2008) and others viewing resilience more as a personality trait or outcome (e.g., Cortes & Buchanan, 2007). Resilience, whether a process or trait, is concerned with how people, as active agents, use and develop their strengths and resources in the face of adversity. Moreover, a resilience perspective takes into account the social context as well as the interdependence of social, emotional, cognitive, and behavioural factors that contribute to resilience.

Cortes and Buchanan (2007), for example, analyzed the narrative accounts of six children who had been child soldiers in Colombia and who had emerged from their war experiences with minimal or no trauma-related symptoms. What appeared to facilitate the children's resilience was their sense of personal agency; their social intelligence and affect regulation; their ability to connect with others; their hopeful attitude toward the future and perspective on the past; their spirituality; and their abiding respect for human life. In other examples of Canadian research framed within a resilience perspective, Van Vliet (2008) conducted a grounded theory study in which thirteen participants were interviewed about how they recovered from significant experiences of shame. The findings revealed how participants rebuilt their damaged identity through social connection, emotional acceptance, understanding or insight, redirection of attention and action, and resisting judgment. Borgen et al. (2004) explored how participation in a career portfolio workshop facilitated the career resilience of two groups of government employees, where career resilience was defined as the ability to cope with the challenges of everyday work life. From focus group interviews with participants, the researchers found that participants enhanced their career resilience through developing a sense of personal agency; maintaining an attitude that was hopeful and positive; and becoming

more aware of their strengths and resources. In addition, resilience
was fostered through supportive relationships, flexibility and creativity, and the development of learning plans.

to see the △, progression
proce dural reflection on strengths

Hope

Hope has been the focus of empirical research and theory development among a number of Canadian counselling psychology researchers. In a qualitative study that explored hope among twelve adults
who were recently diagnosed with HIV, as noted above, Harris
and Larsen (2007, 2008) found that participants experienced hope
through receiving support from family, friends, and peer counsellors;
engaging in experiences that provided a sense of meaning and purpose; gaining information about HIV/AIDS and developing options;
receiving medical treatment and counselling; and maintaining or
increasing life quality. Furthermore, based on participant accounts,
high-risk behaviours diminished as participants became more hopeful that they could live a long and meaningful life. In an earlier study,
Wong-Wylie and Jevne (1997) also explored hope in HIV-positive
individuals, within the specific context of patient-physician interactions. From the critical incident accounts and interviews with eight
people diagnosed with HIV, interactions that most fostered hope
were ones characterized by physician behaviours and attitudes that
helped patients feel welcomed, cared for, and respected as human
beings. Participants also felt greater hope when physicians showed
that they were well-informed about HIV and where the physician
described rather than prescribed options.

Larsen, Edey, and Lemay (2007) developed a model for intentionally addressing hope in therapeutic conversations between clients
and therapists. The model focused on the implicit and explicit manners in which hope may be brought into these conversations. To
further elucidate the implicit and explicit hope-focused practices
used in psychotherapy, Larsen and Stegge (2010a, 2010b) video-
recorded the one-on-one therapy sessions of five psychotherapists
and their eleven clients. Each therapist and client then watched a
playback of their individual sessions, while they commented on
hope-related moments that they remembered occurring during therapy. Thematic analysis of the data revealed that hope was implicitly
fostered through the therapeutic relationship or joining between the
client and therapist, through focusing on the client's strengths, and

active processes

through the use of reframing, metaphor, and humour (Larsen & Stegge, 2010a). Explicitly, hope was addressed in therapy through naming hope, focusing on its multiple dimensions, teaching about hope, and framing challenges as threats to hope (Larsen & Stegge, 2010b).

Some researchers have also brought a hope perspective to bear on research involving the experiences of refugee and immigrant populations. Yohani and Larsen (2009) conducted a qualitative study involving ten children who recently arrived in Canada as refugees or immigrants from Sierra Leone, Sudan, Iraq, China, or the Philippines. Sources and experiences of hope were explored through analyses of participant narratives and artwork. For the children in the study, hope was engendered through self-empowering activities, secure relationships with other people, and relationships with the natural world.

Mindfulness and Self-Compassion

In recent years, several counselling psychology researchers have turned their attention to mindfulness, which is typically defined as the intentional and non-judgmental observation of one's experience in the present moment, with an attitude of acceptance and non-judgment (Kabat-Zinn, 1994). Not only have researchers focused on mindfulness-based interventions for emotion regulation in clinical and non-clinical client populations (e.g., Koszycki, Benger, Shlik, & Bradwejn, 2007), but they have also contributed to an understanding of how helping professionals and trainees can develop their own mindfulness practices. Paré, Richardson, and Tarragona (2009) argued that mindfulness, as a form of reflexivity, is a crucial part of ethical practice and counsellor education. Counsellors and students who are mindful of both their internal and external experiences during therapeutic conversations have greater awareness of their blind spots, are more intentional in their interventions, and make better decisions when working with their clients. Thus, there is less chance of causing harm. Paré and Lysack (2006) described an exercise they use regularly in counsellor training as a means of promoting mindfulness. In this exercise, students write down their inner dialogue, in real time, as they practice counselling with their peers.

Irving, Dobkin, and Park (2009) conducted a comprehensive literature review on mindfulness-based stress reduction (MBSR) programs aimed at enhancing self-care and preventing burnout in health care professionals (e.g., physicians, nurses, psychologists, and social workers). The researchers concluded that there is strong support for the effectiveness of mindfulness practice in reducing stress among clinicians and trainees. However, Irving, Dobkin, and Park (2009) highlighted a need for more qualitative and mixed-methods studies on clinicians' and trainees' experiences of mindfulness-based practice to help illuminate the processes through which mindfulness contributes to positive physical and mental health. The researchers also suggested that future studies investigate some of the potentially harmful effects of mindfulness, include the use of physiological measures (e.g., salivary cortisol levels) in addition to self-reported outcomes, and make use of more homogeneous samples (e.g., with a focus specifically on mindfulness among psychologists rather than health professionals in general).

Also related to mindfulness research has been work in the area of self-compassion. Patsiopoulos and Buchanan (2011) interviewed fifteen Canadian counsellors about how they practiced self-compassion in the context of counselling-related situations. In their narrative accounts, participants reported that self-compassion contributed to healthy physical and psychological functioning and helped them to manage the many stresses that accompanied their work. Moreover, many participants believed that self-compassion improved their work effectiveness by helping them accept their fallibility, develop a better balance between the needs of clients and their own needs, monitor and adjust their own actions when appropriate, and proactively engage in self-care. Focusing on counselling approaches that help foster self-compassion in clients, Van Vliet and Kalnins (2011) described how compassion-focused therapy, as first introduced by Gilbert and his colleagues (Gilbert, 2009; Gilbert & Procter, 2006), can be adapted in working with adolescents and young adults who self-injure. Van Vliet (2008, 2010) also highlighted the important role that self-compassion may play in helping people recover from shame and trauma.

COUNSELLING PSYCHOLOGY PREVENTION RESEARCH

Prevention research in counselling psychology has spanned across a wide range of areas related to health and wellness, including the prevention of eating disorders (Piran, 2005; Piran & Thompson,

2008; Russell-Mayhew, 2007), anxiety disorders (Miller, Gold, Laye-Gindhu, et al., 2011; Miller, Laye-Gindhu, Bennett, et al., 2011), bullying/violence (Leschied et al., 2006; Leschied & Cummings, 2002; Smith, Cousins, & Stewart, 2005), suicide (Gredeinus & Everall, 2010), substance abuse (Fallu, Janosz, Brière, et al., 2010); and counsellor burnout (Grafanaki et al., 2005; Patsiopoulos & Buchanan, 2011); and the promotion of physical and mental health among Aboriginal and Métis people (Stewart, 2008; Stewart, Riecken, Scott, Tanaka, & Riecken, 2008). Emphasis has been on primary prevention, which attempts to forestall the emergence of physical and mental health issues, and secondary prevention, which targets people who are at risk or in the early stages of developing problems. A major strength of Canadian prevention research has been its emphasis on systemic and environmental interventions that, in conjunction with individual interventions, help enhance resilience and bring about social changes that support well-being.

For instance, in her review of outcome studies on eating disorder prevention programs for children, adolescents, and young adults, Piran (2005) concluded that primary prevention programs are most effective when they target both the individual and the social system. At the university level, it may be particularly important to incorporate social cognitive interventions and critical theory into prevention programs, in order to help young people challenge internalized socially constructed cognitions about body ideals. In a later study, Piran and Thompson (2008) found that among independent samples of university students and community members, the development of eating disorders was related to experiences of prejudicial treatment, including weightism and sexism. Consequently, the researchers suggested that in addition to promoting healthy habits and attitudes in individuals, primary prevention programs need to target social norms regarding body weight and educate teachers to recognize weight prejudice. The importance of integrating the social and environmental into prevention efforts is also apparent in a model developed by Russell-Mayhew (2007) for understanding and preventing eating disorders. Her model presented a continuum of behaviours and attitudes that arise within a sociocultural context and that may lead to eating disorders. Eating disorder prevention, according to Russell-Mayhew, must target sociocultural factors such as media messages and peer teasing, in order to promote healthy eating habits and a positive body image at the level of the individual.

Several Canadian counselling psychologists have directed their attention to understanding how violence and bullying can best be prevented (Jaffe, Wolfe, & Campbell, 2012; Leschied, Chiodo, Whitehead, & Hurley, 2006; Smith, Cousins, and Stewart, 2005). A systemic and socio-economic perspective on prevention is evident in a study by Leschied et al. (2006), who studied the relationship between poverty, family status, and violence in the families of 693 children seen at a children's aid society in Ontario. The findings pointed to the cumulative risks associated with poverty, including domestic violence and child abuse/maltreatment, especially in homes with single mothers living below the poverty line. For prevention efforts to be effective, structural changes and government-initiated programs, such as high-quality daycare and more support for women experiencing domestic violence, are needed to mitigate the effects of poverty.

Smith et al. (2005) explored the role of schools in preventing bullying. Principals from 395 elementary and secondary schools completed a survey on the schools' efforts to reduce bullying. Schools that put time and resources into anti-bullying initiatives were associated with safer and more peaceful environments for children, as reported by the principals. Moreover, prevention efforts were more effective in the long term than in the short term, with researchers suggesting that bullying reduction depends upon long-term changes to school culture and social attitudes. These findings are consistent with the recommendations of Jaffe, Crooks, and Watson (2009), who argued that school violence prevention programs need to intervene at the level of individual students, parents, teachers, and the school environment.

Stewart and her colleagues (Stewart, 2008; Stewart, Riecken, Scott, Tanaka, & Riecken, 2008) have contributed to an understanding of how to promote health literacy among Indigenous youth in Canada. In an innovative participatory action research project (Stewart et al., 2008), a group of Canadian Indigenous youth created educational videos on health issues for use in their communities. The achievement of greater health literacy was only one of the many benefits that accrued to the participants. Through the process of developing the videos, the youth also developed stronger connections to their peers, families, and communities, along with a deeper understanding and appreciation of their cultural heritage and community knowledge – all of which help foster resilience and promote well-being. In another study aimed at promoting health and healing among Aboriginal peoples, Stewart (2008) interviewed five counsellors from First Nations or Métis backgrounds about their understanding of mental health and healing for Indigenous clients and how culture informs their counselling practices. Participants identified four main and interrelated aspects of mental health promotion and healing for Indigenous peoples, including the necessity of community as a foundation for mental health and healing, finding or strengthening a Native identity, taking a holistic approach to mental health and healing, and establishing relationships based on interdependence.

CHALLENGES AND FUTURE DIRECTIONS

We align with the members of the MHCC who believe "that a dynamic, broadly based social movement is essential to realizing [our] vision of a profoundly transformed mental health system" (MHCC, 2009, p. 101). This vision includes: the promotion of mental well-being and prevention; development of a responsive "culturally-safe" mental health system; recognition and support for families in promoting recovery and well-being; equitable access to appropriate and effective programs for all; defining Commission actions according to appropriate evidence-based, measured outcomes in research; and elimination of stigma and discrimination against people living with mental health problems. We see this vision as a challenge for all counselling psychology researchers, because our research plays an important role in informing and guiding the future of Canadian mental health care through the actions taken and priorities set by the MHCC.

In this regard, our review of the literature in light of the goals set by the MHCC reveals gaps in counselling psychology health research in Canada. It is our challenge to take a role in filling these gaps. For example, aging and issues of the elderly appear to be under-represented in counselling psychology health research. Abuse toward the elderly is certainly an area of current concern in our aging population, along with transitions into retirement, elder care for family members, transitions into care institutions, and so on. Additionally, there appears to be a shortage of research examining the impact of mental health issues on family relationships, particularly in the context of vicariously traumatized populations (e.g., emergency workers, journalists, medical care professionals, and other front-line workers), people with severe mental illness, or family members who are injured or dealing with significant or chronic illness. Further, it is important for researchers to explore how multiculturalism and social justice influence individual, family, and community health and well-being, with a focus on the unique contexts in which people live; this may include culture and tradition, environmental factors, spirituality and religion, or economic limits to care. These types of context-specific factors also need to be considered when researching specific issues related to health and mental health, especially when enhancing or developing new treatments, interventions, or programs as a result of research outcomes. Health and wellness is a dynamic process that demands creative solutions for promoting prevention and resilience.

In terms of effective and appropriate services, our literature review shows a gap in counselling psychologists presenting and offering programs or interventions that will draw boys and men to access services when they are needed. As noted above, there is a shortage of research on gender-sensitive and evidence-based interventions in this area, as well as a lack of counselling services tailored for males. In addition, there is a need for more research and services for people from sexual minorities. Such research could help ensure that the health and wellness needs of all Canadians are served. Given its emphasis on diversity, Canadian counselling psychology is well-poised to expand knowledge and understanding in these areas.

Another challenge for counselling psychology researchers is bringing the outcomes of research not only to other researchers and practitioners in the field, but also to study participants and the community at large. The Canadian government's interest in promoting mental health as a key factor influencing all health issues is a prompt for us to step forward and find or create venues where our research can be available and understandable to everyone who may be influenced by the topics at issue. This would demand that our research be relevant and useful so that the audience will act on what they learn. Furthermore, with an eye on stigma and mental health, researchers may also need to look at how the health issues studied are framed in the media and in other social networks, so that we can respond to how the topics are depicted, how the people who are dealing with the issues are described, and what types of information are available to the public. With its strength in considering the contexts in which health and wellness issues are embedded, counselling psychology research may help provide a deeper and more nuanced understanding of these issues.

Actions in all of these areas would help to place counselling psychology researchers at the forefront of the process initiated by the MHCC, so that the vision of good mental health for all Canadians can be realized.

NOTE

1 All authors have equally contributed their expertise to this chapter.

8

Towards a Definition of
Canadian Career Psychology

WILLIAM A. BORGEN,
LEE D. BUTTERFIELD, NICOLA GAZZOLA,
AND LIETTE GOYER[1]

This chapter offers an overview of the changes that have affected work and workers in Canada, drawing on historical events in the field of career psychology in Canada and internationally in order to understand where we are and how we got here. Moreover, the focus of this chapter is on understanding the present Canadian context and offering suggestions about where we go from here. It begins with an overview of career development within Canadian counselling psychology, the importance of work in people's lives, and recent questions related to the suitability of traditional career assumptions in the current Canadian (and international) context. Next we examine the forces of change, including the changing assumptions underlying career development practices, followed by a discussion of the changes experienced by organizations and workers. Theoretical contributions of Canadian scholars are summarized next, followed by a discussion of multiculturalism and social justice within the context of Canadian career psychology. Next we discuss the need for career development services throughout the lifespan and the need for multiple methodologies when studying career psychology. We then offer some thoughts for augmenting recently established theoretical and applied paradigms for career psychology, along with a proposed definition of career psychology. The chapter ends with a look at major challenges and future directions in career psychology in Canada.

CAREER DEVELOPMENT AND
THE IMPORTANCE OF WORK

Career development is a key domain in the specialized field of counselling psychology in Canada (Sinacore, 2011a). Career development and the importance of working with individuals experiencing difficulties or challenges related to career, work, and education issues or transitions are also fundamental to the definition of counselling psychology adopted by the Canadian Psychological Association (Bedi et al., 2011). The function of counselling, within career development, is to provide interventions with individuals, groups, and organizations to assist with occupational choice and professional development by providing resources and support to best guide an individual within their immediate environment, and more specifically within a professional field. This requires evaluating career interests and assisting with job entry and/or work transitions (Savard & Lecomte, 2009), as well as tailoring interventions that address an individual's unique psychological, psychosocial, and societal issues (Goyer, 2012).

Work is fundamental to psychological health and well-being throughout the lifespan (Kelloway & Day, 2005a; Sinacore, Borgen, Daniluk, Kassan, Long, & Nicol, 2011) and it provides meaning to individuals' lives (Young & Collin, 2000). In a recent report, the Mental Health Commission of Canada (2012) states that "[h]aving meaningful work, education, and access to an adequate income contribute to everyone's ability to achieve and sustain a good quality of life" (p. 73). The Commission advocates the implementation of psychological health and safety standards in the workplace for both the public and private sectors in an attempt to prevent the increase in mental health issues, such as depression and anxiety, among Canadian workers.

QUESTIONING EXISTING CAREER
DEVELOPMENT MODELS

Over the past two decades we have witnessed a growing volatility in the employment market which has resulted in unstable incomes for many Canadians. Questions have arisen about the usefulness of existing career development models and services, precipitating a call in Canada and internationally for new career development approaches, models, and services that coincide with the reality of work in the twenty-first century, along with an updated understanding of the term *career* (Borgen & Hiebert, 2006; Gelatt, 1989; Mitchell, Levin, & Krumboltz, 1999; Savickas et al., 2009; Young & Collin, 2000; Goyer, 2003; Riverin-Simard & Simard, 2005, 2011). Historically, Canadian practitioners and researchers in the career development field have been at the forefront of developing theory and repositioning career services in response to political and labour market forces (Counselling Foundation of Canada, 2002). Today, the focus is on finding an approach to career psychology that is continually responsive in multiple change contexts.

Borgen and Hiebert (2014) are among those who believe that career services need to reflect the contemporary needs of society and they ask an important question: "How well is the majority being served?" (p. 4) Their conclusion is that the majority of today's workers are not well served, in part because the assumptions which underlie most traditional career development theories are not as relevant today as they once were. To understand why, we need to review what has changed in the world around us.

Forces of Change

Globalization, competition, increased mobility of people and families, the transformation to a technology- and knowledge-based economy, the increased diversity of workers (including the increased role of women in the workplace), and the rise of social change movements (e.g., human rights, environmentalism, mass migration/immigration) have all changed the ways in which work gets done and, indeed, the very concept of career (Borgen & Hiebert, 2014; Sinacore et al., 2011; Young & Collin, 2000). Since the beginning of career counselling in Canada, and particularly since the end of the Second World War, the main issues and debates within the profession have multiplied, especially within Francophone Canada (L'Allier, Tétreau, & Erpicum, 1981; Tremblay, 1994a, 1994b). Overall, the professional identity and ethical practice of career counsellors have evolved with the changing practices of counselling and the competency requirements of becoming a career counsellor, which include learning new psychometric instruments and approaches (Bacon, 2007).

Canadian sociologists Maranda and Comeau (2000) offer an excellent summary of the changes affecting work and workers since the 1950s. They suggest that positivism, which seeks the truth through scientific investigation and a focus on statistical and quantitative approaches, encouraged the use of matching in career counselling. This involved assigning a label to individuals and then matching them with a corresponding environment for their category. Borgen and Hiebert (2014) suggest that this led to career development interventions that focused on the point of entry into careers, primarily the transition from school to work. Maranda and Comeau (2000) further suggest that the natural extension of this practice is the expectation that people would adapt to their environments and would stay put even when the environments were dysfunctional or toxic and not psychologically sustainable over time. Riverin-Simard (2000) suggests that the current socio-economic reality has resulted in people needing to transition their careers many times during the course of their adult lives. There is evidence that workers no longer remain loyal to their employers. Rather, they are loyal to their careers and career aspirations (Guichard, 2010; Munro, n.d.). Thus the concepts of matching and *person-environment* fit that have organized many of Canada's career development services and activities in the past may need to be reconsidered in order to meet the needs of today's workers.

As other researchers have pointed out, Parsons' true reasoning trait and factor paradigm for matching an individual to the environment relied on stable and predictable occupations and career paths, which no longer exist (e.g., Le Bossé, 2011; Riverin-Simard, 2000; Savickas, 2000). Borgen and Hiebert (2006) suggest that the traditional assumptions are no longer valid and that career development theories and services therefore need to be changed to reflect the current environment. Assumptions that underlie traditional career development theories are: (a) there are individual attributes or traits that draw people to certain occupations and these are pivotal to effective occupational, vocational, and career-related decision-making; (b) occupations that match the vocational interest of individuals are accessible to them; (c) occupations are stable enough in their characteristics that assessment instruments for matching individual traits with occupational characteristics are valid over time; and (d) once desired occupations are secured, individuals have the capability to stay involved in them (Borgen & Hiebert, 2006).

The need to review and adjust career development services and the role of counselling psychologists has been evident throughout the history of career development in Canada. The Counselling Foundation of Canada (2002), in its overview of the history of Canadian career counselling, makes the point that career development initiatives historically have changed to address political imperatives such as the advent of rapid industrialization at the start of the twentieth century, the return of veterans following World Wars I and II, the adjustment to the post-war economy, changes in the government's role in the economy, and upheavals in the workplace due to technological advances and recessions. Hurley and Doyle (2003) have also documented the ways in which counselling psychology, and particularly career development / vocational guidance practices, have adjusted in reaction to changes occurring in Canadian society. Thus, it is not surprising that in a rapidly changing environment, just how career theories and practitioners support Canadians needs to be revisited. Although different forces are shaping Canada from the ones faced by our young nation in 1900, there are nonetheless parallels between the sweeping changes occurring today and those that heralded the dawn of the Industrial Age. The concept of *career* needs to adjust to meet the realities of a new century. Now, as then, Canada is facing rapid change that requires innovation, action, and commitment by governments, employees, employers, and taxpayers to effect the kind of change needed to support people's needs for career development services throughout their lives (Maranda & Comeau, 2000; Riverin-Simard, 2000).

Changing Assumptions Underlying Career Development Practices

Hurley and Doyle (2003) highlight the traditional focus in the United States (which is also true in Canada) on vocational guidance and assessment interventions that were developed primarily to assist workers leaving the agricultural regions of the country, people inducted into the armed forces during the world wars, returning war veterans, and others affected by changing demographics and industrialization. The trait-factor theory suggested by Frank Parsons in the United States in the early 1900s was built on the assumptions mentioned above (Borgen & Hiebert, 2006) that arose from the social needs at the time. Trying to fit people into jobs was appropriate then, but less so now given the unpredictability of the labour market and of organizations, and the role of work itself. Borgen and Hiebert (2014) report that about eighty percent of jobs people hold today did not exist ten years ago. They also report that the top ten jobs in demand in 2010 did not exist in 2004. The cradle-to-grave experience of generations of workers, whereby work was guaranteed as long as workers attended regularly and were able to fulfill the functions of the job, has all but disappeared. It is estimated that Canadians today will change occupations between six and ten times during their working lives (Borgen & Hiebert, 2014). The idea of having one occupation for life is therefore no longer expected or even possible in many cases, and helping Canadian workers decide what to do for the rest of their working lives at the point of entering the workforce from school or university is no longer a viable approach.

If it is true that the traditional assumptions are no longer applicable in the current Canadian context, what assumptions are more useful? Borgen and Hiebert (2006), based on their experiences in many different countries and their awareness of the social, economic, political, and cultural influences in Canada, have proposed a revised set of assumptions that they believe will be more useful for contemporary work-related decision-making processes. These new assumptions are: (a) several factors influence choice of occupations or career paths, including individual attributes or traits, family perspectives, and rapidly evolving cultural influences such as poverty, addiction, conflict, displacement, and discrimination, along with internationalization and rapid change in labour market opportunities; (b) these factors are differentially important within and across cultural contexts; (c) occupations of choice may not be accessible; (d) many tasks and processes related to occupations are unstable; and (e) people need the skills and attitudes required to successfully manage the rapid and unpredictable changes that characterize many occupations and career trajectories (Borgen & Hiebert, 2006).

ISSUES AND CHANGES AFFECTING ORGANIZATIONS AND WORKERS

Organizational Issues

Estimates of costs related to absenteeism and lost productivity in Canada due to mental health–related disability a decade ago were $33–45 billion annually (Dewa, Lesage, et al., 2004; Disability management forum, 2005), suggesting that our current Canadian workplaces were not sustainable (Finlayson, 2005; Hewitt Associates, 2005). Recent estimates of costs related to absenteeism and lost productivity in Canada due to mental health–related disability have now risen to $51 billion annually (Mental Health Commission of Canada, 2010). These figures are sobering and concerning, given the needs of organizations to recruit and retain highly skilled workers who are healthy, engaged, innovative, and productive (Amundson, 2007; Law, Flood, & Gagnon, 2008).

In addition, Duxbury and Higgins (2009) reported that conditions within Canadian corporations have declined, citing a threefold increase in job stress and absenteeism over a ten-year period. During this period, employees' job satisfaction and organizational commitment have declined, as well as their mental and physical health. These researchers conclude that although the world has changed significantly, organizations have not. They suggest that organizations are reactive rather than proactive, employer-centric, and built on the mistaken belief that workers' personal and work lives are separate, and that they design supportive policies and procedures to deal with abusers of these programs rather than those who need them and do not abuse them. The net result is a Canadian workforce that is overtaxed and in declining health, and an economy that is experiencing falling productivity in the face of increasing global competition.

In light of the challenges faced by Canadian workers, systemic approaches have been called for by a number of researchers. Amundson and Morley (2002) highlight the benefits of providing healthy workplace programs and provide examples of interventions, but point out that these are usually offered in larger organizations, while workers in small businesses or with lower income levels often do not have access to such programs. A Canadian healthy workplace model has been proposed by Kelloway and Day (2005a) that includes the following elements: safety in the work environment; work-life balance; a culture of support, respect, and fairness; employee involvement and development; appropriate work content and characteristics; and healthy interpersonal relationships at work. Individuals, organizations, and society stand to benefit from psychologically healthy workplaces, with an emphasis on prevention through job redesign and leadership training (Kelloway & Day, 2005b). The need for more than just treatment (such as Employee Assistance Programs [EAP] and stress management training) is key if we do not want to just continue "healing the wounded" (Kelloway & Day, 2005b, p. 310).

On a national level, the Mental Health Commission of Canada (2012) has called for organizations in both the public and private sectors to initiate workplace promotion, prevention, and anti-stigma initiatives, training for managers to help prevent mental illness from arising in the workplace, and support for re-entry into the workplace for those who do experience mental illness. This is consistent with Shain's (2010) call for psychologically healthy workplaces and the legal imperative for organizations to support workers' well-being.

Adult Workers' Issues

Until recently, little research had been conducted on the impact of change on mainstream workers (those without special needs or who are not experiencing barriers to employment) in Canada or other industrialized countries. The focus historically appears to have been on marginalized or special populations, the chronically unemployed, women and other minorities, and those facing barriers or challenges related to finding and keeping paid employment. The impact of unemployment on people has been well documented (e.g., Amundson & Borgen, 1987; Borgen & Amundson, 1987; Limoges, Lahaie, & Martiny, 2008). However, the common belief appears to have been that employed, mainstream workers were doing well, despite the workplace instability that has affected workers at all levels and in all industries. A few of the recent studies that have focused on mainstream workers are reviewed next.

Neault (n.d.) and Neault and Pickerell (2011) surveyed 181 management employees at one of Canada's largest telecommunications companies who were survivors of major downsizing and restructuring. They investigated the factors that these employees attributed to their career success (external attributes such as salary, status, and prestige) as well as to their job satisfaction (subjective perception of happiness or contentment). Their findings suggest that employee optimism and flexibility were the best predictors of career success and that optimism, continuous learning, and (surprisingly) a less planful approach were the best predictors of job satisfaction. In addition, a satisfied worker was persistent, was willing to take risks, and had achieved a level of work-life balance.

Other research with mainstream workers (e.g., Amundson, Borgen, Jordan, & Erlebach, 2004; Borgen, Butterfield, & Lalande, in press; Butterfield & Borgen, 2005; Butterfield, Borgen, Amundson,

& Erlebach, 2010; Goyer, Dorion, & Veilleux, 2010; Maglio, Butterfield, & Borgen, 2005) had different findings. Taken together, these
studies suggest that workers are experiencing challenges related to
changes that are affecting their work. Participants involved in the
above-mentioned studies reported: (a) They are changing jobs, organizations, and occupations several times throughout their careers;
(b) Career support is not just needed at the point of entry to the
workforce or because of layoff or downsizing, but is needed on an
ongoing basis to help navigate these career-related changes; (c) Many
workers were utilizing the services of personal coaches rather than
Employee Assistance Program counsellors or other professional counsellors, including career counsellors; (d) Organizations' best workers
were choosing to leave when interactions with managers/supervisors
hindered their ability to do their best work; (e) Many workers who
had not left their organizations were planning to leave as a result of
unsatisfactory interactions with managers/supervisors; (f) Workers
wanted to matter to their managers and organizations; they wanted
to have a voice, and to feel connected to the organization; (g) There
is a need for counselling services to help workers deal with both
personal and career-related psychological issues related to career
transitions and change.

These results are no doubt a reflection, at least in part, of the bond
of trust having been broken between workers and employers when
the psychological employment contract changed (Rousseau, 1995),
profoundly affecting Canadian workers as well as workers internationally. Trevor-Roberts (2006) suggested the new contract opened
the doors for an increasingly volatile work environment in Western
industrialized economies, including Canada. This could be at least
partly responsible for the disconnect between workers' experience of
work and employers' need to attract and retain highly skilled workers, decrease turnover and absenteeism, and increase productivity
(e.g., Amundson, 2007).

Duxbury and Higgins (2009) conducted research on workers'
work-life conflict experiences, comparing data collected a decade
apart, and concluded that time spent at work has increased over the
years, with many Canadians being unable to complete their work
during regular working hours. This has resulted in longer hours at
work, bringing work home, increased overtime (much of which is not
paid), and role overload. It has also resulted in less time being devoted
to non-work activities, including child-care, home chores, and leisure

time. Canadian workers are also facing increased elder-care responsibilities that make it challenging to balance work-life demands. The researchers concluded that workers are struggling and that organizations have a responsibility to be proactive in helping workers.

Borgen, Butterfield, and Amundson (2009) asked mainstream workers who self-reported as doing well what changes they had experienced that impacted their work, and what the impacts were of those changes. The impacts of the changes they reported mirrored the burnout, unemployment, and post-traumatic stress literature even though these individuals had not experienced an adverse event as defined by Carver (1998). Instead of thriving, as had been anticipated at the outset of the research project, participants reported oscillating between positive reactions (e.g., feeling competent, challenged, enthusiastic, and engaged), and negative reactions (e.g., feeling discouraged, angry, alienated, and burned out), with negative emotional reactions cited three times more often than positive emotional reactions.

Environics (2010) recently conducted a survey on behalf of the Canadian Education and Research Institute for Counselling (CERIC). In it they reported that only two in ten workers (19 percent) stated that they had a good understanding of what they needed to do in order to advance their careers within their organizations. They found that the majority of Canadians (49 percent) have only some idea, or little idea at all (25 percent), about what they need to do in order to advance their careers. In addition, the survey highlighted that while 79 percent of Canadians said professional career counselling programs were valuable, few said they would use these services. Colleagues and associates were the number-one source for Canadians seeking career advice and guidance, followed closely by family, friends, and neighbours. This suggests Canadian career specialists and programs have work to do to make their services known, accessible, and helpful to workers.

THEORETICAL CONTRIBUTIONS
OF CANADIAN SCHOLARS

The changes facing Canadian workers and organizations just described have contributed to the need to update and revise conceptual models related to career development. Canadian scholars have made some important contributions to the development of career choice and development theories, in particular to postmodern, social construction approaches that better fit the realities experienced by today's workers. Several of the theorists and their contributions are high-lighted next.

Vance Peavy

Vance Peavy is considered to be an early leader in promoting a constructivist approach to understanding career development. Peavy's (2000) sociodynamic theory adopts a holistic view of career counselling, suggesting that it offers "a general method of life planning" (p. 4). There are three key constructivist assumptions underpinning Peavy's (2000) perspective: (a) people construct all aspects of societies and relationships; realities are constructed, not discovered, and help-seekers interpret their own experiences; (b) the counselling process is a co-construction; and (c) counsellors should be real and genuine, rather than expert advice-givers. Peavy's (1992, 1996, 1998, 2004) meaning-making approach reflects a move away from the logical positivism and causation that had formed the basis of traditional trait-factor approaches to career interventions.

Peavy (1992) described the key goals of his approach: (a) reducing the conceptual gap between life and career; (b) having meaning as the central focus of counselling; (c) promoting the role of client agency; (d) viewing individuals as self-authors in the context of socio-historical influences; (e) taking a constructivist epistemological stance of personal, social, constructed, and negotiated realities; (f) helping clients to engage in reflexivity and envision alternatives; and (g) avoiding reductionistic views of individuals, including clients and counsellors. Peavy (1992) also suggested a need to reconsider the general counselling process and encouraged counsellors to consider their work with clients as experiments rather than interventions. His approach is also culture-centred (Peavy, 2001), emphasizing life planning and the creation of personal meaning as being central to all career-related counselling (Peavy, 1996). Peavy has contributed to the conceptualization of career choice being inextricably linked with an individual's whole life, and emphasized the need to connect career counselling with the client's perception of their life situation.

Larry Cochran

Larry Cochran (1992, 1997) also emphasized agency and meaning in the career counselling process. He describes the notion of career projects as involving a combination of both life and personal tasks to express a life theme. The structure of a career project is such that "several life tasks which involve a course of action make up a coordinated series of actions" (Cochran, 1992, p. 193) and goes beyond task completion to include "an extension, refinement or revision of a personal theme" (p. 194). He adopted Little's (1983) concept of a personal project, which represents a set of interrelated actions over a period of time that provide the individual with a means to channel abilities. He also references Emmons' (1989) notion that personal themes and strivings organize a person's goals and make them collectively significant, persisting regardless of success or failure. According to Cochran (1992), personal projects are significant for a career and have some important characteristics: (a) they yield a variety of achieved outcomes that have a significant impact on the future (e.g., obtaining a degree, entering into a relationship, obtaining employment); (b) they cultivate skills, virtues, mastery of a role, and identity; (c) the very act of participating in a career project leads to many possible constructed life experiences which integrate various parts of a person; this process leads to crystallization of a life plan as themes become integrated as one career project informs the next; and (d) participation in career projects can be an end in itself, regardless of outcomes.

Cochran (1997) conceptualizes career as a drama wherein an individual plays a character developing their own career plot. The emphasis is on creating life meaning and the developing story extends well beyond obtaining occupations. In creating career narratives, the individual also develops a sense of agency. The counselling psychologist's role is to assist the client in the process of co-authoring career experiences (i.e., not just in completing specific tasks). Thus, Cochran embraces a position that values context and personalized life meaning rather than the perspective that tasks are normative and follow a sequential, linear path (Cochran, 1992).

Richard Young

Richard Young and his colleagues have adopted a key postmodern premise that fits well with the contributions of Vance Peavy and Larry Cochran: we can only understand individuals in the context of their environments as they experience the environments and make meaning from these experiences (Young, Valach, & Collin, 2002). They also have contributed to the notion that careers are constructed over time through a series of goal-directed action systems (Young & Valach, 2004; Young et al., 2002).

Actions are goal-directed and have three parts: (a) manifest, observable behaviours; (b) unobservable, internal processes (cognitive and emotional); and (c) meaning as interpreted by individuals and those around them (Young et al., 2002). There are three constructs associated with action: joint action, project, and career. A joint action is not merely a summation of individual actions; it includes the individual's sense of manifest behaviours, internal processes, and meaning. A project goes beyond actions and may have its own manifest behaviours. According to Young et al. (2002), career is "a superordinate construct that allows people to construct connections among actions, to account for effort, plans, goals, and consequences, to frame internal cognitions and emotions; and to use feedback to fast forward processes" (p. 217). Career cannot be separated from the context of culture, given the multicultural nature of society. Young et al. (2002) suggest that even the term *career* has a cultural context (e.g., economics, occupations, capitalism, etc.). Further, the authors caution us to consider gender issues in career. For instance, gender considerations include some structural disadvantages, how women interact in the workforce, and different career meanings (e.g., the meaning of success) (Young et al., 2002; Young, Marshall, & Valach, 2007).

In keeping with the constructivist nature of the theory, Young et al. (2002) suggest that actions are co-constructed (i.e., joint action) whereby goals are formed based on joint goals that have both personal and societal meanings. Thus, actions are inseparable from social context. The career psychologist's role in the career counselling process is to assist clients in developing their career narratives through a therapeutic bond that helps to energize the narrative (Brown, 2012). The joint action is spontaneously constructed in the moment (i.e., it is a co-constructed meaning-making process). This theory emphasizes the role of interpretation – i.e., "the process by which people make sense of action and context" (Young et al., 2002, p. 219) – as well as meaning-making.

Charles Chen

Charles Chen is another Canadian counselling psychologist who has contributed to the emerging, constructivist views of career psychology as well as to the promotion of theoretical integration in career counselling. Like the other scholars already discussed, Chen (2001a, 2002, 2003, 2006a) advocates considering the individual in context, and one of his key focus areas is enhancing human agency. Chen (2002) proposes an integration of action theory and human agency in career contexts and emphasizes the importance of helping clients find meaning in the career counselling process (Chen, 2001b). His views are in line with those of Young et al. (2002) and Betz and Hackett (1987), who emphasize goal-directedness, purposefulness, persistence, and intentionality within a given context. Chen (2003) integrates traditional career theories that are positivistic in nature with emerging theories that are guided by constructivist principles. Chen believes that both perspectives are important in the career counselling process and suggests that a combination of perspectives would enrich our understanding of the individual. Chen (2003) identified some commonalities among theoretical approaches:

- *Career as self-realization.* This is a focus of many traditional career theories that suggest the career process leads to self-realization. Self-efficacy and human agency (Bandura, 1977, 2001) can also promote self-realization.
- *Career as a reflection of growing experiences.* Here, career is seen as a biographical and narrative process that also includes significant others and society. This view can also be combined with the more traditional approaches that consider career development as a series of developmental tasks (e.g., Super, 1990).
- *Career as context conceptualization.* This is a key premise in constructivist theories such as action theory (Young et al., 2002) but is also present in Holland's theory, the Theory of Work Adjustment, and in Social Learning Theory, all of which consider the influence of the environment on the individual.

Chen (2001a, 2001b) also makes the case for the importance of integrating career and personal counselling. Similar to Cochran (1997) and Amundson (2009, 2010), Chen suggests that career, life, personal, and social issues are intertwined and therefore we must adopt a holistic approach rooted in the client's life context. Although many counsellor education programs in Canada, the United Kingdom, and the United States include training in both personal and career issues, Chen (2001b) suggests that more emphasis be placed on the integration of personal and career issues in counsellor and counselling psychologist training. Chen's perspectives on career, which are narrative and constructivist, also have implications for working across cultures with immigrant clients (Chen, 2004), women, and families (Coogan & Chen, 2007).

Mildred Cahill

Mildrid Cahill has made a noteworthy contribution to our understanding of applications of career theory in Canada by focusing on remote rural areas. Cahill and Martland (1993) brought to light the lack of relevance that traditional career counselling theories have for these areas. Career theories are rooted in assumptions such as the urban-industrial structure and mass-production economies, and they value career in the context of paid work (Cahill & Martland, 1993). These authors suggest that individuals who live in rural communities have a different conceptualization of career from those in urban centres. Using Newfoundland as an example, they propose the following key differences in rural areas: (a) the meaning of work goes beyond formal, paid work and includes household and life maintenance activities (e.g., hunting, building) that form workers' rural identity; (b) career involves multitracking (vs. specialization), which creates varied and unstable work patterns due to resource-based industries and lack of local opportunities; (c) career choices are greatly influenced by geographical preferences vs. mobility, which implies the need to respect the life choices made by individuals who choose to live and work in rural areas; (d) in rural areas there are varied employment arrangements that include short-term work, mainland-to-home patterns for seasonal work, and a need to change career goals due to the discourse in theories that values the stable, long-term occupation; and (e) career skill development is needed that addresses barriers to entrepreneurship in rural areas (see Cahill & Martland, 1993, 1995a, 1995b).

Cahill and Martland (1995a) challenged the often negative discourse regarding career drifters, whom they defined as individuals who have completed high school and/or have been out for at least four years and have made at least three voluntary changes in the last ten years. They further defined five different types of career drifters: (a) those who are chronically indecisive or have lacked the opportunities to develop skills; (b) those who are drifters by necessity (e.g., cycles of migration of working to and from home in order to earn money; (c) occupational drifters (e.g., construction to self-employment); (d) drifters who value their multipotentiality (e.g., those unwilling to sacrifice options and anxious about narrowing their choices); and (e) those who strive for intrinsic rewards and growth and who also take lower-level jobs. These researchers have contributed to the understanding of career counselling of individuals in rural areas and have shed light on the shortcomings of existing career development theories. Consistent with other scholars discussed in this section, Cahill and Martland emphasize the importance of meaning and life context in their conceptualization of career counselling.

Centre de Recherche et d'Intervention sur l'Éducation et la Vie au Travail

The University of Laval houses the largest number of researchers in Canada dedicated to the study of career development and training, known as CRIEVAT (Centre de recherche et d'intervention sur l'éducation et la vie au travail). CRIEVAT's founder, Geneviève Fournier, is a prominent researcher who has examined the instability of career paths, individual and social factors contributing to this instability, and professional and personal consequences of instability. One of Fournier's hallmarks has been her engagement in longitudinal studies with large sample sizes (up to 150 workers). Her goal has been to reconstruct participants' career paths, taking into account their work histories, subjective experiences, personal temperaments, and personal life events. Fournier's expertise is recognized nationally and internationally. She has assisted in the development of employment programs both in Quebec (Programme Interagir) and in France.

Several other professors at the University of Laval have made important contributions in the field of career counselling. Yvon Pépin created a psychosocial career counselling approach that looks at career in the context of social interactions, workplace integration, and career interventions. Over the last twenty-five years, Pépin has tracked the evolution of career counselling practices and has trained generations of career practitioners to engage in and analyze career counselling counselling strategies with the goal of empowering the individuals and communities with whom they work (Pépin, 2009;

Le Bossé, 2011). Other major contributors include Denis Pelletier (educational approach to career counselling); Charles Bujold (career trajectories and journeys); Marcelle Gingras (assessment and career fit); Danielle Riverin-Simard (developmental approach to career and defining career within the perspective of life-long learning and participation); Armelle Spain (women's career development and the establishment of *Devenir*, career services for immigrants); Jimmy Ratté (fundamental dimensions of counselling and psychotherapy); Marie-France Maranda (psychodynamic perspectives and investigations of work); and Liette Goyer (My Career GPS, skills assessment, and the use of the career counselling process in promoting efficacy). Taken together, these Francophone researchers have made a significant national and international impact on expanding our understanding of the nature and processes of effective career-based interventions, as they affect individuals and communities.

MULTICULTURALISM AND SOCIAL JUSTICE

Multiculturalism and social justice in the field of counselling psychology has evolved from being thought of as a consideration in applying traditional counselling approaches, to being conceptualized as central to any intervention. (For a more in-depth discussion of multiculturalism and social justice please see chapters 3 and 11 in this book.) Further, Canada has an increasingly diversified population and workforce, and counselling interventions require not just an awareness of culture, but a knowledge that culture must be central to conceptualizations of the individual. Diversity will continue to become increasingly complex due to the changing world, and it exists on multiple dimensions: age, sex, nationality, cultural background, language, socio-economic status, sense of personal identity, spirituality, disabilities, and so on (Poehnell & Amundson, 2011). Hargrove, Creagh, and Kelly (2003) noted that increasing diversification, coupled with the global changes being observed, will require that counselling psychologists develop specific guidelines and further training to meet basic multicultural requirements. Within the field of career development, Arthur (2005) has also identified two key trends: (a) the changing societal demographics resulting from multicultural immigration; and (b) the interdependence of national economies due to the increasing demand for skilled labour. These imply (a) a need to work more proactively with specific groups

(Arthur, 2005); (b) a need for a multicultural, rather than a mono-cultural, perspective (Arthur, 2005); and (c) a need for the development of multicultural competencies in career counselling (Arthur, 2005; Arthur & Collins, 2011; Goyer, 2003; Hargrove, Creagh, & Kelly, 2003). The first implication highlights the importance of not defining culture solely in terms of race and ethnicity, and suggests that career practitioners must consider how various dimensions of culture intersect and impact career development. They must be aware of systemic barriers, and they must develop an awareness of the impact of their own personal cultures (Arthur, 2005). Second, culturally appropriate interventions ought to be guided by an awareness of the limitations of the theories that reflect the dominant culture, and efforts must be made to attend to the interaction between the individual and the system. Third, multicultural career counselling core competencies include self-awareness, knowledge, skills, and organizational development within a Canadian context (Arthur, 2005; Arthur & Collins, 2005). However, as Horne and Matthews (2006) remind us, it is very difficult to become culturally competent and the best we can become is "informed not knowers" (Laird, 1998, p. 3).

Further to infuse social justice into counselling, counselling psychologists have long focused their social advocacy efforts in career areas because work was considered a vehicle to social equity (Fouad, Gerstein, Toporek, et al., 2006, p. 3). Indeed, many believe the centrality of career interventions is to empower individuals (Le Bossé, 2011; Le Bossé, Chamberland, Bilodeau, & Bourassa, 2007). To that end, Arthur and Collins (2011) proposed a tripartite model for culture-infused career counselling (CICC) that includes: (a) cultural self-awareness; (b) awareness of cultural identities; and (c) the development of a culturally sensitive working alliance. The model is based on six principles: (1) culture is relevant for all clients based on unique experiences, issues, and resources; (2) culture is relevant for all counselling psychologists and includes notions of career, work, and on/off-track, and definition of problems, interventions, and actions; (3) career and career issues are culturally defined; (4) theories/models of career development contain cultural assumptions that are based on Western values; (5) there is a need to collaboratively define the goals and processes of career counselling; and (6) there is a need to incorporate multiple levels of intervention beyond the individual and to use a social justice perspective (Arthur & Collins, 2011). These authors also express a need to incorporate social justice in career counselling and emphasize that there ought to be an awareness of the social, economic, and political issues that shape career development, including opportunities and barriers. Further, they suggest that the focus of career interventions needs to also include prevention, not just remediation, and that practitioners use a cultural auditing guide.

Richardson (2012) uses a feminist and social justice lens to challenge the traditional discourse of career, work, and family. Richardson argues that *career as choice* does not fit the reality of market work; that vocational guidance is built on the fallacy of choice; that career progress is viewed as a vertical advancement through linear stages; and that personal care has "invisible status" and is devalued in society (Richardson, 2012, p. 198). Richardson calls for a holistic, societally contextualized lens that moves away from linear, developmental conceptualizations of career. Richardson (2012) suggests "a shift in focus from how careers develop to how people develop in relation to multiple social contexts" (p. 200–1), a view that is supported by Blustein, Medvide, and Kozan (2012) and expressed by others (Arthur & Collins, 2011; Fouad, 2006; Toporek & McNally, 2006). Finally, according to Richardson (2009a, 2009b), a person's thought processes influence all aspects of life, including work life. Therefore, felt experiences come into play not only during times of professional transition, but at all times over the course of an adult's life. Career development proceeds through the pursuit of all types of work activities, both paid and non-paid: "What is recommended for vocational psychology and vocational guidance is ... to broaden attention to include the multiple social contexts of lives that goes beyond consideration of these contexts as factors affecting work trajectories" (Richardson, 2009b, p. 78).

Herr (1997) contends that theories should be developed to address cross-cultural concerns, with a focus on the "specific forms of obstacles, barriers, reinforcements, received messages, and other variables affecting the career behavior of women, racial and ethnic groups, persons with disabilities, and people of alternative sexual orientations, by levels of education, socioeconomic level, and other indices" (Super & Knasel, 1979, p. 243). Amundson (2007) states that clients have become more diverse and multi-barriered, supporting the need for multicultural models. There is an abundance of research supporting the need for multicultural counselling, as Western frameworks of career development cannot ethically be applied across cultures (Fitzgerald & Betz, 1994; Gysbers, Heppner, & Johnston, 2003; Leong & Hartung, 2000; Leung, 1995).

Given the movement toward recognizing the impact of contextual influences on career behaviour, it is logical to consider the contexts in which career psychology is applied. The emergence of the constructivist approach in Canada and internationally necessitates the expansion of career counselling settings to include people and places that have bearing on the client's self-construction. Patton and McMahon (2006) suggest:

> Systems theory encourages interventions at levels of the system other than that of the individual, and raises the potential for career counselors to be more proactive at this broader systems level. For example, career counselors may work with a family or an organization in the belief that interventions anywhere in the system will interact with other elements of the system to bring about change. (2006, para. 21)

The presence of older workers in the workforce also warrants consideration as to where career counselling services should be offered. It is no longer adequate to focus career counselling services in high school or university settings where only younger members of the population are being served. A new model that has emerged is that of the one-stop centre. One-stop centres were created by the Workforce Investment Act of 1998 in the United States. These one-stop centres provide integrated services for both job-seekers and employers. Integration of services is achieved with the integration of various career guidance counsellor groups, which typically work in isolation from each other. Amundson and colleagues state that "integration of these groups was necessary at both a practical and theoretical level" (Amundson, Parker, & Arthur, 2002). The provision of career counselling services must also be expanded to reach members of all socioeconomic levels, not just the middle to upper class. Amundson (2006) suggests blending a counselling model with a business model to create "social enterprises" to address the needs of clients facing multiple barriers.

One possible remedy for reaching clients facing geographic barriers would be the use of a virtual guidance centre. Amundson and colleagues suggest four components for such a centre: links to existing websites, locally developed information, access to web counselling, and an overall monitoring function (Amundson, Harris-Bowlsbey, & Niles, 2005). Sampson (1999) suggests using an integrated website in a career centre in order to (1) provide educational and employment information; (2) supplement some services such as resume writing, career exploration, and assessment; (3) provide up-to-date operational information about the running of the centre; and (4) provide links to commercial and non-commercial resources and services. The development of web-based services should be subjected to equal levels of scrutiny and evaluation as services, assessments, and interventions that are provided in person. Despite their growing popularity, evaluations of web-based assessments are seldom performed (Chope, 2011).

CAREER DEVELOPMENT SERVICES THROUGHOUT THE LIFESPAN

Research in the past decade has highlighted the need for career development services throughout people's lives, not just at the point of entry to the workforce. This was briefly mentioned in the previous section but is expanded here.

Research Highlights

In a study on out-placement counselling services, Butterfield and Borgen (2005) found that participants at all stages of their careers needed support, skills development, and connection when facing unexpected unemployment and navigating the transitions from employment, to unemployment, back to employment. These findings were consistent with those of Amundson, Borgen, Jordan, and Erlebach (2004) who studied the effects of downsizing on those remaining in the organization. Amundson et al. (2004) highlighted many areas with which counselling psychologists could assist survivors, either individually or in work groups. It was clear that these individuals needed counselling services that could assist them with both the personal and career issues they were facing.

Maglio et al. (2005) discussed the employment and unemployment transitions experienced by people by looking at themes arising from several unrelated research projects regarding individuals' needs for full-service career counselling services. They urged career practitioners to put the "counselling" back into career counselling by ensuring clients' emotional as well as skills development needs were met. The need for this was highlighted by the fact that fifteen percent of participants in one study stated they were experiencing suicidal thoughts following a work transition or loss of employment.

Riverin-Simard (2000) looked at career development needs in the second part of adults' working lives. She describes the careers of people aged forty and older as being characterized by "numerous ruptures, new departures, and intense moments of suffering, by continual redefinitions of vocational projects, and by novel means of carrying out these projects" (p. 126). She calls for career practitioners to take seriously their responsibility to attend to the needs of this population, as the more traditional view of older workers voluntarily disengaging from work/career activities is no longer accurate. She also suggests there is a need to support workers who are questioning their chosen career and are considering new career options. More recently, Fournier, Gauthier, and Zimmermann (2011) and Fournier, Zimmermann, and Gauthier (2011) studied the experiences of workers forty-five years of age and older who were experiencing work instability. The wish for professional integration was the feeling most strongly observed in the study.

Finally, Borgen and Hiebert (2014) discuss the concept of *Education for All, Across the Lifespan*. They suggest *Education for All* needs to be disengaged from career and more focus placed on people's intrinsic interests, creativity, and motivation. That way, if career transitions or job losses occur, individuals have the tools they need to undertake the journey initiated by the change. Their assertion is that for life-long learning to be effective, life-long career guidance and counselling services need to be provided.

Considering Personal, Social, and Cultural Contexts

When advocating for career services to be available throughout people's lifespans, it is crucial to keep in mind the individuals' personal, social, and cultural contexts. What works for the Baby Boomers will not necessarily work for Generation Y (individuals born between 1981 and 2000; Munro, n.d.). Munro created a *Blueprint for Generation Y Transitioning from Academia to Workplace* that promotes a phased introduction to the workforce that facilitates the transition from school to work and ultimately increases recruitment and selection of this group by employers who are able to create a Generation Y–friendly work environment.

Cognizant of this need for career development services to be made available across the lifespan, Canadian researchers cited in the following sections of the chapter have drawn attention to three key perspectives: (a) the importance of developing an ability to see the situation from the perspective of the individual experiencing it; (b) the importance of individuals developing a sense of career agency; and (c) the importance of recognizing the integrations of life spheres in career decision-making. A more detailed discussion of these three perspectives follows.

Subjectivity, Personal Representations, and Personality Temperament

There are authors who propose that subjectivity (Heiz et al., 2009; Lalive D'Épinay, 2005) and personal representations (Guichard, 2009, 2012; Young & Valach, 2004; Young, 2010) are influential in understanding transitions throughout a person's lifespan. Consequently, no event (such as a strained relationship or employment loss) can be judged beneficial or harmful, nor positive or negative. Instead, events are to be understood by the meaning that is created by a person's view of themselves, their lives, their aspirations, and the career stage they are in. Transitions and life challenges can be more deeply understood by taking a person's self-concept into account. As such, educational and professional undertakings can be viewed through a life-long perspective, from past to present to future, along our lifespan. An important event that marks a person's life is to be understood in the light of events that preceded it, as much as the person's goals or apprehensions (Guichard, 2010; Heinz et al., 2009; Young & Valach, 2008; Peterson et al., 2005).

Agency, Social Structures, and Social Context

More and more, individuals are considered agentic; they participate in the construction of their life paths by goal-setting, making choices, engaging in strategy – often based on how they view themselves. The idea of agency rests on the concept of intentionality. It is necessary to further understand that actions are influenced by social structures and contexts (both locally and globally), which are ever-changing and vary in importance throughout a person's lifespan (Fournier, Goyer, & Masdonati, 2010). Social structures and contexts can facilitate or restrain a person's development, depending on their situation (Krumboltz, 2009; Settersten & Gannon, 2009; Vondracek & Porfeli, 2008).

Interdependent Life Spheres

According to Canadian and international researchers (e.g., Blustein, 2011; Richardson, 2009a, 2009b; Riverin-Simard & Simard, 2011; Savickas et al., 2009; Young, 1996), it is imperative to consider all aspects or spheres of a person's life in order to better support their career development. Events or transitions experienced in one area of a person's life impact other areas as well. This is why it is also important to consider the contributions of non-work-related experiences to a person's life path. The more precarious or uncertain work opportunities are, the more important it becomes to examine the interdependence of life spheres (Peavy, 2004; Goyer, 2011; Savickas et al., 2009; Sapin et al., 2007). According to Riverin-Simard (2011), the following life spheres influence our direction the most: professional demands, informal organizational contributions, volunteer work, hobbies, and existential ponderings. Identifying what factors mobilize an individual in their everyday life helps a person situate themselves in the here and now, manage unpredictability, and seize opportunities as they present themselves. This is why career counselling must consider all experiences in a person's life, both work-related and not, across the lifespan. With this approach, a person can better understand and integrate the meanings they make with regard to their continuous or interrupted career path. They can also better prepare to meet their career goals in the face of predictable or unpredictable events. The research is clear that people's experiences have an impact on their career decisions, and that predictable and unpredictable events can happen at any point in a person's career. Therefore having career services accessible to all workers throughout their lifespan is needed and important.

USE OF MULTIPLE METHODOLOGIES IN STUDYING CAREER PSYCHOLOGY

In the field of career psychology, in Canada and elsewhere, there has been a push toward qualitative research methods to elucidate the subjective experience of clients (Hiebert, Domene, & Buchanan, 2011; Rennie, 2002; Savickas et al., 2009). For some, objective measures fall short of explaining the human experience. Rennie (2002) explains his view of the shift toward qualitative research:

> Qualitative researchers are skeptical of this objectivism. We maintain that it keeps distant the complexities and nuances of what it means to be human, both in terms of those being researched and those doing the research ... The upshot is that qualitative research occupies a middle ground between the sciences and humanities, which goes against established research practice in psychology and most related social and health science disciplines. (p. 139)

The contribution of Canadian researchers to various qualitative research approaches has afforded us an expanded understanding of people's career development and related issues. For example, Richard Young and his colleagues have enlarged the focus of career research by exploring contextual factors as well as individual factors, allowing for a fuller understanding of the context in which careers are lived and experienced (Collin & Young, 1986; Young & Valach, 2004). This led to the development of the contextual action theory of career and counselling, and the related qualitative action project method already described (Young, Valach, & Collin, 1996, 2002). This approach is based on the premise that careers are constructed over time and are the result of a series of actions and projects undertaken in an intentional, goal-directed manner, and that the context in which decisions are made is critically important to understanding individuals' career experiences and decisions.

Research in the field of career counselling has grown in both quantity and diversity over recent years, marked by the emergence of different models and scientific methods, each one trying to tackle the complex challenges of our ever-changing society. Bourassa, Fournier, and Goyer (2013) present a number of these research methodologies that have served to advance knowledge in the field as well as to empower individuals and communities. The approach of these methodologies is to conduct research *with* participants rather than *on* participants. These methods are referred to by various names such as action research, cooperative research, action science, and participatory research. They investigate career issues and social and professional assimilation, based on collaborative efforts between researchers and participants. These methodologies are being increasingly recognized and used both in Canada and around the world (Bourassa et al., 2013). Young and colleagues' contributions have already been discussed earlier in this chapter. Another methodology that has been further developed in Canada is the Critical Incident Technique, which is discussed next.

The Critical Incident Technique

The Critical Incident Technique, initially arising out of industrial and organizational psychology to understand flight crews' success in World War II bombing missions (Flanagan, 1954), was embraced and adapted for counselling psychology research by Woolsey (1986) and others at the University of British Columbia. It has been used extensively to study people's career experiences, to look at other counselling psychology–related areas of interest (Butterfield, Borgen, Amundson, & Maglio, 2005), and most recently to examine professional practice transformations (Fournier, Goyer, & Bourassa, 2011; Goyer, Landry, & Leclerc, 2006; Leclerc, Bourassa, & Filteau, 2010). It has recently been modified to include the use of credibility checks, contextual information against which to understand the critical incidents, and "wish list" items as additions to things that actually helped or hindered someone's experience of the phenomenon of interest. Now known as the Enhanced Critical Incident Technique (ECIT) (Butterfield, Borgen, Maglio, & Amundson, 2009), it has allowed researchers to explore career-related issues by first inviting people to share their phenomenological narratives of their experiences, which in turn prepares them for the critical incident component of the qualitative research interview and elicits large amounts of rich and meaningful data.

The ECIT has also facilitated the introduction of quantitative elements (for example, pre- and post-test scaling questions), resulting in mixed-methods research designs related to career issues and experiences. This is consistent with research trends in the health care and psychology literature, to name just two disciplines, where multiple approaches to inquiry are being used to explore complex real-world situations and social phenomena in Canada and elsewhere (Creswell, Plano Clark, Gutmann, & Hanson, 2003; Forthofer, 2003; Twinn, 2003; Waszak & Sines, 2003). Qualitative and quantitative methods can be mixed such that they have complementary strengths, compensate for the weaknesses of each, and allow for triangulation of results that increase validity and strengthen a study's findings (Cozby, 1997; Creswell et al., 2003; Palys, 1997; Tashakkori & Teddlie, 2003; Teddlie & Tashakkori, 2003). They also increase the breadth of understanding we have about a construct or experience that each approach alone could not elicit.

Challenges and Proposed Approaches Related to Career Psychology Research

Despite the complications with quantitative research, and the move by some researchers to conduct qualitative research as it applies to clients' individual needs or the ability to translate quantitative data into practice, there still appears to be a preference for quantitative research. A review of Canadian publication journals revealed a paucity of qualitative and mixed-methods research (Hiebert, Domene, & Buchanan, 2011). These findings stimulated two very important questions for the researchers: "Is there truly a diversity of methods in counselling psychology in Canada?" and "Where are Canadian counselling psychology researchers publishing their work?" (p. 268) Hiebert et al. (2011) state:

> Our basic position is that by more strongly embracing the use of diverse research approaches, and expanding the scope of acceptable evidence to include a broader range [of] data sources, we will be able to develop a more relevant and more inclusive approach to demonstrating the value of counselling psychology interventions. (p. 271)

In the spirit of keeping research relevant to career counselling clients, research should include a long-term approach. Longitudinal studies are needed to explore life-long interest development in a population that is living and working longer (Chope, 2011; Masdonati & Goyer, 2012). Traditionally, studies of interest are performed during adolescence and again in middle adulthood, which neglects changes occurring later in life. Not much is known about older workers and longitudinal research may prove informative for interventions with this population.

Expanding the methods for researching the efficacy of career psychology interventions will have implications for preparing counselling psychologists for practice, as well as training those already in practice. Although courses in program evaluation, statistics, and qualitative research are *offered* in all CPA-accredited doctoral programs in counselling psychology, none of the programs *require* the completion of a qualitative research course for graduation and not all programs *require* program evaluation (Hiebert et al., 2011). Hiebert et al. suggest making these courses mandatory instead of electives, incorporating them into master's-level coursework, and/or offering them as continuing education for counselling psychologists who are already in the field.

DEVELOPMENT OF AUGMENTED AND NEW THEORETICAL AND APPLIED PARADIGMS FOR CAREER PSYCHOLOGY

Career Development as Psychological Transition

Career development can no longer be viewed as distinct from other areas of clients' lives. Clients must be understood within the context of their circumstances across the lifespan. Career development is embedded in the contexts of the personal, the self, the family, and the society over time. Career decisions lead to, and are the product of, psychological transitions. It is imperative that career practitioners and counselling psychologists recognize this relationship and work collaboratively to support clients through these transitions. Riverin-Simard (2000) suggests that "career specialists must continue to combine their efforts in order to support adults in their vocational transitions, their career development, and, above all, their continuing search for work" (p. 127). She describes adult careers in the twenty-first century as being a series of "new beginnings and career transitions" (p. 115) that are not supported by current models of career development. Riverin-Simard also suggests that this career life cycle of "comings and goings" (p. 119) has replaced the twentieth-century notion of three phases of career – education, work, and retirement.

Savickas et al. (2009) recommend a shift from offering "simple advice for vocational decision making to an expertise in co-construction and accompaniment of a more holistic life design." It is a matter of asking "How do we construct our lives though our work?" (p. 243) This position is consistent with the writings of several other Canadian and international career experts. Amundson (2006) posits that work and educational organizations no longer direct career planning but, rather, that people have begun to focus on their employability and "self-organizing" behaviour (p. 5). This trend has been noted using terms such as the "boundaryless" (Arthur & Rousseau, 1996), "portfolio" (Handy, 1994), and "protean" (Hall, 1996) career. These terms reflect a holistic approach that recognizes the clients' active role in shaping their lives and work.

The Evolution of a Canadian Approach

In considering a definition for career psychology, it is important to go back to some of the early initiatives and movements that led us to where we are today. One of the major bases for career psychology is vocational psychology, which many believe began with the vocational guidance movement. We have taken some time to review the development of the vocational guidance movement within a North American context, which began about a hundred years ago, since it had a clear intention to help individuals but also to create awareness in the broader society of issues related to vocational/career development that would benefit the individual and the broader society. The original goal was to achieve for individuals a less conflictual and more harmonious interaction with their school and/or work environments for the betterment of themselves and their environments.

Over the last century, much of the focus has been on how to enhance or fine-tune assessment, intervention, and counselling processes or procedures so that we may better understand salient psychological factors, in order to increase the probability of individuals achieving a successful match with an occupation. There has also been increasing recognition of the need to address the needs of women, immigrants, individuals with disabling conditions, and those who are economically disadvantaged.

In the special edition of the *Journal of Vocational Behavior* in 2001, which considered the future of vocational psychology in Western industrialized economies (including Canada), Mark Savikas defined vocational psychology as follows:

The study of vocational behavior and its development in careers, particularly emphasizing issues of occupational choice and work adjustment. The discipline focuses on the perspective of individual workers not the perspectives of the organization or occupation. The focus on individuals differentiates vocational psychology from the fields of I/O psychology, organizational behavior, and occupational sociology. Of course, vocational psychologists work in organizations, yet when they do they concentrate on individual workers and their careers rather than on the organization and its leadership. (p. 167)

It is interesting to note in the definition of vocational psychology provided by Savickas that the words *occupational, vocational,* and *career* are all used. The focus seems to be clearly on work and work adjustment that would centre the work of vocational psychologists more in the area of occupational choice, perhaps with prominence given to a sense of vocation or passion for the occupation being chosen, rather than taking the longer view implied by the word *career*. The definition also appears to rest on the series of historical assumptions discussed earlier in this chapter that have been long held in the area of occupational/vocational/career development (Borgen & Heibert, 2006).

In recognizing the important historical and ongoing contribution of vocational psychology and in considering the perspective of career, which encompasses meaningful life activities inside and outside of paid employment as highlighted by many of the Canadian researchers discussed above, it is important to consider two major factors: (a) rapid and unpredictable changes in labour market opportunities; and (b) the increasing recognition of issues of equity and multiculturalism in Canadian society. The first factor suggests a move away from the traditional emphasis on the area of occupational/vocational/career development among younger people and their initial entry into the labour market, toward the current reality where throughout adulthood increasing numbers of Canadians will be engaged in life transitions precipitated by changing opportunities for paid work (Borgen et al., 2011; Riverin-Simard, 2000). There is also abundant evidence demonstrating the level of challenge and emotional turmoil often experienced by Canadian workers who voluntarily or involuntarily enter these transitions. The second factor is the greater range of perspectives regarding the nature of meaningful life activities and the processes that are important to take into account when seeking and securing employment.

Within this context of ongoing and escalating occupational or cultural change in Canada and other parts of the world, it may be worthwhile to consider the revised set of assumptions noted earlier in the chapter as a helpful way to underpin the concept of occupational/vocational/career development (Borgen & Hiebert, 2006). These proposed new assumptions recognize the increasing level of fluidity in occupational opportunities, which may or may not be tied to individuals' vocational interest, and which need to be considered within the broader perspective of a person's career trajectory over time. This context likely increases the level of complexity in the number of variables that an individual may need to take into account in making a decision. Also, there may be a number of psychological challenges that arise for individuals who find themselves in protracted experiences of career/life transition (Borgen, 1997).

In considering a definition of career psychology it is important to take into account its potential fit within the recently developed Canadian definition of counselling psychology, which is described as "being concerned with using psychological principles to enhance and promote the positive growth, well-being, and mental health of individuals, families, groups, and the broader community" (CPA, 2009b). Also, components of the definition will likely centre on the definition of key concepts, the central aim of career psychology, the processes involved, and the intended outcomes of career psychology. With these parameters in mind and in light of the forces of change affecting the Canadian landscape and workers, we offer an initial definition of career psychology to meet the needs of people in today's context.

A Proposed Definition of Career Psychology

Career psychology is concerned with psychological principles and processes that develop, promote, and enhance effective decision-making with respect to engagement in meaningful life activities over time. These activities may include but are not limited to paid employment. Core concepts involved in career psychology include: *occupation*, which typically implies paid employment; *vocation*, which refers to an individual's sense of passion or interest in an activity; and *career*, which refers to meaningful life activities over time (Borgen & Hiebert, 2006).

Core processes in career psychology include *advising, guidance,* and *counselling*. According to Borgen and Hiebert (2006), *advising* involves the provision of information related to an occupation or other meaningful life activity of interest to the individual. During the Information Age, knowing how to access up-to-date and accurate information is increasingly valuable. *Guidance* most often historically has involved the use of some form of assessment process with the aim of assisting an individual to better understand their abilities, aptitudes, and interests in effectively seeking and attaining satisfying employment. Within the current context this continues to be a viable process, with the understanding that the desired occupation may not be available at any given point, and that the nature of occupations may be shifting so rapidly that instruments may no longer be normed on their current requirements. *Counselling* involves developing a relationship with an individual, hearing the individual's perspective within their cultural context, appropriately challenging that perspective utilizing a variety of evidence-informed and evidence-based interventions, and assisting the individual in engaging in action-planning activities appropriate to their circumstances. This process has assumed increasing importance within career psychology given the number of individuals who require assistance with managing and moving through voluntary or forced career/life transitions at many different stages of their careers. Career psychology services are offered on an individual and group basis.

The intended outcomes of career psychology services include individuals who are more informed about their career options and who are more confident in their ability to engage in achieving the career goals that they have set, and are more robust in meeting the challenges and opportunities of future career/life transitions. They are also able to seek and have available career help when needed throughout their working lives. They also have the skills needed to access information that is up-to-date in order to help them make career decisions. The broader societal outcomes include greater numbers of people who are able to constructively interact in their places of employment, in their families, and in society more broadly.

As proposed by Canadian (Collin & Young, 2000; Riverin-Simard & Simard, 2011) and international (Blustein, 2011; Savickas et al., 2009; Richardson, 2009a, 2009b) advocates of the postmodern approach to career intervention, consideration must be given to all areas of an adult's life to facilitate their career development. A person's identity cannot be determined by one occupation or profession. Identifying what inspires a person in their everyday life helps connect them with the here and now, assisting them to manage the unknown and seize opportunities as they are presented (Boivin &

Goyer, 2006). As a person's whole life sphere is the focal point in counselling psychology, it is necessary to acquire a *"mode of intervention that integrates work and non-work issues in a seamless and conceptual matter"* (Blustein, 2011, p. 15). This allows a person to engage in *meaning-making*, where they embrace the interpretation and understanding of their experiences (applicable to both predictable and unpredictable events). Career counselling is thus redefined to examine a person's professional identity, organizational attachment, volunteer work, hobbies, and existential realities (Riverin-Simard & Simard, 2011).

MAJOR CHALLENGES AND FUTURE DIRECTIONS IN CAREER PSYCHOLOGY

Following the work of Danvers (2009), in developing the definition for career psychology we endeavoured to pursue the development and maintenance of a common language in career psychology, beyond the boundaries of language and nationalities. The mix of clinical, interdisciplinary, and systemic approaches necessitates an integration of career-related interventions. In this context, an analysis of the conceptual framework, protocols, and emerging practices of educational and professional guidance is vital. This final section of the chapter focuses on the issues, challenges, and future directions for Canadian career psychology within the Canadian and international contexts.

Public Policy and Career Development

A new field of research is studying the use of educational and career counselling by governments (Herr, 2003; Watts, 2008). This research is based within European Union countries or led by the Organization for Economic Co-operation and Development (OECD, 2003, 2004; Watts, Sultana, & McCarthy, 2010). The International Centre for Career Development and Public Policy was formed to study public policy and career development. Canada has contributed research to this topic (Bezanson & Kellett, 2001; Bezanson & O'Reilly, 2002; OECD, 2003), particularly as it relates to career development. The Canadian Research Working Group for Evidence Based Practice in Career Development and the Forum of Labour Market Ministers (2009) are investigating the connections between career development and public policy (Bélisle, 2010). At this time, however, no systematic study has been undertaken pertaining to the creation of educational and professional action plans within the academic or work sectors.

Governments have an interest in career counselling services. In the educational and labour sectors, public policy views such services as a means to efficiently meet governmental goals (OECD, 2003, 2004). This interest emerges from the potential effects of career services to bridge education with the realities of the job market; to enhance social inclusion and increase graduation rates; to improve the competencies of the population to support prosperity; or to ensure the proper delivery of services funded by taxpayer money. Public policy views career counselling services on the one hand as a public resource – as a way to facilitate a qualified workforce to aid economic growth – and on the other hand as a private resource – to help workers individually grow and prosper in the job market (Picard & Masdonati, 2012).

Towards Long-Term Social and Occupational Support

To support a person's social and occupational participation while valuing their freedom of choice, there needs to be an examination of their capabilities and adjustment to change factors in order to provide comprehensive guidance (Picard & Masdonati, 2012). An examination of a person's capabilities allows for a realistic set of options to be presented, and from there a concrete action plan can be developed with the individual for attaining them (Sen, 1992, 2009). Sen's approach to examining capabilities (the Capability Approach) emphasizes a person's resources and social supports as contributing factors to their dispositional character (Olympio, 2012; Verhoevan et al., 2007).

Change factors encompass a person's nature. Influenced by societal and environmental factors that facilitate or discourage a person from adequately making use of career services, these factors have the potential to transform opportunity into a concrete action plan. The Capability Approach allows for an assessment of a person's change factors (both positive and negative) so that they can be taken into consideration in the career decision-making process. The Capability Approach is a complex and formidable framework. However, it can allow for a critical analysis (through Sen's approach [2009]) of the actual effects of career services on diverse populations, and in turn assess whether interventions are fulfilling the mandates envisioned by public policy. The results can inform the restructuring of career services to better anchor their usefulness.

Recognition of Diverse Research Methodologies in Career Psychology

Over the course of the last few years, as already discussed, research in career psychology has evolved and diversified. Its development has been marked by the emergence of different research methodologies aiming to understand complex and continually changing problems within society. Certain research methods purport to advance our knowledge and empower both individuals and communities. Their approach is to conduct research *with* participants, not *on* participants. These methods include action research, co-operative research, action science, and participatory research. They rely on the collaboration between researchers and participants and they are being used and recognized more and more within Canada and around the world (Bourassa et al., 2013). Other research methodologies are also used in career psychology and take the form of evaluative, narrative, or experimental research. Furthermore, based on the conclusions of Masdonati and Goyer (2012), certain topics within career psychology, such as career trajectories, could benefit from longitudinal studies.

Evaluation Framework, Best Practices, and Persuasive Findings

Despite the importance accorded to evaluating career counselling services, in reality not many studies have been conducted. The majority of data collected does not investigate what interventions were most effective for clients nor how counsellors most effectively employed these interventions (Lalande & Magnusson, 2007; Magnusson & Lalande, 2005; Michaud, Goyer, Baudouin, & Turcotte, 2006). Studies emphasize employment placement statistics or the number of workers who returned to school. The evaluations of career services are often measured by observable and quantifiable changes.

Over and above the international consensus on the importance of career counselling, there is the desire to establish an evidence base to demonstrate the effectiveness of services to the highest scientific standard (Hiebert et al., 2011). Over the past ten years, two principal approaches have appeared in career psychology literature related to service provision for individuals and communities: evidence-based interventions, and interventions founded by best practices. Evidence-based interventions are interested in documenting the changes experienced by clients after they have received career services. Evidence-based interventions ask: what proof is there that the interventions succeeded? On the other hand, interventions formed through best practices are founded on the empirical evidence of their efficacy. They ask the question: what program (intervention or process) would be most appropriate for this particular client? More and more, we find that service providers and policy-makers want answers to both these questions. For their part, clients hope for both probable results and tailored interventions. These two approaches warrant further discussion. One of the objectives of the evidence-based approach is to render more explicit the connections between the services offered by agencies and the results obtained. More and more career counselling service providers must account for this connection: from the reporting requirements and expectations of policy-makers and third-party insurers to addressing the hopes of the clients they serve (Hiebert, 2010).

Increased Emphasis on Evidence-Based Approaches

As already mentioned, paradoxically research indicates strong support for evaluating the outcome of services without actual evaluations being performed (CRWG, as cited in Hiebert, 2002). What constitutes evidence of success is elusive and typically includes variables that are not amenable to being measured (Hiebert, n.d.). Much to the chagrin of respondents, contextual variables and societal impacts are often not included in the evaluation of services (Magnusson & Lalande, 2005). Client variables deemed important in considering career counselling service success include client intrapersonal factors such as internal locus of control, self-confidence, motivation, self-esteem, client self-reliance and initiative, belief that change is possible, and opportunity awareness (Magnusson & Lalande, 2005). Other factors practitioners wished could have been considered in service evaluation were client goal attainment, client skill acquisition, independent client use of resources provided in career service centres, and client acquisition of non-job-related skills

(Magnusson & Lalande, 2005). Michaud et al. (2006) came to the same conclusions.

Hiebert (2002) offers suggestions to various stakeholders to promote evidence-based practice. He contends that evaluation needs to be central in professional training programs for career psychology practitioners. The academic community is responsible for conducting and disseminating applied research that links outcomes with practices. Program designers should couple program evaluation with program delivery, with a focus on intrapersonal variables that are integral components influencing services delivered. Program evaluation experts should collect evidence of client change, with the recognition that merely evaluating change will, in itself, produce change. He challenges policy developers, program administrators, and funders to provide leadership by funding service evaluation and being open to negotiating what constitutes evidence of client change. Practitioners are asked to view their role as a service evaluator equally to their role as a service provider. This position has been referred to as a *local clinical scientist* approach (Stricker & Trierwieler, 1995). In embracing their service-evaluator role, practitioners will need to develop a means to collect evidence of client outcomes:

> A likely result of adopting a *Local Clinical Scientist* perspective is that counselling psychology practitioners will see their professional roles as involving a combination of both process and outcome, thereby bridging the main components of evidence-based practice and outcome-focused intervention. (Hiebert et al., 2011, p. 271)

Lastly, Hiebert (2002) states that agency managers and supervisors will need to support practitioners in their roles as service providers and evaluators by providing in-service and professional training that develops the necessary skills and knowledge to assess and document client outcomes. Hiebert (2002) contends that "[w]hen people begin to take ownership for their part of the situation, then change becomes more probable. The lack of evaluation could create a crisis in the career development field" (p. 5).

The CRWG developed a framework for evaluation of career development services. The framework consists of inputs, processes, and

outcomes. Inputs include the resources available to the career development program. Processes include activities such as generic and
specific interventions, and quality service factors that affect the operation of the agency but not necessarily the outcomes. Outcomes
include indicators of client change. Programs are evaluated on the
basis of their ability to produce outcomes. Outcomes occur as a result
of the inputs enacting processes. Although it can be a linear process
where input leads to process, which then leads to outcomes, there is
also an interactive relationship among the three components. For
instance, inputs can directly affect outcomes. Bearing this framework
in mind, evaluation of career development services should include the
evaluation of all three components (Baudouin et al., 2007). A vari-
ance in the process component, such as straying from the intervention plan by the service provider or client, will taint the evaluated
effectiveness of the intervention plan. Baudouin and colleagues suggest that agencies should be clear about the client outcomes they
wish to be held accountable for and should design processes based
on this determination. Once the appropriate processes are identified,
the availability of inputs should be considered (Baudouin et al.,
2007). Further research related to the effectiveness of applying this
model to the outcomes of career interventions and services is needed.

Increased Emphasis on the Regulation of
the Practice of Career Psychology

Amundson (2006) contends that new developments within the
career guidance field present issues with implementation, necessitating training, career specialization, and accreditation. The International Centre for Career Development and Public Policy (ICCDPP)
was created to address such issues. Career development services have
expanded to include various types of career practitioners. The training and expertise of various career coaches and career development facilitators is variable and often does not match the extensive
training of a career counsellor or counselling psychologist. This can
be confusing to potential clients who may seek assistance from
these related service providers at a lower cost than that of a career
counsellor or counselling psychologist. Niles (2003) suggests several
questions career counsellors must address: "Can career counsellors
demonstrate their centrality to career services when others provide
related services (often at a lower cost)?" "How effectively has the

career counselling profession communicated what it has to offer to the public?" and "Do consumers understand the distinction between career counselling and other services, such as career coaching?" (p. 71) Regulation of career development services, including professional designations (registration), would likely clarify these ambiguities by informing potential clients (consumers) of the services available from each practitioner and her/his qualifications.

Adding to the confusion of the multitude of career development practitioners is the variety of designations, training, and experiences within the counselling psychology profession. Counsellors and psychologists are licenced at the provincial level (Gazzola, Smith, King-Andrews, & Kearney, 2010), which leads to some inconsistency across Canada (Hall & Hurley, 2003). Specialities within mental health disciplines are not necessarily licensed. This can be problematic across provinces, particularly when language and cultural differences exist. For instance, the term *counselling psychology* in English does not have a French equivalent. In Quebec, guidance counselling and professional psychology are treated separately and regulated by different boards: the *Ordre des Conseillers et Conseillères d'Orientation du Québec* (Order of Guidance Counsellors of Quebec; occoQ) and the *Ordre des Psychologues du Québec* (Order of Psychologists of Quebec; oPQ), respectively.

Increased Emphasis on Career Psychology in Graduate Programs in Canada

Some have argued that career development is "one of the defining factors" for counselling psychology and, therefore, should be an integral part of counselling training (Lalande, 2004, p. 280). Yet, one cPA-accredited doctoral program does not require the completion of a career development course (Young, 2002). Certificate and diploma programs have more career-specific content than most graduate-level programs in counselling psychology, except in Quebec. For instance, degree programs do not typically include career information, work trends, or work search techniques (Burwell & Kalbfleisch, 2011). They also tend to be oriented toward the individual, rather than the macro-systems involved in career concerns. In recognition of this point, Hiebert, McCarthy, and Repetto (2001) state: "Career counsellor education primarily stems from a psychological background (versus a career development, adult transition, or labour market background), and does not address the diverse career paths and complex labour market that clients encounter" (p. 1). Of additional concern is the fact that the majority of these certificate and diploma programs do not have supervision requirements, as counselling psychology programs do. McMahon (2003) also noted the lack of emphasis on supervision in career counselling internationally. This lack of supervision may lead to an assumption that career work is not complex or difficult enough to warrant supervision.

The establishment of a professional identity of career counselling and career psychology requires training (McCarthy, 2001). The identity of career counselling has been likened to that of a client lacking "vocational identity and clearly articulated goals" (Niles, 2003, p. 73). Increasing emphasis on career counselling in graduate programs in Canada and elsewhere would work in concert with the regulation of career development services to promote the professional identity of career counsellors and counselling psychologists, and distinguish them from other career development practitioners.

CONCLUDING COMMENTS

Career psychology today is at a major turning point, influenced by work settings, the needs of workers, efficiency expectations, the influence of third-party insurance, new legislation, and increased governmental control. Not only does career psychology have to respond to new demands that place it at the centre of educational and work concerns, the latter also put pressure on career psychology to make life more predictable and uniform. The societal importance of career psychology is recognized internationally (AIOSP, 2009; Danvers, 2009; McCarthy, 2011). Career psychology has large expectations, both with younger and older members of a population, to help increase a person's power to act (Brown et al., 2011; Le Bossé, 2011), to give meaning to their participation in the work force (Riverin-Simard & Simard, 2005, 2010), and to engage in a culture of life-long learning (Bélisle, 2010; Boivin & Goyer, 2007). Career psychology plays an important role in society's collective challenges, including an increase in educational expectations and curtailing drop-out rates. Such contributions increase social and occupational integration in society and as a result strengthen human and social capital (Kamanzi, 2006). Challenges can be found with regard to improving both positive organizational dynamics and the organizational commitment of workers (Goyer, Savard, Bilodeau, & Veilleux, 2008; Vandenberghe, 2009). This requires making quality career psychology services available to all members of society, at any stage of their lives. This is a means of guaranteeing the social and occupational participation of all, particularly in a culture that necessitates life-long career and educational support (Danvers, 2009; Vuorinen & Watts, 2010).

NOTE

1 Authors are listed alphabetically. We would like to thank our research assistants, Stephanie Conn, Jessica Isenor, Kate Kearney, Ellen Schlesinger, and Jacqueline Synard, for their diligent work in the preparation of this text.

9

Assessment in Canadian Counselling and Counselling Psychology

SHARON E. ROBERTSON AND
MARVIN J. MCDONALD

Canadian literature in counselling and counselling psychology is largely silent on the matter of assessment, and where it does exist, it tends to be scattered among innovative practices, training activities, and literature addressing other professional issues of various kinds. Our first goal in this chapter is to highlight various ways in which assessment is conceptualized in counselling and counselling psychology in Canada, drawing primarily on the work of Canadian authors, while offering a contextual framework within which various approaches can be positioned. The Canadian Psychological Association's (CPA) recently approved definition of counselling psychology characterizes assessment, diagnosis, and case conceptualization as core aspects of the discipline (Bedi et al., 2011). The development of this definition provides an invaluable opportunity to identify, describe, and cultivate emerging resources in this area. Testing and assessment are multidisciplinary and multiprofessional sets of domains with profound significance for personal and social well-being. So the pluralistic, advocacy values of counselling psychology provide a crucial motivation for tracking emerging practices and paradigms. Our second goal is to provide a Canadian resource upon which educators, practitioners, and researchers in professional counselling and counselling psychology can draw. Toward that end we provide a brief history of assessment in counselling psychology. We follow this by describing both traditional, analytic and more recent, contextualist models of assessment being pursued by counselling psychologists in Canada. We conclude with a brief discussion of ethical responsibilities in assessment practice.

HISTORY AND PURPOSES OF ASSESSMENT IN COUNSELLING PSYCHOLOGY

Historically, assessment and testing have served as important parts of Canadian counsellors' and, to a greater extent, counselling psychologists' roles. As noted by Beatch et al. (2009), areas of assessment practice for counselling psychologists vary, often depending on work environments, and overlapping with other specialties within psychology (e.g., clinical psychology, industrial/organizational psychology). Indeed, some areas of assessment may overlap with other professional groups such as school counsellors, professional mental health counsellors, marriage and family therapists, clinical social workers, and psychiatrists (cf. Young & Nicol, 2007). Although many assessment methods are not unique to counselling psychologists, what does appear to be distinctive is a core philosophical orientation that guides their practice and the way in which assessments are carried out.

Four traditions have commonly been identified as having a significant influence on the development of both counselling and counselling psychology: (a) the vocational guidance movement founded by Frank Parsons; (b) the psychometric tradition and the study of individual differences originating with the work of people such as Alfred Binet; (c) the mental hygiene movement begun by Clifford Beers; and (d) the development of the client-centred approach to counselling and psychotherapy by Carl Rogers. In a review of the historical influences on the use of assessment in counselling, Watkins (1992) argued that these diverse traditions coalesced in such a way as to provide a unique counselling psychology perspective on the assessment process and counselling psychologists' testing and assessment activities. In keeping with this diverse background, counselling approaches to assessment allow for a multiplicity of methods while adhering to a client-centred orientation with a common goal of helping clients better understand and help themselves. Similarly, Duckworth (1990) noted that a counselling psychology approach to assessment is carried out in collaboration with the client, with the client's stated goals driving the assessment, and with the client as an active participant throughout the process, including test selection and interpretation. The process focuses on normalcy, strengths as well as weaknesses, and the promotion of self-assessment. These descriptions are in keeping with the core values outlined in the definition of counselling psychology adopted by the CPA (2009b).

> Counselling psychology adheres to an integrated set of core values: (a) counselling pre-existing strengths and resourcefulness and the therapeutic relationship as central mechanisms of change; (b) the counselling psychology approach to assessment, diagnosis, and case conceptualization is holistic and client-centred; and it directs attention to social context and culture when considering internal factors, individual differences, and familial/systemic influences; and (c) the counselling process is pursued with sensitivity to diverse sociocultural factors unique to each individual.

This definition "is centred on a philosophy and worldview that posits a definable perspective on professional psychology practice rather than a discipline-specific set of skills or a wholly unique knowledge base" (Bedi et al., 2011, p. 130). This philosophy and worldview informs all aspects of assessment in counselling psychology.

While assessment is seen to be part of the counselling role, various purposes have been identified for engaging in the assessment process. Duckworth (1990) identified four purposes of assessment: (a) to enhance short-term treatment; (b) to help in focusing on developmental issues; (c) to aid in decision-making; and (d) to enhance client exploration and self-reflection. According to Hood and Johnson (2007), psychological assessment enables counsellors to identify the nature of a client's concern, to consider possible treatment approaches, and to engage in program planning and evaluation. Assessment results can be used by clients to promote self-understanding and to make future plans. The comprehensive review by Meyer et al. (2001) identified purposes of assessment that include (a) describing current functioning; (b) confirming, refuting, or modifying impressions of a client; (c) identifying counselling needs, issues likely to emerge, interventions that might be used, and possible outcomes; (d) helping in differential diagnosis; (e) monitoring and evaluating effectiveness of interventions and emerging concerns; (f) managing risk and identifying negative responses to counselling; and (g) using assessment feedback as an intervention. This expansion of assessment purposes allows professionals to recognize a larger range of contexts in which professional assessment can flourish.

According to Sinacore-Guinn (1995a), the ways in which assessment has been integrated into the counselling psychologist's role have been significant. Assessment is any activity that is designed to further the process of gathering information through formal and/or informal techniques to describe the psychological, social, biological, and cultural factors that influence an individual's behaviour (Sattler & Hoge, 2006; Stewart, 2010). It is a complex process and includes more than formal testing and/or diagnosis. Psychological assessment consists of the entire process of collecting, organizing, and interpreting psychological data about clients. It may result in a formal report or be used to develop counselling goals, plan interventions, or assess outcomes. In contrast, testing is defined as the use of formal tests (e.g., personality or vocational tests). Assessment may involve various informal methods to gather information such as interviews, rating scales, and observations. Talley (1995a, p. 9, cited by Sinacore-Guinn, p. 268) suggested that "assessment [should be] looked upon as an evolving procedure rather than a static one-time procedure, and testing is [to be viewed as] only one means of understanding a person's abilities or personality structure." As such, assessment is an ongoing aspect of counselling processes across time. Assessment is different from formulating a diagnosis in that it involves both personality dispositions and contextual factors (Stewart, 2010). The requirement of contextual sensitivity (Meyer et al., 2001) shifts criteria of assessment adequacy to encompass intersections of multiple social identities (gender, class, ethnicity, sexual orientation, and so on; Cole, 2009; McCall, 2005; Sinacore-Guinn, 1995b). For any specific purpose of assessment, varying identities and relationships may be salient to the person(s) being assessed. Moreover, since social identities are mutually constitutive, contextual sensitivity cannot be addressed through mere listing of aspects of human diversity in categories. Instead, connections among those identities salient for a particular person in a specific assessment process need to be clarified. Different assessment purposes reflect the social identities that are most important for the person being assessed in his or her own situation. Cole (2009) demonstrates one way to clarify connections between social identities and assessment purposes by asking three orienting questions. For each assessment purpose, we need to clarify how each identity category (e.g., gender) is relevant. When gender is relevant for exploring vocational directions, we can ask: (a) Who is included in the appropriate gender category (man, woman, transman, transwoman, etc.)? (b) What role does inequality play in each category (e.g., transwomen may experience different oppressions than do cisgendered women)? (c) What commonalities are there across categories (e.g., some oppressions of transwomen may be similar to those experienced by cisgendered women)? These three questions help the professional and the client track connections between the purpose of a particular assessment (e.g., vocational guidance) with salient identities (e.g., transwoman). The resources of critical race theory and feminist theory are thus particularly helpful for counselling psychologists in formulating assessment purposes while acknowledging the impacts of oppression and empowerment resources. These historical and paradigm considerations come together in a contextual assessment approach for counselling psychology.

ANALYTIC MODELS OF ASSESSMENT

The most common strategies for organizing assessment practices operate on the basis of models for information-gathering and decision-making in the helping professions. For clients and professionals that share similar cultural and social backgrounds, decision-making can often be facilitated by analytic tools that effectively organize, summarize, and communicate relevant insights. Two common versions of analytic assessment highlight problem-solving principles and biopsychosocial backgrounds.

Problem-Solving Models of Assessment

A number of problem-solving models of assessment are commonly used within the Canadian counselling context. The most commonly used ones appear to be those put forward by Hood and Johnson (2007), Groth-Marnat (2009), and Sattler and Hoge (2006).

Hood and Johnson (2007) use a five-step problem-solving model as part of their approach to assessment in counselling. The five steps consist of (a) problem orientation, (b) problem identification, (c) generation of alternatives, (c) decision-making, and (e) verification. In this model, various assessment methods are used to facilitate the process during each step through client-assessor collaboration.

Consistent with the model proposed by Hood and Johnson, Bedi and Rawdah (2009) describe career assessment as "a broad process of systematic information gathering using multiple methods to answer career-related questions. A common question addressed in career assessment is, 'What career options provide the best fit for this individual?'" (p. 67) Although clients often expect counsellors and counselling psychologists to provide a definitive answer as to the best career for them based on standardized test results, in keeping with the core values of counselling, in actual practice the process is one of career exploration and planning in which the counsellor and the client work together to reach the client's goal. The domains most frequently addressed in career assessment include personality, aptitude, academic achievement, values, career interests, career-related thinking, and stage of career development. Increasingly, an assessment of the client's personal problems and clinical symptoms is carried out as well with the increased recognition that career issues can affect mental health and mental distress and vice versa (Bedi & Rawdah, 2009). The methods normally used include interviews, standardized tests and inventories, record review, and a range of self-assessment activities such as card sorts, self-monitoring, and rank-ordering tasks as well as those proposed by Peavy (1996, 1997). The reader is referred to Bedi and Rawdah (2009) and Hood and Johnson (2007) for a more extensive description of commonly used domains, methods, and instruments.

According to Groth-Marnat (2009), "the ultimate goal of psychological assessment is to help solve problems by providing information and recommendations relevant to making the optimum decisions related to the client" (p. 535). Groth-Marnat described a four-phase conceptual framework to guide clinical assessment: (a) evaluating the referral question, (b) acquiring knowledge relating to the content of the problem, (c) collecting data, and (d) interpreting the data. He noted that, although the four phases have been separated for conceptual convenience, in actuality they often occur at the same time and interact with one another. In the first phase, the clinician needs to clarify the reasons for the referral, the expectations of the referring source, and the specific questions to be addressed through the assessment. In the second phase, the clinician needs to carefully consider the problem to be addressed, the adequacy of the tests to be used, and the appropriateness of the test for an individual's particular situation. In the third phase, the clinician proceeds to collect information from a wide variety of sources, primarily personal history, test results, behavioural observations, and interviews. Depending on the referral question, other sources of information may also be accessed. Multiple sources of information should be relied upon to aid problem-solving and decision-making. In the last phase, the clinician engages in a process of analyzing the data, developing hypotheses, obtaining support for the hypotheses, and integrating the conclusions. The outcome of the assessment should consist of a description of the client's present level of functioning and considerations pertaining to etiology, prognosis, and treatment recommendations.

Sattler (Sattler & Hoge, 2006; Sattler, 2008) has outlined an eleven-step problem-solving model for the cognitive, behavioural, social, and clinical assessment of children. The steps involved in this multistage assessment process consist of (a) reviewing referral information; (b) deciding whether to accept the referral; (c) obtaining relevant background information; (d) considering the influence of relevant others; (e) observing the child in several settings; (f) selecting and administering an appropriate assessment battery; (g) interpreting the assessment results; (h) developing intervention strategies and recommendations; (i) writing a report; (j) meeting with parents, the examinee (if appropriate), and other concerned individuals; and (k) following up on recommendations and conducting a re-evaluation.

It is worthwhile to note the similarities and differences between these three models. As mentioned previously, all three are considered to be problem-solving models of assessment. They contain components of problem identification, gathering relevant information, generating alternatives, and decision-making. However, there are differences in the way this is done, particularly between the counselling approach to assessment put forward by Hood and Johnson (2007) and the clinical approach to assessment described by Groth-Martnat (2009) and Sattler (2006, 2008). In the Hood and Johnson approach, assessment is part of an ongoing relationship in which both the counsellor and counsellee are actively engaged in working to resolve the client-defined problem. In both the Groth-Marnat and Sattler approaches, assessment is a process of problem identification, data collection, hypotheses generation, and decision-making by the examiner leading to recommendations provided to a referral source, which in Groth-Marnat's approach might be the person being assessed. Such assessments may inform treatment, but in Sattler's model another practitioner carries out the treatment. Hood and Johnson identified the counsellor-counsellee relationship as a collaborative one. Sattler (2006) distinguished between two states of the examiner-examinee relationship: restrictive and collaborative. He clearly stated that the examiner-examinee relationship should be an open and responsible collaborative partnership. All three approaches appear to be used by counselling psychologists in Canada and may vary depending upon the reason for the assessment and the context in which the assessment is to be conducted.

The need for a contextualized approach to assessment in counselling was raised by Amundson, Borgen, and Tench as early as 1995 when they examined the role of personality and intelligence in counselling, illustrating their concerns through a specific focus on the area of vocational development and career counselling. Traditional models of vocational development and career and employment counselling were based on the notion of developing a fit between the person and the environment through matching intelligence and personality with work/educational environments (e.g., job characteristics). Most of these endeavours had as an underlying assumption that there existed a stable or expanding labour market, and in much of the developed world up to the early 1980s, this assumption was correct. It allowed counsellors to assist clients in assessment of personality, intelligence, and other personal attributes and to link those personal characteristics with the jobs and broader career paths that the characteristics suggested. However, with structural changes to the labour market such as changes in the global economy and various major and minor recessions, labour market demands were not only reduced or altered but increasingly uncertain. Traditional assumptions regarding education and work no longer seemed viable and the idea of *vocational choice* seemed to have increasingly less applicability, as there was no guarantee that a suitable job would be available. "The whole notion that the individual can select from a wide range of occupations and simply plug or be plugged into a job is seriously in question" (Amundson et al., 1995, p. 614). Amundson et al. (1995) questioned the value of decontextualized theory and assessment practices and suggested that traditional theory and assessment of personality, intelligence, and environmental factors in vocational contexts be revised to combine and contextualize these factors. Their criticisms and suggestions continue to be applicable in today's professional and social environments.

Biopsychosocial Models of Assessment

Historically, the biomedical model of health and illness with its emphasis on biological (physiological, biochemical, and/or genetic) causes of disorder and disease has dominated Canadian health care for a century. In keeping with this approach, most or all abnormal behaviour is attributed to biological causes and is primarily treated through physically based (somatic) methods, including medication and surgery. For both physical and mental health problems, the focus is on the diagnosis and treatment of disease, disorder, or injury.

Engel (1977) challenged the medical community to re-evaluate the prevailing biomedical paradigm, arguing that important psychological and sociocultural factors were not addressed within the model and that by confining their views on patients' illnesses to only biological causes, physicians were restricting their ability to understand and effectively treat patients. Indeed, according to Engel, such a reductionist approach did not take into account the multiple interacting causal influences on disorders. Instead, he provided a new way of conceptualizing human health and illness, the biopsychosocial (BPS) approach. According to Meyer and Melchert (2011), the BPS approach is "one of the most comprehensive, integrative, and well known approaches to conceptualizing the mental health assessment process" (p. 70–71). The biopsychosocial model, based on general systems theory (von Bertalanffy, 1968), has been formulated as a holistic, systemic approach that allows practitioners and researchers to address major areas of presenting issues across three areas (physical, psychological, and sociocultural) and to examine the reciprocal and interactive effects between them. According to Meyer and Melchert (2011) and Kaplan and Coogan (2005), the BPS approach can be used by mental health practitioners to inform both assessment and intervention processes.

Kaplan and Coogan (2005, p. 18) argued that the biopsychosocial model is a robust framework for counsellor use as it is applicable across different types of counselling and client problems. They defined each of the three areas as follows: *bio* refers to biology and reflects the physical, biochemical, and genetic factors that influence a client's problem; *psycho* refers to developmental, psychological, and psychopathological factors that need to be considered; and *social* refers to areas such as family systems, diversity, and social justice, which are central to the counselling identity. Kaplan and

Coogan examined each of the three areas (physical, psychological, and sociocultural) from a counselling perspective and described how the model might be applied to the assessment and treatment of various client problems (e.g., adolescent depression, failing grades, career indecisiveness, bulimia, low self-esteem, smoking cessation, and death of a spouse) across the lifespan.

An important and controversial issue associated with the biomedical and biopsychosocial models is medical diagnosis of mental disorders. In the early 1950s, the American Psychiatric Association published the first edition of the *Diagnostic and Statistical Manual of Mental Disorders* (D S M) (American Psychiatric Association, 1952), which provided a means of classifying psychiatric and psychological disorders for treatment and research purposes. The D S M aims to be atheoretical and classifies medical disorders according to descriptive, not etiological, factors. Since the initial publication, the manual has been revised a number of times and is widely used in classifying mental disorders in most medical and psychological settings in Canada, the United States, and elsewhere. When the American Psychiatric Association published the third edition of the D S M in 1980, it added the multi-axial system, which supports the comprehensive biopsychosocial assessment of clients' psychiatric concerns. In the fourth edition of the D S M, the D S M-I V-T R (American Psychiatric Association, 2000), the multi-axial system was retained along with updated information regarding many of the mental disorders. A detailed description of the D S M-I V-T R is beyond the scope of this chapter. Suffice it to say that the influence of the biopsychosocial model is evident in the multi-axial classification system used in the D S M-I V-T R.

Hood and Johnson (2007) provide an overview of the D S M-I V-T R together with points that should be considered in using it in counselling. In order to reduce variability in the amount and type of information derived from interviews with clients, structured interview schedules have been developed based on various versions of the D S M. The Structured Clinical Interview for the D S M-I V (S C I D; First, Spitzer, Gibbon, & Williams, 1997) is the most frequently used structured interview and it adheres closely to the D S M-I V-T R decision trees for psychiatric diagnosis (Groth-Marnat, 2009).

Various arguments have been made for using the D S M-I V-T R, including the fact that it provides a common classification system and an integrated language for talking about clients' concerns by various mental health professionals (Hood & Johnson, 2007; Strong, 2012). With the increased prevalence of psychopathology within the general population and the increased focus on counselling and counselling psychology as health professions, there has been increased pressure to become knowledgeable about the D S M-I V-T R in order to recognize pathology when presented with it and also to be able to communicate with other professionals about client disorders. In addition, as counsellors and counselling psychologists increasingly find jobs within settings (e.g., health care and medical settings) where the D S M-I V-T R is commonly used, it behooves them to be well informed about the D S M-I V-T R classifications, as they are integral to understanding and engaging in providing services to clients in these settings.

At the same time, since its first introduction, there has been strong criticism of the D S M, particularly as it is seen as being increasingly aligned with the medical model (Kawa & Giordano, 2012). According to Kaplan and Coogan (2005), despite being based on the bio-psychosocial model, the emphasis in the D S M-I V-T R remains on the Axis I and II diagnostic categories, which are rooted in the biomedical, disease model of mental illness. In addition, across time there has been strong criticism of the D S M approach to classification (see for example Malik, Johannsen, & Beutler, 2008).

Within the Canadian context, several counsellors and counselling psychologists have expressed serious reservations about the D S M-I V-T R and its predecessor, the D S M-I V. Sinacore-Guinn (1995b) provided a thoughtful critique of the D S M-I V, arguing that it was based on a Western male-modelled standard that neglected to adequately consider cultural or gender aspects of clients' presenting problems, resulting in some groups (e.g., gay men and lesbians, ethnic minorities, women, and non-traditional men) being over-diagnosed with certain disorders or misdiagnosed altogether. To alleviate some of these difficulties, Sinacore-Guinn put forward a gender- and culturally-sensitive interview protocol and general diagnostic model for use with all clients. More recently, Gazzola, Smith, King-Andrews, and Kearney (2010) traced the ongoing and increasing conflict for counsellors between the traditional counselling discourse of holism, wellness, prevention, social justice, multiculturalism, and person-environment interaction with the medical model of practice. Similarly, Strong (2012) and Strong, Gaete, Sametband, French, and Eeson (2012) argued that for counsellors and therapists, particularly those practicing from narrative and other social constructionist perspectives, "systems or constructionist discourses as well as social justice, existential, or normal problem-solving discourses are inconsistent with a psychiatric discourse that exclusively locates client concerns as deficits or pathologies within them" (Strong, 2012, p. 55). Furthermore, counsellor and client conversational work is increasingly being constrained by the D S M and medicalized discourses of practice as clients' concerns and experiences are "mapped onto a language and logic stripped from clients' context of living and meaning" (Strong, 2012, p. 55).

There is a great deal of variation among Canadian counselling psychologists' work settings as well as their knowledge, attitudes, and practice with respect to diagnostic assessment. In some settings, the use of standardized tests is discouraged altogether, while in others (e.g., mental health clinics, hospitals, and correctional facilities), diagnostic assessment of psychopathology is standard practice (Bedi et al., 2011). Many counselling psychologists are inclined to emphasize assessment of normal personality functioning rather than severe clinical pathology (Beatch et al., 2009, p. 35). Concern has been expressed that counsellors and counselling psychologists working in health care settings are at risk of changing their values and orientations and being assimilated into the medical culture (e.g., Gazzola et al., 2010). At the same time, there are those (e.g., Sinacore-Guinn, 1995b) who argue for the potential for making changes within the health care system. However, all Canadian doctoral programs in counselling psychology include education and training in psychopathology, clinical diagnosis, and psychological assessment as part of their curriculum, although the emphasis and amount of coursework varies across programs (Beatch et al., 2009, p. 35; Bedi et al., 2011, p. 131; Haverkamp et al., 2011). Many counselling psychologists who provide mental health services to clients with diagnosable clinical disorders are able to do so within a contextual perspective (Bedi et al., 2011).

> Counselling psychologists, from their core philosophical orientation, are trained to see beyond diagnostic labels, to focus on environmental/socio-cultural causes that can create/perpetuate/contribute to psychopathology, and to avoid unnecessary diagnostic labeling of individuals (Sinacore-Guinn, 1995[a]).
> However, that does not mean that counselling psychologists are

unable to provide clinical diagnoses, when this serves the best interests of their clients. Some counselling psychologists intentionally work within diagnostic systems to ensure clients are actively involved in the diagnostic process. These psychologists work with clients to help them understand diagnostic labels critically and to facilitate empowerment and growth. (Beatch et al., 2009, p. 35)

For Bedi and Domene (2008), focusing on strengths does not suggest a particular scope of practice. Instead, it is an example of an occasion where counselling psychology's philosophical orientation pervades multiple areas of its practice.

CONTEXTUAL ASSESSMENT PARADIGM: ANALYTIC MODELS AND HOLISTIC MODELS

Problem-solving and biopsychosocial models are most likely to be effective and appropriate in situations where a large degree of cultural and social identity is shared or familiar, and empowering, respectful relationships are sustainable for all participants in professional interactions. Yet even when contexts are shared, oppressive traditions may well constitute features of familiar traditions or settings. Because privilege of position is often invisible to those benefiting from power and because access to professional status is often associated with privilege, professional standards and education emphasize a high priority for addressing privilege and oppression. In assessment, Richard Dana's work is exemplary for the systematic manner in which he transforms professional practice and models (e.g., 2005, 2008). A central feature of his multicultural assessment-intervention process is the clarifying of cultural orientations at the outset, especially for the person or group being assessed. This focus reconstructs the entire assessment process, directly evaluating the adequacy of assessment protocols for a clear assessment purpose with (a) specific person(s) being assessed in a particular situation. When client cultural orientation fits with available assessment protocols and instruments, then analytic strategies such as problem-solving or biopsychosocial models are likely to be helpful. (Power considerations are still important in guiding assessment practices, of course.) But when client cultural orientation reflects emic features that constrain the viability of typical protocols or instruments, then more holistic strategies need to be mobilized in the assessment process to identify relevant contexts and to adapt assessment protocols accordingly. We turn now to descriptions of contextual paradigms of assessment that emphasize holistic approaches.

Contextual Assessment: Purpose and Holism

Stewart (2010, p. 190) defines assessment as "using formal and/or informal techniques to accurately describe the psychological, social, biological, and cultural factors that influence the behaviour of" people, families, or groups. (We have replaced Stewart's term *individuals* in this passage to emphasize the range of possibilities and settings for assessment practice in counselling psychology.) He then formulates a core outcome of assessment as "accurate and comprehensive description of the individual within the individual's context." Focusing on individuals-in-context or families-in-context, for instance, helps to clarify assessment purposes as shaped by settings and relationships jointly with the person(s) being assessed. Clarifying purposes, in turn, helps to shape selection of appropriate units for assessment (person, family, group, etc.) and of relevant constructs (climate, relationship quality, introversion, etc.). Contextual models are holistic in formulation, so "the psychological, social, biological, and cultural factors" are listed not as separate dimensions or features, but as aspects of dynamic processes that are intrinsically interconnected and thus open for alternative formulations (cf. Beatch et al., 2009).

The heart of contextual assessment – tracing contexts as a holistic means of clarifying assessment principles and purposes – contrasts with analytic stances typical of many models of assessment. Analytic frameworks increase the potential for misreading contextual models in compartmentalized, segmented fashions. This potential for misreading is present even in formulations of contextual assessment models, which emphasize holistic paradigms to counter compartmentalization. For instance, listing psychological, social, biological, and cultural factors in definitions such as Stewart's can be taken to imply *necessary* ways to trace *exhaustive, universal* features of assessment practices – in contradiction to contextual principles sustaining a plurality of alternative versions of holistic formulations. Without presuming necessity or uniformity, Stewart's list can be treated as distinguishable dimensions or facets to be used in guiding practice by suggesting different assessment activities of value for a particular assessment. The case vignettes and illustrations employed by Stewart are offered to clarify a range of possibilities for different sources of useful information. Typically, then, insights can be integrated from multiple sources to approximate a more complete grasp of a person or group being assessed, while recognizing organic and dynamic interconnections that jointly shape those multiple sources of information. Again, short vignettes and cases illustrate processes for combining observations in helpful ways.

The practices employed by professionals to distinguish aspects of the person (e.g., Stewart's list) typically draw upon frameworks and procedures established within mainstream disciplines as adequate ways for understanding human life and functioning. Stewart's use of this list is well connected to professional literature in just this manner. Moreover, a guiding principle emphasized by Stewart is the value of adapting the distinctions, activities, and frameworks in ways that fit more adequately with each particular person, setting, and assessment purpose. Within mainstream professional environments, the deployment of established distinctions, activities, and frameworks in flexible ways is typically assumed to be possible and adequate for the full range of people, settings, and communities encountered in the professional practice of assessment. It is doubtful that many mainstream professionals would hesitate to use a list such as "psychological, social, biological, and cultural factors."

Unfortunately, a strategy of "flexible application of established practices and distinctions" can become difficult to critique if established practices or models are presumed to be uniformly applicable or necessary. Even Stewart's list of psychological, social, biological, and cultural factors can be reified in professional and academic settings in ways that undermine the core requirement of flexible, adaptable practices. In Dana's approach to multicultural assessment mentioned above, he addressed this concern by performing a cultural orientation assessment early in an assessment process (2005, 2008). This strategy opens assessment practice to reformulation in the service of sensitivity to contexts. One model of Indigenous assessment (Zolner, 2000) helps to trace the horizons involved and is discussed a little later in this chapter. What follows, therefore, is a selection of models that together demonstrate a variety of possibilities for contextual assessment paradigms.

INDIGENOUS ASSESSMENT PRACTICES Theresa Zolner (2000, 2003) has provided a rich exposition of profound possibilities for openness that are available through these early phases of professional assessment practices. In Zolner's work, Dana's (2008) first step in assessment, "cultural identity assessment," is transformed into taking "a step over to their worldview." Through the documentation of her collaborations with Sandra Antimoyoo and Colin Rope in the context of work with the Health and Social Development Commission (HSDC) of the Federation of Saskatchewan Indian Nations (FSIN; Zolner, 2000), Zolner goes beyond exercises with vignettes and case analyses to demonstrate a fundamental reframing of assessment activities required for successfully engaging First Nations people and communities. Through this demonstration, she clarifies how professionals can prevent recolonizing First Nations people through mainstream practices of professional assessment. In her dissertation project, Zolner asked, "How can I come to understand a First Nations perspective on assessment and what it means for me, as a member of mainstream, academic Psychology, to perform an assessment with a First Nations person?" (p. xi) And in several publications, she shared further implications (e.g., 2003, 2004) of postcolonial engagement with traditional First Nations worldviews for professional and academic practice.

In this work, Zolner (2000) shares a "deep learning" about the heritage of First Nations peoples in collaboration with HSDC partners, demonstrating ways in which a relational matrix of respect profoundly transforms the work of assessment. She describes the perspective she developed through this work as standing at a point between three cultures – First Nations, Ukrainian (her own heritage), and psychological. That is, a first phase of engagement involves holistic positions reflecting heritages of the person being assessed and the assessor being jointly addressed, while examining the formal and informal resources of psychology and professional assessment. "The psychologist must [also] be willing to enter into a process of self-examination in order to understand what beliefs, heritage, training, and experiences he or she is personally bringing to the assessment process" (p. iii). The range and depth of conversations presented (2000) go far beyond the partial summaries available in vignettes and case summaries of typical textbooks and workshops, displaying processes in deep intercultural learning. These conversations concretely embody (a) reflexive awareness and critique of professional training and practices, (b) reflective tracing of bicultural trajectories for multiple participants, (c) confrontations of colonial and postcolonial voices, and (d) pathways of engagement imbued with contexts of respect. In short, Zolner offers a template for reorienting professional practices in ways that help avoid recolonizing.

Zolner's (2000, 2003) template for respectful professional assessment of First Nations people does not yield a uniform set of practices. Instead, the documentation of her own journey offers direction for each of us as professionals to pursue deep learning as the core of holistic postcolonial practice: to learn about First Nations people and their heritage in relationship, to learn about our own heritage in conversation, and to learn about the cultures undergirding professional practices of assessment as they connect with intercultural learning. Through her recognition of the embeddedness of assessment practices within professional cultures, Zolner highlights the coherence of professional assessment with the institutions of counselling, education, and health care. This emphasis reminds the professional community of the rich and expanding literature on counselling and psychology being authored by members of Aboriginal communities (e.g., McCabe, 2007; McCormick, 1997; Stewart, 2009). Thus holistic templates for Indigenous assessment like that promoted by Zolner recognize the immediate and direct relevance of the broad proposals for Indigenizing psychology, counselling, and health care for assessment practice. Whether or not a particular principle or guideline is formulated as an "assessment practice," accounts of transformed professional activities in close concert with Aboriginal peoples can foster parallel transformations of formal and informal features of assessment. The holistic nature of worldviews and First Nations community traditions is such that partitions among disciplines, professions, or institutions often become secondary to maintaining fidelity of care and integrity of relationships in partnership practices.

CULTURALLY SENSITIVE ASSESSMENT While Zolner cultivated contextual sensitivity to address assessment among First Nations people, Sinacore-Guinn (1995b) focused instead on cultivating contextual sensitivity pertaining to a widespread professional practice: diagnosis. She developed pedagogical tools for counsellors-in-training to cultivate contextual sensitivity to culture, gender, and

diversity issues when distinguishing psychopathology from problems in living that are indicative of stressful situations rather than
dysfunctional coping. By situating the diagnostic process within
larger considerations of cultural values, cultural systems and struggles, and encounters with traumatic events, counsellors-in-training
are helped to distinguish dysfunctional or exaggerated coping from
behaviour that reflects alternative frameworks of meaning. Moreover, her pedagogical model directly engages the backgrounds of
educators and graduate students while highlighting the flexibility
required to address intersections among multiple social identities of
clients and professionals. In this way, her "diagnostic window" serves
a parallel function in professional education, as does Zolner's deep
learning, while focusing more broadly at a level that encompasses
multiple dimensions of culture and diversity.

ECOLOGICAL ASSESSMENT   Alderson (2003, 2010) proposed a
theory of development called the Ecological Model of Gay Male
Identity (EMGMI). As an ecological model, the EMGMI is holistic
in that "it seeks to identify all influences affecting the person ...
including internal factors (physical and psychological) and external
factors (social and environmental)" (2010, p. 403). The model
focuses on coming out, which Alderson refers to as "the process of
self-identifying as gay." Within the model, Alderson proposed three
developmental stages: (a) before coming out, (b) during coming out,
and (c) beyond coming out. Each stage has its own processes.

  According to Alderson (2010), many clients, especially soon after
they come out, wonder about their sexual identity (i.e., whether they
are gay, lesbian, or bisexual) and whether their sexual orientation is
consistent with their label. Because sexual identity is self-chosen, it
can be assessed by simply asking clients what labels they use to
describe their sexual identity. Alderson suggested that the ecological
model of gay male identity might help the counsellor and client
make an assessment of sexual orientation. Alderson provided a series
of questions to assess sexual behaviour, sexual cognition, and sexual
affect based on the ecological model. Alternatively, he suggested the
counsellor might use a modified version of a sexual orientation scale
developed by Shively and De Cecco (as cited in Alderson, 2010).
Alderson advised the use of caution in using some of the available
quantitative measures with gay clients, as they may contain examples of heterosexism or some form of heterosexist bias; have

inappropriate theoretical underpinnings that do not apply to all gay men; or be of questionable validity for use with this group.

CONSTRUCTIVIST ASSESSMENT Peavy's (1996, 1997) Socio-Dynamic Counselling provides another important example of a contextualist approach to counselling and assessment. Emerging out of his dissatisfaction with existing theories of career counselling specifically and counselling generally in a time of rapid social change and labour market uncertainty, Peavy's intent was to develop a theory of counselling to meet the needs of people struggling with the doubts, uncertainties, and conflicts of the postmodern era. His theory, grounded in the human sciences and a constructivist perspective, views individuals as capable of constructing their own lives based on what has personal meaning for them. Drawing on developing ideas in counselling and vocational development including narrative, holism, voice, multiple realities, difference, social construction, and unpredictability, Peavy attempted to build a new form of counselling focusing on counselling skills and techniques that emphasize the client's search for meaning; life planning; identification of client strengths, values, and assumptions; and the use of mapping, metaphor, and mindfulness in helping clients tell their stories. A major assumption in this approach is that "individuals are always situated, or are always socially located, in a specific context and thus will give voice to their concerns from that particular perspective ... As contexts change, stories change. As situations change, so do we" (Peavy, 1997, p. 43).

In outlining his approach to career-related assessment, Peavy (1996) stated:

It should be borne in mind that two primary objectives of constructivist assessment are 1) to generate personal meaning and 2) to promote reflection on the implications of both new and old self-knowledge in relation to the concern under consideration (such as career planning). New meaning and reflection are part of the self construction and reconstruction process. (p. 11)

Peavy (1997) believed that most of the time, assessment is best done through dialogue and interview methods rather than through tests of general characteristics that do not capture individual uniqueness. With this strategy in mind, he developed a set of eight clusters of questions, which help to guide the counsellor in assessing the client's experience, concern, and preferred counselling plan. Further, he suggested that there are various activities that the counsellor and client can engage in during the counselling session that have an assessment function, including mapping the client's life-space; developing a lifeline of critical events and experiences in the client's life; using meaning-creating questions; reflecting on personal narratives and life stories and other forms of autobiographical work (e.g., journaling, writing letters, self-characterization); conceptual and word-sculpturing; and portfolio assessment (Peavy, 1996, 1997).

Constructivists vary in their advocacy for and against the use of formal tests, and in general, constructivist counselling makes much less use of testing than some other counselling approaches. As Stewart (2010) points out, the use of formal tests can be adapted to contextualist assessment paradigms. And Zolner makes clear a cultural inertia in formal practices of assessment that can deflect cultural sensitivity. Although there are a variety of reasons for this, one of the major objections lies in, for example, an assumption that traits are universal and that test results can be usefully interpreted regardless of context across all developmental and social identities; this can readily lead to contextual insensitivity. Peavy (1996) called for diversity in career-related assessment and a cautionary attitude toward the use of standardized tests and questionnaires as assessment tools in this area. He did, however, see a place for questionnaire-type assessment tools: (a) tools such as the Myers-Briggs Type Indicator (Myers & McCaulley, 1985) could be used as devices for assisting clients to explore their own life experiences and ways of thinking about those experiences and their reactions to items on the test; and (b) tools such as the Career Beliefs Inventory (Krumboltz, 1994) could be used to help clients consider the implications of their own interests, values, attitudes, dispositions, and preferences as well as the implications and meaning of these beliefs for the conduct of their everyday activities. Neimeyer and Neimeyer (1993) and Stewart (2010) provided a discussion of the various ways in which tests and other formal assessment tools can be used by construct.

According to Peavy (1997), constructivist counsellors rarely use the concept of diagnosis, and then only with caution, as they have concerns about the stigma and disempowerment that can result from such categorization and labelling, along with the focus on deficits rather than assets. This is contrary to the aim of assessment

(planning) in constructivist counselling, which is "to open up ave-
nues of movement, promote empowerment, support transitions, and
assist the client to gain eligibility for more participation in social
life" (Peavy, 1996, p. 11).

PSYCHOMETRICS   The formal and psychometric aspects of assessment present a complementary set of difficulties, challenges, and
opportunities for contextual assessment that are also being addressed
by scholars and professionals who adopt models congruent with
counselling psychology in Canada. For example, the work of Bruno
Zumbo and his colleagues on revising and extending unified validity
theory (UVT; e.g., Hubley & Zumbo, 2011; Zumbo, 2009) exem-
plifies current developments in psychometrics that directly embody
priorities for contextual assessment paradigms. Moving beyond traditional psychometric preoccupations with individual differences
between individuals, they integrate the theory of multilevel constructs into UVT. And since values have implications for all facets
of test development (theory, construct definition, test construction,
and test use), thoughtful examination of assumptions and values as
they are embodied in formal psychometric procedures is needed.
Furthermore, the meaning of test scores is directly informed by the
intended and unintended social consequences, the intended and
unintended personal consequences, and the social and personal side
effects of legitimate test interpretation. UVT is not addressing test
misuse, but rather the legitimate use of formal tests in the promotion
of social and personal change. Thus careful analysis of psychometric
theory shows direct implications of values, intended and unintended
social consequences, and multilevel constructs for formal test interpretation and use. At times, UVT involves thorough examination of
technical topics such as construct- and test-equivalence. In other
cases, the focus is more on conceptual background or neglected
assumptions behind the work of test development and use. In all
cases, Hubley and Zumbo's revised unified view of validity and validation invites professionals and researchers "to be more reflective,
more thoughtful, and more aware of how values, theory, practice,
and consequences are linked" (p. 229).
    Additional models of assessment with particular relevance for
adaptation by counselling psychologists in Canada include therapeutic and collaborative assessment models (Meyers et al., 2001;

see also Fischer & Finn, 2008). By refocusing traditional problem-solving models through explicit examination of values and consequences, not only is validity enhanced but also the relational integrity of the professionals with test-takers and other stakeholders is strengthened.

ETHICS IN ASSESSMENT

Fundamental to any professional practice, regardless of which model or approach is used, is the requirement that practitioners adhere to principles of ethical conduct and professional behaviour set by the professional and regulatory bodies of which they are members. This is no less true in the practice of assessment in counselling and counselling psychology. Within Canada, professional associations such as the CPA and the provincial colleges of psychologists, as well as the Canadian Counselling and Psychotherapy Association (CCPA), have adopted codes of ethics and standards of practice, which govern all professional activities in which their members are engaged. Such codes articulate principles, values, and standards to guide members whether they are engaged in direct service, research, teaching, supervision, consultation, administration, or any other role related to the discipline. For example, the *Canadian Code of Ethics for Psychologists* (CPA, 2000) articulates principles in four areas (respect for the dignity of persons, responsible caring, integrity in relationships, and responsibility to society) and then specifies values and ethical standards pertaining to each area. The CPA *Code* is also intended to serve as an umbrella document for the development of codes of conduct or other more specific codes or schedules (e.g., guidelines for the provision of psychological services, control and use of tests, child custody assessment). Similarly, the CCPA code (CCPA, 2007) articulates principles in the areas of beneficence, fidelity, nonmaleficence, autonomy, justice, and social interest. The CCPA code contains six main sections that address the following areas: professional responsibility; counselling relationships; consulting and private practice; evaluation and assessment; research and publications; and counsellor education, training, and supervision. Relevant ethical mandates are outlined in the articles in each section. While the principles and ethical mandates cross areas of practice, there are specific mandates/guidelines in the area of evaluation and assessment with respect to

(a) general orientation of the client, (b) informing the client about the purposes and results of an evaluation and assessment, (c) the counsellors' evaluation and assessment competence, (d) administrative and supervisory conditions, (e) use of technology, (f) the appropriateness of the evaluation or assessment, (g) reporting evaluation and assessment results, (h) releasing evaluation and assessment data, (i) maintaining the integrity of evaluation and assessment instruments and procedures, (j) demonstrating sensitivity to diversity when assessing and evaluating, and (k) ensuring the integrity and security of evaluation and assessment instruments and procedures consistent with any legal and contractual obligations. These have been further addressed in standards of practice (CCPA, 2011) and in case studies demonstrating application of the ethical guidelines for evaluation and assessment (Haverkamp, 2006). Both the CPA and the CCPA have adopted models of ethical decision-making to help guide practitioners in their everyday conduct, thinking, and planning, and in the resolution of ethical dilemmas.

SUMMARY

Counselling psychologists in Canada promote and adapt assessment approaches from a variety of sources in manners that cohere with the values, priorities, and principles framed in the disciplinary definition. Counsellors, educators, psychologists, and career development professionals have developed contextually sensitive strategies and resources for engaging the intersections of social identities in the lives of clients and community members in Canada today. These frameworks display complementary and overlapping directions for guiding professional practice, research, and professional education. The range and diversity of promising projects is quite impressive. The Unified Validity Theory of Zumbo and his colleagues is enhancing and promoting developments in psychometric theory, while the profoundly transformative practices of collaboration are documented by Zolner, Peavy, and their colleagues. Creative integration into professional development and training resources emerges repeatedly, as shown by Stewart, Sinacore, and their colleagues.

One of the major limitations of this chapter is the failure of our attempts to collaborate with a partner familiar with the Francophone literature on assessments and testing in Canada. Disconnections in the patterns of contextual assessment models seem to reflect the discipline, domain of application, setting, and social diversity of those being assessed. It may well be that Francophone literature may address distinctive intersections of consideration that are not well disseminated in Anglophone literature. Nor have we addressed substantial English-language literatures on bilingual assessment, bilingualism, dynamic assessment, or disabilities assessment, among other gaps. The list of omissions is lengthy and incomplete, in part reflecting the loose integration among many domains of research and practice. One value of noting the many directions needing attention is to reiterate a key point with which we opened this chapter. Assessment in counselling psychology is not being addressed consistently and systematically in the literature despite the social and human significance of this topic. We hope this brief review will foster additional attention to this area, thus facilitating more effective and widespread observance of the advocacy and empowerment principles guiding the field.

Training and Supervision
in Counselling Psychology

MARILYN FITZPATRICK, SHARON CAIRNS,
AND LOUISE OVERINGTON

EMERGING ISSUES AND CHALLENGES
IN TRAINING AND SUPERVISION

There are currently five doctoral-level counselling psychology programs in Canada. They are located within faculties of education in the University of Alberta, the University of British Columbia, the University of Calgary, McGill University, and the University of Toronto. The programs all operate within the Boulder model scientist-practitioner framework and are accredited by the Canadian Psychological Association (CPA); the University of British Columbia and McGill University programs are also accredited (until 2015) by the American Psychological Association (APA). While the spirit of the Boulder model is to allow program-to-program differences in how training is offered, all programs share certain challenges based on the shifting landscape of professional training in psychology. Canadian counselling psychology programs must respond effectively to the challenge of these shifts.

In this chapter, we will focus on three important aspects of training and supervision that are of current concern in counselling psychology in Canada: student funding, evidence-based practice, and gatekeeping. Each of these challenges bears on how Canadian programs attract and retain the best students, the nature of training in counselling psychology, and how the programs ensure that the students they accept attain professional competence. The first issue – funding – has become a greater challenge during the financial crisis, as tuition costs increase, university budgets are squeezed, and available tri-council funding is diminishing. These shifts create a climate of funding uncertainty for students. The second issue – training in evidence-based practice – is part of an emerging reality within all health-related disciplines. Because counselling psychology doctoral programs endorse the scientist-practitioner model, they must develop methods of training that are consistent with new definitions of what constitutes evidence in the discipline. Finally, while the issue of gatekeeping is not new, it is one that urgently requires clarification. This issue was the subject of extensive discussion at the Inaugural Canadian Counselling Psychology Conference in 2010. In spite of this, very little Canadian research literature addresses gatekeeping issues. Related to these three issues, this chapter will review the current situation, begin a dialogue about present challenges, and propose some next steps.

THE CHALLENGE OF FUNDING

In considering the major challenges to counselling psychology training in Canada, funding may not be the issue that springs most readily to mind. However, if the viability of the discipline is to be judged on the contribution of its researchers to knowledge and the contribution of its practitioners to the health and well-being of Canadians, our training programs must attract a diverse group of highly competent students who are interested in the foundational elements of our discipline: research and practice. The students who are accepted to programs need the means to complete their training successfully – including funding. To attract the best students, we must fund them at rates that are comparable to other schools that train helping professionals. American research suggests that graduate school applicants make decisions about where to attend based on school rankings and financial aid (Rosenberg, 2008). Even more convincing is evidence that indicates that funding is a major factor in retaining graduate students (Guraraj, Heilig, & Somers, 2010). Although no Canadian studies have investigated these issues, we would suggest that sufficient funding is, in all likelihood, as important an element of graduate success in Canada as it is in the US.

Successfully completing programs means more, however, than just graduation. It also means having the time to explore the discipline, and to absorb its literature, its ethos, and its values. Funding is important in this vein because it ensures that students do not have to work in ways that pull their focus away from training. The requirements of the C P A for accrediting psychology programs (C P A, 2011) and the requirements of funding agencies across Canada limit the hours that students may work outside their program of study, in recognition of the importance of maintaining student focus on program requirements during the degree years.

Finally, funding students reflects one of the core commitments of counselling psychologists – social justice (Beatch et al., 2009). Recent empirical findings suggest that the social justice commitment of our trainees is influenced by their perceptions of their training environments over and above their personal orientation to activism (Beer, Spanierman, Greene, & Todd, 2012). If we want the trainees of today to be counselling psychologists committed to social justice tomorrow, we need to model this commitment in our programs. In terms of financial aid, this means creating funding models that give students who are not economically privileged access to counselling psychology graduate training.

The Current Funding Context

COSTS OF GRADUATE EDUCATION   Canadian counselling psychology programs operate in a context in which university education is subsidized. Graduate education in Canada is still substantially less expensive than in the United States. Data from the A P A Centre for Workforce Studies (A P A, 2010) indicate that in a recently reported year (2008–09), the median tuition cost of doctoral education in psychology in Canada was $5,249 for residents compared to $7,104 at American public and $27,072 at American private institutions; the median for non-residents in Canadian universities was $10,800. Clearly Canadian universities remain less costly than their American counterparts; however, tuition is only part of the cost of education. C P A-accredited counselling psychology programs are located in Vancouver, Toronto, Calgary, Montreal, and Edmonton. Toronto, Vancouver, and Calgary are the cities with the highest cost of living in Canada; Montreal and Edmonton are less expensive but still rank as costly places to live in Canada (Schwarz, 2008).

In addition, professional programs are typically longer than other graduate programs because they have both research and applied components. A recent survey of accredited counselling psychology programs in Canada indicated that course credit requirements range from forty-eight to ninety-one at the doctoral level; practicum hours were a minimum of 600 and internship an additional 1600 hours minimum (Haverkamp, Robertson, Cairns, & Bedi, 2011). Having completed an undergraduate degree, students in counselling psychology programs in Canada will typically spend an additional two years completing an MA and invest four to five years, or more, to graduate with a PhD. The commitment to graduate training in counselling psychology is a substantial investment for students. In order for counselling psychology programs to support students in this investment, funds need to be allocated for both their research and their applied training throughout the duration of the degree.

RESEARCH FUNDING   Although every form of aid helps to retain graduate students, a recent American study indicates that receiving grant money (as opposed to funding through research or teaching assistantships) is the largest predictor of student success in graduate school regardless of the background characteristics of the students (Guraraj, Heilig, & Somers, 2010). Grant or fellowship funding allows students to remain focused on their own research without devoting hours as research assistants to projects that may be outside their research area or working as teaching assistants in courses that may not relate to their program of study. The major sources of fellowships in Canada are university fellowship programs and government agencies at both the federal and the provincial levels.

In 2011–12, funding in CPA-accredited doctoral programs was generally composed of packages that were combinations of fellowships and money allocated from research assistantships or teaching assistantships. OISE, University of Toronto, guaranteed funding for four years, the University of Calgary for two years, and McGill University for one year. The University of Alberta and the University of British Columbia did not guarantee funding to all students but had packages for individual students that ranged from zero to four years. One of the factors that may influence this funding picture is the fact that there are no undergraduate counselling programs in these universities. While clinical psychology programs are typically located in psychology departments that have large undergraduate enrolments, counselling psychology programs are located within faculties of education. The undergraduate programs in faculties of education typically train students as teachers, whereas students in counselling psychology graduate programs have often completed their undergraduate training in psychology departments. Although the funding models vary across universities, it may be that the large pools of funds from undergraduate teaching that are available to psychology graduate departments to train clinical psychology graduate students are not typically available to the counselling psychology programs located within faculties of education.

In addition to university support, students in counselling psychology programs typically look to federal and provincial agencies for funding to support their research. The agency that has historically funded students in counselling psychology programs has been the Social Sciences and Humanities Research Council (SSHRC). In 2011–12, SSHRC funded 10.5 percent of the doctoral awards applications it received (SSHRC, 2012). Since 2009, health-related counselling research – for example, research in psychotherapy – has been moved under the mandate of the Canadian Institutes of Health Research (CIHR). In 2011–12, the CIHR funded 12 percent of the 1,512 applications it received for the Canada Graduate Fellowship (CIHR University Delegate, 2012). In addition, international students are usually ineligible for Canadian agency funding. Given the value of inclusiveness and diversity to counselling psychology, excluding international students means that Canadian programs may make offers to students who will receive inadequate support. Furthermore, out-of-province students may be ineligible for provincial agency fellowships. Clearly these funding levels leave a large proportion of students without support.

For students to prosper in this competitive environment, they must have excellent grades and references, but also convincingly demonstrate the ability to develop a strong research proposal and to be productive in the research domain. In order to win funding, counselling psychology faculty members must be both productive researchers and superior research mentors. Currently, students in counselling psychology programs perceive that they receive higher levels of socioemotional mentoring than their counterparts in other psychology graduate programs. However, experimental psychology students report greater levels of instrumental mentoring, and it is instrumental support that correlates with higher levels of research productivity (Taylor & Niemeyer, 2009). The situation on both the university and the funding agency fronts indicates that research funding of counselling psychology students in Canada is a major challenge.

FUNDING FOR CLINICAL TRAINING In CPA-accredited programs, students are either required or encouraged to complete internships accredited by the CPA or the APA (Haverkamp et al., 2011). In order to attain these accreditations, internship sites must pay interns during their pre-doctoral internship year. Although this would appear to solve the problem of student funding during the final year of training, the situation is more complex. There are not enough accredited internships in Canada and the United States to accommodate the number of students who apply for training. A survey conducted by the Canadian Council of Professional Psychology Programs (CCPPP) in 2012, and reported at their annual meeting, indicated that Canadian students typically stay in Canada. As there are currently only three accredited counselling psychology sites in Canada, most counselling psychology students will complete their training either at accredited sites that are not strongly oriented to counselling psychology or at non-accredited sites that may or may not pay them.

The history of recent efforts to address the internship shortage includes a meeting in September 2008 of several stakeholder groups in the US. The result of the meeting was a proposal that had eleven action steps and identified the organizations that needed to take action for each step. One action item was to create new/funded internships (Grus, McCutcheon, & Berry, 2011). To facilitate that process, the APA is seeking public comment on policy change concerning a stepped process of accrediting new internship sites. The proposed first level would allow sites to seek accreditation eligibility status prior to accepting interns. The second would grant contingent accreditation while the site collected outcome data. Contingent accreditation would confer accreditation status on the site and its interns. The third proposed level is full accreditation.

In Canada, an ad-hoc Committee for Counselling Psychology Pre-doctoral Internships with representatives from each of the doctoral programs in Canada was formed in July 2011. The committee members represented accredited programs in counselling psychology from across Canada. Committee members conducted a series of interviews with the directors of training at accredited and constructed (non-accredited) internship sites across Canada. The majority of constructed sites have been training students for many years (range seven to twenty). At the time of the survey, two sites were actively pursuing accreditation, although most expressed interest in belonging to a counselling psychology consortium. The sites recognized many of the benefits of accreditation, such as attracting high-quality interns, improving program quality, and supporting the development of staff expertise; however, substantial barriers to accreditation were also noted. Barriers clustered around the resources required: financial costs and time costs to complete and retain accreditation and the lack of university resources in support of the process. The committee identified two sets of recommendations that it communicated to the CPA's Counselling Psychology Section at its Halifax meeting in June 2012. This first set of recommendations focused on simplifying the application process and mentoring sites to complete it. The Counselling Psychology Section voted to request that the CPA Accreditation Panel consider implementing a stepped accreditation process similar to that of the APA reported above. A list of doctoral and internship training directors who have volunteered to assist local agencies in developing internships has been compiled and is available (Council of Chairs of Training Councils, n.d.). Currently the list contains only six names from Canada. Training directors with expertise in accreditation in different Canadian areas might add their names to this list in order to extend the reach of this initiative across the country. The second set of recommendations of the ad-hoc committee focused on outreach activities for the CPA and the Special Section for Counselling Psychology to educate sites about the benefits of accreditation. Well-organized and sustained efforts are needed to realize the objectives of these recommendations. The CPA Section requested that the ad-hoc Counselling Psychology Pre-doctoral Internships Committee become a permanent committee.

Clearly funding is a core element of graduate success and a challenge that our profession must continue to address to ensure the success of counselling psychology training in Canada. Funding is needed to support both the research and the applied components of student preparation. There are no magic solutions for increasing this support. However, sustained attention to the issues, the commitment of counselling psychology directors to raising the awareness of the problem and of faculty members to increasing their fellowship mentoring skills, and partnerships of accrediting bodies with programs to create more accredited and funded sites are needed to improve the funding situation in Canadian counselling psychology training. Research also is needed to investigate the optimal levels of funding that lead to success in counselling psychology graduate programs. As governments in Canada already make an enormous investment in graduate education, such research would be a useful tool in lobbying to increase funding levels in order to maximize the return on the investments in education.

EVIDENCE-BASED PRACTICE AND CANADIAN COUNSELLING PSYCHOLOGY

Worldwide, the field of mental health is experiencing ever greater demands for accountability and an increased focus on demonstrable treatment outcomes. Internationally, the notion of evidence-based practice in psychology (E B P P) has strengthened over the last decade. In the United Kingdom, governing bodies have stressed the need for evidence-based practices in order to fulfil the effectiveness agenda (Lucock et al., 2003), and the Australian Psychological Society (A P S) has endorsed an evidence-based practice model for psychological services in 2003 (A P S, 2003, 2010). In the United States, the A P A embraced E B P P, defining it as "the integration of the best available research with clinical expertise in the context of patient characteristics, culture, and preferences" (A P A, 2006, p. 273).

In Canada, C P A accreditation standards for doctoral-level psychology training programs mandate that students receive training in evidence-based interventions (C P A, 2011). Former C P A president David Dozois created a task force on Evidence-Based Practice of Psychological Treatments (E B P P T; Dozois, 2011a). This task force has released a document with an initial statement on E B P P T, seeking feedback from Canadian clinicians and researchers in order to reach consensus on a final definition (C P A, 2012). The proposed definition of E B P P T states that "psychologists apply their knowledge of the best available research in the context of specific client characteristics, cultural backgrounds, and treatment preferences ... respect for the dignity of persons is imperative in evidence-based practice ... communication and collaboration between the psychologist and the client is crucial in the process of achieving informed consent and reflects best practice based on current evidence" (CPA, 2012, p. 1).

It is important to differentiate evidence-based practice from the widely known paradigm of empirically supported treatments (ESTs). ESTs refer to those treatments that have been tested under controlled trials and have produced clinically significant change (Chambless et al., 1996; Chambless & Ollendick, 2001). Initially, counselling psychologists in Canada were part of the controversy surrounding ESTs. The randomized controlled trial (RCT) designs of the supporting studies generally fail to account for culture and have raised concerns related to the applicability and generalizability of findings. Indeed, clinicians seem to pay little attention to the results of ESTs (Stewart & Chambless, 2010). Conversely, evidence-based practice takes culture into account. It is a "process by which the best available evidence available is used to make optimal clinical decisions" (Dozois, 2012, p. 7) and is not limited to one source of evidence (e.g., RCTs and meta-analyses). This distinction is particularly relevant for counselling psychology, due to its emphasis on viewing the client as a unique individual requiring treatment that takes into account a diverse array of factors, rather than following a one-size-fits-all approach.

As with every paradigm shift there is a certain amount of uncertainty and discomfort (Hunsley, 2007); however, although controversy still surrounds ESTs, EBP is firmly establishing itself as a necessary and accepted part of Canadian counselling psychology. For example, the CPA Counselling Psychology Section (Section 24) definition recognizes the role of evidence-based practice, stating that counselling psychologists "employ a variety of evidence-based and theoretical approaches grounded in psychological knowledge" (Bedi et al., 2011, p. 13). Additionally, the practice of counselling psychology is founded on collaboration, a focus on individual client characteristics, and culturally competent practice. Clearly, the core elements of evidence-based practice strongly resonate with the core values of Canadian counselling psychology. However, moving from the level of values and aspirations to the real world of practice is complex.

To date, there is limited scholarship on evidence-based practice in a Canadian context. Although the CPA is only now in the process of defining EBPPT, a recent edition of *Psynopsis* (a CPA

publication) dedicated to discussing E B P P T in a Canadian setting
and several publications by Canadian counselling psychologists
(Hiebert, Domene, & Buchannan, 2012; Overington & Ionita, 2012)
suggest that interest in E B P is growing in counselling psychology in
Canada. Undoubtedly over the next decade much more attention
will be devoted to the area as it applies to Canadian psychology.
Until then we must rely on scholars in other parts of the world.
Although the following sections dedicated to E B P draw on Canadian
resources when possible, primarily US sources are cited, as those
are the sources available. Given the "extensive exposure to American
C N P S Y and psychotherapy literature" (Beatch et al., 2009, p. 34)
the US arguably has a strong impact on Canadian counselling psychology. Although E B P is composed of many parts, we are going to
emphasize one specific aspect: systematic monitoring of client
change. In the following sections, we will argue that ongoing monitoring is both an essential part of E B P and a practice in line with
training future Canadian counselling psychologists.

Progress Monitoring Measures: An Evidence-Based Approach

Research indicates that practitioners rely on clinical judgment over
empirical evidence in assessing client progress and making treatment
decisions (e.g., Raine et al., 2004; Stewart & Chambless, 2010).
However, there is evidence that judgment can be flawed (e.g., Garb,
2005) and that clinicians are particularly poor at detecting clients
who are not progressing or, in fact, deteriorating (Hannan et al., 2005;
Hatfield, McCullough, Frantz, & Krieger, 2010). Although psychotherapy outcomes are generally positive, deterioration rates range
from five to ten percent in clinical trials (Lambert & Ogles, 2004) and
from three to fourteen percent in routine care (Hansen, Lambert, &
Forman, 2002). There is considerable room for improvement.

A promising method of helping counselling psychologists to identify deterioration and potentially prevent clinical errors is through
the use of standardized tools referred to as Progress Monitoring
(P M) measures. P M measures are instruments that clinicians imple-
ment on a regular basis to track client progress (Lambert &
Shimokawa, 2011; Overington & Ionita, 2012; Whipple & Lambert,
2011). These brief, psychometrically sound tools provide clinicians
working from various theoretical orientations with information

regarding changes in client functioning (Lueger & Barkham, 2010). PM measures generally assess several domains, including psychological symptoms (e.g., anxiety, depression, sleep), subjective well-being (e.g., life satisfaction) and overall functioning (e.g., school, work, sexual functioning). There are a growing number of studies linking the use of systematic feedback to improved treatment outcomes (e.g., Miller, Duncan, Sorrell, & Brown, 2005; Reese, Norsworthy, & Rowlands, 2009; Shimokawa, Lambert, & Smart, 2010). PM measures are increasingly recognized as important tools that contribute to an evidence-based practice (e.g., Higa-McMillan, Powell, Daleiden, & Mueller, 2011; Hunsley, 2007; Lambert & Cattani, 2012; Whipple & Lambert, 2011).

The use of PM measures has been specifically endorsed by the CPA: "psychologists should be prepared to alter the treatment being provided based on data from ongoing treatment monitoring (including both in-session and between-session client reactions and changes to symptoms and functioning)" (CPA, 2012, p. 4). Our values as a discipline, the stance of our flagship professional organization, and the empirical evidence point to the idea that progress monitoring should become an important part of evidence-based practice in counselling psychology in Canada. For this to happen, students need training and supervision in PM measures and usage.

Progress Monitoring and Counselling Psychology Training

Current research indicates that students who are trained to use PM measures have improved treatment outcomes compared to those who do not receive feedback from these tools (Reese, Usher, et al., 2009). Specifically, trainees who received PM feedback were almost twice as effective ($d = .92$) as trainees without feedback ($d = .23$). They also improved more in the second semester of training (from $d = .70$ to $d = .97$) than those in the no-feedback condition (from $d = .30$ to $d = .37$). All trainees experienced an increased sense of self-efficacy from training; however, trainees who received feedback had self-efficacy scores that correlated with client outcome. We need to consider how the training of our students can be organized to realize these benefits and still remain faithful to our core values and aspirations. Canadian counselling psychology aspirations have already been defined.

Counselling psychologists bring a collaborative, developmental, multicultural, and wellness perspective to their research and practice ... Counselling psychology adheres to an integrated set of core values: (a) counselling psychologists view individuals as agents of their own change and regard an individual's pre-existing strengths and resourcefulness and the therapeutic relationship as central mechanisms of change; (b) the counselling psychology approach to assessment, diagnosis, and case conceptualization is holistic and client-centred. (Bedi et al., 2011, p. 130)

While we recognize that the definition is holistic, for the sake of clarity, we will consider how the individual elements fit with training in progress monitoring.

TRAINING IN THE THERAPEUTIC ALLIANCE AND COLLABO-RATION   The therapeutic alliance is both a cornerstone of counselling psychology and a key variable contributing to positive therapeutic outcomes (e.g., Horvath & Bedi, 2002; Martin, Garske, & Davis, 2000; Norcross, 2002). A recent special issue of *Psychotherapy* (2011, volume 48) focused on evidence-based therapeutic relationships and concluded that collecting client feedback, through the use of a PM measure, is a "demonstrably effective" element of the therapeutic alliance (Norcross & Wampold, 2011, p. 99). Results from a meta-analysis of nine studies indicates that progress monitoring is an evidence-based component of the relationship that contributed to improved treatment outcomes as well as lowered dropout and deterioration rates for clients at risk (Lambert & Shimokawa, 2011).

Counselling psychology training programs have traditionally focused on preparing students to be competent at establishing good alliances. Integrating training in progress monitoring can help trainees to improve their skills in this area. For example, the popular Partners for Change Outcome Management System (PCOMS; Miller et al., 2005) includes a Session Rating Scale (SRS) which assesses the therapeutic relationship based on Bordin's (1979) definition of the alliance and the client's theory of change. Areas covered in the SRS include the relational bond and the degree of agreement between the client and therapist on the goals, methods, and overall approach of therapy (Miller et al., 2005). Session-by-session concrete feedback from clients helps to focus trainees' attention on these key elements of the therapeutic process. This has the dual purposes of alerting trainees to potential ruptures and providing reassurance when the relationship is going well; "such monitoring leads to increased opportunities to reestablish collaboration, improve the relationship, modify technical strategies, and avoid premature termination" (Norcross & Wampold, 2011, p. 99).

A related value of counselling psychology is the collaboration between client and therapist. This construct too is strongly linked to outcome (e.g., Tyron & Winograd, 2011). Progress monitoring can improve collaboration as well as increasing goal consensus by engaging client and therapist together in the assessment of progress (Lambert & Cattani, 2012). PM measures include alerts and/or benchmarks to signal when a client is not progressing as expected (Overington & Ionita, 2012). Teaching trainees how to use these markers of client progress or deterioration offers them a tool for increasing collaboration with clients. Findings from a recent qualitative study suggest that progress monitoring can open discussions of "progression and change," and conversations that express "experiences, meanings, and perspectives about the therapeutic work" (Sundet, 2012, p. 126). Additionally, when therapy was not progressing as expected, the measures legitimized talk about frustrations; without the scales, discussions related to recovery and change might have been overlooked. Counselling psychology training should focus on the data from PM measures as a way to help trainees learn to give voice to the client. Directing attention to a lack of progress can help trainees to engage in collaborative problem-solving with clients to inform treatment decisions (Sparks, Kisler, Adams, & Blumen, 2011).

WELLNESS, CLIENT-CENTRED, AND HOLISTIC TRAINING
Counselling psychology emphasizes wellness, focusing on client strengths and growth (e.g., Beatch et al., 2009). In helping trainees to focus on these issues, we must ensure that they do not systematically ignore symptoms and fail to note client deterioration. PM measures give trainees a simple and accessible method to maintain a dual focus on symptoms and subjective well-being (Overington & Ionita, 2012). By offering a quick test of client "vital signs" (Whipple &

Lambert, 2011), including self-harm, suicide risk, and drug/alcohol problems, P M can help trainees to build confidence. Research has indicated that trainee self-efficacy is more strongly linked to client outcome when they receive feedback than when they do not, which may suggest that feedback can assist trainees to more accurately evaluate their own skills (Reese, Usher, et al., 2009). Trainees themselves have indicated that feedback from P M provided "an incentive for expanding beyond one's comfort zone and for learning new skills" (Sparks et al., 2011, p. 12).

Secure in the knowledge that clients are on track, trainees can work with strengths and wellness knowing that risk and harm are not issues in the session (Sparks et al., 2011). In a qualitative investigation of the use of the Outcome Questionnaire-45 at the Centre for Psychological Services at the University of Ottawa, focus groups had generally positive reactions from clients who were using these measures. Client comments such as "allows a bit of a rubric for judging personal emotional progress" (Yamin, Rosval, Byrne, Burr, & Aubry, 2011, p. 24) indicate that clients appreciate the opportunity to see positive changes. Discussions of improvements with clients teach trainees how to incorporate a strength-based approach into their work.

Counselling psychology is client-centred, privileging the client perspective. When administering tests or ongoing assessment measures, counselling psychologists need to select tools that are in line with client goals and that involve them as active participants in the work (Bedi et al., 2011; Duckworth, 1990). Obtaining feedback and adjusting services accordingly are "part and parcel of client-based assessment" (Murphy, 2008, p. 241). Most P M systems, however, have clinical cut-offs based on normed samples. Counselling psychology programs rightly teach trainees to be wary of evaluating a client in comparison to a group to which they do not belong. Although work needs to continue to understand the validity of these measures across different cultural groups, the focus in P M measurement is on how the clients change compared to where they started (Lambert & Cattani, 2012). Training students to take a holistic approach means helping them to consider the multiplicity of factors that might be at play at any point in treatment. P M measures assess a broad range of factors and provide a snapshot of the client in context, as opposed to narrowing in on symptoms.

CULTURALLY COMPETENT PRACTICE   Culturally competent practice is another cornerstone of Canadian counselling psychology. Diagnosis and assessment tools have been widely criticized for cultural biases that can compromise their reliability and validity. Increasingly, studies outside Canada are examining the use of various PM measures across cultural groups. The Outcome Questionnaire-45 has been used to determine how clients from different ethnic minority groups (Native American, Latino/a, African American, or Asian / Pacific Islander) progress in psychotherapy (Lambert et al., 2006). Outcomes were similar, and in some cases superior, to outcomes for the Caucasian control group. While these results may be helpful in informing training practices in culturally sensitive psychotherapy, there are still limited studies investigating the validity of the OQ-45 with diverse groups (e.g., Gregersen, Nebeker, Seely, & Lambert, 2004; Nebeker, Lambert, & Huefner, 1995). A recent assessment of the psychometric properties and sensitivity to change of the Behavior and Symptom Identification Scale (BASIS-24; Eisen, Normand, Belanger, Spiro, & Esch, 2004) in a group of Whites, African-Americans, and Latinos (Eisen, Gerena, Ranganathan, Esch, & Idiculla, 2006) indicated that despite particular exceptions (e.g., Latinos and emotional lability), results generally supported the use of the BASIS-24 across groups. Canada is a culturally diverse society. PM research must continue to test the applicability of these measures across cultures and identify cultural biases. As multicultural competence is a key piece of Canadian counselling psychology, we must ensure that we are training students to provide culturally appropriate and sensitive psychotherapeutic services.

In deciding to integrate progress monitoring throughout training in a marriage and family therapy program in the United States, Sparks et al. (2011) have noted, "With clients' voices guiding clinical work, trainees could learn from and better assist persons whose social and cultural locations are outside from their own. The outcome assessment measures chosen are content-free dimensions, requiring therapists to invite clients to clarify their views regarding their unique journeys of change" (p. 5). Progress monitoring gives trainees a method to involve the client in the decision-making process by using client feedback to direct therapy. Culturally competent practice involves working in collaboration with clients and tailoring goals and services to them (Sue & Sue, 2008). Training that focuses on teaching trainees to consider the validity of measurement in each session has the potential to increase awareness and competence not only in assessment but also in the cultural applicability of measurement strategies.

Progress Monitoring in Canadian Counselling Psychology Today

We believe that progress monitoring is a useful training tool that is consistent with the values of Canadian counselling psychology. It is an evidence-based approach that can be used to help trainees build and repair the alliance, increase collaboration, focus on client strengths, and develop a culturally competent practice. As counselling psychologists, it is our ethical responsibility to ensure that trainees are educated in the use of these measures. Discussions with clinical training faculty at doctoral counselling psychology programs in Canada suggest that progress monitoring is not a strong focus of most curricula at the moment (M. Fitzpatrick, personal communication, 11 April 2012). As counselling psychology continues to grow as a discipline in Canada, it is one of our challenges to articulate our approach to evidence-based practice. Progress monitoring is a research-based and value-consistent method to train Canadian counselling psychologists.

GATEKEEPING IN COUNSELLING PSYCHOLOGY

In their history of ethical codes and licensure, Sinclair, Simon, and Pettifor (1996) describe the characteristics of professions. A number of these characteristics are relevant to gatekeeping, including: controlling entry to training; providing training that is lengthy and challenging and requires particular knowledge and skills; and socializing trainees into the values and practices of the profession. Gatekeeping refers to the professional responsibility of training programs to: (1) limit access to training in professional psychology to candidates who have the requisite background education and experience, intellectual ability, and interpersonal skills such that success in the program is likely; (2) ensure that students have the requisite skills and competencies to work with clients before they are permitted to engage in practica and internships; and (3) ensure that students demonstrate adequate competency in coursework, practica, and internships before graduating from the program. The first issue speaks to how programs *select* the students who will receive training in counselling psychology. The second and third points address the issue of how programs *develop student competency* during the training sequence.

In Canada, the discourse on gatekeeping issues is primarily located within documents on ethics, training standards, and supervision. The documents that have particular relevance for gatekeeping include: the *Canadian Code of Ethics for Psychologists, 3rd ed.* (Canadian Psychological Association, 2000), *Ethical Guidelines for Supervision in Psychology: Teaching, Research, Practice, and Administration* (CPA, 2009a), *Accreditation Standards and Procedures for Doctoral Programmes and Internships in Professional Psychology, 5th revision* (CPA, 2011), *Guidelines for Non-Discriminatory Practice* (CPA, 1996/2001), and the *Mutual Recognition Agreement of the Regulatory Bodies for Professional Psychologists in Canada – as Amended June, 2004* (MRA, 2004).

According to the CPA (CPA, 2009a), the ethical issues in training and supervision exist across specializations (e.g., clinical, counselling, school) and "involve learning and ensuring the safety, effectiveness, and quality of psychological performance" (p. 3). "[S]upervisors have an obligation to ensure that successful supervisees meet at least minimal standards of competence for their level of training in their area of activity by the end of supervision; moreover, supervisors assume responsibility for addressing problematic areas of concern identified during the supervisory relationship and for not passing or certifying supervisees who are not meeting developmentally appropriate standards" (p. 4–5).

CPA Accreditation Standards specify a process for asking students to leave a program. Standard II J specifies that programs have policies and procedures for handling students' academic, practice, and interpersonal difficulties. These policies and procedures require mechanisms for developing, implementing, and monitoring remediation plans that must be communicated in writing at the start of graduate training and reviewed at orientation. Students who experience difficulties should be counselled and offered remediation plans. Students whose difficulties persist should be made aware of career alternatives and, if necessary, withdrawn (p. 22). Clearly this is a step in the process that both trainees and programs hope to avoid. By selecting students who have the requisite skills and values and focusing on competency development, programs would be expected to reduce the need to remove students from training. Because there is minimal Canadian empirical literature on gatekeeping (Francophone literature

could not be located) our discussion references foundational literature from outside Canada.

Selecting Successful Students

The ultimate goal of the admission process is to ensure that the students who are selected have the aptitudes to develop professional
competence. The recent development of a values statement for counselling psychology in the US offers criteria and tools for selecting
those with the greatest potential for success (Loewy, Juntunen, &
Duan, 2009). The authors propose that the admission process is the
optimal time to ensure that we select students who are self-aware,
open to alternative viewpoints, and respectful of others. Deficits in
these basic characteristics are best dealt with when both program
and student have made relatively minimal investments in the process. Attending to these issues during admission is consistent with
the emphases on prevention and vocational well-being that are central to counselling psychology. Canadian programs can provide
statements of their training philosophies and the Canadian definition of counselling psychology on their websites to allow students to
inform themselves of these important issues and to help them to
speak to these issues in their applications.

The admission interview is an important step with a long history
in the selection process. Research in Sweden has shown that compared to students who were admitted based only on a review of application materials, a smaller proportion of those who were interviewed
at admissions left (11 percent compared to 18 percent) or interrupted (17 percent compared to 39 percent) their programs (Sundin
& Ögren, 2011). Selection interviews have been criticised for their
potential bias and unreliability. Twenty-one directors of Australian
training programs saw interviews as having at least some value, with
the opportunity to evaluate interpersonal skills being one of the
most commonly mentioned advantages (Helmes & Pachana, 2008).
Interview questions that can indicate the fit of students to the values
of the profession include questions about early experiences or recent
development in thinking about diversity, questions about changes
in thinking, and questions that probe the candidates' ideas about
their fit with program values (Loewy et al., 2009). To ensure the
selection process is relatively unbiased, faculty members can examine their own cultural and personal biases. This is consistent with a

counselling psychology model that considers both the individual and the context as elements that contribute to student success. Programs that publicly articulate their values, examine their consistency with those values, and select students who are interested in those values would be expected to have fewer problems related to students' unsuitability for the profession of counselling psychology. Research is needed to investigate this assertion.

Developing Students' Professional Competencies

Once programs have selected students who have values consistent with the profession, there remains the issue of how they develop student competencies during the training sequence. This is a very large question and beyond the scope of this chapter. Relative to gate-keeping, the issue is what to do when students fail to develop competencies. In their review of the literature, Forrest, Elman, Gizara, and Vacha-Haase (1999) noted the minimal empirical literature addressing issues associated with trainee professional competence problems. From 1975 to 1995 they located only ten survey studies that investigated the issue of impaired trainees. In that earlier literature, the term *impairment* was used and did not make distinctions between trainees who were impaired, incompetent, and unethical, tending to focus on personality rather than problematic behaviours. There has been increased attention to behavioural issues in recent years (Gaubatz & Vera, 2006). In training, distinctions need to be made in terms of trainees who have not yet acquired professional competency, and those who are impaired or who act unethically (Elman & Forrest, 2007; Vacha-Haase, Davenport, & Kerewsky, 2004). In the US the term *professional competence problems* has become the recommended way to describe the issue because it focuses attention on specific behaviours that require remediation (Elman & Forrest, 2007, p. 505). The advantage of addressing behaviours is that they are more measureable and can be addressed earlier in the training sequence. Competency frameworks are relatively new in psychology but are well established in education, human resource management, dentistry, medicine, and nursing (Falender & Shafranske, 2012). A recent workshop at the CPA's annual convention focused on professional competency assessment and feedback (Heath, Hurley, & Ritchie, 2012).

In the current context, professional competence problems are frequent. A recent review in the US reported that 66 to 95 percent of doctoral programs had reported at least one trainee with competency problems in the previous five years (Forrest et al., 2008). A survey of clinical, counselling, and school psychology training directors indicated that 52 percent of programs had removed a student within the previous three years (Vacha-Haase et al., 2004). Gaubatz and Vera (2002) suggest that the incidence of competency problems may be closer to 10 percent of MA-level trainees if the estimate includes concerns about suitability as well those with formal remediation plans or recommended withdrawal.

As stated by Miller, Forrest, and Elman (2009), "Counseling psychology has demonstrated leadership on multicultural issues through serious and committed attention to diversity in scholarship, conferences, and training and recruitment. Yet a survey of the literature on trainees with competence problems resulted in limited references to race/ethnicity and/or gender (REG)" (p. 482). In their survey of fourteen doctoral counselling training directors, eight of twelve directors indicated that REG was a factor in remediation decisions. Of 47 case descriptions of competency problems, 38 percent identified REG information but the role of REG was not examined in 41 percent of the cases identifying REG. These training directors identified significant emotions associated with race/ethnicity in remediation. Although Canada has professional *Guidelines for Non-Discriminatory Practice* (CPA, 1996/2001), the empirical literature in Canada is silent on this issue in the area of competency problems. This is certainly a concern given our valuing of diversity and the multiplicity of issues such as power differentials, conflicting value systems, and English as a second language.

A variety of challenges face training programs in identifying and addressing competency problems. These include difficulty with identifying mental health problems, lack of agreement on impairment/deficit, training faculty with the same problems, desire to be nurturing and supportive, lack of training in dealing with competency problems, and avoidance of adversarial or potentially litigious situations (Forrest et al., 1999). The fear of litigation increased when there was disagreement among faculty and when the competency issues involved interpersonal skills or difficulty in supervision (Vacha-Haase et al., 2004). Addressing trainee competency concerns is also stressful for faculty members and supervisors (Forrest et al., 1999): "One of the most complex and emotionally stressful problems faced by educators in professional psychology training programs is the dilemma of the trainee who is not making adequate professional progress and the training program's educational, ethical, and legal response" (p. 628). The balance between faculty members' developmental and gatekeeping roles is complex (for a review see Johnson et al., 2008). The previously mentioned workshop by Heath et al. (2012) focused on the competencies identified in the Mutual Recognition Agreement (MRA, 2004). The MRA is an agreement between the regulatory bodies for professional psychologists in Canada that defines six core competencies and identifies the attendant knowledge and skills. Heath et al. proposed that these competencies could be used to determine when remediation or gatekeeping activities might need to be implemented and presented an evaluation rubric developed by Memorial University. Focusing on competencies and using an evaluation rubric avoids some of the difficulties identified with impairment and personality.

The bigger issue is how to address professional competence problems. In their 1999 review, Forrest et al. only identified two studies that looked at what happened when students were identified as having competency problems. At that time, reasons for dismissal included academic or clinical performance, interpersonal skills, and unethical behaviour; however, not all students were provided with opportunities for remediation. More recently, Vacha-Haase et al. (2004) have described a range of responses to trainee competency issues including: terminating the program, escalating supervision, recommending a leave of absence from the program, requiring the repeating of practica, supplementing coursework or practica, and recommending personal counselling.

A more holistic and proactive approach to competency concerns has been outlined by Forrest, Miller, and Elman (2008), who applied Bronfenbrenner's (1979) ecological model to problems in professional competence. The model considers individual behaviour within the context of the microsystem (peers, supervisor, instructors, faculty, and peer and supervisors' interactions), exosystem (professional standards and ethics, accreditation and licensure standards, program policies, and evaluation), and macrosystem (cultural beliefs and values). By considering the context instead of locating all of the problems within the individual, the approach is congruent with the values of counselling psychology. Best practices for programs using an ecological framework begin with preparation through development of appropriate policies and creating a culture of communication, accountability, and preventative training experiences. When problems emerge, programs can assess contextual influences and design remediation that integrates the individual and addresses problems within the system (Forrest, Miller, & Elman, 2008). Currently, research has not linked training problems to later difficulties in professional practice. This is clearly an area in which research is needed.

Gatekeeping is one of the important skills of supervisors (CPA, 2009a; Pettifor, McCarron, Schoepp, Stark, & Stewart, 2011). Pettifor et al. (2011) discuss this issue relative to clinical supervision. They recommend that supervisors reveal the implications of their gatekeeping and evaluative roles during the process of informed consent with trainees. When supervising students who are struggling, they suggest, supervisors should increase the frequency of oral and written feedback (Pettifor et al., 2011). In summary, Canadian scholars have primarily contributed to the gatekeeping issues in the form of documents on ethics, competencies, and guidelines. Counselling psychology researchers in Canada need to investigate issues associated with gatekeeping in order to provide data-based recommendations for the future.

A FIVE-YEAR PLAN: DIRECTIONS FOR TRAINING IN CANADIAN COUNSELLING PSYCHOLOGY

As counselling psychology grows in the Canadian context, the quality of our attention in training to funding issues, to evidence-based practice, and to gatekeeping will help to shape the future of our discipline. In the next five years, we need to engage in discussion, in lobbying, and in concerted actions to ensure the development of our discipline. Funding is important to students because it allows them to maintain their focus on training requirements and gives them time to explore the discipline and become strong counselling psychologists. In the next five years, counselling psychology programs need to work to ensure that students are funded at levels that reflect a strong commitment to social justice. This commitment demands that programs advocate within their universities for better funding models to support student success and within the CPA for better access to accredited and funded training. For counselling psychology faculty members, a strong commitment to being the kind of productive researchers and superior research mentors who increase student success in funding competitions is imperative. The CCPPP and CPA need to take up the call to develop methods of increasing the pool of accredited counselling psychology internships so that students can be funded during the final year of training. Finally, students need to be active and informed participants relative to funding issues, not only to secure their own research and clinical funding but also to ensure that the discipline moves in directions that allow for the success of future students.

As a mental health profession, counselling psychology in Canada faces increasing demands for accountability. We must pay attention to data that indicate that students who are trained to use PM measures have improved treatment outcomes. Our discipline has a long tradition of training students to develop strong therapeutic relationships, of focusing on the client as an individual, and of collaborations that prioritize the client's voice. We recommend expanding that training to include data-based collaborative conversations that focus on client strengths and growth and offer security for trainees to work with client deterioration using PM measures. Training in these measures offers an avenue for students to consider the validity of a measurement strategy within each session for each individual client. As we grow as a discipline in Canada, we must continue to articulate an approach to evidence-based practice that is consistent with our values. Progress monitoring is such an approach.

Canadian counselling psychology is founded on a collaborative, developmental, multicultural, and wellness perspective (Young & Lalande, 2011). The challenge is to maintain that focus while fulfilling our gatekeeping roles. We need to devise methods consistent with our foundational principles for selecting students who have the potential to develop their interpersonal skills and then help them develop those skills into the competencies needed for working with clients. Our accrediting bodies have suggested the policies and procedures to support this role but our discipline must engage more directly with the challenges of this work. In particular, we must focus research on investigating the effectiveness of different policies and create a dialogue in our professional forums for understanding the implication of those policies relative to our professional identity. Canadian research is required on the use and effectiveness of interviews in the selection process, the frequency and types of competency problems encountered, how competency is evaluated, challenges in identifying and addressing competency problems, remediation outcomes, and what role diversity plays in competency concerns.

As students represent the future generation of our discipline, we must ensure that they are provided with training that models counselling psychology values and allows for the adoption of these values in their own work as clinicians and researchers. It is only through appropriate training that our discipline will strengthen as a unique speciality within the helping profession in Canada.

Articulating a Social Justice Agenda for Canadian Counselling and Counselling Psychology

FREDA GINSBERG AND ADA L. SINACORE[1]

The practice of social justice is a central feature of the Canadian identity and political landscape. In fact, Canada has a global reputation as a nation founded upon the values of tolerance, benevolence, and diversity, and for promoting the ideal of a justice orientation for both its citizens and those around the world (Joshee & Johnson, 2005). Notably, Canada ranks tenth among twenty-one countries in extending its support to poorer countries in the form of aid, trade, and investments, primarily in Asia and Africa (Centre for Global Development, 2006).

To explore the relative fact or fiction of Canadian social justice, in this chapter the authors will first outline the socio-political context of Canadian society, and the relationship of that context to the provision of mental health services. Next, an analysis of the scholarship conducted by Canadian counsellors and counselling psychologists that directly relates to social justice psychology and service provision will be covered. Finally, a discussion of how counsellors and counselling psychologists can contribute to realizing a social justice agenda with regard to mental health service provision within a Canadian context will be presented.

To begin, Joshee (2007) explains that social justice in actuality "is a broad term that is used to talk about both a general sense of fairness and more particular notions of how to achieve fairness" (p. 171). Other Canadian scholars (see Nagy, 2000) expand upon traditional definitions of social justice and include the notion of compensating past wrongs and healing deep divisions in society. Canadian human rights scholars Basok, Ilcan, and Noonan (2006) also contend that a socially just society promotes a fundamental respect for human dignity and diversity and does not undermine minority groups' aspirations, thereby enabling all people to voice their concerns. In this light, the practice of social justice is not only an ideal to be promoted, but also entails the realization of both individual and community empowerment. Accordingly, the reality of Canadian social justice can be measured by the extent to which deep societal inequities are addressed, economic resources are fairly distributed, citizens are gainfully employed, and all Canadians are successful in their pursuit of legal justice. Simply put, the practice of social justice in Canada "focuses on the relative position of one social group in relationship to others in a society as well as on the root causes of disparities and what can be done to eliminate them" (Edwards & MacLean Davison, 2008, p. 130).

To realize the Canadian ideal of a just society, Howard and Donnelly (1986, 1988) explain, the protection of human rights must be central. Specifically, these authors posit that there are four types of fundamental human rights that must be enforced, namely: (a) survival rights, which guarantee individuals' right to life, food, and health care; (b) membership rights, which assure families' rights and freedom from societal discrimination; (c) protection rights, which prevent abuses of governments and guarantee an independent judiciary; and last, (d) empowerment rights, which guarantee individuals' right to an education, a free press, and freedom of association.

Similarly, scholars have argued that for human rights to be protected, social justice must be realized at all levels of Canadian society – that is, at the levels of the individual, the community, and the broader macro or national milieu. At the individual level, social justice indicates experiences of personal competence, empowerment, and freedom of self-determination leading to positive life outcomes. At the community level, social justice manifests itself in the protection and valuing of a community's norms and customs, and community members' ability to influence those broader socio-political arenas designed to justly govern and provide for the community's needs. Last, social justice at the macro level requires that all national and governmental processes ensure the fundamental equity and protection of human rights at all levels (Ginsberg, 2012b; Horvath, 1999; Prilleltensky, 1994; Sinacore, 2011c; Stoltz, Collins, Arthur, & Audet, 2009) .

GOVERNMENT POLICIES AND ACTS

Over the past fifty years, as evidence of social justice at the macro level, the Canadian government has enacted a number of policies and acts to protect and promote diversity and human rights for its citizens. Generally speaking, many of these policies were initiated in the 1960s and over time have been revised or replaced with a more progressive version of the original policy. A brief (but not exhaustive) review of these policies will be discussed next.

To begin, one of the most significant policies of the 1960s, known as the *Bill of Rights*, was established to grant rights to First Nations people, and also represents the first Canadian immigration policy to directly forbid racial discrimination (Joshee & Johnson, 2005; Lai & Ishiyama, 2004). The *Bill of Rights*, a federal statute, with limited provincial legal scope, was ultimately replaced in 1982 by the *Canadian Charter of Rights and Freedoms*, which in turn was incorporated into the first part of the *Canadian Constitution Act*, thereby allowing Supreme Court judges to strike down discriminatory laws. Thus, the *Canadian Charter of Rights and Freedoms* guarantees the political, human, and social justice rights of Canadian citizens, and most recently was amended to include the rights of lesbian, gay, and bisexual people (Parliament of Canada, 2013).

While the *Canadian Charter of Rights and Freedoms* is one of the most significant social justice advances for Canada, it is also complemented by other legislative human rights initiatives. In particular, in 1971, Canada instituted the *Multiculturalism Policy of 1971*, which was replaced by the *Official Multicultural Act* (1988). This policy and act ultimately resulted in the creation of the Department of Multiculturalism and Citizenship, administered by the Department of Canadian Heritage (Ungerleider, 1992). The *Official Multicultural Act* ensures civic participation, identity development, and cultural and lingual preservation, as well as the promotion of social justice and tolerance for all ethnic groups (Berry & Laponce, 1994; Department of Canadian Heritage, 2002). As well, in 1982, the Minister of State for Multiculturalism established a Race Relations

Unit to address the inherent racism in Canadian institutions, specifi-cally the legal system and media (Multiculturalism Canada, 1983).

In addition to Canadian multicultural policies, due to growing pressure from women's and feminist groups, the Royal Commission on the Status of Women was established in 1969, which led to the *Federal Policy on the Status of Women* in 1972. In 1983, the Special Parliamentary Committee on the Participation of Visible Minori-ties in Canadian Society was established, and in 1984, the Royal Commission on Equality of Employment Opportunity issued a report substantiating how women, visible minorities, Indigenous people, and persons with disabilities were victims of systemic discrimina-tion. To remedy these inequities, the Royal Commission on Equality of Employment Opportunity prescribed measures to correct this social justice problem. Eventually, the Royal Commission's report led to Canada's first *Employment Equity Act* in 1986.

In addition to the special federal attention given to women and minority equity issues, the Royal Commission on Bilingualism and Biculturalism was founded in 1963 and resulted in the *Official Languages Act* (1969) and the *Multiculturalism Within a Bilingual Framework* policy (Esses & Gardner, 1996), designed to ensure French Canadians' demands for political and cultural fairness were met (Esses & Gardner, 1996; Joshee & Johnson, 2005). Further in 1976, the *Quebec Charter of Human Rights and Freedoms* was adopted.

Thus, the history of federal human rights and social justice legisla-tions has resulted in Canada having some of the most progressive laws in the world. For example, Canada is one of the few countries in the world that recognizes same-sex common-law unions and civil marriage (Alderson, 2004b). As well, Canada has a variety of pro-grams in place to help those who are economically vulnerable, including the Old Age Pension, the Canada Pension, the Guaranteed Income Supplement, the Family Allowance Child Tax Credit, and Employment Insurance, among others (Swift & Callahan, 2009).

HISTORICAL AND CURRENT INJUSTICES

Yet, despite the federal government's initiatives to ensure and pro-mote Canadian social justice and human rights, Canadian history is replete with social injustice and countless human rights violations. While an accounting is beyond the scope of this chapter, many authors have documented the vast discriminatory practices and blatant human rights violations committed against Indigenous people and Black, Chinese, Jewish, and Italian Canadians, to name just a few. (For a full discussion of these brutal historical realities, see Ungerleider, 1992, and the chapters in this book discussing LGBT people, immigration, multiculturalism, and Indigenous peoples.)

Poverty

Unfortunately, many of these historical social injustices are still entrenched in Canadian society today. For illustrative purposes, a consideration of Canadian economic realities aptly depicts one of the many gross social inequities faced by many Canadians. Specifically, experts have demonstrated that relative to other first-world countries, Canadian poverty rates are both high and persistent (Valetta, 2006). Although Canadians are proud to view their country as a land of possibility, it is also a country of longstanding inequality regarding the distribution of personal wealth (Kersetter, 2002). Moreover, studies indicate that nearly sixteen percent of Canadians can be categorized in the low-income bracket (Statistics Canada, 2006), and notably, rates of low-income status are considerably higher for single-parent mothers, immigrants, Indigenous people, people with disabilities, and seniors (Canadian Council on Social Development, 2006; National Council of Welfare, 2006).

In Canada, the hierarchy of wealth distribution and poverty has become steeper in the past several decades. That is, the rich have become richer and the poor, poorer, and the gap between them has widened (Swift & Callahan, 2009). In fact, in 1999, 50 percent of family units in Canada held 94.4 percent of the wealth, leaving only 5.6 percent to the bottom 50 percent (Kersetter, 2002). Between 1999 and 2005, a period when total wealth increased greatly in Canada, the overall gains were not shared equally as the highest quintile received 71 percent of the total increase in wealth, where by contrast, the lowest quintile saw its median real net wealth fall by 9.1 percent (Drummond & Tulk, 2006). This trend of unequal wealth distribution continues on with the gap in earnings between the wealthy and the poor now wider than it has been for thirty years (Yalnizyan, 2005).

As a result, Canada is home to many who live in poverty and ongoing deprivation. For instance, it is estimated that about 1.2 million children, approximately one in six, live in families whose income is below the poverty line, a figure that has not declined since 1980 (Campaign 2000, 2006). Similarly, the reality of the longstanding poverty endured by Indigenous people living in some of the most remote areas of Canada as well as those living in urban centres (Canadian Council for Social Development, 2006) is becoming increasingly visible and disheartening (Lee, 2000). More specifically, Indigenous youth aged fifteen to twenty-four had a poverty rate of 37 percent in 2001, compared to 19 percent among non-Indigenous youth; and 42 percent of immigrant children under age fifteen were poor in 2001, compared to 17 percent of those born in Canada (Canadian Council on Social Development, 2006; Paul-Sen, de Wit, & McKeown, 2007; Rothman, 2007).

Notably, single mothers and their children have the highest rates of poverty in Canada (Canadian Research Institute for the Advancement of Women, 2005). It is very important to highlight that children who live in deep and enduring poverty are less likely to be ready to start school and/or succeed academically, and sadly these children live with greater emotional distress (Canadian Council of Social Development, 2006). Thus, the existence of such abject poverty and marginalization in a country as wealthy and politically stable as Canada is particularly unjust.

Homelessness

In a similar vein, experts report that the street counts of homeless people have nearly tripled in the past few decades. The Sheldon Chumir Foundation for Ethics in Leadership (Laird, 2007) released a report estimating Canada's homeless population to be somewhere between 200,000 and 300,000 people, with another 1.7 million struggling with housing affordability issues. Canada's homeless population is also increasingly younger, with nearly one in seven users of emergency shelters across Canada being children and almost one-third of Canada's homeless population being youths aged sixteen to twenty-four (Laird, 2007). Further, it is estimated that of these homeless children and youth, at least twenty percent identify as a sexual minority, further highlighting the pervasive discrimination faced by this population (Ginsberg, 2013).

Moreover, research has demonstrated that the homeless, and certainly homeless youth, suffer greatly from life on the streets and in shelters and may engage in sex work, drug use, and crime just to survive (Alvi, Scott, & Stanyon, 2010; MacDonald, Fisher, Wells, Doherty, & Bowie, 1994). As well, some experts have estimated that half of all homeless individuals suffer from mental distress or illness, and in particular, many homeless and residentially disadvantaged people suffer from a range of maladies including depression, anxiety, malnutrition, anemia, respiratory ailments, alcohol and drug addiction, and other physical and psychological problems (Frankish, Hwang, & Quantz, 2005; Public Health Agency of Canada, 2002).

SOCIAL DETERMINANTS OF HEALTH

Needless to say, the lack of economic and social mobility amongst low-income Canadians is a major determinant of poor physical and mental health outcomes (Canadian Council on Social Development, 2006; Canadian Institute for Health Information, 2004; Raphael, 2004). Currently, it is estimated that seven million Canadians struggle with mental health problems, and many of these individuals come from economically disadvantaged populations. As such, it is safe to say that life as a disadvantaged individual may in and of itself lead to mental distress (Public Health Agency of Canada, 2002). In fact, economic, racial, and a host of other oppressions are being referred to as *social determinants of health*, a term which obviates the symbiotic, cyclical relationship between larger systemic realities and physical and mental health (Health Canada, 2002). Those who coined the phrase *social determinants of health*, namely four hundred experts hailing from a broad cross-section of medicine and the social sciences, identified a host of specific social determinants that lead to poor health outcomes, even more so than medical or personal health care behaviours, including: income inequality, social inclusion and exclusion, employment and job security, working conditions, early childhood care, education, food security, and housing (Health Canada, 2002). In fact, current evidence suggests that social determinants of health are likely the best predictors of population health – that is, disparities in social and economic status between groups directly affect the health status of the entire population, whereby the larger the social inequity, the lower the health status of the population of Canada (Health Canada, 2002).

Hence, addressing and mediating social determinants of mental health may, in fact, promote mental health and inoculate against the occurrence of mental illnesses (Public Health Agency of Canada,

2002). This fact is clearly noteworthy, as currently one in five
Canadians experiences severe psychological distress, and one in ten
confirms suffering from a mental disorder. More specifically, low-
income populations, racialized minorities, women, single, separated,
or divorced individuals, immigrants, and Indigenous people showed
higher rates of suffering from psychological distress or mental disorders than the mainstream (Caron & Lui, 2010; Williams, 2001).

Equally relevant is the reality that mental illness in the lives of
youth, and in particular marginalized youth, is the most prevalent
and chronic medical condition causing disability for this population,
often leading to substantial negative life outcomes. These negative
life outcomes include: poor academic and occupational success; substantial personal, interpersonal, and family difficulties; increased
risk for physical illnesses; shorter life expectancy; and greater familial economic burden. Likewise, most young people, as well as those
in the general population, who need specialized mental health care
do not receive it, a sad reality that is further complicated by these
individuals suffering from the stigma associated with having a mental disorder (Child and Youth Advisory Committee of the Mental
Health Commission of Canada, 2010).

Similarly, seniors are a growing Canadian demographic that will
be in need of increasingly greater mental health services, since the
proportion of Canadians over sixty-five years old rose from one in
twenty in 1921, to one in eight in 2001, and will likely reach a rate
of one in four by 2041 (Health Canada, 2002). Currently, experts
contend that one in five individuals over the age of sixty-five may
have a mental health disorder (Jeste et al., 1999), and given that the
percentage of the population aged sixty-five and over is expected to
increase from thirteen percent to twenty-two percent between 2006
and 2026 (Trucotte & Schellenberg, 2007), there will be an increasing number of seniors who will experience or who will be at risk of
experiencing mental health problems (Macourt, 2008; Sullivan,
Kessler, LeClair, Stolee, & Whitney, 2004).

A MENTAL HEALTH STRATEGY FOR CANADA

To address the need for mental health services that directly attend
to the social determinants of health and population diversity, the
Mental Health Commission of Canada (MHCC) devised a forward-
thinking national mental health strategy outlined in a document

entitled *Toward Recovery & Well Being: A Framework for a Mental Health Strategy for Canada* (2009). Broadly speaking, this strategy calls for a revamp of Canada's broken mental health system, which currently costs the Canadian economy fifty billion dollars annually. As aforementioned, of particular concern is the fact that only one-third of Canadian adults and one-quarter of Canadian children who need mental health services receive them (Mental Health Commission of Canada, 2009). In formulating this federal strategy, the MHCC identified that those who are at the highest risk for mental health problems and inadequate service provision are people from marginalized groups, such as Indigenous people, those of a minority ethnocultural background, the poor, immigrants, sexual and religious minorities, those who are differently abled, and/or those who are enduring social violence. In fact, the MHCC acknowledges that individuals in these groups continue to experience worse mental health outcomes than the overall population, and often, these disparities in mental health are severe. Similarly, the MHCC highlights how mental health must be put into cultural context, and when this does not occur, misdiagnosis and harmful treatment are likely to ensue. Likewise, the MHCC identified the existence of significant barriers that face marginalized people in their pursuit of mental health services. Overall, the MHCC recognized that societal power imbalances and discrimination directly contribute to poor mental health outcomes, and ultimately restrict access to quality mental health care (Mental Health Commission of Canada, 2009).

To remedy these profound mental health realities, the MHCC recommends that more community- and school-based prevention programs be put in place and that services be founded upon a wellness model, in order to improve access to treatment across a person's lifespan. Moreover, the MHCC proposes that mental health initiatives target individuals and communities at risk for poor mental health outcomes. Further, they suggest that prevention and service initiatives be targeted to meet the unique needs of diverse communities by simultaneously drawing upon community strengths and resources and taking into account the unique historical and current social, political, and spiritual challenges at play regarding housing, employment, and education. Ultimately, Canada's most recent mental health strategy aims to address the social determinants of health and vastly improve the quality of service delivery for all Canadians (Mental Health Commission of Canada, 2009).

CREATING A SOCIAL JUSTICE AGENDA FOR
COUNSELLING AND COUNSELLING PSYCHOLOGY

The spirit and mandate set out in the document *Toward Recovery & Well Being: A Framework for a Mental Health Strategy for Canada* (Mental Health Commission of Canada, 2009) shares much in common with the multicultural counselling competencies covered in the multiculturalism chapter of this book, as well as with the philosophy and values embedded in the recent official definition of counselling psychology,which explicitly directs attention to social context, thereby identifying counselling psychologists as well suited to consider individuals in the context of the oppressive systemic structures in which they live (Bedi et al., 2001; see Introduction, chapter 1).

Similarly, the Canadian Psychological Association's Code of Ethics (CPA Code of Ethics, 2000), Principle I: Respect for the Dignity of Persons mandates that counselling psychologists adopt a social justice orientation:

> Psychologists appreciate that the innate worth of human beings is not enhanced or reduced by their culture, nationality, ethnicity, colour, race, religion, sex, gender, marital status, sexual orientation, physical or mental abilities, age, socioeconomic status, or any other preference or personal characteristic, condition or status. Psychologists also recognize that as individual, family, group or community vulnerability increase, or as the power of individual persons to control their environment or their lives decreases, psychologists have an increasing responsibility to seek ethical advice and establish safeguards to protect those less able to protect themselves. These responsibilities have special significance in a society which is becoming more diverse culturally and economically and which has not achieved gender equality. (p. 8)

Accordingly, the CPA Ethics Code highlights counselling psychologists' ethical requirement to safeguard and work on behalf of those whose lives are affected by social inequities, a requirement which echoes the call put forth by the MHCC urging service providers to actively attend to broader social inequities in Canada.

As well, throughout this book authors have highlighted counselling psychologists' orientation toward strength-based counselling, with a particular focus on health, wellness, and prevention. Additionally, authors in this book have presented counselling psychologists' contributions to multicultural competence development and services provision for marginalized populations, namely immigrants, sexual minorities, Indigenous people, people from diverse ethnic and racial backgrounds, and people suffering from economic and employment challenges. As such, it is evident that the plethora of scholarship produced by counsellors and counselling psychologists, as reviewed in this book, is testimony to the ways Canadian counsellors and counselling psychologists are attending to the social determinants of health, and specifically the strategy and mental health mandate put forth by the Mental Health Commission of Canada (2009).

Yet, in order to fully, and wholeheartedly, address the MHCC's strategy and related service delivery recommendations, counselling and counselling psychology's current disciplinary orientation toward multiculturalism may not be adequate. As such, the counselling disciplines' more recent movement towards a social justice orientation may, in fact, be a more apt philosophical and epistemological orientation to address the myriad ways that social determinants of mental health can be remedied, thereby preventing long-term mental health struggles for Canadians. Simply put, some scholars have suggested that even though social justice is foundationally implied in a multicultural zeitgeist, multiculturalism does not entirely describe what social justice is, and thus, social justice in counselling and counselling psychology has yet to be fully articulated and practiced (e.g. Arthur, 2005a; Sinacore, Ginsberg, & Kassan, 2013). In other words, while most counselling and counselling psychology multiculturalism experts concur that multicultural and feminist analyses serve as a partial theoretical cornerstone required for a robust social justice agenda in the discipline, they also acknowledge that multiculturalism and feminism alone are inadequate, and render a social justice plan for the discipline unrealized (Palmer & Parish, 2008; Sinacore, Ginsberg, & Kassan, 2013).

In addition, scholars have argued that a pervasive adherence to traditional psychological theory, and the interventions thereby practiced, merely reproduces the dynamics of social exclusion, marginalization, and oppression for those already underserved in Canada's mental health system (Arthur, 2005a, 2005b; Prilleltensky & Nelson, 2002). That is, current conceptualizations of mental health, even

through the lens of wellness, are still often accompanied by treatment and service delivery that are intra-psychically focused, thereby
ignoring broader socio-political forces impacting client symptomol-
ogy. Alternatively, some argue for the utilization of a social justice
paradigm that employs new theoretical conceptualizations of distress (Ginsberg, 2013). Palmer and Parish (2008) contend that counsellors and counselling psychologists are ideally suited to accomplish
this goal and propose that

> [c]ounsellors and psychologists are in a position to recognize and
> work to change the systemic nature of oppression, being cogni-
> zant of the ways in which social, cultural, political, and economic
> inequities negatively impact on individuals' and communities'
> psychological and emotional well-being. (p. 280)

As such, it is clear that counsellors and counselling psychologists
have the basic philosophical predisposition to do social justice work
consistent with the MHCC's mandate. However, to date, only a few
Canadian counsellors and counselling psychologists have been at the
forefront of social justice work in the discipline. Nonetheless, there
are those who are actively contributing to the literature on social
justice and their work is important to consider as the discipline
embarks toward the goal of articulating a social justice agenda for
itself.

To this end, it is important to consider what is meant exactly by
social justice work in counselling. Accordingly, Arthur, Collins,
MacMahon, & Marshall (2009) began with that consideration in
their study of one hundred and fifty-one career counsellors. In this
unique research, these authors identified ten components that their
practitioner participants reported that their practice of social justice
comprised, including advocacy, equality, self-fulfillment, equal opportunity, inclusion, and equal access. As well, in the pursuit of creating
a social justice agenda for counsellors, Arthur and Stewart (2001)
suggest that "[c]ounsellors need to possess knowledge about the
history, values, and socialization practices of cultural groups within
Canadian society and how their heritages, including the socio-political
issues facing these groups[,] may have influenced their personal and
social development" (p. 7). These authors posit that it is essential for
counsellors to "understand the political, economic, historical, social
and psychological development specific to a particular cultural

group" (p. 8) and that "[c]ounsellors have an advocacy role to influence the policies and procedures of organizations and to create positive changes for the delivery of services to culturally diverse clients"
(p. 10). Last, a robust definition of social justice implores counsellors
and counselling psychologists to reflect upon their own prejudices
and biases as they work toward broader social change (Sinacore,
Ginsberg, & Kassan, 2013; Sinacore & Kassan, 2011).

MODELS OF SOCIAL JUSTICE

In addition to attempting to formulate a definition of social justice
for the counselling discipline, certain Canadian authors have built
upon models hailing from the United States (e.g. Toporek, Gerstein,
Fouad, Roysircar, & Israel, 2006) and have conceived models of
social justice that can be used to guide service delivery in different
settings. For the organizational realm, Sinacore (2011c) designed the
Integrated Social Justice Consultation Model (ISJCM) that speaks
to policy development and implementation in organizations and
comprises four main principles (Sinacore, 2011c). The first principle
of the ISJCM explains that inequities within institutions are by-
products of broader socio-cultural climates and contexts. The second principle notes that power dynamics in institutions contribute
to, and result in, the silencing and marginalizing of certain individuals. The third principle contends that rules that govern social interactions and decision-making processes in institutions must take into
account individuals' multiple intersecting identities, such as gender,
biological sex, and sexual orientation. Finally, the fourth principle
reminds us that institutional, social, and structural change may
result in controversy, which can productively lead to positive change
through dialogue and education (Sinacore, 2011c).

this being the a process of structural

Additionally, Arthur (2005a, 2005b) designed a model for social
justice competency for career counsellors, comprising five domains,
including: (a) knowledge of systemic forces and oppression; (b) consultation with local community groups regarding career development
services; (c) expansion of career development interventions to include
multiple roles and multiple levels of intervention; (d) increased access
to culturally appropriate career resources; and (e) professional development for social justice career development competency.

As well, Ginsberg (2012a) posits that social justice work must
not only be theoretical, but be realized via service delivery at the

individual, community, and macro levels of society (see earlier discussion in this chapter). Thus, to practice social justice work at the individual level, one must (a) educate oneself about multiculturalism and oppression; (b) empower oneself and clients to develop and use advocacy skills; (c) seek out supervision with knowledgeable social justice experts; (d) critically examine the limitations of traditional counselling theories; (e) conceptualize client problems based on broad societal realities; (f) normalize client problems with their socio-cultural context; (g) do pro-bono work; and (h) use one's personal privilege and connections to help clients access resources. Likewise, at the community level, counsellors must: (a) seek feedback from community experts and members; (b) organize grassroots initiatives; (c) run prevention programs, support groups, and psychoeducation programs, and participate in outreach; and (d) conduct program evaluation and action research on behalf of the communities being served. Last, at the macro level, counsellors should: (a) use the media and internet to raise awareness; (b) network with stakeholders to build coalitions, alliances, and task forces; (c) educate policy-makers, public figures, and legislators; (d) conduct research to generate data to support policy change and service creation; and (e) engage in peaceful protests and circulate and sign petitions (Ginsberg, 2012b).

FUTURE DIRECTIONS: TRAINING FOR SOCIAL JUSTICE WORK

As previously discussed, the Mental Health Commission of Canada has proposed an innovative national mental health strategy that is consistent with the emerging social justice frameworks conceptualized by counsellors and counselling psychologists in Canada. Simply put, the call from the MHCC to mental health professionals is to be ready to wholeheartedly target individuals and communities at risk; apply strength-based, culturally safe, and competent approaches; take social, political, linguistic, and spiritual realities into account; avoid stereotyping when providing mental health services; and address power, discrimination, and structural barriers. Further, the MHCC mandates service providers to reflect critically upon their own cultural values, and take historical and political contexts into account when considering clients' concerns. Each one of these recommendations is consistent with practicing social justice and requires a strategy that addresses deep societal inequities, particularly in the distribution of economic resources, social and political power, employment opportunities, and systemic legal justice at the individual and community levels. Thus, the current zeitgeist of mental health professionals in the disciplines of counselling and counselling psychology uniquely qualifies them to meet the mandate put forth by the MHCC. That is, the official definition of counselling psychology (Bedi et al., 2011) specifically refers to the role of advocacy and the need to attend to the social and cultural contexts of clients presenting concerns. Further, social justice is not a new concept in counselling and counselling psychology and it represents efforts to make psychology more inclusive (Young and Lalande, 2011). However, adopting a social justice agenda has a number of challenges and barriers that must be addressed.

To facilitate future counsellors' and counselling psychologists' ability to apply social justice frameworks in their work, a consideration of how counsellors and counselling psychologists are trained is essential. Palmer and Parish (2008) contend that "fundamental changes in graduate student education, training, and research [are] key toward increasing social justice in counselling psychology" (p. 279). To this end, these authors suggest that graduate counselling psychology programs move beyond traditional training paradigms and expose students to the discourses and debates of critical psychology, grassroots feminism, and multiculturalism, as these schools of thought are informed by the work of activists and broader systemic forces that impact clients' lives. Likewise, counselling and counselling psychology training and practice do not necessarily promote a focus on topics outside the discipline, nor on interventions that do not take place in traditional settings (Sinacore et al., 2013). To remedy this, Palmer and Parish (2008) propose that "graduate student engagement with these debates is key to placing social justice aims at the heart of counselling psychology" (p. 279).

Similarly, Sinacore and colleagues (2013) propose that the graduate training of counsellors and counselling psychologists must employ a scientist-advocate model, rather than a pure scientist-practitioner one, so as to articulate the link between science and advocacy for students and to prepare them for grassroots advocacy work. These scholars note that the scientist-practitioner model and the move towards evidence-based practice may, in fact, serve as barriers to integrating a social justice framework into training programs, as these models do not always allow for an examination of social inequalities and contextual variables, nor do they promote advocacy and social action (Sinacore et al., 2013). Moreover, the broader values of academia, which emphasize knowledge and data production, and not necessarily social action, may be incongruent with social justice ideologies. As a result, current training models, which largely depend upon theoretical analysis and scientific evidence to inform service delivery, do not necessarily require an examination of societal injustice. Hence, as the field is increasingly emphasizing the use of science or evidence to inform clinical practice, there needs to be a careful consideration as to whether or not that research was conducted or that evidence was collected in a manner that attended to social justice factors. Alternatively, if counsellors and counselling psychologists employed a scientist-advocate approach, it would be compulsory for them to seek solutions to mental health problems that are informed by data gathered using unconventional approaches.

Likewise, training programs for counsellors and counselling psychologists do not necessarily take into consideration social action and advocacy as core competencies needing to be developed by trainees (Arthur, 2005b). That is, though social justice is implied in diversity and multicultural competencies, it has not always been explicitly articulated (Arthur et al., 2008). As such, social justice principles and related competencies should be explicitly articulated and integrated into the curriculum. To the contrary, the emphasis on standard coursework, clinical hours, supervision, and assessment does not necessarily lend itself to training students in social justice work at the community and macro levels. For example, training in policy evaluation and implementation, which may be essential to bringing about systemic change, is not necessarily part of the counselling or counselling psychology curriculum. Further, while programs may require a course in program evaluation and consultation, these courses do not necessarily include social justice frameworks when training students to evaluate programs and systems.

In addition to philosophical training considerations, Sinacore and Enns (2005a) suggest that pedagogical frameworks, optimal for achieving social justice, should emphasize combining social and individual change, transforming knowledge and knowers, analyzing multiple intersecting oppressions and privileges, and situating self-awareness in the analysis of power systems. Similarly, Sinacore and Enns (2005a) outline a social justice pedagogy for training counsellors and counselling psychologists which teaches students to work toward: (a) empowerment and social change; (b) empowering ignored and marginalized individuals and communities; (c) conceptualizing multiple and intersecting identities, privileges, and oppressions; and (d) reflecting on and self-awareness of personal biases, assumptions, and attitudes.

More practically speaking, Sinacore et al. (2013) also suggest that social justice frameworks be integrated into all courses in the counselling curriculum, and caution against training programs that rely on a stand-alone course on multiculturalism. Accordingly, these authors suggest that counsellor educators and counselling psychologists need to "articulate and apply social justice pedagogy in the classroom and clinical training such that the students' learning environments are reflective of the values put forth in the discipline" (Sinacore et al., 2013, p. 430). That is, a training curriculum that is based on a social justice orientation speaks directly to a counselling identity, as articulated in the official definition of Canadian counselling psychology and the requirement for social justice work mandated in the CPA Code of Ethics. In sum, all of these authors who are working to conceptualize a Canadian social justice training paradigm, strive to develop the next generation of social action agents who will dedicate their work to bringing about social change for Canadians.

Yet Palmer and Parish (2008) caution that the movement toward employing social justice training models is not without risk and challenge. Specifically, these authors note that trainees may face social and professional censure from either students or faculty in their training programs who do not support a social justice orientation. Additionally, faculty who employ a social justice paradigm may be at risk for professional consequences. In particular, Sinacore et al. (2013) suggest that the constraints of tenure and promotion require educators to stay engaged in traditional academic activities, and not focus on work in the broader community. Further, activities relevant to advocacy and social action are not necessarily rewarded when assessing counsellor educators and counselling psychologists' contributions to the discipline and the university. Sinacore et al. (2013) contend that "typically the number of publications, number of courses taught, number of students graduated, and amount of university service provided are highly valued in the evaluation of tenure and promotion, while activities related to social action and community service are oftentimes overlooked" (p. 429). Moreover, course evaluations are an important variable in the assessment of professors' teaching, yet research has linked lower course evaluations, lower student satisfaction, and backlash to using diversity pedagogies in the classroom (e.g. Sinacore & Boatwright, 2005; Sinacore, Healy, & Justin, 2002). As such, university teachers may be reluctant to apply pedagogical strategies that attend to diversity and social justice for fear of reprisal.

Furthermore, practitioners working as social activists in counselling and counselling psychology environments may be at risk for negative job outcomes, while employing a more traditional route is likely to be rewarded (e.g. Arthur et al., 2009; Toporek & McNally, 2006). For example, Arthur et al. (2009), in a study of career counsellors, identified a number of individual and systemic barriers to putting social justice work into practice that the participants in their study reported. Specifically, the career counsellors in this study reported individual barriers to doing social justice work, which included a lack of time, interest, training, and support from colleagues and supervisors. The systemic barriers these service providers reported included lack of financial resources and professional influence, as well as a fear of challenging the status quo, losing agency funding, and job loss. In addition, American social justice scholars have identified that there is often an emotional toll that those who do social justice work must pay, and this price is often a costly inhibitor for those who wish to work within a social justice framework (Goodman et al., 2004).

In conclusion, the mandate put forth by the Mental Health Commssion of Canada is explicitly linked to applying social justice models and frameworks toward the betterment of mental health services for marginalized and at-risk individuals and communities. In order for Canadian counsellors and counselling psychologists to play their role in the roll-out of this national mental health mandate, the structural, educational, and personal barriers that limit the ability of trainees, educators, and practitioners to engage in social justice work and advocacy must be addressed. Therefore, for a social justice orientation to move into the mainstream in the disciplines of counselling and counselling psychology, those invested in advancing a social justice zeitgeist must engage in new ways of thinking and must generate critical dialogues in their respective professional circles to address the gross inequities in mental health service provision in

Canada today. To this end, practitioners, educators, and trainees who take up the call to centralize a social justice paradigm in the counselling discipline must rally for support at the individual and systemic levels to ensure that the barriers to social justice teaching, research, and clinical practice do not stand in their way.

NOTE

1 Order of authorship is alphabetical and does not indicate level of contribution.

Contributors

KEVIN ALDERSON is an associate professor of counselling psychology at the University of Calgary. During his twenty-nine years as a practicing psychologist, Dr Alderson has counselled hundreds of LGBTI clients. He is currently an elected council member with the College of Alberta Psychologists. He is also the editor-in-chief of the *Canadian Journal of Counselling and Psychotherapy* and the author of eight books, most recently *Counseling LGBTI Clients* (Sage) and *Breaking Out II: The Complete Guide to Building A Positive LGBTI Identity* (Insomniac Press).

NANCY ARTHUR is a professor in the Department of Educational Studies in Counselling Psychology, the associate dean of research, Werklund School of Education, University of Calgary, and former Canada Research Chair in Professional Education. Dr Arthur is a registered psychologist in Alberta and she provides consultation and training services. Her teaching and research interests focus on culture-infused counselling, career development, international transitions, and professional education for working in global contexts. She serves on the Board of Governors of the International Association for Educational and Vocational Guidance and the Canadian Career Development Foundation.

WILLIAM BORGEN is a professor of counselling psychology and head of the Department of Educational and Counselling Psychology and Special Education at the University of British Columbia. Dr Borgen is a registered psychologist in BC and Alberta, and has conducted research and has developed programs in the areas of life transitions and career development for several years. His work has been translated and adapted for use in Bhutan, Denmark, Finland, Hungary, and Sweden. In 2005 Dr Borgen was awarded an honorary doctorate from the University of Umea for his leadership in the development of counsellor education in Sweden.

MARLA BUCHANAN is a professor in the Department of Educational and Counselling Psychology and Special Education at the University of British Columbia. She teaches in the counselling psychology graduate program with specialization in advanced qualitative research methods. Her research interests include studies in traumatic stress and narrative research methodologies.

ERIN BUHR is a doctoral student in counselling psychology at the University of Alberta. She is currently working on a variety of qualitative, quantitative, and mixed-methods research projects. Her primary interests include motivation in therapy with adults, factors contributing to successful therapeutic outcomes, grief, relationships, trauma, and cultural issues. As a practitioner, she has worked with youth who have developmental and behavioural disorders, and with adults presenting with depression, anxiety, and relationship problems.

LEE D. BUTTERFIELD is a registered psychologist in British Columbia. She currently works as a psychologist at Simon Fraser University's Health and Counselling Centre and in private practice. Her research interests include career counselling, women and work, outplacement counselling, employee wellness / worker well-being, and the impact of workplace policies and change on workers. Prior to becoming a psychologist, Dr Butterfield worked for more than twenty-five years in human resource management in a variety of industries.

SHARON CAIRNS is an associate professor in counselling psychology at the University of Calgary, where she serves as chair of counselling psychology as well as graduate program director for educational psychology. Prior to her faculty appointment, she worked in post-secondary counselling, where she provided direct service and supervised practicum students. Dr Cairns' current research is focused on student mental health in the post-secondary context.

SANDRA COLLINS is a professor in the Graduate Centre for Applied Psychology at Athabasca University. She focuses her research and teaching in the areas of culture-infused counselling, social justice, women's issues, sexual orientation and gender identity, and counsellor education. Dr Collins is a registered psychologist in Alberta and a registered clinical counsellor in British Columbia, with a private practice in Victoria. She is a member-at-large of the Social Justice Chapter of the Canadian Counselling and Psychotherapy Association.

JOSÉ F. DOMENE is a professor and Canada Research Chair in School to Work Transition in the Faculty of Education at the University of New Brunswick, Fredericton. His research interests include the relational contexts of career development, university student mental health, and research practices in counselling and counselling psychology in Canada. Dr Domene has served on the executives of the Counselling Psychology Section of the Canadian Psychological Association and the Counsellor Educators Chapter of the Canadian Counselling and Psychotherapy Association.

MARILYN FITZPATRICK is a professor and director of the Counselling Psychology Program at McGill University. Her research interests focus on effective psychotherapy processes, including the alliance and client engagement. She is currently conducting a series of studies on the use of values work to promote change. She is affiliated with two Practice Research Networks (PPRN, York University) and is active in developing initiatives to encourage practitioners to adopt evidence-based practices.

NICOLA (NICK) GAZZOLA is an associate professor of counselling and the vice-dean and faculty secretary of the Faculty of Education at the University of Ottawa. His research interests focus on clinical supervision, the professional identity of counselling, and psychotherapist self-doubt. He is a licensed psychologist in the province of Quebec, where he has a private practice, and is also a Canadian Certified Counsellor.

FREDA GINSBERG is an assistant professor and the director of the Ward Hall Counseling Center in the Counselor Education Department at SUNY Plattsburgh. Dr Ginsberg's scholarly expertise includes counselling and teaching for social justice and critical peda-gogies. She has been an active member of the Canadian Psychological Association's Section for Counselling Psychology since 2009 and currently serves on the section's executive; she also spearheaded the creation of the section's on-line interactive archive. In 2010, she served as the coordinator for the Inaugural Canadian Counselling Psychology Conference.

LIETTE GOYER is a professor at Laval University. She holds a PhD with a specialization in education and counselling, and teaches undergraduate and graduate programs in science orientation. She is a regular member of the Centre de recherche et d'intervention sur l'éducation et la vie au travail (CRIEVAT). She has conducted col-laborative and evaluative research in connection with the govern-ment's policy on adult education and continuing training with the Ministry of Education. She is currently associated with the Pan-Canadian Research Group on Evidence in Career Development. Her research interests focus on innovative practices, guidance proce-dures, and guidance processes with youth and adults.

BRYAN HIEBERT is a professor emeritus of education at the University of Calgary, adjunct professor in educational psychology and leadership studies at the University of Victoria, and docent of education (research and training of counselling) at the University of Jyväskylä, Finland. He has served as both vice-president and presi-dent of the International Association for Educational and Vocational Guidance. In 2007, Dr Hiebert was awarded the Stu Conger Gold Medal and Diamond Pin for leadership in career development. He has published more than 180 professional papers and eight books dealing with career counselling, stress control, and counsellor education.

GEORGE HURLEY is a registered psychologist and a past profes-sor and past residency training director at the Memorial University Counselling Centre in St. John's, Newfoundland. Since his retire-ment in 2013, he continues to be interested in program develop-ment, supervision, and outreach/consultation to the university and the community at large (as well as sailing and gardening). George is a fellow of the CPA and APA and was recently named as a distin-guished member of the Section on Counselling Psychology, CPA.

ANUSHA KASSAN is an assistant professor in the Counselling Psychology Program in the Werklund School of Education at the University of Calgary. Her scholarly interests include multicultural counselling competencies, immigration, and adolescent development, as well as training and supervision. She is presently conducting immigration research with adolescents and same-sex binational couples who immigrate to Canada. She has recently published in the *Journal of LGBT Issues in Counselling, Training and Education in Professional Psychology*, and *Women & Therapy*.

PATRICE KEATS is an associate professor of counselling psychology at Simon Fraser University. She is the current academic coordinator of the program and the clinical director of the SFU Surrey Counselling Centre. She has conducted research, published, and presented scholarly papers on witnessing trauma, and on primary and secondary traumatic stress in a variety of populations, including journalists, sex abuse survivors, and traumatized children. She also conducts research in counsellor education and supervision. She is currently interested in international human development in the areas of counselling, counsellor training, and education.

AUDREY KINZEL is a registered doctoral psychologist practicing in Saskatchewan. She is a member of the Canadian Psychological Association and the Saskatchewan College of Psychologists. She has a private practice where she assists children, teens, adults, couples, and families with a range of issues including chronic illness and persistent pain. She also provides psychological services, including assessment and treatment, at physical rehabilitation centres where she assists clients who have been injured on the job or in motor vehicle collisions. She is involved in research projects on topics such as persistent pain, cyberbullying, and women on the tenure track.

VIVIAN LALANDE is a consulting psychologist (Alberta), a registered clinical counsellor (BC), an associate professor emerita in counselling psychology at the University of Calgary, and a Fellow of the Canadian Psychology Association (CPA). She is the former editor of the *Canadian Journal of Counselling* and was awarded the Canadian Counselling Association (CCA) Professional Contribution Award in 2008 and the CPA Section of Counselling Psychology Distinguished Member Award in 2009. With the CPA, she is the past chair of the

Section on Counselling Psychology and the past chair of the Section on Women and Psychology. With CCA, she served on the Board of Directors as the Alberta and NWT representative and as the treasurer.

SASHA LERNER is completing a doctorate in counselling psychology at McGill University under the supervision of Dr Ada L. Sinacore. She is also currently working at the University Counseling Center at the University of Albany in New York. Her research interests include immigration, cultural transitioning, and LGBTQ familial experiences, as well as gender and sexually focused bullying. She has contributed to recent publications such as *The cultural transitioning and educational challenges faced by first generation immigrant undergraduate students in Canada* (2013); *Lesbian mother–heterosexual daughter relationships: Toward a postmodern feminist analysis* (2012); and *Cultural transition of Jewish immigrants: Occupation, education, and integration* (2009).

ANNE MARSHALL is a professor of counselling psychology in educational psychology and leadership studies (Faculty of Education) and director of the Centre for Youth & Society at the University of Victoria. She is a co-developer of the Indigenous Communities Counselling Psychology graduate program, the first of its kind in Canada. Dr Marshall's community-engaged research focuses on youth well-being, transitions, and mental health in cultural and community contexts, especially among Indigenous communities and marginalized youth. She is the co-author of *Knowledge Translation in Context: Indigenous, Policy, and Community settings* (2011), published by University of Toronto Press.

MARVIN MCDONALD is the director of and a faculty member in the MA program in counselling psychology at Trinity Western University. His recent research focuses on collaborations for investigating bicultural identity, traumatic stress, compassion satisfaction, spiritual health, and close personal relationships. He is currently developing methodology and protocols drawn from French phenomenology and hermeneutics to enrich empirical inquiry into human thriving and flourishing. He is also involved in shared projects to adapt psychometric and assessment protocols with extended mixed-methods frameworks, collaborative assessment paradigms, and international, multilingual settings of application.

LOUISE OVERINGTON is completing her PhD in the Counselling Psychology Program at McGill University. She conducts research that informs, and is informed by, clinical practice, including how to improve the process and outcome of therapy, and psychotherapy training. Her dissertation research examines the use of evidence-based practices, such as progress monitoring measures, in training contexts; she published a comparison of PM measures in *Canadian Psychology* in 2012. Her work identifies and explores ways to improve training to facilitate the adoption of evidence-based practices that lead to better therapeutic outcomes.

JANE OXENBURY is a registered psychologist with a private practice in Calgary, where she works extensively with the LGBT communities, especially in the areas of same-sex domestic violence, the bullying and harassment of LGBT youth, and gender dysphoria. She is a member of the Psychologists' Association of Alberta, the College of Alberta Psychologists, the Canadian Psychological Association, the Canadian Register of Health Service Providers in Psychology, and the Canadian Society of Clinical Hypnosis – Alberta Division. She co-chairs the Safety Under the Rainbow capacity-building project. She is co-author of "Counselling Lesbians" in *Culture-Infused Counselling: Celebrating the Canadian Mosaic* (2005).

SHARON E. ROBERTSON is a professor and director of training, Counselling Psychology Program, Werklund School of Education, University of Calgary. She holds a PhD in counselling and school psychology from the University of Alberta and is a registered psychologist in Alberta. Her areas of research include psychosocial transitions, stress, coping, and social support; loss, grief, and bereavement; counselling women; counsellor education and supervision; and program development and evaluation. She is co-author of the CCPA accreditation standards for master's programs in Canada. Dr Robertson has served as president of the Canadian Counselling and Psychotherapy Association and as vice-president of the International Association for Counselling.

ADA L. SINACORE is an associate professor of counselling psychology at McGill University, a fellow of the Canadian Psychological Association, a past chair of the Canadian Psychological Association's Section on Counselling Psychology, a licensed professional counsellor

(Michigan), and an expert consultant. She founded and chaired the Inaugural Canadian Counselling Psychology Conference in 2010 and edited the first special section on counselling psychology published in *Canadian Psychology*. She is internationally recognized for her research, which focuses on feminist pedagogy, social justice, gender diversity and oppression, and immigration. For this work she was awarded the Oliva Espin Award for Social Justice Concerns in Feminist Psychology: Immigration and Gender, from the Association for Women in Psychology.

SUZANNE STEWART is a member of the Yellowknife Dene Nation. She is an associate professor of counselling psychology in the Department of Applied Psychology and Human Development at OISE–University of Toronto and Canada Research Chair in Aboriginal Homelessness and Life Transitions. Dr Stewart is also special advisor to the dean of OISE on Aboriginal education and research, as well as faculty chair of the Indigenous Education Network (IEN) at OISE. Her research focuses on cultural education and healing, Indigenous research methodologies, and Indigenous post-secondary success. Dr Stewart also practices as a counselling psychologist in Toronto.

K. JESSICA VAN VLIET is an associate professor in counselling psychology at the University of Alberta. Her primary research interests are in the areas of compassion and acceptance-based approaches for emotion regulation, especially in working with shame, trauma, and depression. Her most recent research has explored the impact of compassion-focused interventions on emotional regulation and mental health. She has also been part of an interdisciplinary research team studying the use of Mindfulness-Based Stress Reduction for youth with behavioural and emotional concerns. Dr Van Vliet currently maintains a small private practice where she counsels adult individuals and couples with a range of issues.

References

Abada, T., & Tenkorang, E.Y. (2009). Pursuit of university education among the children of immigrants in Canada: The roles of parental human capital and social capital. *Journal of Youth Studies, 12,* 185–207. doi:10.1080/13676260802558870

Aboriginal Healing Foundation. (2002). *The healing has begun: An operational update from the Aboriginal Healing Foundation.* Ottawa, ON: Aboriginal Healing Foundation.

Absolon, K. (1994). Building health from the medicine wheel: Aboriginal program development. A resource paper for theNative Physicians Association Conference at Winnipeg.

Ackbar, S., & Senn, C.Y. (2010). What's the confusion about fusion? – Differentiating positive and negative closeness in lesbian relationships. *Journal of Marital and Family Therapy, 36*(4), 416–430.

Adam, B.D. (2006). Relationship innovation in male couples. *Sexualities, 9*(1), 5–26. AIOSP. (2009). Époques prospères ou sombres: les apports de l'orientation en période de crise économique. Association internationale d'orientation scolaire et professionnelle (AISOP), communiqué, 5 June 2009. http://www.iaevg.org

Alderson, J. (2004). Intersex: A sad postscript. *The Psychologist, 17*(11), 629.

Alderson, K. (2000). *Beyond coming out: Experiences of positive gay identity.* Toronto: Insomniac Press.

Alderson, K. (2003). The ecological model of gay male identity. *Canadian Journal of Human Sexuality, 12*(2), 75–85.

Alderson, K. (2004a). A different kind of outing: Training counsellors to work with sexual minority clients. *Canadian Journal of Counselling, 38*(3), 193–210.

Alderson, K. (2004b). A phenomenological investigation of same-sex marriage. *Canadian Journal of Human Sexuality, 13*(2), 107–122.

Alderson, K. (2010). From madness to mainstream: Counselling gay men today. In N. Arthur and S. Collins (Eds.), *Culture-infused counselling: Celebrating the Canadian mosaic* (2nd ed., pp. 395–422). Calgary, A B: Counselling Concepts.

Alderson, K. (2012). *Breaking out II: The complete guide to building a positive L G B T I identity.* London, O N: Insomniac Press.

Alderson, K. (2013). *Counseling L G B T I clients.* Thousand Oaks, C A: Sage.

Alderson, K.G., Orzeck, T.L., & McEwen, S.C. (2009). Alberta high school counsellors' knowledge of homosexuality and their attitudes toward gay males. *Canadian Journal of Education, 32*(1), 87–117.

Alfred, T. (1999). *Peace, power and righteousness: An Indigenous manifesto.* Don Mills, O N: Oxford University Press.

Alves, S., & Gazzola, N. (2011). Professional identity: A qualitative inquiry of experienced counsellors. *Canadian Journal of Counselling and Psychotherapy, 45,* 189–207. doi:10.1080/09515070.2011.630572

Alvi, S., Hannah, S., & Stanyon, W. (2010). "We're locking the door": Family histories in a sample of homeless youth. *The Qualitative Report, 15*(5), 1209–1226.

American Psychiatric Association. (1952). *Diagnostic and statistical manual of mental disorders.* Washington, D C: Author.

American Psychiatric Association. (2000). *Diagnostic and statistical manual of mental disorders* (4th ed., text rev.). Washington, D C: Author.

American Psychiatric Association. (2013). *Diagnostic and statistical manual of mental disorder* (5th ed.). Washington, D C: Author.

American Psychological Association. (2006). Evidence-based practice in psychology. *American Psychologist, 61*(4), 271–285. doi:10.1037/0003-066X.61.4.271

American Psychological Association. (2010). Applications, acceptances, enrolments, and degrees awarded to master's- and doctoral-level students in U.S. and Canadian graduate departments of psychology: 2008–2009. http://www.apa.org/workforce/publications/10-grad-study/applications.aspx

Amundson, N.E. (2006). Challenges for career interventions in changing contexts. *International Journal for Educational and Vocational Guidance, 6,* 3–41. doi:10.1007/-s10775-006-0002-4

Amundson, N.E. (2007). The influence of workplace attraction on recruitment and retention. *Journal of Employment Counseling, 44*(4), 154–162.

Amundson, N.E. (2009). *Active engagement: The "being" and "doing" of career counselling*. Richmond, B C: Ergon Communications.

Amundson, N.E. (2010). *Metaphor making: Your career, your life, your way*. Richmond, B C: Ergon Communications.

Amundson, N.E., & Borgen, W.A. (1987). Coping with unemployment: What helps and what hinders. *Journal of Employment Counseling*, 24(3), 97–106.

Amundson, N.E., Borgen, W.A., Jordan, S., & Erlebach, A.C. (2004). Survivors of downsizing: Helpful and hindering experiences. *Career Development Quarterly*, 52, 256–271.

Amundson, N.E., Borgen, W.A., & Tench, E. (1995). Counselling and the role of personality and intelligence. In D.H. Saklofske and M. Zeidner (Eds.), *International handbook of personality and intelligence* (pp. 603–619). New York: Plenum Press.

Amundson, N.E., Harris-Bowlsbey, J., & Niles, S.G. (2005). *Essential elements of career counseling: Processes and techniques*. Upper Saddle River, NJ: Pearson/Merrill/Prentice-Hall.

Amundson, N.E., & Morley, J. (2002). Workplace wellness and worker well-being. In B. Hiebert & W. Borgen (Eds.), *Technical and vocational education and training in the twenty-first century: New roles and challenges for guidance and counselling* (pp. 103–114). Paris: United Nations Educational, Scientific, and Cultural Organization.

Amundson, N.E., Parker, P., & Arthur, M.B. (2002). Merging two worlds: Linking occupational and organizational career counselling. *Australian Journal of Career Development*, 11, 26–35.

Amundson, Yeung, Sun, Chan, & Cheng, J. (2011). The transition experiences of successful Chinese immigrants. *Journal of Employment Counseling*, 48(3), 129–135. doi:10.1002/j.2161-1920.2011.tb01119.x

Anderson, C.A. (2001). *The voices of older lesbian women: An oral history*. PhD thesis, Social Work. Calgary, A B: University of Calgary.

Andersen, R., & Fetner, T. (2008). Cohort differences in tolerance of homosexuality: Attitudinal change in Canada and the United States, 1981–2000. *Public Opinion Quarterly*, 72(2), 311–330.

Anisef, P., Sweet, R., & Adamuti-Trache, M. (2010). Impact of Canadian postsecondary education on recent immigrants' labour market outcomes. http://www.cic.gc.ca/english/resources/research/impact_postsecondary.asp

Archibald, J., Jovel, E., McCormick, R., Vedan, R., & Thira, D. (2006). Creating transformative Aboriginal health research: The B C A C A D R E at three years. *Canadian Journal of Native Education*, 29(1), 4–11.

Armstrong, P., Westwood, M., & Black, T.G. (2008). Case incident 17: Counseling military personnel following traumatic events. In N. Arthur & P. Pedersen (Eds.), *Case incidents in counseling for international transitions* (pp. 281–295). Alexandria, VA: American Counseling Association.

Arredondo, P., & Perez, P. (2003). Expanding multicultural competence through social justice leadership. *Counseling Psychologist, 31*(3), 282–289. doi:10.1177/0011000000303 1003003

Arredondo, P., & Perez, P. (2006). Historical perspectives on the multicultural guidelines and contemporary applications. *Professional Psychology: Research and Practice, 37*(1), 1–5. doi:10.1037/0735-7028.37.1.1

Arredondo, P., Toporek, R., Brown, S., Sanchez, J., Locke, D.C., Sanchez, J., & Stadler, H. (1996). Operationalization of the multicultural counseling competencies. *Journal of Multicultural Counseling & Development, 24*(1), 42–78.

Arredondo, P., Tovar-Blank, Z.G., and Parham, T.A. (2008). Challenges and promises of becoming a culturally competent counsellor in a socio-political era of change and empowerment. *Journal of Counseling & Development, 86,* 261–268.

Arthur, N. (2005a). Building from diversity to social justice competencies in international standards for career development practitioners. *International Journal for Educational and Vocational Guidance, 5*(2), 137–148.doi:10.1007/s10775-005-8791-4

Arthur, N. (2005b). Social justice competencies of career development practitioners. Paper presented at the National Consultation on Career Development (NATCON), Ottawa. http://www.natcon.org/natcon/papers/natcon-papers_2005_e4.pdf

Arthur, N. (in press). Career development and international transitions. In M. McMahon & M. Watson (Eds.), *Career development: Global issues and challenges.* Hauppauge, NY: Nova Science.

Arthur, N., & Achenbach, K. (2002). Developing multicultural counseling competencies through experiential learning. *Counselor Education and Supervision, 42*(1), 2–14.

Arthur, N., Anchan, J.P., Este, D., Khanlou, N., Kwok, S., & Mawani, F. (2004). Managing faculty-student collaborations in research and authorship. *Canadian Journal of Counselling, 38,* 177–192.

Arthur, N., & Collins, S. (2005). Expanding culture-infused counselling in professional practice. In N. Arthur & S. Collins (Eds.), *Culture-infused counselling* (pp. 151–212). Calgary, AB: Counselling Concepts.

Arthur, N., & Collins, S. (Eds.). (2010a). *Culture-infused counselling.* Calgary, A B: Counselling Concepts.

Arthur, N., & Collins, S. (2010b). Culture-infused counselling supervision. In N. Pelling, J. Barletta, & P. Armstrong (Eds.), *Practice of supervision* (pp. 267–295). Bowen Hills, Q L D: Australian Academic Press.

Arthur, N., & Collins, S. (2010c). Introduction to culture-infused counselling. In N. Arthur & S. Collins (Eds.), *Culture-infused counselling* (2nd ed., pp. 3–25). Calgary, A B: Counselling Concepts.

Arthur, N., & Collins, S. (2010d). Social justice and culture-infused counselling. In N. Arthur & S. Collins (Eds.), *Culture-infused counselling* (2nd ed., pp. 139–164). Calgary, A B: Counselling Concepts.

Arthur, N., & Collins, S. (2011). Infusing culture in career counselling. *Journal of Employment Counseling, 48*(3), 47–49. doi:10.1016/j. jvb.2003.12.006

Arthur, N., & Collins, S. (2012, May). Multicultural counselling and social justice: From concepts to practice. Pre-conference workshop at the Canadian Counselling and Psychotherapy Association 2012 Annual Conference, Calgary, A B.

Arthur, N., Collins, S., & Kennedy, B. (2011, May). *Social justice: Multiple meanings and practices.* Presentation at the annual conference of the Canadian Counselling Association, Ottawa.

Arthur, N., Collins, S., McMahon, M., & Marshall, C. (2009). Career practitioners' views of social justice and barriers for practice. *Canadian Journal of Career Development / Revue canadienne de developpement de carrière, 8,* 22–31.

Arthur, N., & Flynn, S. (2011). Career development influences of international students who pursue permanent immigration to Canada. *International Journal of Education and Vocational Guidance, 11*(3), 221–237.

Arthur, N., & Januszkowski, T. (2001). Multicultural competencies of Canadian counsellors. *Canadian Journal of Counselling, 35*(1), 36–48.

Arthur, N., & Lalande, V. (2009). Diversity and social justice implications for outcome approaches to evaluation. *International Journal for the Advancement of Counselling, 31*(1), 1–16. doi:10.1007/ s10447-008-9063-z

Arthur, N., & McMahon, M. (2005). Multicultural career counseling: Theoretical applications of the Systems Theory Framework. *The Career Development Quarterly, 53,* 208–222.

Arthur, N., Merali, N., & Djuraskovic, I. (2010). Facilitating the journey between cultures: Counselling immigrants and refugees. In N. Arthur &

S. Collins (Eds.), *Culture-infused counselling* (2nd ed., pp. 285–314). Calgary, A B: Counselling Concepts.

Arthur, N., & Pedersen, P. (Eds.). (2008). *Case incidents in counseling for international transitions.* Alexandria, V A: American Counseling Association.

Arthur, N., & Popadiuk, N. (2010). A cultural formulation approach to counseling international students. *Journal of Career Development,* 37(1), 423–440. doi:10.1177/0894845309345845

Arthur, N., & Rousseau, D.M. (1996). *The boundaryless career: A new employment principle for a new organizational era.* New York, N Y: Oxford University Press.

Arthur, N., & Stewart, J. (2001). Multicultural counselling in the new millennium: Introduction to the special theme issue. *Canadian Journal of Counselling, 35*(1), 3–14.

Arvay, M.J. (2001). Secondary traumatic stress among trauma counsellors: What does the research say? *International Journal for the Advancement of Counselling, 23*(4), 283–293.

Assembly of First Nations. (2002). *Top misconceptions about Aboriginal peoples.* Retrieved 15 December 2005 from http://www.afn.ca

Aston, S., Comeau, J., & Ross, N. (2007). Mapping responses to women with substance use problems in rural Canada. In N. Poole & L. Greaves (Eds.), *Highs and lows: Canadian perspectives on women and substance use* (pp. 111–122). Toronto: Centre for Addiction and Mental Health.

Australian Psychological Society. (2003). Endorsed psychological treatments in mental health. http://www.psychsociety.com.au/members/evidence/default.asq

Australian Psychological Society. (2010). Evidence-based psychological interventions in the treatment of mental disorders: A literature review (3rd ed.). Finders Lane, V I C: Author.

Ayala, J., & Coleman, H. (2000). Predictors of depression among lesbian women. *Journal of Lesbian Studies, 4*(3), 71–86.

Aycan, Z., & Berry, J.W. (1996). Impact of employment-related experiences on immigrants' psychological well-being and adaptation to Canada. *Canadian Journal of Behavioral Science, 28*(3), 240–251. http://psycnet.apa.org/journals/cbs/28/3/240.html

Bacon, C. (2007). L'interrelation identité professionnelle–éthique professionnelle. Doctoral thesis. Quebec: Université de Sherbrooke. https://www.usherbrooke.ca/cirea/documentation/theses_doc.html

Bagley, C., Wood, M., & Khumar, H. (1990). Suicide and careless death in young males: Ecological study of an Aboriginal population in Canada. *Canadian Journal of Community Mental Health, 29,* 127–142.

Balsam, K.F., & Szymanski, D.M. (2005). Relationship quality and domestic violence in women's same-sex relationships: The role of minority stress. *Psychology of Women Quarterly, 29,* 258–269.

Bandura, A. (1977). *Social learning theory.* Englewood Cliffs, N J: Prentice-Hall.

Bandura, A. (2001). Social cognitive theory and clinical psychology. In N.J. Smelser & P.B. Baltes (Eds.), *International encyclopedia of the social and behavioral sciences* (Vol. 21, pp. 14250–14254). Oxford, U K: Elsevier Science.

Barbara, A.M., Quandt, S.A., & Anderson, R.T. (2001). Experiences of lesbians in the health care environment. *Women & Health, 34*(1), 45–62.

Barret, B., & Logan, C. (2002). *Counseling gay men and lesbians: A practice primer.* Pacific Grove, C A: Brooks/Cole.

Basok, S., Ilcan, T., & Noonan, J. (2006). Citizenship, human rights, and social justice. *Citizenship Studies, 10*(3), 267–73.

Baudouin, R., Bezanson, L., Borgen, B., Goyer, L., Hiebert, B., Lalande, V., … Turcotte, M. (2007). Demonstrating value: A draft framework for evaluating the effectiveness of career development interventions. *The Canadian Journal of Counselling, 41*(3), 146–157. http://cjc-rcc.ucalgary.ca

Beatch, R., Bedi, R.P., Cave, D., Domene, J.F., Harris, G.E., Haverkamp, B.E., & Mikhail, A. (2009). *Counselling psychology in a Canadian context: Final report from the Executive Committee for a Canadian Understanding of Counselling Psychology.* Ottawa: Counselling Psychology Section of the Canadian Psychological Association. http://www.cpa.ca/aboutcpa/cpasections/counsellingpsychology/counsellingsectionbusiness/

Becker, J.M. (2012, 25 April). Exclusive: Dr. Robert Spitzer apologizes to gay community for infamous 'ex-gay' study. *Truth Wins Out.* http://www.truthwinsout.org/news/2012/04/24542/

Becklum, P., & Elgersma, S. (2008). *Recognition of the foreign credentials of immigrants.* (Publication No. PRB-04-29E). http://www.parl.gc.ca/Content/LOP/researchpublications/prb0429-e.pdf.

Bedi, R.P. (2006). Concept mapping the client's perspective on counseling alliance formation. *Journal of Counseling Psychology, 53*(1), 26–35. doi:10.1037/0022-0167.53.1.26

Bedi, R.P., & Domene, J.F. (2008). Counseling, definition of. In F.T. Leong (Ed.), *Encyclopedia of counseling* (pp. 119–120). Thousand Oaks, CA: Sage Publications.

Bedi, R.P., Haverkamp, B.E., Beatch, R., Cave, D.G., Domene, J.F., Harris, G.E., & Mikhail, A.M. (2011). Counselling psychology in a Canadian context: Definition and description. *Canadian Psychology – Psychologie Canadienne, 52*(2), 128–138. doi:10.1037/a0023186

Bedi, R.P., Klubben, L.M., & Barker, G.T. (2012, 9 July). Counselling vs. clinical: A comparison of psychology doctoral programs in Canada. *Canadian Psychology.* Advance online publication. doi:10.1037/a0028558

Bedi, R.P., & Rawdah, N. (2009).Career assessment. In B.T. Erford (Ed.), *The ACA encyclopedia of counseling* (pp. 67–70). Alexandria, VA: American Counseling Association.

Beer, A.M., Spanierman, L.B., Greene, J.C., & Todd, N.R. (2012). Counseling psychology trainees' perceptions of training and commitments to social justice. *Journal of Counseling Psychology 59*, 120–133. doi:10.1037/a0026325

Beharry, P., & Crozier, S. (2008). Using phenomenology to understand experiences of racism for second-generation South Asian women. *Canadian Journal of Counselling, 42*(4), 262–277.

Belanger, A., & Caron Melenfant, E. (2005). Population projections of visible minority groups, Canada, provinces and regions, 2001–2017. Cat. no. 91-541. Ottawa: Statistics Canada.

Belisle, R. (2010). *Can public policy support career development in a complex, compartmentalized and harsh world?* Traduction de la Conférence d'ouverture du Symposium pancanadien sur le développement de carrière et les politiques publiques organisé par le Groupe de travail sur les services de développement de carrière du Forum des ministres du marché du travail (FMMT), Winnipeg, 29 October 2009.

Bell, L.A. (1997). Theoretical foundations for social justice education. In M. Adams, L.A. Bell, & P. Griffin (Eds.), *Teaching for diversity and social justice: A sourcebook* (pp. 3–15). New York: Routledge.

Berenson, C. (2002). What's in a name? Bisexual women define their terms. *Journal of Bisexuality, 2*(2–3), 9–21.

Bergeron, S.M., & Senn, C.Y. (1998). Body image and sociocultural norms: A comparison of heterosexual and lesbian women. *Psychology of Women Quarterly, 22*(3), 385–401.

Bergeron, S., & Senn, C.Y. (2003). Health care utilization in a sample of Canadian lesbian women: Predictors of risk and resilience. *Women & Health, 37*(3), 19–35.

Berry, J.W. (1984). Multicultural policy in Canada: A social psychological analysis. *Canadian Journal of Behavioural Science, 16,* 353–370. doi:10.1037/h0080859

Berry, J.W. (1997). Immigration, acculturation, and adaptation. *Applied Psychology, 46,* 5–34. doi:10.1111/j.1464-0597.1997.tb01087.x

Berry, J.W. (2001). A psychology of immigration. *Journal of Social Issues, 57,* 613–651. doi:10.1111/0022-4537.00231

Berry, J.W. (2003). Conceptual approaches to acculturation. In K.M. Chun, P.B. Organista, & G. Marin (Eds.), *Acculturation: Advances in theory, measurement, and applied research* (pp. 17–38). Washington, D C: American Psychological Association.

Berry, J.W. (2005). Acculturation: Living successfully in two cultures. *International Journal of Intercultural Relations, 29,* 697–712. doi:10.1016/j.ijintrel.2005.07.013

Berry, J.W. (2008). Acculturation and adaptation of immigrant youth. *Canadian Diversity, 6*(2), 50–53.

Berry, J.W., & Laponce, J.A. (1994). Evaluating research in Canada's multiethnic and multicultural society: An introduction. In J.W. Berry & J.A. Laponce (Eds.), *Ethnicity and culture in Canada: The research landscape* (pp. 3–16). Toronto: University of Toronto Press.

Bezanson, L., & Kellett, R. (2001). Integrating career information and guidance services at a local level. Paris: O E C D.

Bezanson, L., & O'Reilly, E. (Eds.). (2002). *Making waves: Volume 2, Connecting career development with public policy.* Ottawa: Canadian Career Development Foundation.

Black, T.G. (2006). Teaching trauma without traumatizing: Principles of trauma treatment in the training of graduate counselors. *Traumatology, 12*(4), 266–271. doi:10.1177/1534765606297816

Black, T.G. (2008). Teaching trauma without traumatizing: A pilot study of a graduate counseling psychology cohort. *Traumatology, 14*(3), 40–50. doi:10.1177/1534765608320337

Black, T., Westwood, M., & Sorsdahl, M. (2007). From the front line to the front of the class: Counseling students who are military veterans. In J. Lippincott & R . Lippincott (Eds.), *Special populations in college counseling: A handbook for mental health professionals* (pp. 3–20). Alexandria, V A: American Counseling Association.

Blair, K.L., & Holmberg, D. (2008). Perceived social network support and well-being in same sex versus mixed-sex relationships. *Journal of Social and Personal Relationships, 25*(5), 769–791.

Blanchard, R. (1989). The concept of autogynephilia and the typology of male gender dysphoria. *Journal of Nervous and Mental Disease,* 177(10), 616–623.

Blanchard, R. (1994). A structural equation model for age at clinical presentation in nonhomosexual male gender dysphorics. *Archives of Sexual Behavior,* 23(3), 311–320.

Blanchard, R., & Collins, P.I. (1993). Men with sexual interest in transvestites, transsexuals, and she-males. *Journal of Nervous and Mental Disease, 181*(9), 570–575.

Bloxom, J.M., Bernes, K.B., Magnusson, K.C., Gunn, T.T., Bardick, A.D., ... McKnight, K.M. (2008). Grade 12 student career needs and perceptions of the effectiveness of career development services within high schools. *Canadian Journal of Counselling,* 42, 79–100.

Blue, A.W. (1977). A study of Native elders and student needs. *United States Bureau of Indian Affairs Education and Research Bulletin,* 5, 15–24.

Blue, A.W., & Darou, W. (2005). Counseling First Nations peoples. In N. Arthur and S. Collins (Eds.), *Culture-infused counselling* (pp. 303–330). Calgary, A B: Counselling Concepts.

Blue, A., Darou, W., & Ruano, C. (2010). Engaging the elder within: Bridging and honouring the cultural spaces in counselling with First Nations. In N. Arthur & S. Collins (Eds.), *Culture-infused counselling* (2nd ed., pp. 259–284). Calgary, A B: Counselling Concepts.

Blustein, D.L. (2011). A relational theory of working. *Journal of Vocational Behavior,* 79, 1–17. doi:10.1016/j.jvb.2010.10.004

Blustein, D.L., Medvide, M.B., & Kozan, S. (2012). A tour of a new paradigm: Relationships and work. *The Counseling Psychologist,* 40(2), 243–254. doi:10.1177/-0011000011429032

Bockting, W.O., Knudson, G., & Goldberg, J.M. (2006). Counseling and mental health care for transgender adults and loved ones. *International Journal of Transgenderism,* 9(3–4), 35–82.

Bohn, D.K. (2003). Lifetime physical and sexual abuse, substance abuse, depression, and suicide attempts among Native American women. *Issues in Mental Health Nursing,* 24, 333–352.

Boisvert, J.A., & Harrell, W.A. (2009). Homosexuality as a risk factor for eating disorder symptomatology in men. *The Journal of Men's Studies,* 17(3), 210–225.

Boivin, M.D., & Goyer, L. (2007). *L'orientation: quels défis pour les pratiques en orientation. Revue française Pratiques et analyses de formation.* Sous la coordination de F. Lesourd. Les temporalités éducatives, Approches plurielles, 51–52.

Bolton, S.-L., & Sareen, J. (2011). Sexual orientation and its relation to mental disorders and suicide attempts: Findings from a nationally representative sample. *The Canadian Journal of Psychiatry / La Revue canadienne de psychiatrie, 56*(1), 35–43.

Bopp, M., & Lane, P. (2000). *The Nuxalk plan*. Lethbridge, A B: Four Worlds International.

Bordin, E.S. (1979). The generalizability of the psychoanalytic concept of the working alliance. *Psychotherapy: Theory, Research & Practice, 16*(3), 252–260.

Borgen, W.A. (1997). People caught in changing career opportunities. *Journal of Employment Counseling, 34*, 133–143.

Borgen, W.A., & Amundson, N.E. (1987). The dynamics of unemployment. *Journal of Counseling and Development, 66*, 180–184.

Borgen, W.A., Amundson, N.E., & Reuter, J. (2004). Using portfolios to enhance career resilience. *Journal of Employment Counseling, 41*(2), 50–59. doi:10.1002/j.2161-1920.2004.tb00878.x

Borgen, W.A., Butterfield, L.D., & Amundson, N.E. (2010). The experience of change and its impact on workers who identify as doing well with change that affects their work. *Journal of Employment Counseling, 47*(1), 2–11. doi:10.1002/j.2161-1920.2010.tb00085.x

Borgen, W.A., Butterfield, L.D., & Lalande, V. (in press). Career conversations in small-to-medium sized businesses: A competitive advantage. Special issue: Changes occurring in the practice of counselling and career development. *Canadian Journal of Counselling and Psychotherapy*.

Borgen, W.A., & Hiebert, B. (2006). Career guidance and counselling for youth: What adolescents and young adults are telling us. *International Journal for the Advancement of Counselling, 28(4)*, 389–400. doi:10.1007/s10447-006-9022-5

Borgen, W.A., & Hiebert, B. (2014). Orienting educators to contemporary ideas for career counseling: An illustrative example. In G. Arulmani (Ed.), *Handbook of career development: International perspectives* (pp. 689–708). New York: Springer.

Bourassa, B., Fournier, G., & Goyer, L. (2013). Introduction. In B. Bourassa, G. Fournier, and L. Goyer (Eds.), Construction de savoirs et de pratiques professionnelles: Le double jeu de la recherche collaborative (pp. 9–40). Quebec: Les presses de l'Université Laval. Collection "Pratiques d'accompagnement professionnel".

Bower, J., Gurevich, M., & Mathieson, C. (2002). (Con)tested identities: Bisexual women reorient sexuality. *Journal of Bisexuality, 2*(2–3), 23–52.

Bowman, C., & Goldberg, J.M. (2007). Care of the patient undergoing sex reassignment surgery. *International Journal of Transgenderism, 9*(3–4), 135–165.

Bowman, M. (2000). The diversity of diversity: Canadian-American differences and their implications for clinical training and A P A accreditation. *Canadian Psychology, 41*(4), 230–243. doi:10.1037/h0086871

Bradshaw, R.A., Cook, A., & McDonald, M.J. (2011). Observed & Experiential Integration (O E I): Discovery and development of a new set of trauma therapy techniques. *Journal of Psychotherapy Integration, 21*, 104–171. doi:10.1037/a0023966

Braun, V., & Clarke, V. (2006). Using thematic analysis in psychology. *Qualitative Research in Psychology, 3*, 77–101. doi:10.1191/1478088706qp0630a

Brennan, D.J., Crath, R., Hart, T.A., Gadalla, T., & Gillis, L. (2011). Body dissatisfaction and disordered eating among men who have sex with men in Canada. *International Journal of Men's Health, 10*(3), 253–268.

Bridges, S.K., Selvidge, M.M.D., & Matthews, C.R. (2003). Lesbian women of color: Therapeutic issues and challenges. *Journal of Multicultural Counseling and Development, 31*, 113–130.

Brittain, D.R., Baillargeon, T., McElroy, M., Aaron, D.J., & Gyurcsik, N.C. (2006). Barriers to moderate physical activity in adult lesbians. *Women & Health, 43*(1), 75–92.

Bronfenbrenner, U. (1979). *The ecology of human development: Experiments by nature and design.* Cambridge, M A: Harvard University Press.

Brosseau, D.C., McDonald, M.J., & Stephen, J.E. (2011). The moderating effect of relationship quality on partner secondary traumatic stress among couples coping with cancer. *Families, Systems, & Health, 29*(2), 114–126. doi:10.1037/a0024155

Brotman, S., Ryan, B., Jalbert, Y., & Rowe, B. (2002). Reclaiming space – regaining health: The health care experiences of Two-Spirit people in Canada. *Journal of Gay & Lesbian Social Services: Issues in Practice, Policy & Research, 14*(1), 67–87.

Brotto, L.A., Knudson, G., Inskip, J., Rhodes, K., & Erskine, Y. (2010). Asexuality: A mixed methods approach. *Archives of Sexual Behavior, 39*(3), 599–618.

Brown, D. (2012). *Career information, career counseling, and career development* (10th ed.). Boston, M A: Pearson.

Brown, G.R., Wise, T.N., Costa, P.T., Herbst, J.H., Fagan, P.J., & Schmidt, C.W. (1996). Personality characteristics and sexual functioning of 188 cross-dressing men. *Journal of Nervous and Mental Disease, 184*(5), 265–273.

Brown, P., & Hasketh, A. (with Williams, S.). (2004). *The mismanagement of talent: Employability and jobs in the knowledge economy.* New York, NY: Oxford University Press.

Brown, S.D., Lent, R.W., Telander, K., & Tramayne, S. (2011). Social cognitive career theory, conscientiousness, and work performance: A meta-analytic path analysis. *Journal of Vocational Behavior, 79*, 81–90.

Buchanan, M., & Keats, P. (2011). Coping with traumatic stress in journalism: A critical ethnographic study. *International Journal of Psychology, 46*(2), 127–135. doi:10.1080/00207594.2010.532799

Buhr, E., & Domene, J.F. (2012, March). *Counselling Psychology Research Practices in British Columbia: Evidence from Journal Publications.* Paper presented at the 2nd Annual Counselling Psychology Research Conference, Langley, BC.

Buhrich, N., & McConaghy, N. (1977). Clinical comparison of transvestism and transsexualism: An overview. *Australian and New Zealand Journal of Psychiatry, 11*(2), 83–86.

Bujold, C., & Gingras, M. (2010). Un nouveau paradigme pour l'orientation: Perspectives, limites et défis. *L'Orientation Scolaire et Professionnelle, 39*, 73–86.

Bullough, V.L., & Bullough, B. (1993). *Cross dressing, sex, and gender.* Baltimore, MD: University of Pennsylvania Press.

Burgoyne, R.W. (1994). Counselling gay male couples living with HIV. *Canadian Journal of Human Sexuality, 3*(1), 1–14.

Burnett, R. (2009, 23 October). *Montreal's Sex Garage raid: A watershed moment.* http://www.xtra.ca/public/National/Montreals_Sex_Garage_raid_A_watershed_moment-7735.aspx

Burwell, R., & Kalbfleisch, S. (2011). Deliberations on the future of career development education in Canada. *Canadian Journal of Career Development, 10*(1), 354–369.

Butt, J.A., & Guldner, C.A. (1993). Counselling bisexuals: Therapists' attitudes towards bisexuality and application in clinical practice. *Canadian Journal of Human Sexuality, 2*(2), 61–70.

Butterfield, L.D., & Borgen, W.A. (2005). Outplacement counselling from the client's perspective. *The Career Development Quarterly, 53*(4), 306–316. doi:10.1002/j.2161-0045.2005.tb00661.x

Butterfield, L.D., Borgen, W.A., Amundson, N.E., & Erlebach, A.C. (2010). What helps and hinders workers in managing change. *Journal of Employment Counseling, 47*, 146–156.

Butterfield, L.D., Borgen, W.A., Amundson, N.E., & Maglio, A.T. (2005/2009). Fifty years of the Critical Incident Technique: 1954–2004 and beyond. *Qualitative Research, 5*, 475–497. Reprinted in Peter Griffiths (Ed.), *Nursing Research Methods*. Thousand Oaks, CA: Sage Publications.

Butterfield, L.D., Borgen, W.A., Maglio, A.T., & Amundson, N.E. (2009). Using the enhanced critical incident technique in counselling psychology research. *Canadian Journal of Counselling, 43*, 265–282.

Cahill, M., & Martland, S. (1993). Career counselling in rural areas. *Guidance & Counseling, 8*(3), 11–19.

Cahill, M., & Martland, S. (1995a). Counseling career drifters. ERIC Digest. Retrieved from ERIC Database. (ED401498)

Cahill, M., & Martland, S. (1995b). Extending the reach: Distance delivery in career counseling. ERIC Digest. Retrieved from ERIC database. (ED414513)

Cain, R. (1991). Relational contexts and information management among gay men. *Families in Society, 72*(6), 344–352.

Cairns, K.V. (1997). Counselling the partners of heterosexual male cross-dressers. *Canadian Journal of Human Sexuality, 6*(4), 297–306.

Calam, B., Varcoe, C., & Buchanan, M.J. (in press). *Report on the Rural Aboriginal Women's Maternity Care Project*. BC Centre for Excellence.

Calderwood, K., Harper, K., Ball, K., & Liang, D. (2009). When values and behaviors conflict: Immigrant BSW students' experiences revealed. *Journal of Ethnic and Cultural Diversity in Social Work, 18*, 110–128. doi:10.1080/15313200902874995

Campaign 2000. (2011). *Revisiting family security in insecure times: 2011 report card on child and family poverty in Canada*. http://www.campaign2000.ca/reportCards/national/2011EnglishRreportCard.pdf

Canadian Broadcasting Corporation. (13 December 2002). Canada's wealth disparity rivals third world. http://www.cbc.ca/canada/story/2002/12/13/disparity021213.html

Canadian Centre for Policy Alternatives. (2006). Growing gap, growing concerns: Canadian attitudes toward income inequality. Ottawa: Author.

Canadian Council for Social Development. (2006). The progress of Canada's children and youth. Ottawa: Author. http://www.ccsd.ca/pccy/2006/

Canadian Counselling and Psychotherapy Association. (2007). *Code of ethics*. Ottawa: Author.

Canadian Counselling and Psychotherapy Association. (2011). *Standards of practice for counsellors*. Ottawa: Author. http://www.ccpa-accp.ca/en/standardsofpractice/

Canadian Institute for Health Information. (2004). *Improving the health of Canadians*. Ottawa: Author.

Canadian Institute for Health Information. (2006). *Improving the health of Canadians: Promoting healthy weights*. https://secure.cihi.ca/estore/productSeries.htm?pc=PCC278

Canadian Psychological Association. (1996/2001). *Guidelines for non discriminatory practice*. Ottawa: Author. http://www.cpa.ca/cpasite/userfiles/Documents/publications/NonDiscPractrev%20cpa.pdf

Canadian Psychological Association. (2000). *Canadian code of ethics for psychologists* (3rd ed.). Ottawa: Author.

Canadian Psychological Association. (2009a). *Ethical guidelines for supervision in psychology: Teaching, research, practice, and administration*. Ottawa: Author.

Canadian Psychological Association. (2009b). *Definition of Counselling Psychology*. Ottawa: Author. http://www.cpa.ca/cpasite/userfiles/Documents/sections/counselling/Definition%20of%20Counselling%20Psychology.pdf

Canadian Psychological Association. (2011). *Accreditation standards and procedures for doctoral programmes and internships in professional psychology (5th revision)*. Ottawa: Author.

Canadian Psychological Association. (2012). *CPA's definition of evidence-based practice of psychological treatments*. Ottawa: Author.

Canadian Research Institute for the Advancement of Women. (2005). Fact sheet: Women and poverty. http://www.criaw-icref.ca/indexFrame_e.htm

Cardu, H. (2008). Career nomadism and the building of a professional identity in female immigrants. *Journal of International Migration and Integration, 8*, 429–439.doi:10.1007/s12134007-0031-y

Cardu, H., & Bouchamma, Y. (2000). *Identité et insertion socio-professionnelle: Un outil de counselling interculturel auprès de femmes immigrants*. Quebec: Les actes du CONAT.

Cardu, H., & Sanschagrin, M. (2002). Les femmes et la migration: les representations identitaires et les stratégies devant les obstacles à l'insertion socioprofessionnelle à Québec. *Recherche Feministe, 15*(2), 87–122. http://www.erudit.org/revue/RF/2002/v15/n2/006512ar.html

Cardu, H., & Sanschagrin, M. (2005). Agir auprès des femmes immigrantes: analyse des représentations identitaires professionnelles des conseillers d'orientation. *Canadian Journal of Counselling, 39*, 215–230.

Caron, J., & Lui, A. (2010). A descriptive study of the prevalence of psy-
chological distress and mental disorders in the Canadian population:
Comparison between low-income and non-low-income populations.
Chronic Diseases in Canada, 30(3), 84–94.

Caron, N.R. (2004). Getting to the root of trauma in Canada's Aboriginal
population. *Canadian Medical Association Journal, 172*, 8. doi:10.1503/
cmaj.050304

Carr-Stewart, S. (2006). First Nations education: Financial accountability
and educational attainment. *Canadian Journal of Education, 29*, 1–21.
doi:10.2307/1602197

Carver, C.S. (1998). Resilience and thriving: Issues, models, and linkages.
Journal of Social Issues, 54(2), 245–266. doi:10.1111%2Fj.1540-4560.
1998.tb01217.x

Casas, J.M., Park, Y.S., & Cho, B. (2010). The multicultural and internationalization counseling psychology movements: When all is said and
done, it's all multicultural, isn't it? In J.G. Ponterotto, J.M. Casas, L.A.
Suzuki, & C.M. Alexander (Eds.), *Handbook of multicultural counseling* (3rd ed., pp. 189–211). Thousand Oaks, CA: Sage.

CBC News. (2002, 20 December). *Bathhouse raid angers Calgary gay
community*. http://www.cbc.ca/canada/story/2002/12/20/bathhouse_
raid021220.html

CBC News. (2007, 1 March). *Same-sex rights: Canada timeline*. http://
www.cbc.ca/news/background/samesexrights/timeline_canada.html

Centre for Global Development. (2006). Commitment to development
index. http://www.cgdev.org/section/initiatives/_active/cdi

Chambless, D.L., & Ollendick, T.H. (2001). Empirically supported psychological interventions: Controversies and evidence. *Annual Review of
Psychology, 52*, 685–716. doi:10.1146/annurev.psych.52.1.685

Chambless, D.L., Sanderson, W.C., Shoham, V., Bennett Johnson, S., Pope,
K.S., Crits-Christoph, P., … McCurry, S. (1996). An update on empirically validated therapies. *Clinical Psychologist, 49*, 5–18.

Chandler, M.J., & Lalonde, C. (1998). Cultural continuity as a hedge
against suicide in Canada's First Nations. *Transcultural Psychiatry, 35*,
191–219.

Chen, C.P. (2001a). Career counselling as life career integration. *Journal of
Vocational Education and Training, 53*(4), 523–542. doi:10.1080/
13636820100200175

Chen, C.P. (2001b). On exploring meanings: Combining humanistic and
career psychology theories in counselling. *Counselling Psychology
Quarterly, 14*(4), 317–330. http://www.tandf.co.uk/journals/carfax/
09515070.html

Chen, C.P. (2002). Integrating action theory and human agency in career development. *Canadian Journal of Counselling, 36*(2), 121–135. http://cjc-rcc.ucalgary.ca/cjc/index.php/rcc

Chen, C.P. (2003). Integrating perspectives in career development theory and practice. *The Career Development Quarterly, 51*(3), 203–216. http://associationdatabase.com/aws/NCDA/pt/sp/cdquarterly

Chen, C.P. (2004). Transforming career in cross-cultural transition: The experience of non-Western culture counsellor trainees. *Counselling Psychology Quarterly, 17*, 137–154. doi:10.1080/09515070410001728299

Chen, C.P. (2006a). Strengthening career human agency. *Journal of Counseling & Development, 84*(2), 131–138. doi:10.1002/j.1556-6678.2006.tb00388.x

Chen, C.P. (2006b). Career endeavour: Pursuing a cross-cultural life transition. Aldershot, U K: Ashgate.

Chen, C.P. (2008). Career guidance with immigrants. In J. Athanasou & R.V. Esbroeck (Eds.), *International handbook of career guidance* (pp. 419–442). New York: Springer. doi:10.1007/978-1-4020-6230-8_21

Chen, C.P., & Asamoah, A. (2007). Vocational psychology of immigrant women: Special issues and practical implications. *Baltic Journal of Psychology, 8*(1&2), 67–75.

Child and Youth Advisory Committee of the Mental Health Commission of Canada. (2010). Evergreen: A child and youth mental health framework for Canada. Calgary, A B: Mental Health Commission of Canada.

Chirkov, V. (2009). Summary of the criticism and of the potential ways to improve acculturation psychology. *International Journal of Intercultural Relations, 33*, 170–180. doi:10.1016/j.ijintrel.2009.03.005

Chope, R.C. (2011). Reconsidering interests: The next big idea in career counseling theory, research, and practice. *Journal of Career Assessment, 19*(3), 343–352. doi:10.1177/1069072710395540

Christ, T.J. (2007). Experimental control and threats to internal validity of concurrent and nonconcurrent multiple baseline designs. *Psychology in the Schools, 44*, 451–459.

Christopher, J.C., & Hickinbottom, S. (2008). Positive psychology, ethnocentrism, and the disguised ideology of individualism. *Theory & Psychology, 18*(5), 563–589. doi:10.1177/0959354308093396

C I H R University Delegate. (2012). I J G O T P W C I H R and they were updating on salary awards with numbers. http://www.cattinilab.mb.ca/Lab_Site/CIHR_Delegate/Entries/2012/2/19_IJGOTPW_CIHR_and_they_were_updating_on_salary_awards_with_numbers.html

Citizenship and Immigration Canada. (2002). Immigration and Refugee Protection Act. *Canada Gazette: Part II, 36*(9).

Citizenship and Immigration Canada. (2009). *A survey of recent research on religious diversity and implications for multiculturalism policy.* http://policyresearch.gc.ca/page.asp?pagenm=2009-0008_15

Citizenship and Immigration Canada. (2011). *Canada facts and figures: Immigration overview permanent and temporary residents.* (Catalogue No. Ci1-8/2010E-PDF). http://publications.gc.ca/site/eng/393243/publication.html

Cochran, L. (1992). The career project. *Journal of Career Development, 18*(3), 187–197. doi:10.1177/089484539201800303

Cochran, L. (1997). *Career counseling: A narrative approach.* Thousand Oaks, CA: Sage.

Cohen, J.N. (2011). Minority stress, resilience, and sexual functioning in sexual-minority women. *Dissertation Abstracts International: Section B: The Sciences and Engineering, 72*(2-B), 1161.

Cohen, J.N., Byers, E.S., & Walsh, L.P. (2008). Factors influencing the sexual relationships of lesbians and gay men. *International Journal of Sexual Health, 20*(3), 162–176.

Cole, E.R. (2009). Intersectionality and research in psychology. *American Psychologist, 64*, 170–180. doi:10.1037/a0014564

Collin, A., & Young, R.A. (2000). The future of career. In A. Collin & R.A. Young (Eds.), *The future of career* (pp. 276–300). Cambridge, UK: Cambridge University Press.

Collins, S. (2010a). The complexity of identity: Appreciating multiplicity and intersectionality. In N. Arthur & S. Collins (Eds.), *Culture-infused counselling* (2nd ed., pp. 247–258). Calgary, AB: Counselling Concepts.

Collins, S. (2010b). Women on the margins: Honouring multiple and intersecting cultural identities. In L. Ross (Ed.), *Counselling women: Feminist issues, theory and practice* (pp. 21–50). Toronto: Canadian Scholars' Press / Women's Press.

Collins, S., & Arthur, N. (2007). A framework for enhancing multicultural counselling competence. *Canadian Journal of Counselling, 41*(1), 31–49.

Collins, S., & Arthur, N. (2010a). Culturally sensitive working alliance. In N. Arthur & S. Collins (Eds.), *Culture-infused counselling* (2nd ed., pp. 103–138). Calgary, AB: Counselling Concepts.

Collins, S., & Arthur, N. (2010b). Culture-infused counselling: A fresh look at a classic framework of multicultural counseling competencies. *Counselling Psychology Quarterly, 23*(2), 203–216. doi:10.1080/09515071003798204

Collins, S., & Arthur, N. (2010c). Culture-infused counselling: A model for developing multicultural competence. *Counselling Psychology Quarterly, 23*(2), 217–233. doi:10.1080/09515071003798212

Collins, S., Arthur, N., & Wong-Wylie, G. (2010). Enhancing reflective practice in multicultural counseling through cultural auditing. *Journal of Counseling & Development, 88*(3), 340–347.

Collins, S., & Oxenbury, J. (2010). Affirming women who love women: Principles for counseling lesbians. In N. Arthur & S. Collins (Eds.), *Culture-infused counselling* (2nd ed., pp. 363–394). Calgary, A B: Counselling Concepts.

Conlin, D., & Smith, J. (1981–82). Group psychotherapy for gay men. *Journal of Homosexuality, 7*(2–3), 105–112.

Coogan, P., & Chen, C.P. (2007). Career development and counselling for women: Connecting theories to practice. *Counselling Psychology Quarterly, 20*, 191–204. doi:10.1080/09515070701391171

Cortes, L., & Buchanan, M. (2007). The experience of Columbian child soldiers from a resilience perspective. *International Journal for the Advancement of Counselling, 29*(1), 43–55. doi:10.1007/s10447-006-9027-0

Costigan, C.L., & Dokis, D.P. (2006). Similarities and differences in acculturation among mothers, fathers, and children in immigrant Chinese families. *Journal of Cross-Cultural Psychology, 37*(6), 723–741. doi:10.1177/0022022106292080

Costigan, C., Su, T.F., & Hua, J.M. (2009). Ethnic identity among Chinese Canadian youth: A review of the Canadian literature. *Canadian Psychology / Psychologie Canadienne, 50*(4), 261–272. doi:10.1037/a0016880

Council of Chairs of Training Councils. (n.d.). Match imbalance survey: Volunteer resources for doctoral internships. http://www.psychtraining-councils.org/Documents/VolunteersforImbalancefromSurvey.doc

Counselling Foundation of Canada. (2002). *A coming of age: A history of counseling Canadians for work in the 20th century*. Toronto: Canadian Education and Research Institute for Counselling.

Cozby, P.C. (1997). *Methods in behavioral research* (6th ed.). Mountain View, C A: Mayfield Publishing.

Creswell, J.W., Plano Clark, V.L., Gutmann, M.L., & Hanson, W.E. (2003). Advanced mixed methods research designs. In A. Tashakkori & C. Teddlie (Eds.), *Handbook of mixed methods in social & behavioral research* (pp. 209–240). Thousand Oaks, C A: Sage.

Daley, A. (2006). Lesbian and gay health issues: O U T side of Canada's health policy. *Critical Social Policy, 26*(4), 794–816.

Daley, A.E. (2008). Telling, knowing, and being understood: Negotiating lesbian in/visibility within the spaces of psychiatric and mental health services. *Dissertation Abstracts International: Section B: The Sciences and Engineering, 69*(6-B), 3503.

Daley, A. (2010). Being recognized, accepted, and affirmed: Self-disclosure of lesbian/queer sexuality within psychiatric and mental health service settings. *Social Work in Mental Health, 8*(4), 336–355.

Dana, R.H. (2005). *Multicultural assessment: Principles, applications, and examples.* Mahwah, NJ: Lawrence Erlbaum.

Dana, R.H. (2008). Clinical diagnosis in multicultural populations. In L.A. Suzuki and J.G. Ponterotto (Eds.), *Handbook of multicultural assessment: Clinical, psychological, and educational applications* (3rd ed., pp. 107–131). New York: Wiley.

Daniluk, J. (1996). When treatment fails: The transition to biological childlessness for infertile women. *Women & Therapy, 19,* 81–98. doi:10.1300/J015v19n02_07

Daniluk, J. (2001). "If we had it to do over again...": Couples' reflections on their experiences of infertility treatments. *The Family Journal, 9,* 122–133. doi:10.1177/1066480701092006

Daniluk, J., & Browne, N. (2008). Traditional religious doctrine and women's sexuality: Reconciling the differences. *Women & Therapy, 31,* 129–142. doi:10.1300/02703140802145284

Daniluk, J., & Fluker, M. (1995). Fertility drugs and the reproductive imperative: Assisting the infertile woman. *Women & Therapy, 16,* 31–47. doi:10.1300/J015v16n01_03

Daniluk, J., & Hurtig-Mitchell, J. (2003). Themes of hope and healing: Infertile couples' experiences of adoption. *Journal of Counseling & Development, 81,* 389–399. doi:10.1002/j.1556-6678.2003.tb00265.x

Daniluk, J.C., Koert, E., & Cheung, A. (2012). Childless women's knowledge of fertility and assisted human reproduction: Identifying the gaps. *Fertility & Sterility, 97,* 420–426. doi:10.1016/j.fertnstert.2011.11.046

Daniluk, J., & Tench, E. (2007). Long-term adjustment of infertile couples following unsuccessful medical intervention. *Journal of Counseling & Development, 85,* 89–100. doi:10.1002/j.1556-6678.2007.tb00448.x

Danvers, F. (2009). *S'orienter dans la vie: une valeur suprême?* Essai d'anthropologie de la formation. Dictionnaire de sciences humaines (500 entrées). Préface: G. Solaux; Postface: J. Saint-Fleur. Villeneuve d'Ascq, Presses universitaires du Septentrion, Collection "Métiers et pratiques de formation", 656 p.

Davidson, M.M., & Huenefeld, N. (2002). Struggling with two identities: The case of Eileen. *The Career Development Quarterly, 50,* 306–310.

Daya, R. (2000). Buddhist psychology, a theory of change processes: Implications for counsellors. *International Journal for the Advancement of Counselling, 22*(4), 257–271. doi:10.1023/A:1005648127301

Daya, R. (2001). Changing the face of multicultural counselling with principles of change. *Canadian Journal of Counselling, 35*(1), 49–62.

DeLuzio Chasin, C.J. (2011). Theoretical issues in the study of asexuality. *Archives of Sexual Behavior, 40*(4), 713–723.

Department of Justice Canada. (2012). Table of Contents: Canada Health Act (R.S.C., 1985, c. C-6). http://laws-lois.justice.gc.ca/eng/acts/C-6/index.html

Devor, H. (2002). Who are "we"? Where sexual orientation meets gender identity. *Journal of Gay & Lesbian Psychotherapy, 6*(2), 5–21.

Dewa, C.S., Lesage, A., Goering, P., & Caveen, M. (2004). Nature and prevalence of mental illness in the workplace. *HealthcarePapers, 5*(2). http://www.longwoods.com

Diamond, L.M. (2008). Female bisexuality from adolescence to adulthood: Results from a 10-year longitudinal study. *Developmental Psychology, 44*(1), 5–14.

Dickason, O.P. (1997). *Canada's First Nations: A history of founding peoples from earliest times*. Toronto: Oxford University Press.

Disability management forum: Tackling depression and mental health. (2005). *Benefits Canada, 29*(8), 1 (Special Supplement).

Djuraskovic, I., & Arthur, N. (2009). The acculturation of former Yugoslavian refugees. *Canadian Journal of Counselling, 43*, 18–34.

Docter, R.F. (1988). *Tranvestites and transsexuals: Toward a theory of cross-gender behavior*. New York: Plenum Press.

Domene, J.F. (2011). Sense of "calling" in post-secondary students: Implications for educational and counselling practice. Public lecture presented at the University of New Brunswick, 17 November, Fredericton, N B.

Domene, J.F., & Bedi, R.P. (2012). Counselling and psychotherapy in Canada: Diversity and growth. In R. Moodley, U.P. Gielen, & R. Wu (Eds.), *Handbook of counseling and psychotherapy in an international context* (pp. 106–116). New York: Routledge.

Domene, J.F., & Young, R.A. (2008). Expanding the action project method to encompass comparative analyses. *International Journal of Qualitative Methods, 7*, 54–80. http://ejournals.library.ualberta.ca/index.php/IJQM/index

Donnelly, J., & Howard, R. (1988). Assessing national human rights performance: A theoretical framework. *Human Rights Quarterly, 10*(2), 214–248.

Dozois, D.J. (2011a). Message from the president. http://www.cpa.ca/aboutcpa/presidentsmessage/

Dozois, D.J. (2011b). Training in professional psychology: The content and process of learning. *Psynopsis, 33*(4), 7.

Drapeau, M. (2004). Les critères de scientificité en recherche qualitative. *Pratiques Psychologiques, 10,* 79–86.

Drummond & Tulk. (2006). Lifestyles of the rich and unequal: An investigation into wealth inequality in Canada. Toronto: Toronto Dominion Bank Financial Group. Special Report. http://www.td.com/economics/special/dt1206_wealth.pdf

Duckworth, J. (1990). The counseling approach to the use of testing. *Counseling Psychologist, 18*(2), 198–204. doi:10.1177/0011000090182002

Dumont, M., Pronovost, J., & Leclerc, D. (2004). Les stratégies adaptatives des adolescents: Comparaison d'un groupe scolaire et d'un groupe desservi en centres jeunesse. *Revue de psychoéducation, 33*(1), 137–155.

Dunn, J.C., Whelton, W.J., & Sharpe, D. (2012). Retreating to safety: Testing the social risk hypothesis model of depression. *Evolution and Human Behavior.* doi:10.1016/j.evolhumbehav.2012.06.002

Dupras, A. (1994). Internalized homophobia and psychosexual adjustment among gay men. *Psychological Reports, 75*(1, Pt 1), 23–28.

Duran, E. (2006). *Healing the soul wound.* New York: Teachers College, Columbia University.

Duran, E., & Duran, B. (l995). *Native American postcolonial psychology.* Albany: State University of New York Press.

Duxbury, L., & Higgins, C. (2009). *Key findings and conclusions from the 2001 National Work-Life Conflict Study.* Ottawa: Health Canada. http://www.hc-sc.gc.ca/ewh-semt/pubs/occup-travail/balancing_six-equilibre_six/index-eng.php

Dyer, B. (in press). The action of mindfulness: Mindfulness and counselling from an action-theoretical perspective. In R.A. Young, L. Valach, & J.F. Domene (Eds.), *Counselling and action: Towards life enhancing work, relationships, and identity.* New York: Springer.

Dze L K'ant Friendship Centre and Society. (2006). Medicine wheel model for mental health. Retrieved 10 September 2006 from http://www.bcaafc.com/centres/smithers/Mental.html

Eady, A., Dobinson, C., & Ross, L.E. (2011). Bisexual people's experiences with mental health services: A qualitative investigation. *Community Mental Health Journal, 47*(4), 378–389.

Edwards, N.C., & MacLean Davison, C. (2008). Social justice and core competencies for public health. *Revue Canadienne de Sante Publique, 99*(2), 130–132.

Eisen, S.V., Gerena, M., Ranganathan, G., Esch, D., & Idiculla, T. (2006). Reliability and validity of the BASIS-24 (c) mental health survey for Whites, African-Americans, and Latinos. *Journal of Behavioral Health Services & Research, 33*(3), 304–323. doi:10.1007/s11414-006-9025-3

Eisen, S.V., Normand, S.L., Belanger, A.J., Spiro, A., & Esch, D. (2004). The revised behavior and symptom identification scale (BASIS-r) – reliability and validity. *Medical Care, 42*(12), 1230–1241. doi:10.1097/00005650-200412000-00010

Elizabeth, A. (2013). Challenging the binary: Sexual identity that is not duality. *Journal of Bisexuality, 13*(3), 329–337.

Ellis, S.J., & Peel, E. (2011). Lesbian feminisms: Historical and present possibilities. *Feminism & Psychology, 21*(2), 198–204.

Elman, N.S., & Forrest, L. (2007). From trainee impairment to professional competence problems: Seeking new terminology that facilitates effective action. *Professional Psychology: Research and Practice, 38*(5), 501–509. doi:10.1037/0735-7028.38.5.501

Emmons, R.A. (1989). The personal striving approach to personality. In L.A. Pervin (Ed.), *Goal concepts in personality and social psychology* (pp. 87–126). Hillsdale, NJ: Erlbaum.

Engel, G.L. (1977). The need for a new medical model: A challenge for biomedicine. *Science, 196,* 129–136.

Enns, C., Sinacore, A.L., & Ancis, J.R. (2004). Toward integrating feminist and multicultural pedagogies. *Journal of Multicultural Counseling & Development, 32,* 414–427.

Environics Survey Group. (2010). *Online survey on public perceptions about career development and the workplace.* Toronto: Author.

Esses, V.M., Deaux, K., LaLonde, R.N., & Brown, R. (2010). Psychological perspectives on immigration. *Journal of Social Issues, 66,* 635–647. doi:10.1111/j.1540-4560.2010.01667.x

Esses, V.M., Dietz, J., & Bhardwaj, A. (2006). The role of prejudice in the discounting of immigrant skills. In R. Mahalingam (Ed.), *Cultural psychology of immigrants* (pp. 113–130). Mahwah, NJ: Lawrence Erlbaum.

Esses, V.M., Dovidio, J.F., Jackson, L.M., & Armstrong, T.L. (2001). The immigration dilemma: The role of perceived group competition, ethnic prejudice, and national identity. *Journal of Social Issues, 57,* 389–412. doi:10.1111/0022-4537.00220

Esses, V.M., & Gardner, R.C. (1996). Multiculturalism in Canada: Context and current status. *Canadian Journal of Behavioural Science / Revue canadienne des sciences du comportement, 28,* 145–152. doi:10.1037/h0084934

Everall, R.D., Altrows, K.J., & Paulson, B.L. (2006). Creating a future: A study of resilience in suicidal female adolescents. *Journal of Counseling & Development, 84*(4), 461–470. doi:10.1002/j.1556-6678.2006.tb00430.x

Everall, R.D., Bostik, K.E., & Paulson, B.L. (2006). Being in the safety zone: Emotional experiences of suicidal adolescents and emerging adults. *Journal of Adolescent Research, 21*(4), 370–392. doi:10.1177/0743558406289753

Everall, R.D., & Paulson, B.L. (2004). Burnout and secondary traumatic stress: Impact on ethical behaviour. *Canadian Journal of Counselling, 38*(1), 25–35.

Fadden, R., & Townsend, T. (2009). Dealing with religious diversity: Opportunities and challenges. *Horizons, 10*(2), 4–5.

Falender, C.A., & Shafranske, E.P. (2012). The importance of competency-based clinical supervision and training in the twenty-first century: Why bother? *Journal of Contemporary Psychotherapy, 42,* 129–137. doi:10.1007/s10879-011-9198-9

Fallu, J.-S., Janosz, M., Brière, F.N., Descheneaux, A., Vitaro, F., & Tremblay, R.E. (2010). Preventing disruptive boys from becoming heavy substance users during adolescence: A longitudinal study of familial and peer-related protective factors. *Addictive Behaviors, 35*(12), 1074–1082. doi:10.1016/j.addbeh.2010.07.008

Fassinger, R.E. (1991). The hidden minority: Issues and challenges in working with lesbian women and gay men. *The Counseling Psychologist, 19,* 157–176.

Fergus, S., Lewis, M.A., Darbes, L.A., & Kral, A.H. (2009). Social support moderates the relationship between gay community integration and sexual risk behavior among gay male couples. *Health Education & Behavior, 36*(5), 846–859.

Finlayson, J. (2005, 26 July). Canada's productivity GAP. *The Vancouver Sun.*

Finn, E. (2011, 1 March). No excuse for inequality: Canada can easily afford to create a truly just society. *The CCPA Monitor, 17*(8), 4.

First, M.B., Spitzer, R.L., Gibbon, M., & Williams, J.B.W. (1997). *Structured clinical interview for DSM-IV Axis I disorders (SCID-I) – Clinician version.* Washington, DC: American Psychiatric Press.

Fischer, C.T., & Finn, S.E. (2008). Developing the life meaning of psychological test data: Collaborative and therapeutic approaches. In R.P. Archer and S.R. Smith (Eds.), *Personality assessment* (pp. 379–404). New York: Routledge.

Fitzgerald, L.E., & Betz, N.E. (1994). Career development in cultural context: The role of gender, race, class, & sexual orientation. In M.L. Savickas & R.W. Lent (Eds.), *Convergence in career development theories: Implications for science and practice* (pp. 103–117). Palo Alto, C A: Consulting Psychologists Press.

Flanagan, J.C. (1954). The critical incident technique. *Psychological Bulletin, 51*(4), 327–358.

Fleras, A., & Elliott, J.L. (1992). *Multiculturalism in Canada: The challenge of diversity.* Scarborough, O N: Nelson Canada.

Fontaine, J.H. (2002). Transgender issues in counseling. In L.D. Burlew & D. Capuzzi (Eds.), *Sexuality counseling* (pp. 177–194). Hauppauge, N Y: Nova Science. Forrest, L., Elman, N., Gizara, S., & Vacha-Haase, T. (1999). Trainee impairment: A review of identification, remediation, dismissal, and legal issues. *The Counseling Psychologist, 27*(5), 627–686. doi:10.1177/0011000099275001

Forrest, L., Miller, D.S., & Elman, N.S. (2008). Psychology trainees with competence problems: From individual to ecological conceptualizations. *Training and Education in Professional Psychology, 2*(4), 183–192. doi:10.1037/1931-3918.2.4.183

Forthofer, M.S. (2003). Status of mixed methods in the health sciences. In A. Tashakkori & C. Teddlie (Eds.), *Handbook of mixed methods in social & behavioral research* (pp. 527–540). Thousand Oaks, C A: Sage.

Foster, D.B., & Kelly, M.T. (2012). Integrative interventions for men with concurrent substance misuse and trauma: Roles for mindfulness and masculinities. *Canadian Journal of Counselling and Psychotherapy, 46*(4), 298–312.

Fouad, N.A. (2006). Social justice in career and vocational aspects of counselling psychology. In R.L. Toporek, L.H. Gerstein, N.A. Fouad, G. Roysircar, & T. Israel (Eds.), *Handbook for social justice in counseling psychology: Leadership, vision, & action* (pp. 251–255). Thousand Oaks, C A: Sage.

Fouad, N.A., Gerstein, L.H., & Toporek, R.L. (2006). Social justice and counseling psychology in context. In R.L. Toporek, L. Gerstein, N.A. Fouad, G. Roysircar, & T. Israel (Eds.), *Handbook for social justice in counseling psychology: Leadership, vision, & action* (pp. 1–16). Thousand Oaks, C A: Sage.

Foucault, M. (1971). *The order of things: An archaeology of the human sciences.* New York: Pantheon Books.

Four Directions. (2005). *Native American Indian General Service Office Newsletter, 4,* 2. Retrieved 15 May 2005 from http://www.naigso-aa.org/index.htm

Fournier, G., Gautier, C., & Zimmermann, H. (2011). Vers une définition du sentiment d'intégration professionnelle: Le cas des travailleurs et des travailleuses de 45 ans et plus en situation d'instabilité d'emploi. *Canadian Journal of Counselling and Psychotherapy, 45*, 280–305.

Fournier, G., Goyer, L., & Bourassa, B. (2011). *Analyse des pratiques dans un centre de placement étudiant.* Cannexus, January 2011, Ottawa.

Fournier, G., Goyer, L. & Masdonati, J. (2010). *Vers une compréhension renouvelée des parcours professionnels.* CRIEVAT. Document inédit.

Fournier, G., Lachance, L., & Bujold, C. (2009). Nonstandard career paths and profiles of commitment to life roles: A complex relation. *Journal of Vocational Behavior, 74*, 321–331. doi:10.1016/j.jvb.2009.02.001

Fournier, G., Zimmermann, H., & Gauthier, C. (2011). Unstable career paths among workers 45 and over: Insight gained from long-term trajectories. *Journal of Aging Studies, 25*, 316–327. http://www.sciencedirect.com/science/article/pii/S0890406510001222

Fowler, D.M., Glenwright, B.J., Bhatia, M., & Drapeau, M. (2011). Counselling expectations of a sample of East Asian and Caucasian Canadian undergraduates in Canada. *Canadian Journal of Counselling and Psychotherapy, 45*(2), 151–167.

France, H., & McCormick, R. (1997). Helping circles: Theoretical and practical considerations of a using a First Nations peer support network. *Guidance & Counselling, 12*(2), 27–31.

Frank, B.W. (1999). Searching for support and community: Experiences in a gay men's psychoeducational group. *Canadian Journal of Counselling, 33*(2), 127–141.

Frankish, C.J., Hwang, S.W., & Quantz, D. (2005). Homelessness and health in Canada. *Canadian Journal of Public Health, 96*, 23–29.

Franks, C.M., Wilson, G.T., Kendall, P.C., & Brownell, K.D. (1982). *Annual review of behaviour therapy: Theory and practice.* New York: Guilford.

Frenette, M., & Morissette, R. (2005). Will they ever converge? Earnings of immigrant and Canadian born workers over the last two decades. *International Migration Review, 39*(1), 5–24. http://www.statcan.gc.ca/pub/11f0019m/11f0019m2003215-eng.pdf

Fuertes, J.N., & Gretchen, D. (2001). Emerging theories of multicultural counseling. In J.G. Ponterotto, J.M. Casas, L.A. Suzuki, & C.M. Alexander (Eds.), *Handbook of multicultural counseling* (2nd ed., pp. 509–541). Thousand Oaks, CA: Sage.

Galarneau, D., & Morisette, R. (2008). Immigrants' education and required job skills. *Perspectives on Labour and Income, 9*(12), 5–18. http://www.statcan.gc.ca/pub/75-001-x/2008112/article/10766-eng.htm

Galassi, J.P., Stoltz, R.F., Brooks, L., & Trexler, K.A. (1987). Improving research training in doctoral programs. *Journal of Counseling and Development, 66,* 40–44. doi:10.1002/j.1556-6676.1987.tb00780.x

Garb, H.N. (2005). Clinical judgment and decision making. *Annual Review of Clinical Psychology, 1,* 67–89. doi:10.1146/annurev.clinpsy.1.102803.143810

Garrett, M.T., & Barret, B. (2003). Two spirit: Counseling Native American gay, lesbian, and bisexual people. *Journal of Multicultural Counseling and Development, 31,* 131–142.

Gaubatz, M.D., & Vera, E.M. (2002). Do formalized gatekeeping procedures increase programs' follow-up with deficient trainees? *Counselor Education and Supervision, 41,* 294–305. doi:10.1002/j.1556-6978.2002.tb01292.x

Gaubatz, M.D., & Vera, E.M. (2006). Trainee competence in master's-level counselling programs: A comparison of counselor educators' and students' views. *Counselor Education and Supervision, 46,* 32–43. doi:10.1002/j.1556-6978.2006.tb00010.x

Gauthier, J., Pettifor, J., & Ferrero, A. (2010). The universal declaration of ethical principles for psychologists: A culture-sensitive model for creating and reviewing a code of ethics. *Ethics & Behavior, 20*(3–4), 179–196. doi:10.1080/10508421003798885

Gazzola, N., De Stefano, J., Audet, C., & Theriault, A. (2012). Professional identity among counselling psychology doctoral students: A qualitative investigation. *Counselling Psychology Quarterly, 24*(4), 257–275. doi:10.1080/09515070.2011.630572.

Gazzola, N., Smith, J.D., King-Andrews, H.L., & Kearney, M.K. (2010). Professional characteristics of Canadian counsellors: Results of a national survey. *Canadian Journal of Counselling, 44*(2), 83–99.

Gelatt, H.B. (1989). Positive uncertainty: A new decision-making framework for counseling. *Journal of Counseling Psychology, 36*(2), 252–256. doi:10.1037/0022-0167.36.2.252

Georgas, J., Berry, J.W., Shaw, A., Christakopoulou, S., & Mylonas, K. (1996). Acculturation of Greek family values. *Journal of Cross-Cultural Psychology, 27,* 329–338. doi:10.1177/0022022196273005

Gerstein, L.H., Heppner, P., Ægisdóttir, S., Leung, S., & Norsworthy, K. (2009). *International handbook of cross-cultural counseling.* Thousand Oaks, CA: Sage.

Gilbert, P. (2009). *The compassionate mind.* London: Constable & Robinson.

Gilbert, P., & Procter, S. (2006). Compassionate mind training for people with high shame and self-criticism: Overview and pilot study of a group therapy approach. *Clinical Psychology and Psychotherapy, 13*, 263–325. doi:10.1002/cpp.507

Ginsberg, F. (2012a). *Honoring Frank Parsons' legacy: Social justice in career psychology*. Paper presented in the Department of Educational and Counseling Psychology, McGill University, Montreal, Q C.

Ginsberg, F. (2012b). *Counseling for social justice in tough economic times*. Paper presented in the Counselor Education Department, S U N Y Plattsburgh, New York.

Ginsberg, F. (2013). *Becoming an ally for L G B T T 2 S Q Q I people*. Paper presented in the Counselor Education Department, S U N Y Plattsburgh, New York.

Goldstein, A., & Flett, G. (2009). Personality, alcohol use, and drinking motive: A comparison of independent and combined internal drinking motives groups. *Behavior Modification, 33*, 182–198. doi:10.1177/0145445508322920

Goldstein, A., Flett, G., & Wekerle, C. (2010). Child maltreatment, alcohol use, and drinking consequences among male and female college students: An examination of drinking motives as mediators. *Addictive Behaviors, 35*, 636–639. doi:10.1016/j.addbeh.2010.02.002

Goldstein, A., Flett, G., Wekerle, C., & Wall, A. (2009). Personality, child maltreatment, and substance use: Examining correlates of deliberate self-harm among university students. *Canadian Journal of Behavioural Science, 41*, 241–251. doi:10.1037/a0014847

Goldstein, A., Walton, M., Cunningham, R., Resko, S., & Duan, L. (2009). Correlates of gambling among youth in an inner-city emergency department. *Psychology of Addictive Behaviors, 23*, 113–121. doi:10.1037/a0013912

Goldstein, A.L., Walton, M.A., Cunningham, R.M., Trowbridge, M.J., & Maio, R.F. (2007). Violence and substance use as risk factors for depressive symptoms among adolescents in an urban emergency department. *Journal of Adolescent Health, 40*, 276–279. doi:10.1016/j.jadohealth.2006.09.023

Gone, J.P. (2004). Keeping culture in mind. In D.A. Mihesuah & A.C. Wilson (Eds.), *Indigenizing the academy* (pp. 124–142). Lincoln, N E: University of Nebraska Press.

Gone, J.P. (2011). The red road to wellness: Cultural reclamation in a Native First Nations community treatment center. *American Journal of Community Psychology, 47*(1–2), 187–202.

Goodman, L.A., Liang, B., Helms, J.E., Latta, R.E., Sparks, E., & Weintraub, S.R. (2004). Training counseling psychologists as social justice agents:

Feminist and multicultural principles in action. *The Counseling Psychologist, 32*(6), 793–837. doi:10.1177/0011000004268802

Goodwill, A., & McCormick, R. (2012). Giibinenimidizomin: Owning ourselves – critical incidents in the attainment of Aboriginal identity. *Canadian Journal of Counselling and Psychotherapy, 46*(1), 21–34.

Government of Canada. (1991). *Agenda for First Nations and Inuit mental health.* Retrieved 1 May 2005 from http://www.hc-sc.gc.ca/fnih-spni/pubs/ads/literary_examen_review/rev_rech_6_e.html

Goyer, L. (2003). *Dynamiques interculturelles en espace carriérologique: défis posés à la profession des conseillers et des conseillères en orientation.* Doctoral thesis. Montreal, QC: UQAM.

Goyer, L. (2005). Intervenir en situation interculturelle: exigences multipliées en orientation. *En pratique 3*(June), 12–14.

Goyer, L. (2007). Faut-il repenser l'information et l'orientation professionnelle auprès des jeunes? In M. Vultur & S. Bourdon (Eds.), *Les jeunes et le travail* (pp. 115–123). Quebec: University of Laval Press.

Goyer, L. (2011). Préambuleen Peavy, R.V. *Counseling socioconstructiviste: la construction de sens.* Septembre éditeur: Québec, p. I–IV.

Goyer, L. (2012a). Counseling de carrière axé sur les parcours de vie: vers une redéfinition holistique. June 2012. http://www.liettegoyer.ca

Goyer, L. (2012b). Parcours universitaire et parcours migratoire: une étude qualitative de l'expérience des étudiants internationaux. In F. Picard and J. Masdonati (Eds.), *Parcours scolaires et professionnelles des jeunes* (pp. 255–276). Quebec: Les Presses de l'Université Laval.

Goyer, L., Dorion. M.A., & Veilleux, A.D. (2010). *Modalités d'accompagnement en matière de développement da carrière dans le contexte des PME: une recension des écrits.* GDRC-FCDC, Quebec.

Goyer, L., Landry, C., & Leclerc, C. (2006). Regard sur une expérimentation du bilan des acquis relatifs à la formation de base en éducation des adultes au Québec. In Rodriguez, F.G., P. Alves, M.P., and Valois, P. (Eds.), *Évaluation des compétences et apprentissages expérientiels. Savoir modèles et méthodes* (pp. 61–73). Lisbon: EDUCA in association with l'ADMEE-Europe-Canada.

Goyer, L., Savard, R., Bilodeau, C., & Veilleux, A. D. (2008). *Le développement de carrière dans les petites et moyennes entreprises: recension des écrits.* Résumé de communication accepté dans le cadre du au congrès de l'AIPTLF, Québec.

Grace, A.P. (2008). The charisma and deception of reparative therapies: When medical science beds religion. *Journal of Homosexuality, 55*(4), 545–580.

Grace, A.P., & Wells, K. (2005). The Marc Hall prom predicament: Queer individual rights v. institutional church rights in Canadian public education. *Canadian Journal of Education, 28*(3), 237–270.

Grafanaki, S., Pearson, D., Cini, F., Godula, D., Mckenzie, B., Nason, S., et al. (2005). Sources of renewal: A qualitative study on the experience and role of leisure in the life of counsellors and psychologists. *Counselling Psychology Quarterly, 18*(1), 31–40. doi:10.1080/09515070500099660

Graham, S.R., & Liddle, B.J. (2009). Multiple relationships encountered by lesbian and bisexual psychotherapists: How close is too close? *Professional Psychology: Research and Practice, 40*(1), 15–21.

Grant, A. (2000). And still, the lesbian threat: Or, how to keep a good woman a woman. *Journal of Lesbian Studies, 4*(1), 61–80.

Grant, K.J., Henly, A., & Kean, M. (2001). The journey after the journey: Family counselling in the context of immigration and ethnic diversity. *Canadian Journal of Counselling, 35,* 89–100.

Green, A.I. (2006). Until death do us part? The impact of differential access to marriage on a sample of urban men. *Sociological Perspectives, 49*(2), 163–189.

Green, A.I. (2008). Health and sexual status in an urban gay enclave: An application of the stress process model. *Journal of Health & Human Behavior, 49*(4), 436–451.

Greenspan, N.R., Aguinaldo, J.P., Husbands, W., Murray, J., Ho, P., Sutdhibhasilp, N., ... Maharaj, R. (2011). "It's not rocket science, what I do": Self-directed harm reduction strategies among drug using ethno-racially diverse gay and bisexual men. *International Journal of Drug Policy, 22*(1), 56–62.

Gregersen, A.T., Nebeker, R.S., Seely, K.I., & Lambert, M.J. (2004). Social validation of the Outcome Questionnaire: An assessment of Asian and Pacific Islander college students. *Journal of Multicultural Counseling and Development, 33*(2), 194–205. doi:10.1002/j.2161-1912.2004.tb00627.

Grégoire, S., Baron, C., & Baron, L. (2012). Pleine conscience et counselling. *Canadian Journal of Counselling and Psychotherapy, 46,* 161–177.

Groth-Marnat, G. (2009). *Handbook of psychological assessment* (5th ed.). Hoboken, NJ: Wiley.

Grove, D. (2012). Male midlife depression: Multidimensional contributing factors and renewed practice approaches. *Canadian Journal of Counselling and Psychotherapy, 46*(4), 313–334.

Grube, J. (1990). Natives and settlers: An ethnographic note on early interaction of older homosexual men with younger gay liberationists. *Journal of Homosexuality, 20*(3–4), 119–135.

Grus, C.L., McCutcheon, S.R., & Berry, S.L. (2011). Actions by professional psychology education and training groups to mitigate the internship imbalance. *Training and Education in Professional Psychology, 5,* 193–201. doi:10.1037/a0026101

Guichard, J. (2005). Life-long self-construction. *International Journal for Educational and Vocational Guidance, 5,* 111–124.

Guichard, J. (2009). Self-constructing. *Journal of Vocational Behavior, 75*(3), 251–258.

Guichard, J. (2010). L'entretien constructiviste de conseil en orientation: une méthode pour aider les personnes à développer leurs compétences pours'orienter dans les sociétés de la modernité tardive? Séminaire invité au CRIEVAT, Université Laval, Québec.

Guichard, J. (2012). L'organisation de l'école et la structuration des intentions d'avenir des jeunes. In F. Picard and J. Masdonati (Eds.), *Parcours scolaires et professionnelles des jeunes* (pp. 15–50). Quebec: Les Presses de l'Université Laval.

Guo, S., & Jamal, Z. (2007). Nurturing cultural diversity in higher education: A critical review of selected models. *Canadian Journal of Higher Education, 37*(3), 27–49. http://www.ingentaconnect.com/content/csshe/cjhe

Gururaj, S., Heilig, J.V., & Somers, P. (2010). Graduate student persistence: Evidence from three decades. *Journal of Student Financial Aid, 40,* 31–46.

Gustafson, D. (2007). White on whiteness: Becoming radicalized about race. *Nursing Inquiry, 14*(2), 153–161.

Gwyn, R. (1995). *Nationalism without walls: The unbearable lightness of being Canadian.* Toronto: McClelland and Stewart.

Gysbers, N.H., Heppner, M.J., & Johnston, J.A. (2003). *Career counseling process, issues, & techniques* (2nd ed.). New York: Allyn & Bacon.

Hall, D.T. (1996). *The career is dead: Long live the career.* San Francisco, CA: Jossey-Bass.

Hall, J.E., & Hurley, G. (2003). North American perspectives on education, training, licensing, and credentialing. In I.B. Weiner, G. Striker, & T.A. Widiger (Eds.), *Handbook of psychology: Vol. 4 Clinical psychology* (pp. 471–496). Hoboken, NJ: Wiley.

Handy, C. (1994). *The age of paradox.* Boston, MA: Harvard Business School Press.

Hannan, C., Lambert, M.J., Harmon, C., Nielsen, S.L., Smart, D.W., Shimokawa, K., & Sutton, S.W. (2005). A lab test and algorithms for identifying clients at risk for treatment failure. *Journal of Clinical Psychology, 61*(2), 155–163. doi:10.1002/jclp.20108

Hansen, N.B., Lambert, M.J., & Forman, E.V. (2002). The psychotherapy dose response effect and its implications for treatment delivery services. *Clinical Psychology: Science and Practice, 9*, 329–343. doi:10.1093/clipsy.9.3.329

Haq, R., & Ng, S.W. (2010). Employment equity and workplace diversity in Canada. In A. Klarsfeld (Ed.), *International handbook of diversity management at work: Country perspectives on diversity and equal treatment* (pp. 68–82). Cheltanham, UK: Edward Elgar Publishing Limited.

Hargrove, B.K., Creagh, M.G., & Kelly, D.B. (2003). Multicultural competencies in career counseling. In D.B. Pope-Davis, L.K. Coleman, W.M. Liu., & R.L. Toporek (Eds.), *Handbook of multicultural competencies in counseling & psychology* (pp. 392–405). Thousand Oaks, CA: Sage.

Harris, G.E. (2009). Reflections on ideological consistency between community-based research and counselling practice. *Canadian Journal of Counselling, 43*, 3–17.

Harris, G.E., & Alderson K. (2006). Gay men living with HIV/AIDS: The potential for empowerment. *Journal of HIV/AIDS & Social Services, 5*, 9–24. doi:10.1300/J187v05n03_02

Harris, G.E., Camerson, J.E., & Lang, J. (2011). Identification with community based HIV agencies as a correlate of turnover intentions and general self-efficacy. *Journal of Community & Applied Social Psychology, 21*, 41–54. doi:10.1002/casp.1059

Harris, G.E., & Larsen, D. (2007). HIV peer counseling and the development of hope perspectives from peer counselors and peer counseling recipients. *AIDS Patient Care & STDs, 21*(11), 843–860. doi:10.1089/apc.2006.0207

Harris, G.E., & Larsen, D. (2008). Understanding hope in the face of an HIV diagnosis and high-risk behaviors. *Journal of Health Psychology, 13*, 401–415. doi:10.1177/1359105307088143

Harvey, M.T., May, M.E., & Kennedy, C.H. (2004). Nonconcurrent multiple baseline designs and the evaluation of educational systems. *Journal of Behavioral Education, 13*, 267–276. doi:10.1023/B:JOBE.0000044735.51022.5d

Hatfield, D.R., McCullough, L., Frantz, S.H.B., & Krieger, K. (2010). Do we know when our clients get worse? An investigation of therapists' ability to detect negative client change. *Clinical Psychology & Psychotherapy, 17*(1), 25–32.

Haverkamp, B.E. (2005). Ethical perspectives on qualitative research in applied psychology. *Journal of Counseling Psychology, 52*, 146–155. doi:10.1037/0022-0167.52.2.146

Haverkamp, B.E. (2006). Case studies in evaluation and assessment. In W.E. Schulz, G.W. Sheppard, R. Lehr, & B. Shepard (Eds.), *Counselling ethics: Issues and cases.* Ottawa: Canadian Counselling Association.

Haverkamp, B., Robertson, S., Cairns, S., & Bedi, R. (2011). Professional issues and Canadian counseling psychology: Identity, education, and professional practice. *Canadian Psychology, 5*(4), 256–264. doi:10.1037/a0025214

Health Canada. (2002). *Canada's aging population.* Ottawa: Minister of Public Works and Government Services.

Health Canada. (2003). *Acting on what we know: Preventing youth suicide in First Nations.* Ottawa: Author.

Health Canada. (2006). *Health Promotion: Mental health promotion for people with mental illness.* Retrieved 1 November 2006 from http://www.phac-aspc.gc.ca/publicat/mh-sm/mhp02-psm02/1_e.html

Health Canada. (2011a). *About Health Canada.* http://www.hc-sc.gc.ca/ahc-asc/index-eng.php

Health Canada. (2011b). *Health care system: Canada's health care system.* http://www.hc-sc.gc.ca/hcs-sss/pubs/system-regime/2011-hcs-sss/index-eng.php

Health Canada. (2011c). *Environmental and workplace health: Trauma response services.* http://www.hc-sc.gc.ca/ewh-semt/occup-travail/empl/trauma-traumatique-eng.php

Health Canada. (2011d). *Health concerns: Violence and abuse.* http://www.hc-sc.gc.ca/hc-ps/violence/index-eng.php

Heath, N.L., Ross, S., Toste, J.R., Charlebois, A., & Nedecheva, T. (2009). Retrospective analysis of social factors and nonsuicidal self-injury among young adults. *Canadian Journal of Behavioural Science, 41*(3), 180–186. doi:10.1037/a0015732

Heath, N.L., Toste, J.R., Nedecheva, T., & Charlebois, A. (2008). An examination of nonsuicidal self-injury among college students. *Journal of Mental Health Counseling, 30*(2), 137–156.

Heath, O., Hurley, G., & Ritchie, P. (2012, June). *Best practices for assessing and giving feedback about professional competencies for trainees.* Workshop presented at the annual convention of the Canadian Psychological Association, Halifax, NS.

Heilbron, C., & Guttman, M.A. (2000). Traditional healing methods with First Nations women in group counselling. *Canadian Journal of Counselling and Psychotherapy, 34*(1), 3–11.

Heinz, W.R., Huinink, J., Swader, C.S., & Weymann, A. (2009). General introduction. In W.R. Heinz, J. Huinink, & A. Weymann (Eds.), *The life* course reader: *Individuals and societies across time* (pp. 15–30). Chicago, IL: The University of Chicago Press.

Helmes, E., & Pachana, N.A. (2008). Value of interviews for admission to clinical training programs: Perspective of program directors. *Australian Psychologist, 43*, 249–256. doi:10.1080/00050060802413362

Herek, G.M. (1996). Heterosexism and homophobia. In R.P. Cabaj & T.S. Stein (Eds.), Textbook of homosexuality and mental health (pp. 101–114). Washington, DC: American Psychiatric Press.

Herr, E.L. (1997). Super's life-span, life-space approach and its outlook for refinement. *The Career Development Quarterly, 45*, 238–246. doi:10.1002/j.2161-0045.1997.tb00468.x

Herr, E. (2003). The future of career counseling as an instrument of public policy. *The Career Development Quarterly, 52*(1), 8–17.

Hersen, M., & Barlow, D.H. (1976). *Single case experimental designs: Strategies for studying behaviour change.* Oxford, UK: Pergamon.

Hewitt Associates. (2005, 16 June). Ignoring employee absences may prove costly for Canadian organizations, according to Hewitt. http://www.hewitt.com/hewitt/resource/newsroom/pressrel/2005/06-15-05eng.htm

Hiebert, B. (2002). *Who will step forward? The need for multijurisdictional leadership for increased accountability.* (Canadian Research Working Group). http://www.crwg-gdrc.ca/crwg/wp-content/uploads/2010/10/Who-Will-Step-Forward-Hiebert.pdf

Hiebert, B., Bezanson, L., O'Reilly, E., Hopkins, S., Magnusson, K., & McCaffrey, A. (2012). *Assessing the impact of labour market information: Final report on results of phase two (field tests), phase three (follow up interviews), and phase four (impact on practice).* Report presented to Human Resources and Skills Development Canada. Retrieved from Canadian Working Group website: http://www.crwg-gdrc.ca/crwg/index.php/research-projects/lmi

Hiebert, B., Domene, J.F., & Buchanan, M. (2011). The power of multiple methods and evidence sources: Raising the profile of Canadian counselling psychology research. *Canadian Psychology–Psychologie Canadienne, 52*(4), 265–275. doi:10.1037/A0025364

Hiebert, B., & Johnson, P. (1994). *Changes in counselling skills and cognitive structures of counsellor trainees.* Paper presented at the Annual Meeting of the American Educational Research Association, New Orleans, LA.

Hiebert, B., & Magnusson, K. (in press). The subversive power of evidence: Demonstrating the value of career development services. In B.

Shepard & P. Mani (Eds.), *Canadian career practitioners handbook.*
Toronto: Counselling and Educational Research Institute of Canada.

Hiebert, B., McCarthy, J., & Repetto, E. (2001, March). Synthesis of Issue
5: Professional training, qualifications, and skills. Presentation conducted at the Second International Symposium on Career Development
and Public Policy, Richmond, B C.

Hiebert, B., Simpson, E.H., & Uhlemann, M.R. (1992). Professional identity and counsellor education. *Canadian Journal of Counselling, 26,*
201–209.

Hiebert, B., & Uhlemann, M. (1993). Counselling psychology:
Development, identity, and issues. In K. Dobson & D. Dobson (Eds.),
Professional psychology in Canada (pp. 285–312). Toronto: Hogrefe
& Huber.

Higa-McMillan, C.K., Powell, C.K.K., Daleiden, E.L., & Mueller, C.W.
(2011). Pursuing an evidence-based culture through contextualized feedback: Aligning youth outcomes and practices. *Professional Psychology –
Research and Practice, 42*(2), 137–144. doi:10.1037/a0022139

Hill, D.B., Rozanski, C., Carfagnini, J., & Willoughby, B. (2007). Gender
identity disorders in childhood and adolescence: A critical inquiry.
International Journal of Sexual Health, 19(1), 57–75.

Hirakata, P. (2009). Narratives of dissociation: Insights into the treatment
of dissociation in individuals who were sexually abused as children.
Journal of Trauma & Dissociation, 10, 297–314. doi:10.1080/
15299780902956804

Holman, C.W., & Goldberg, J.M. (2007). Social and medical transgender
case advocacy. *International Journal of Transgenderism, 9*(3–4), 197–217.

Holmberg, D., & Blair, K.L. (2009). Sexual desire, communication,
satisfaction, and preferences of men and women in same-sex versus
mixed-sex relationships. *Journal of Sex Research, 46*(1), 57–66.

Holmberg, D., Blair, K.L., & Phillips, M. (2010). Women's sexual satisfaction as a predictor of well-being in same-sex versus mixed-sex
relationships. *Journal of Sex Research, 47*(1), 1–11.

Holmes, M.M. (2008). Mind the gaps: Intersex and (re-productive) spaces
in disability studies and bioethics. *Journal of Bioethical Inquiry, 5*(2–3),
169–181.

Homma, Y., Chen, W., Poon, C.S., & Saewyc, E.M. (2012). Substance use
and sexual orientation among East and Southeast Asian adolescents in
Canada. *Journal of Child & Adolescent Substance Abuse, 21*(1), 32–50.

Hood, A.B., & Johnson, R.W. (2007). *Assessment in counseling* (4th ed).
Alexandria, V A: American Counseling Association.

Hoover, S., Bedi, R., & Beall, L. (2012). Frequency of scholarship on counselling males in the Canadian Journal of Counselling and Psychotherapy.
Canadian Journal of Counselling and Psychotherapy, 46(4), 292–297.

Horan, J.J. (1980). Experimentation in counselling and psychotherapy
part 1: New myths about old realities. *Educational Researcher, 9*, 5–10.
doi:10.3102/0013189X009011005

Horne, S.G., & Mathews, S.S. (2006). A social justice approach to international collaborative consultation. In R.L. Toporek, L.H. Gerstein, N.A.
Fouad, G. Roysicar, & T. Israel (Eds.), *Handbook for social justice in
counseling psychology: Leadership, vision, and action* (pp. 388–405).
Thousand Oaks, CA: Sage.

Hornjatkevyc, N.L., & Alderson, K.G. (2011). With and with*out*: The
bereavement experiences of gay men who have lost a partner to non-
AIDS-related causes. *Death Studies, 35*, 801–823. doi:10.1080/
07481187.2011.553502

Horvath, A.O., & Bedi, R.P. (2002). The alliance. In J.C. Norcross (Ed.),
Psychotherapy relationships that work (pp. 37–69). New York: Oxford
University Press.

Horvath, P. (1999). The organization of social action. *Canadian
Psychology / Psychologie canadienne, 40*(3), 221.

Howard, R., & Donnelly, J. (1986). Human dignity, human rights, and
political regimes. *The American Political Science Review, 80*(3),
801–817.

Howarth, I. (1989). Psychotherapy: Who benefits? *The Psychologist, 2*,
150–152.

HRSDC (Human Resources and Skills Development Canada). (2011).
*What works in career development services? Measuring the results of
labour market integration services.* Gatineau, QC: HRSDC Policy
Research Directorate.

Hubley, A.M., & Zumbo, B.D. (2011).Validity and the consequences of
test interpretation and use. *Social Indicators Research: An International
Interdisciplinary Journal for Quality of Life Measurement, 103*, 219–
230. doi:10.1007/s11205-011-9843-4

Hudson, P., & Taylor-Henley, S. (2001). Beyond the rhetoric: Implementing
culturally appropriate research projects in First Nations communities.
American Indian Culture and Research Journal, 25(2), 93–105.

Hunsley, J. (2007). Training psychologists for evidence-based practice.
Canadian Psychology – Psychologie Canadienne, 48(1), 32–42.
doi:10.1037/cp2007_1_32

Hurley, G. (2010, November). Recollections of our past. Keynote address presented at the Inaugural Canadian Counselling Psychology Conference, Montreal, Q C.

Hurley, G., & Doyle, M.S. (2003). Counseling psychology: From industrial societies to sustainable development. In S. Carta (Ed.), *Encyclopedia of life support systems*. Oxford, U K: E O L S S Publishers.

Hurley, M.C. (2005, September 14). *Bill C-38: The Civil Marriage Act.* http://www.parl.gc.ca/About/Parliament/LegislativeSummaries/ bills_ls.asp?ls=c38&Parl=38&Ses=1

Iaquinta, M., Amundson, N.E., & Borgen, W.A. (2012). Women's career decision making after brain injury. *Canadian Journal of Career Development, 11,* 38–48.

Igartua, K.J. (1998). Therapy with lesbian couples: The issues and the interventions. *The Canadian Journal of Psychiatry / La Revue canadienne de psychiatrie, 43*(4), 391–396.

Igartua, K.J., & Des Rosier, P. (2004). Transference and countertransference in therapy with lesbian patients: Contrasting views from lesbian and heterosexual therapists. *Journal of Lesbian Studies, 8*(1–2), 123–141.

Igartua, K.J., Gill, K., & Montoro, R. (2003). Internalized homophobia: A factor in depression, anxiety, and suicide in the gay and lesbian population. *Canadian Journal of Community Mental Health, 22*(2), 15–30.

Irving, J.A., Dobkin, P.L., & Park, J. (2009). Cultivating mindfulness in health care professionals: A review of empirical studies of mindfulness-based stress reduction (M B S R). *Complementary Therapies in Clinical Practice, 15*(2), 61–66. doi:10.1016/j.ctcp.2009.01.002

Ishiyama, F. (2003). A bending willow tree: A Japanese (Morita Therapy) model of human nature and client change. *Canadian Journal of Counselling, 37*(3), 216–231.

Ishiyama, I. (1995). Culturally dislocated clients: Self-validation and cultural conflict issues and counselling implications. *Canadian Journal of Counselling and Psychotherapy, 29*(3), 262–275. http://cjc-rcc.ucalgary.ca/cjc/index.php/rcc/article/view/48/913

Iwasaki, Y., Mactavish, J., & Mackay, K. (2005). Building on strengths and resilience: Leisure as a stress survival strategy. *British Journal of Guidance & Counselling, 33*(1), 81–100.

Jaffe, P.G., Crooks, C.V., & Watson, C.L. (2009). *Creating safe school environments: From small steps to sustainable change.* London, O N: Althouse.

Jaffe, P., Wolfe, D.A., & Campbell, M. (2012). *Growing up with domestic violence*. Cambridge, MA: Hogrefe.

James, S. (2002). Agonias: The social and sacred suffering of Azorean immigrants. *Culture, Medicine, and Psychiatry, 26*, 87–110. doi:10.1023/A:1015295013651

James, S., & Clarke, J. (2001). Surplus suffering: The case of Portuguese immigrant women. *Feminist Review, 68*, 167–170. http://www.jstor.org/stable/1395751

James, S., & Foster, G. (2003). Narratives and culture: "Thickening" the self for cultural psychotherapy. *Journal of Theoretical and Philosophical Psychology, 23*(2), 1–25. doi:10.1037/h0091228

Janoff, D.V. (2005). *Pink blood: Homophobic violence in Canada*. Toronto: University of Toronto Press.

Jarvis, P. (n.d.). Formula for success in career building. In R. Shea & R. Joy (Eds.), *A multi-sectoral approach to career development: A decade of Canadian research* (pp. 399–406). Canada: The Canadian Journal of Career Development.

Jeste, D., Alexopoulous, G., Bartels, S., Cummings, J., Gallo, J., Gottlieb, J., et al. (1999). Consensus statement on the upcoming crisis in geriatric mental health research agenda for the next two decades. *Archives of General Psychiatry, 56*, 848–853.

Jewell, L.M., & Morrison, M.A. (2010). "But there's a million jokes about everybody": Prevalence of, and reasons for, directing negative behaviors toward gay men on a Canadian university campus. *Journal of Interpersonal Violence, 25*(11), 2094–2112.

Johnson, W.B., Elman, N.S., Forrest, L., Robiner, W.N., Rodolfa, E., & Schaffer, J.B. (2008). Addressing professional competence problems in trainees: Some ethical considerations. *Professional Psychology: Research and Practice, 39*, 589–599. doi:10.1037/a0014264.

Jordan, J.V. (2010). *Relational-cultural therapy*. Washington, DC: American Psychological Association.

Joshee, R. (2007). Opportunities for social justice work: The Ontario Diversity Policy Web. *EAF Journal, 18*(1/2), 171–199.

Joshee, R., & Johnson, L. (2005). Multicultural education in the United States and Canada: The importance of national policies. In N. Bascia, A. Cumming, A. Datnow, K. Leithwood, & D. Livingstone (Eds.), *International Handbook of Educational Policy*. Great Britain: Springer.

Julien, D., Jouvin, E., Jodoin, E., l'Archeveque, A., & Chartrand, E. (2008). Adjustment among mothers reporting same-gender sexual partners:

A study of a representative population sample from Quebec province (Canada). *Archives of Sexual Behavior, 37*(6), 864–876.

Justin, M. (2010). Intersections of identity: Hybridity, situational ethnicity, and in-between spaces. In N. Arthur & S. Collins (Eds.), *Culture-infused counselling* (2nd ed., pp. 315–337). Calgary, AB: Counselling Concepts.

Kabat-Zinn, J. (1994). *Wherever you go, there you are: Mindfulness meditation in everyday life.* New York: Hyperion.

Kamanzi, P.C. (2006). *Influence du capital humain et du capital social sur les caractéristiques de l'emploi chez les diplômés postsecondaires au Canada.* Thesis. Quebec: Université Laval. Retrieved 5 June 2012 from http://www.collectionscanada.gc.ca/obj/s4/f2/dsk3/QQLA/TC-QQLA-23561.pdf

Kaplan, D.M., & Coogan, S.L. (2005). Article 3: The next advancement in counseling: The bio-psycho-social model. In *VISTAS: Compelling perspectives on counselling* (pp. 17–25). http://counsellingoutfitters.com/vistas/vistas05.art03.pdf

Karmali, S., Laupland, K., Harrop, A.R., Findlay, C., Kirkpatrick, A.W., Winston, B., et al. (2005). Epidemiology of severe trauma among status Aboriginal Canadians: A populations-based study. *Canadian Medical Association Journal, 172*(8), 1007–1011.

Kassan, A., & Sinacore, A. (2011). *Multicultural counseling competencies with immigrant adolescents.* Poster presented at the annual meeting of the American Psychological Association, Washington, DC.

Kawa, S., & Giordano, J. (2012). A brief historicity of the Diagnostic and Statistical Manual of Mental Disorders: Issues and implications for the future of psychiatric canon and practice. *Philosophy, Ethics, and Humanities in Medicine, 7*(2), 1–9.

Keats, P. (2010a). The moment is frozen in time: Photojournalists' metaphors in describing trauma photography. *Journal of Constructivist Psychology, 23*(3), 231–255. doi:10.1080/10720531003799436

Keats, P.A. (2010b). Soldiers working internationally: Impacts of masculinity, military culture, and operational stress on cross-cultural adaptation. *International Journal for the Advancement of Counselling, 32*(4), 290–303. doi:10.1007/s10447-010-9107-z

Keats, P.A., & Buchanan, M.J. (2009). Addressing the effects of assignment stress injury. *Journalism Practice, 3*(2), 162–177. doi:10.1080/17512780802681199

Keats, P.A., & Buchanan, M.J. (2011). Reports of resilience in trauma journalism. In M. Celinski & K. Gow (Eds.), *Continuity versus creative response to challenge: The primacy of resilience & resourcefulness in life & therapy* (pp. 291–306). Hauppauge, NY: Nova Science Publishers.

Kelley, N., & Trebilcock, M. (2010). *The making of a mosaic: A history of Canadian immigration policy* (2nd ed). Toronto: University of Toronto Press.

Kelloway, E.K., & Day, A.L. (2005a). Building healthy workplaces: What we know so far. *Canadian Journal of Behavioural Science, 37*(4), 223–235. doi:10.1037/h0087259

Kelloway, E.K., & Day, A.L. (2005b). Building healthy workplaces: Where we need to be. *Canadian Journal of Behavioural Science, 37*(4), 309–312. doi:10.1037/h0087265

Kersetter, S. (2002). Rags and riches: Wealth inequality in Canada. http://www.policyalternatives.ca/documents/National_Office_Pubs/rags_riches.pdf

Kilbride, K.M., & D'Arcangelo, L. (2002). Meeting immigrant community college students' needs on one greater Toronto area college campus. *Canadian Journal of Higher Education, 32*(2), 1–26. http://www.eric.ed.gov/PDFS/EJ661236.pdf

Kinzel, Audrey L. (2011, May). The journey of accepting chronic pain. Presentation at Canadian Counselling and Psychotherapy Association, Ottawa.

King, J. (1999). Denver American Indian mental health needs survey. *American Indianand Alaska Native Mental Health Research, 8*(3), 1–12.

Kirmayer, L.J. (2012). Cultural competence and evidence-based practice in mental health: Epistemic communities and the politics of pluralism. *Social Science & Medicine, 75,* 249–256.

Kirmayer, L.J., Brass, G.M., & Tait, C.L. (2000). The mental health of Aboriginal peoples: Transformations of identity and community. *Canadian Journal of Psychiatry, 45*(7), 607–617.

Kirmayer, L.J., Brass, G.M., & Valaskakis, G.G. (2009). Conclusion: Healing/Intervention/Tradition. In L.J. Kirmayer & G.G. Valaskakis (Eds.), *Healing traditions: The mental health of Aboriginal peoples in Canada* (pp. 440–472). Vancouver, BC: University of British Columbia Press.

Knapik, M., & Miloti, A. (2006). Conceptualizations of competence and culture: Taking up the post-modern interest in social interaction. *International Journal for the Advancement of Counselling, 28,* 375–387.

Knowles, V. (2007). *Canadian immigration and immigration policy, 1540–2006* (rev. ed.). Toronto: Dundurn Press.

Koehn, C.V. (2007). Experiential work in group treatment for alcohol and other drug problems: The relationship sculpture. *Alcoholism Treatment Quarterly, 25*, 99–111. doi:10.1300/J020v25n03_08

Koehn, C.V. (2010). A relational approach to counseling women with alcohol and other drug problems. *Alcoholism Treatment Quarterly, 28*, 38–51. doi:10.1080/07347320903436185

Koert, E., Borgen, W.A., & Amundson, N.E. (2011). Educated immigrant women workers doing well with change: Helping and hindering factors. *Career Development Quarterly, 59*(3), 94–207. http://readperiodicals. com/201103/2299078961.html#b

Koszycki, D. (2006). Interpersonal psychotherapy for depression in patients with coronary heart disease. In E. Molinari, A. Compare, & G. Parati (Eds.), *Clinical psychology and heart disease* (pp. 369–390). New York: Springer.

Koszycki, D., Benger, M., Shlik, J., & Bradwejn, J. (2007). Randomized trial of a meditation-based stress reduction program and cognitive behavior therapy in generalized social anxiety disorder. *Behaviour Research and Therapy, 45*, 2518–2526. doi:10.1177/153321010731162

Koszycki, D., Lafontaine, S., Frasure-Smith, N., Swenson, R., & Lespérance, F. (2004). An open-label trial of interpersonal psychotherapy in depressed patients with coronary disease. *Psychosomatics, 45*(4), 319–324. doi:10.1176/appi.psy.45.4.319

Kranz, K., & Daniluk, J. (2006). Living outside the box: Lesbian couples with children conceived through the use of anonymous donor insemination. *Journal of Feminist Family Therapy: An International Forum, 18*, 1–23. doi:10.1300/J086v18n01_01

Krumboltz, J. (1994). The Career Beliefs Inventory. *Journal of Counseling and Development, 22*, 424–428.

Krumboltz, J.D. (2009). The happenstance learning theory. *Journal of Career Assessment, 17*(2), 134–154.

Kuo, B., Chong, V., & Joseph, J. (2008). Depression and its psychosocial correlates among older Asian immigrants in North America: A critical review of two decades' research. *Journal of Aging And Health, 20*(6), 615–652. doi:10.1177/0898264308321001

Kuo, B.C.H., Kwantes, C.T., Towson, S., & Nanson, K.M. (2006). Social beliefs as determinants of attitudes toward seeking professional psychological help among ethnically diverse university students. *Canadian Journal of Counselling, 40*(4), 224–241.

Kwast-Welfel, J., Boski, P., & Rovers, M. (2004). Intergenerational value similarity in Polish immigrant families in Canada in comparison to intergenerational value similarity in Polish Canadians and non-immigrant families. In G. Zheng, K. Leung, & J.G. Adair (Eds.), *Perspectives and progress in contemporary cross-cultural psychology: Selected papers from the Seventeenth International Congress of the International Association for Cross-CulturalPsychology* (pp. 193–209). Ottawa: University of Ottawa. http://ebooks.iaccp.org/xian/PDFs/4_4Welfel.pdf

Kwee, A., Dominguez, A., & Ferell, D. (2007). Sexual addiction and Christian college men: Conceptual, assessment, and treatment challenges. *Journal of Psychology and Christianity, 26*, 3–13.

Lachance, L., Brassard, N., & Tétreau, B. (2005). Étude des différences intersexes sur le plan des conflits entre le travail et les rôles familiaux auprès de professionnels. *Canadian Journal of Counselling, 39,* 145–167.

Lahey, K.A., & Alderson, K. (2004). *Same-sex marriage: The personal and the political.* Toronto: Insomniac Press.

Lai, Y., & Ishiyama, F.I. (2004). Involvement of immigrant Chinese Canadian mothers of children with disabilities. *Exceptional Children, 71*, 97–108.

Laird, G. (2007). Homelessness in a growth economy: Canada's 21st century paradox. *A report for the Sheldon Chumir Foundation for Ethics in Leadership.* Retrieved 8 April 2013 from http://www.chumirethicsfoundation.ca/files/pdf/SHELTER.pdf

Laird, J. (1998). Theorizing culture: Narrative ideas and practice principles. In M. McGoldrick (Ed.), *Re-visioning family therapy* (pp. 20–36). New York: Guilford.

Lalande, V. (2004). Counseling psychology: A Canadian perspective. *Counseling Psychology Quarterly, 17*, 273–286. doi:10.1080/09515070412331317576

Lalande, V., & Laverty, S. (2010). Creating connections: Best practices in counselling girls and women. Introduction to culture-infused counselling. In N. Arthur & S. Collins (Eds.), *Culture-infused counselling* (2nd ed., pp. 339–362). Calgary, AB: Counselling Concepts.

Lalande, V., & Magnusson, K. (2007). Measuring the impact of career development services in Canada: Current and preferred practices. *Canadian Journal of Counselling, 41*(3), 133–145.

Lalive d'Epinay, C. (2005). De l'étude des personnes âgées au paradigme du parcours de vie. In D. Mercure (Ed.), *L'analyse du social: les modes d'explication* (pp. 141–167). Quebec: Les Presses de l'Université Laval.

L'Allier, P., Tétreau, B., & Erpicum, D. (1981a). L'orientation professionnelle au Québec depuis le rapport Parent. *L'Orientation Professionnelle, 17*(4), 35–62.

Lambert, M.J., & Cattani-Thompson, K. (1996). Current findings regarding the effectiveness of counseling: Implications for practice. *Journal of Counseling & Development, 74,* 601–608. doi:10.1080/0951507041233131317576

Lambert, M.J., & Cattani, K. (2012). Practice-friendly research review: Collaboration in routine care. *Journal of Clinical Psychology, 68*(2), 209–220. doi:10.1002/jclp.21835

Lambert, M.J., & Ogles, B.M. (2004). *The efficacy and effectiveness of psychotherapy.* New York: Wiley.

Lambert, M.J., & Shimokawa, K. (2011). Collecting client feedback. *Psychotherapy, 48*(1), 72–79. doi:10.1037/a0022238

Lambert, M.J., Smart, D.W., Campbell, M.P., Hawkins, E.J., Harmon, C., & Slade, K.L. (2006). Psychotherapy outcome, as measured by the OQ-45, in African American, Asian / Pacific Islander, Latino/a, and Native American clients compared with matched Caucasian clients. *Journal of College Student Psychotherapy, 20*(4), 17–29. doi:10.1300/J035v20n04_03

Landolt, M.A., Bartholomew, K., Saffrey, C., Oram, D., & Perlman, D. (2004). Gender nonconformity, childhood rejection, and adult attachment: A study of gay men. *Archives of Sexual Behavior, 33*(2), 117–128.

Larose, S., Ratelle, C.F., Guay, F., Senécal, C., & Harvey, M. (2006). Trajectories of science self-efficacy beliefs during the college transition and academic and vocational adjustment in science and technology programs. *Educational Research and Evaluation, 12*(4), 373–393. doi:10.1080/13803610600765836

Larsen, D., Edey, W., & Lemay, L. (2007). Understanding the role of hope in counselling: Exploring the intentional uses of hope. *Counselling Psychology Quarterly, 20*(4), 401–416. doi:10.1080/09515070701690036

Larsen, D., Flesaker, K., & Stege, R. (2008). Qualitative interviewing using interpersonal process recall: Investigating internal experiences during professional-client conversations. *International Journal of Qualitative Methods, 7,* 18–37.

Larsen, D.J., & Stege, R. (2010a). Hope-focused practices during early psychotherapy sessions: Part I: Implicit approaches. *Journal of Psychotherapy Integration, 20*(3), 271–292. doi:10.1037/a0020820

Larsen, D.J., & Stege, R. (2010b). Hope-focused practices during early psychotherapy sessions: Part II: Explicit approaches. *Journal of Psychotherapy Integration, 20*(3), 293–311. doi:10.1037/a0020821

LaTorre, R.A., & Wendenburg, K. (1983). Psychological characteristics of bisexual, heterosexual and homosexual women. *Journal of Homosexuality, 9*(1), 87–97.

Launikari, M., & Puukari, S. (2005). *Multicultural guidance and counselling: Theoretical foundations and best practices in Europe.* Jyväskylä, Finland: University of Jyväskylä, Institute for Educational Research.

Law, S., Flood, C., & Gagnon, D. (2008). *Listening for direction III: National consultation on health services and policy issues, 2007–2010.* Ottawa: Canadian Health Services Research Foundation and Canadian Institutes of Health Research, Institute of Health Services and Policy Research.

Lawrence, A.A. (2008). Gender identity disorders in adults: Diagnosis and treatment. In D.L. Rowland & L. Incrocci (Eds.), *Handbook of sexual and gender identity disorders* (pp. 423–456). Hoboken, NJ: John Wiley & Sons.

Leblond de Brumath, A., & Julien, D. (2007). Facteurs reliés au choix de la partenaire qui portera l'enfant chez de futures mères lesbiennes. [Factors connected to the choice of partner who will carry the child in future lesbian mothers.] *Canadian Journal of Behavioural Science/Revue canadienne des sciences du comportement, 39*(2), 135–150.

Le Bossé, Y. (2011). *Psychosociologie des sciences de l'oientation: Un point de vue interactionniste et stratégique.* Quebec: Éditions Ardis, 557.

Le Bossé, Y., Chamberland, M., Bilodeau, A., & Bourassa, B. (2007). Formation à l'approche centrée sur le développement du pouvoir d'agir des personnes et des collectivités (DPA): Étude des modalités optimales de supervision. *Travailler le social, 38–39–40,* 133–157.

LeBreton, D. (2009). Trajectoire d'insertion socioprofessionnelle de femmes sous l'angle des variables personnelles et sociales. *Canadian Journal of Counselling, 43,* 131–145.

Leclerc, C., Bourassa, B., & Filteau, O. (2010). Utilisation de la méthode des incidents critique dans une perspective d'explicitation, d'analyse critique et de transformation des pratiques professionnelles. *Éducation et francophonie, 38*(1), 11–32. http://www.acelf.ca/c/revue/sommaire.php?id=27

Leclerc, C., Bourassa, B., Picard, F., & Courcy, F. (2011). Du groupe focalisé à la recherche collaborative: Défis et stratégies. *Recherches Qualitatives, 29,* 144–166.

Lee. (2000). *Urban poverty in Canada: A statistical profile.* Ottawa: Canadian Council on Social Development.

Lee, G., & Westwood, M. (1996). Cross-cultural adjustment issues faced by immigrant professionals. *Journal of Employment Counseling, 33,* 29–42.

Lemoire, S.J., & Chen, C.P. (2005). Applying person-centered counseling to sexual minority adolescents. *Journal of Counseling & Development, 83*(2), 146–154.

Leong, F.T., & Hartung, P.J. (2000). Adapting to the changing multiculturalism context of career. In A. Collin & R.A. Young (Eds.), *The future of career* (pp. 212–227). Cambridge, UK: Cambridge University Press.

Lerner, S., & Sinacore, A. L. (in press). Lesbian mother–heterosexual daughter relationships: Toward a postmodern feminist analysis. *Journal of GLBT Family Studies.*

Leschied, A.W., Chiodo, D., Whitehead, P.C., & Hurley, D. (2006). The association of poverty with child welfare service and child and family clinical outcomes. *Community, Work & Family, 9*(1), 29–46. doi:10.1080/13668800500420988

Leschied, A.W., & Cummings, A.L. (2002). Youth violence: An overview of predictors, counselling interventions, and future directions. *Canadian Journal of Counselling, 36*, 256–264.

Lespérance, F., Frasure-Smith, N., & Koszycki, D. (2007). Effects of citalopram and interpersonal psychotherapy on depression in patients with coronary artery disease: The Canadian Cardiac Randomized Evaluation of Antidepressant and Psychotherapy Efficacy (CREATE) trial. *JAMA, 297*, 367–379. doi:10.1001/jama.297.4.367

Leung, S.A. (1995). Career development and counseling: A multicultural perspective. In J.G. Ponterotto, J.M. Casas, I.A. Suzuki, & C.M. Alexander (Eds.), *Handbook of multicultural counseling* (pp. 549–566). Thousand Oaks, CA: Sage.

Levant, R.F. (2005). Evidence-based practice in psychology: Report of the 2005 Presidential Task Force on Evidence-Based Practice. *APA Monitor on Psychology, 36*(2), 5. http://www.apa.org/monitor/feb05/pc.html

Li, J. (2001). Expectations of Chinese immigrant parents for their children's education: The interplay of Chinese tradition and the Canadian context. *Canadian Journal of Education, 26*(4), 477–494. http://www.jstor.org/stable/160217

Liddle, B.J. (2007). Mutual bonds: Lesbian women's lives and communities. In K.J. Bieschke, R.M. Perez, & K.A. DeBord (Eds.), *Handbook of counseling and psychotherapy with lesbian, gay, bisexual, and transgender clients* (2nd ed., pp. 51–69). Washington, DC: American Psychological Association.

Liddle, K. (2005). More than a bookstore: The continuing relevance of feminist bookstores for the lesbian community. *Journal of Lesbian Studies, 9*(1–2), 145–159.

Limoges, J., Lahaie, R., & Martiny, C. (2008). O P T R A: Job entry core program. Montreal, Q C: Éditions Yvon Blais/Thomson.

Little, B.R. (1983). Personal projects: A rationale and method for investigation. *Environment & Behavior, 15*(3), 273–309. doi:10.1177/0013916583153002

Loewy, M.I., Juntunen, C.L., & Duan, C. (2009). Application of the counselling psychology model training values statement addressing diversity to the admission process. *The Counseling Psychologist, 37,* 705–720. doi:10.1177/0011000009331942.

Logan, C.R, & Barret, R. (2005). Counseling competencies for sexual minority clients. *Journal of L G B T Issues in Counseling, 1*(1), 3–22.

Lorber, J. (2004). Preface. *Journal of Homosexuality, 46*(3–4), xxv–xxvi.

Löwenborg, C. (2001). Inspiration across cultures: Reflecting teams among the Métis in Canada. A N Z J F T *Australian and New Zealand Journal of Family Therapy, 22,* 25–27.

Lucock, M., Leach, C., Iveson, S., Lynch, K., Horsefield, C., & Hall, P. (2003). A systematic approach to practice-based evidence in psychological therapies service. *Clinical Psychology and Psychotherapy, 10,* 389–399. doi:10.1002/cpp.385

Lueger, R.J., & Barkham, M. (2010). Using benchmarks and benchmarking to improve quality of practice and service. In M. Barkham, G.E. Hardy, & J. Mellor-Clark (Eds.), *Practice-based evidence: A guide for psychological therapies* (pp. 223–256). Hoboken, N J: Wiley-Blackwell.

MacCourt, P. (2008). *Promoting seniors' well-being: A seniors' mental health policy lens toolkit.* Victoria, B C: British Columbia Psychogeriatric Association.

MacDonald, B.J. (1998). Issues in therapy with gay and lesbian couples. *Journal of Sex & Marital Therapy, 24*(3), 165–190.

MacDonald, N.E., Fisher, W.A., Wells, G.A., Doherty, J.A., & Bowie, W.R. (1994). Canadian street youth: Correlates of sexual risk-taking activity. *The Pediatric Infectious Disease Journal, 13*(0891–3668), 690–697.

MacIntosh, H., Reissing, E.D., & Andruff, H. (2010). Same-sex marriage in Canada: The impact of legal marriage on the first cohort of gay and lesbian Canadians to wed. *Canadian Journal of Human Sexuality, 19*(3), 79–90.

Maglio, A.-S.T., Butterfield, L.D., & Borgen, W.A. (2005). Existential considerations for contemporary career counseling. *Journal of Employment Counseling, 42,* 75–92. doi:10.1002/j.2161-1920.2005.tb00902.x

Magnusson, K., & Lalande, V. (2005). *The state of practice in Canada for measuring career services impact: A C R W G report* [Canadian Research

Working Group]. http://www.crwg-gdrc.ca/crwg/wp-content/
uploads/2010/10/

Mak, A.S., Westwood, M.J., Ishiyama, F., & Barker, M.C. (1999).
Optimising conditions for learning sociocultural competencies for
success. *International Journal of Intercultural Relations*, 23(1), 77–90.
doi:10.1016/S0147-1767(98)00026-1

Malik, M.L., Johannsen, B.E., & Beutler, L.E. (2008). Personality disorders
and the D S M: A critical review. In G.J. Boyle, G. Matthews, and D.H.
Saklofske (Eds.), *The Sage handbook of personality theory and assessment: Vol 1: Personality theories and models*. Thousand Oaks, C A: Sage.

Malone, J. (2004). Working with Aboriginal women: Applying feminist
therapy in a multicultural counselling context. *Canadian Journal of
Counselling and Psychotherapy*, 34(1), 33–41.

Malone, J.L. (2011). Professional practice out of the urban context:
Defining Canadian rural psychology. *Canadian Psychology*, 52(4), 289–
295. doi:10.1037/a0024157

Manthei, R.J. (2005). What can clients tell us about seeking counselling
and their experience of it? *International Journal for the Advancement of
Counselling*, 27, 541–555. doi:10.1007/s10447-005-8490-3

Maranda, M., & Comeau, Y. (2000). Some contributions of sociology to
the understanding of career. In A. Collin & R.A. Young (Eds.), *The future
of career* (pp. 37–52). Cambridge, U K: Cambridge University Press.

Marshall, E.A., Peterson, R., Coverdale, J., Etzel, S., & McFarland, N.
(2014). Learning and living community-based research: Graduate student collaborations in Aboriginal communities. In B. Hall, C. Etmanski,
& T. Dawson (Eds.), *Teaching community-based research: Linking pedagogy to practice* (pp. 206–229). Toronto: University of Toronto Press.

Martin, D.J., Garske, J.P., & Davis, M.K. (2000). Relation of the therapeutic alliance with outcome and other variables: A meta-analytic review.
Journal of Consulting and Clinical Psychology, 68(3), 438–450.
doi:10.1037/0022-006X.68.3.438

Martin, R., Murphy, K.K., Hanson, D.D., Hemingway, C.C., Ramsden,
V.V., Buxton, J.J., ... Hislop, T.G. (2009). The development of participatory health research among incarcerated women in a Canadian prison.
International Journal of Prisoner Health, 5(2), 95–107.
doi:10.1080/17449200902884021

Martin, S.L. (2009, October). An exploration of women's health and healing in the context of intimate partner violence. Poster presented at the
15th International Qualitative Health Research Conference, Vancouver,
B C.

Masdonati, J., & Goyer, L. (2012). Et l'orientation scolaire et professionnelle, dans tout ça? In F. Picard and J. Masdonati (Eds.), *Parcours
scolaires et professionnelles des jeunes* (pp. 281–291). Laval, QC:
l'Université Laval.

Mathieson, C.M., Bailey, N., & Gurevich, M. (2002). Health care services
for lesbian and bisexual women: Some Canadian data. *Health Care for
Women International, 23*(2), 185–196.

Matteson, D.R. (1995). Counseling with bisexuals. *Individual Psychology:
Journal of Adlerian Theory, Research & Practice, 51*(2), 144–159.

Matteson, D.R. (1996). Psychotherapy with bisexual individuals. In R.P.
Cabaj & T.S. Stein (Eds.), *Textbook of homosexuality and mental health*
(pp. 433–450). Washington, DC: American Psychiatric Association.

McBride, D.L. (2010). Issues supervising family violence cases: Advocacy,
ethical documentation, and supervisees' reactions. *Canadian Journal of
Counselling and Psychotherapy, 44*, 283–295.

McBride, D., & Korell, G. (2005). Wilderness therapy for abused women.
Canadian Journal of Counselling, 39, 3–12.

McCabe, G.H. (2007).The healing path: A culture and community-derived
Indigenous therapy model. *Psychotherapy: Theory, Research, Practice,
Training, 44*(2), 148–160. doi:10.1037/0033-3204.44.2.148

McCall, L. (2005). The complexity of intersectionality. *Signs: Journal of
Women in Culture and Society, 30*, 1771–1800.

McCarthy, J. (2001). The skills, training and qualifications of guidance
workers. *International Journal of Educational and Vocational
Guidance, 4*, 159–178.

McCarthy, J. (2011). *Waxing the Gaza: The political role of professional
associations.* IAEVG-PACE Conference, Capetown, South Africa.

McCormick, R.M. (1997). Healing through interdependence: The role of
connecting in First Nations healing practices. *Canadian Journal of
Counselling, 31*, 172–184.

McCormick, R. (1998). Ethical considerations in First Nations counselling. *Canadian Journal of Counselling, 32*, 284–297.

McCormick, R. (2000a). The relationship of Aboriginal peoples with
nature. Paper presented 15 January at the National Consultation on
Vocational Counselling, Ottawa.

McCormick, R.M. (2000b). Aboriginal traditions in the treatment of substance abuse. *Canadian Journal of Counselling, 34*, 25–32.

McCormick, R. (2009). Aboriginal approaches to counseling. In E.
Kirmayer and V. Guthrie Valaskakis (Eds.), *Healing traditions: The men-
tal health of Aboriginal peoples in Canada* (pp. 337–354). Vancouver:
University of British Columbia Press.

McCormick, R., & Gerlitz, J. (2009). Nature as healer: Aboriginal ways of healing through nature. *Counselling and Spirituality, 28*(1), 55–72.

McDonald, C. (2006). Lesbian disclosure: Disrupting the taken for granted. *CJNR: Canadian Journal of Nursing Research, 38*(1), 43–57.

McElwain, A.D., Grimes, M.E., & McVicker, M.L. (2009). The implications of erotic plasticity and social constructionism in the formation of female sexual identity. *Journal of Feminist Family Therapy: An International Forum, 21*(2), 125–139.

McIntosh, C. (2011). Introduction: The medium and the message. *Journal of Gay & Lesbian Mental Health, 15*(3), 318–319.

McKirnan, D.J., Stokes, J.P., Doll, L., & Burzette, R.G. (1995). Bisexually active men: Social characteristics and sexual behavior. *Journal of Sex Research, 32*(1), 65–76.

McLennan, N.A., Rochow, S., & Arthur, N. (2001). Religious and spiritual diversity in counselling. *Guidance & Counseling, 16*(4), 132.

McMahon, M. (2003). Supervision and career counsellors: A little-explored practice with an uncertain future. *British Journal of Guidance and Counselling, 31*, 177–187. doi:10.1080/0306988031000102351

McMahon, M., & Arthur, N. (2008). Social justice and career development: Looking back, looking forward. *Australian Journal of Career Development, 17*(2), 21–29.

Meara, N., Schmidt, L., Carrington, C., Davis, K., Dixon, D., Fretz, B., ... Suinn, R. (1988). Training and accreditation in counseling psychology. *The Counseling Psychologist, 16*, 366–384. doi:10.1177/0011000088163005

Medicine-Eagle, B. (1989). The circle of healing. In N.R. Carlson, B. Shields, & J. Brugh (Eds.), *Healer on healing* (pp. 58–62). New York: J.P. Tarcher/Putnam.

Mental Health Commission of Canada. (2009). *Toward recovery & well-being: A framework for a mental health strategy for Canada.* http://www.mentalhealthcommission.ca/SiteCollectionDocuments/boarddocs/15507_MHCC_EN_final.pdf

Mental Health Commission of Canada. (2010). *Mental health in the workplace: A perfect legal storm.* Ottawa: Author. http://www.mentalhealthcommission.ca/SiteCollectionDocuments/News/en/Tracking%20the%20Perfect%20Legal%20Storm%20news%20release.pdf

Mental Health Commission of Canada. (2012). *Changing directions, changing lives: The mental health strategy for Canada.* Calgary, AB: Author.

Mental Health Commission of Canada. (n.d.). Vision and mission of the MHCC. http://www.mentalhealthcommission.ca/English/Pages/TheMHCC.aspx

Menzies, P. (2009). Homeless Aboriginal men: Effects of intergenerational trauma. In J.D. Hulchanski, P. Campsie, S. Chau, S. Hwang, & E. Paradis (Eds.), *Finding home: Policy options for addressing homelessness in Canada* (e-book, chapter 6.2). Toronto: Cities Centre, University of Toronto. http://www.homelesshub.ca/FindingHome

Merali, N. (2002). Perceived versus actual parent-adolescent assimilation disparity among Hispanic refugee families. *International Journal for the Advancement of Counselling, 24,* 57–68. doi:10.1023/A:1015081309426

Merali, N. (2003). Incorporating Confucian Chinese spiritual beliefs into cognitive-behavioural therapy for post-traumatic stress. In F.D. Harper & J. McFadden (Eds.), *Culture and counseling: New approaches* (pp. 252–255). Needham Heights, M A: Allyn & Bacon.

Merali, N. (2004a). Individual assimilation status and intergenerational gaps in Hispanic refugee families. *International Journal for the Advancement of Counselling, 26,* 21–32. doi:10.1023/B:ADCO.0000021547.83609.9d

Merali, N. (2004b). Family experiences of Central American refugees who overestimate intergenerational gaps. *Canadian Journal of Counselling and Psychotherapy, 38,* 91–103.

Merali, N. (2005). Perceived experiences of Central American refugees who favourably judge the family's cultural transition process. *International Journal for the Advancement of Counselling, 27,* 345–357. doi:10.1007/s10447-005-8198-4;http://cjc-rcc.ucalgary.ca/cjc/index.php/rcc/article/view/248

Merali, N. (2008a). Rights-based education for South Asian sponsored wives in international arranged marriages. *Interchange: A Quarterly Review of Education, 39,* 205–220. doi:10.1007/s10780-008-9060-5

Merali, N. (2008b). Theoretical frameworks for studying female marriage migrants. *Psychology of Women Quarterly, 32,* 281–289. doi:10.1111/j.1471-6402.2008.00436.x

Merali, N. (2012). Arranged and forced marriage. In M. Paludi (Ed.), *The psychology of love: Volume III – Meaning and culture* (pp. 143–168). Santa Barbara, C A: Praegar Academic Publishers.

Merali, N., & Violato, C. (2002). Relationships between demographic variables and immigrant parents' perceptions of assimilative adolescent behaviours. *Journal of International Migration and Integration, 3*(1), 65–82. doi:10.1007/s12134-002-1003-x

Methei, R.J. (2006). What can clients tell us about seeking counselling and their experience of it? *International Journal for the Advancement of Counselling, 27,* 541–553. doi:10.1007/s10447-005-8490-3

Meyer, G.J., Finn, S.E., Eyde, L.D., Kay, G.G., Moreland, K.L., Dies, R.R., ... Reed, G.M. (2001). Psychological testing and psychological assessment. *American Psychologist, 56*, 128–165.

Meyer, L., & Melchert, T.P. (2011). Examining the content of mental health intake assessments from the biopsychosocial perspective. *Journal of Psychotherapy Integration, 21*(1), 70–89.

Meyer-Cook, F., & Labelle, D. (2004). Namaji: Two-Spirit organizing in Montreal, Canada. In S. Wehbi (Ed.), *Community organizing against homophobia and heterosexism: The world through rainbow-colored glasses* (pp. 29–51). Binghamton, NY: Harrington Park Press/Haworth Press.

Michaud, G., Goyer, L., Turcotte, M., & Baudouin, R. (2006). *L'évaluation des services de développement de carrière: Qu'en pensent les praticiens, les responsables de développement de politiques et les employeurs?* Consultation nationale touchant le développement de carrière (CONAT), Ottawa. http://www.natcon.org/natcon/papers/natcon_papers_2006_f2.pdf

Miller, D.S., Forrest, L., & Elman, N.S. (2009). Training directors' conceptualizations of the intersections of diversity and trainee competence problems: A preliminary analysis. *The Counseling Psychologist, 37*(4), 482–518. doi:10.1177/0011000008316656

Miller, L.D., Gold, S., Laye-Gindhu, A., Martinez, Y.J., Yu, C.M., & Waechtler, V. (2011). Transporting a school-based intervention for social anxiety in Canadian adolescents. *Canadian Journal of Behavioural Science, 43*(4), 287–296. doi:10.1037/a0023174

Miller, L.D., Laye-Gindhu, A., Bennett, J.L., Liu, Y., Gold, S., March, J.S., et al. (2011). An effectiveness study of a culturally enriched school-based CBT anxiety prevention program. *Journal of Clinical Child & Adolescent Psychology, 40*, 618–629. doi:10.1080/15374416.2011.581619

Miller, S.D., Duncan, B.L., Sorrell, R., & Brown, G.S. (2005). The partners for change outcome management system. *Journal of Clinical Psychology, 61*(2), 199–208. doi:10.1002/Jclp.20111

Mitchell, K.E., Levin, A.S., & Krumboltz, J.D. (1999). Planned happenstance: Constructing unexpected career opportunities. *Journal of Counseling & Development, 77*, 115–124. doi:10.1002/j.1556-6676.1999.tb02431.x

Mogan, T., & Ness, D. (2003). Career decision-making difficulties of first-year students. *Canadian Journal of Career Development, 2*, 33–39.

Mohr, J.J., & Rochlen, A.B. (1999). Measuring attitudes regarding bisexuality in lesbian, gay male, and heterosexual populations. *Journal of Counseling Psychology, 46*, 353–369.

Moodley, R. (2007a). (Re)placing multiculturalism in counselling and psychotherapy. *British Journal of Guidance & Counselling, 35*, 1–22. doi:10.1080/03069880601106740

Moodley, R. (2007b). Matrices in black and white: Implications of cultural multiplicity for research in counselling and psychotherapy. *Counselling & Psychotherapy Research, 3*, 115–121. doi:10.1080/14733140312331384482

Moodley, R. (2009). Multi(ple) cultural voices speaking "outside the sentence" of counselling and psychotherapy. *Counselling Psychology Quarterly, 22*, 297–307. doi:10.1080/09515070903302364

Moodley, R., Gielen, U.P., & Wu, R. (2012). *Handbook of counseling and psychotherapy in an international context* (pp. 106–116). New York: Routledge.

Morrissette, P.J. (2003). First Nations and Aboriginal counsellor education. *Canadian Journal of Counselling, 37*, 205–215.

Multiculturalism Canada. (1983). *Strategy on race relations.* Ottawa: Author.

Munro, C. (n.d.). Charting workplace transitioning pathways of Generation-Y human resources practitioners. In R. Shea & R. Joy (Eds.), *A multi-sectoral approach to career development: A decade of Canadian research* (pp. 273–287). Canada: *The Canadian Journal of Career Development.*

Murphy, J.J. (2008). Client-based assessment: A fast track to better outcomes. In G. Walz & R. Yep (Eds.), *Compelling counseling interventions: Vistas' fifth anniversary* (pp. 239–248). Alexandria, va: American Counseling Association.

Mussell, B. (2005). Perceptions of First Nations males (Part III). In *Warrior-caregivers: Understanding the challenges and healing of First Nations men.* Ottawa: Aboriginal Healing Foundation.

Mussel, B., Cardiff, K., & White, J. (2004). *The mental health and well-being of Aboriginal children and youth: Guidance for new approaches and services.* Chilliwack, bc: British Columbia Ministry for Children and Family Development.

Mussell, W.J., Nichols, W.M., & Adler, M.T. (1993). *Meaning making of mental health challenges in First Nations: A Freirean perspective, 2nd ed.* Chilliwack, bc: Sal'i'shan Institute Society.

Mutual recognition agreement of the regulatory bodies for professional psychologists in Canada – as amended June 2004. (2004). http://www.cpa.ca/documents/MRA.pdf

Mwarigha, M.S. (2002). Towards a framework for local responsibility: Taking action to end the current limbo in immigrant settlement – Toronto. Toronto: Maytree Foundation.

Myers, I., & McCaulley, M. (1985). *Manual for the Myers-Briggs type indicator.* Palo Alto, CA: Consulting Psychologists Press.

Myers, M.F. (1991). Marital therapy with HIV-infected men and their wives. *Psychiatric Annals, 21*(8), 466–470.

Nagy, R. (2000). Justice and reconciliation: Analysis and response to past human rights violations. In *Seminar on social justice and multiculturalism: Contemporary policy and research issues.* Draft proceedings. Ottawa: Department of Canadian Heritage, n.p.

Nassrallah, C. (2005). *Canada's approach to multiculturalism.* Rome: Canadian Heritage.

National Council of Welfare. (2006). *Poverty profile 2002 and 2003.* Ottawa: Author.

Nayar, K.E., & Sandhu, J.S. (2006). Intergenerational communication in immigrant Punjabi families: Implications for helping professionals. *International Journal for the Advancement of Counselling, 28,* 139–152. doi:10.1007/s10447-005-9005-y

Neault, R.A. (2005). Managing global careers: Challenges for the 21st century. *International Journal for Educational and Vocational Guidance, 5,* 149–161. doi:10.1007/s10775005-8796-z

Neault, R.A. (n.d.). Thriving in the new millennium: Career management in the changing world of work. In R. Shea & R. Joy (Eds.), *A multi-sectoral approach to career development: A decade of Canadian research* (pp. 221–239). Canada: The Canadian Journal of Career Development.

Neault, R.A., & Pickerell, D.A. (2011). Career engagement: Bridging career counselling and employee engagement. *Journal of Employment Counselling, 48*(4), 185–188. doi:10.1002/j.2161-1920.2011.tb01111.x

Nebeker, R.S., Lambert, M.J., & Huefner, J.C. (1995). Ethnic differences on the Outcome Questionnaire. *Psychological Reports, 77,* 875–879. doi:10.2466/pro.1995.77.3.875

Nelson, F. (1996). *Lesbian motherhood: An exploration of Canadian lesbian families.* Toronto: University of Toronto Press.

Nelson, F. (1999). Lesbian families: Achieving motherhood. *Journal of Gay & Lesbian Social Services: Issues in Practice, Policy & Research, 10*(1), 27–46.

Newbury, J.,& Hoskins, M.L. (2010). Girls are so complicated! Re-imaging addiction support in Canada. *Canadian Journal of Counselling, 44*(1), 15–33.

Newring, K.A.B., Wheeler, J., & Draper, C. (2008). Transvestic fetishism: Assessment and treatment. In D.R. Laws & W.T. O'Donohue (Eds.), *Sexual deviance: Theory, assessment, and treatment* (2nd ed., pp. 285–304). New York: Guilford Press.

Nicol, J.J. (2010). Body, time, space and relationship in the music listening experiences of women with chronic illness. *Psychology of Music, 38*, 351–367. doi:10.1177/0305735609351914

Niemeyer, G.J., & Niemeyer, R.A. (1993). Defining the boundaries of constructivist assessment. In G.J. Niemeyer (Ed.), *Constructivist assessment: A casebook* (pp. 1–30). Newbury Park, CA: Sage.

Niles, S.G. (2003). Career counselors confront a critical crossroad: A vision of the future. *The Career Development Quarterly, 52*, 70–77. doi:10.1002/j.2161-0045.2003.tb00629.x

Niles, S.G., Amundson, N.E., & Neault, R.A. (2011). Career flow: A hope-centered approach to career development. Columbus, OH: Pearson.

Norcross, J.C. (2002). *Psychotherapy relationships that work: Therapists' contributions and responsiveness to patient needs*. New York: Oxford University Press.

Norcross, J.C., & Wampold, B.E. (2011). Evidence-based therapy relationships: Research conclusions and clinical practices. *Psychotherapy, 48*(1), 98–102. doi:10.1037/a0022161

Nuttgens, S.A. (2009, July). *Teaching counselling theory amidst changing views on the primacy of theory within counselling practice*. Paper presented at the International Conference on the Teaching of Psychology, Vancouver, BC.

Nuttgens, S.A., & Campbell, A.J. (2010). Multicultural considerations for counselling First Nations clients. *Canadian Journal of Counselling and Psychotherapy, 44*(2), 115–129.

O'Brien, K.M. (2001). The legacy of Parsons: Career counselors and vocational psychologists as agents of social change. *The Career Development Quarterly, 50*(1), 66–76.

O'Byrne, P., & Holmes, D. (2011). Desire, drug use and unsafe sex: A qualitative examination of gay men who attend gay circuit parties. *Culture, Health & Sexuality, 13*(1), 1–13.

Offet-Gartner, K. (2010). Engaging in culturally competent research. In N. Arthur & S. Collins, *Culture-infused counselling* (2nd ed., pp. 209–244). Calgary, AB: Counselling Concepts.

Offet-Gartner, K. (2011). Sharing the stories: Aboriginal women reclaim education as a tool for personal and career development. Saarbrucken, Germany: VDM Verlag Dr. Muller Gmbh & Co.

Olympio, N. (2012). *Les contexts éducatifs européens à l'épreuve de la théorie des "capabilités" d'Amartya Sen*. Quebec: Les Presses de l'Université Laval.

Omidvar, R., & Richmond, T. (2003). *Settlement and social inclusion in Canada. Working paper series: Perspectives on social inclusion.* Toronto: Laidlaw Foundation.

O'Neill, L.K. (2010a). Mental health support in northern communities: Reviewing issues on isolated practice and secondary trauma. *Rural and Remote Health, 10*(2), 1369. http://www.rrh.org.au

O'Neill, L.K. (2010b). Northern helping practitioners and the phenomenon of secondary trauma. *Canadian Journal of Counselling and Psychotherapy, 44*(2), 130–149.

O'Neill, L., Guenette, F., & Kitchenham, A. (2010). 'Am I safe here and do you like me?' Understanding complex trauma and attachment disruption in the classroom. *British Journal of Special Education, 37*(4), 190–197. doi:10.1111/j.1467-8578.2010.00477.x

Ordre Professionel des Conseillers et Conseillères d'Orientation du Québec. (2011a). *Assessment Guide for Career and Guidance Counselling.* Montreal, QC: OCCOQ. http://www.ceric.ca/files/PDFs/Assessment%20Guide%20for%20Career%20and%20Guidance%20Counselling_OCCOQ%202011.pdf

Ordre Professionel des Conseillers et Conseillères d'Orientation du Québec. (2011b). *L'Orientation, 1*(1). http://www.orientation.qc.ca/Communications/Publications/~/media/FAC621EF437F4729AC10861DAF37DABF.ashx

Oreopoulos, P. (2009). Why do skilled immigrants struggle in the labor market? A field experiment with six thousand résumés. (Research Report No. 09 – 03). Retrieved from Metropolis British Columbia, http://riim.metropolis.net/assets/uploads/files/wp/2009/WP09-03.pdf

Organization for Economic Cooperation and Development. (2003). *Analyse des politiques d'éducation.* Paris: Author.

Organization for Economic Cooperation and Development. (2004). *Career guidance and public policy: Bridging the gap.* Paris: Author.

Ornstein, M. (2000). *Ethno-racial inequality in the city of Toronto: An analysis of the 1996 census.* Toronto: Project Steering Committee for the Study on Ethno-Racial Inequality.

Osborne, J.W. (2012). Psychological effects of the transition to retirement. *Canadian Journal of Counselling and Psychotherapy, 46,* 45–58.

Otis, J., Girard, M.-E., Alary, M., Remis, R.R., Lavoie, R., LeClerc, R., … Masse, B. (2006). Drogues, sexe et risques dans la communauté gaie montréalaise: 1997–2003. [Drugs, sex and risks in Montreal's gay community: 1997–2003.] *Drogues, santé et société, 5*(2), 161–197.

Oulanova, O. (2008). *Navigating two worlds: Experiences of Canadian mental health professionals who integrate aboriginal traditional healing practices.* Unpublished master's thesis. Toronto: University of Toronto.

Oulanova, O., & Moodley, R. (2010). Navigating two worlds: Experiences of counsellors who integrate Aboriginal traditional healing practices. *Canadian Journal of Counselling and Psychotherapy, 44*(4), 346–362.

Overington, L., & Ionita, G. (2012). Progress monitoring measures: A brief guide. *Canadian Psychology – Psychologie Canadienne, 53*(2), 82–92. doi:10.1037/a0028017

Page, E.H. (2004). Mental health services experiences of bisexual women and bisexual men: An empirical study. *The Journal of Bisexuality, 4*(1/2), 137–160.

Palmer, A., & Parish, J. (2008). Social justice and counselling psychology: Situating the role of graduate student research, education, and training. *Canadian Journal of Counselling, 42,* 278–292.

Palys, T. (1997). *Research decisions: Quantitative and qualitative perspectives* (2nd ed.). Toronto: Harcourt Brace & Company.

Paré, D. (2008). Discourse, positioning and deconstruction: Response to chapter 5. In G. Monk, J. Winslade, & S. Sinclair (Eds.), *New horizons in multicultural counseling* (pp. 137–140). Thousand Oaks, CA: Sage.

Paré, D., & Lysack, M. (2006). Exploring inner dialogue in counsellor education. *Canadian Journal of Counselling, 40*(3), 131–144.

Paré, M.F. (2009). *History of gay Toronto and birth of Queer West Village.* Retrieved 30 August 2011 from http://queerwest.org/history.php

Parliament of Canada. (2013). *Canadian Charter of Rights and Freedoms.* Retrieved 8 April 2013 from http://www.parl.gc.ca

Pasterski, V. (2008). Disorders of sex development and atypical sex differentiation. In D.L. Rowland & L. Incrocci (Eds.), *Handbook of sexual and gender identity disorders* (pp. 354–375). Hoboken, NJ: John Wiley & Sons.

Patsiopoulos, A.T., & Buchanan, M.J. (2011). The practice of self-compassion in counseling: A narrative inquiry. *Professional Psychology: Research & Practice, 42*(4), 301–307. doi:10.1037/a0024482

Patton, W.A., & McMahon, M.L. (2006). The systems theory framework of career development and counselling: Connecting theory and practice. *International Journal for the Advancement of Counselling, 28,* 153–166. doi:10.1007/s10447-005-9010-1

Paul-Sen, R., de Wit, M.L., & McKeown, D. (2007). The impact of poverty on the current and future health status of children. *Paediatrics & Child Health, 12*(8), 667–673.

Peavy, R.V. (1992). A constructivist mode of training for career counsellors. *Journal of Career Development, 18*(3), 215–228. doi:10.1177/089484539201800305

Peavy, R.V. (1996). Constructivist career counselling and assessment. *Guidance & Counseling, 11*, 8–14.

Peavy, R.V. (1997). Socio-dynamic counselling: A constructivist perspective. Victoria, B C: Trafford.

Peavy, R.V. (1998). When strangers meet: Majority culture counsellors and minority cultural clients, a discussion paper. In *Proceedings of the 3rd International Conference for Trainers of Educational and Vocational Guidance Counsellors* (pp.125–140). Tampere, Finland.

Peavy, R.V. (2000, January). *SocioDynamic perspective and the practice of counselling.* Paper presented at the Annual Conference of National Consultation on Career Development (Natcon Papers 2002).

Peavy, R.V. (2001). A brief outline of SocioDynamic counselling: A co-constructivist perspective on helping. http://www.sociodynamic-constructivist-counselling.com/

Peavy, R.V. (2004). *Sociodynamic counselling: A practical approach to meaning making.* Chagrin Falls, O H: Taos Institute.

Peavy, R., & Li, H. (2003). Social and cultural context of intercultural counselling. *Canadian Journal of Counselling and Psychotherapy, 37*(3), 186–196.

Pedersen, P. (1999). *Multiculturalism as a fourth force.* Philadelphia, P A: Bruner/Mazel.

Pedersen, P.B., Crethar, H.C., & Carlson, J. (2008). *Inclusive cultural empathy: Making relationships central in counseling and psychotherapy.* Washington, D C: American Psychological Association.

Pelling, N. (2004). Introduction. *Counselling Psychology Quarterly, 17*(3), 239–245. doi:10.1080/09515070412331317611

Pendakur, R. (2000). *Immigrants and the labour force: Policy, regulation and impact.* Montreal, Q C: McGill-Queen's University Press.

Pépin, Y. (2009). *Intervention psychosociale.* Recueil de textes. Quebec: Université Laval.

Perreira, K. M., Harris, K. M., & Lee, D. (2006). Making it in America: High school completion by immigrant and native youth. *Demography, 43,* 511–536.

Petersen, L., & Park-Saltzman, J. (2010). Implications for counselling Asian transnational youth: The experiences of Taiwanese youth in Vancouver. *Canadian Journal of Counselling and Psychotherapy, 44*(4), 402–420.

Peterson, C., Seligman, M.E.P., & George, E. (1988). Pessimistic explanatory style is a risk factor for physical illness: A thirty-five year longitudinal study. *Journal of Personality and Social Psychology, 55*, 23–27.

Peterson, G.W., Krumboltz, J.D., & Garmon, J. (2005). Chaos out of order. New perspectives in career development in the information society. In J. Patrick, G. Elisson, & D.L. Thompson (Eds.), *Issues in career development*. Greenwich, CT: Information Age Publishing.

Pettifor, J. (2010). Ethics, diversity, and respect in multicultural counselling. In N. Arthur & S. Collins, *Culture-infused counselling* (2nd ed., pp. 167–188). Calgary, AB: Counselling Concepts.

Pettifor, J., McCarron, M.C.E., Schoepp, G., Stark, C., & Stewart, D. (2011). Ethical supervision in teaching, research, practice, and administration. *Canadian Psychology, 52*(3), 198–205. doi:10.1037/a0024549

Picard, F., & Masdonati, J. (Eds.). (2012). *Parcours scolaires et professionnelles des jeunes*. Quebec: Les Presses de l'Université Laval.

Pieterse, A.L., Evans, S.A., Risner-Butner, A., Collins, N.M., & Mason, L.B. (2009). Multicultural competence and social justice training in counseling psychology and counselor education: A review and analysis of a sample of multicultural course syllabi. *The Counseling Psychologist, 37*, 93–115.

Piran, N. (2005). Prevention of eating disorders: A review of outcome evaluation research. *Israeli Journal of Psychiatry and Related Sciences, 42*(3), 172–178.

Piran, N., & Robinson, S.R. (2011). Patterns of associations between eating disordered behaviors and substance use: A university and a community based sample. *Journal of Health Psychology, 16*, 1027–1037. doi:10.1177/1359105311398681

Piran, N., & Thompson, S. (2008). A study of the adverse social experiences model to the development of eating disorders. *International Journal of Health Promotion & Education, 46*(2), 65–71. doi:10.1080/14635240.2008.10708131

Plumb, A.M. (2011). Spirituality and counselling: Are counsellors prepared to integrate religion and spirituality into therapeutic work with clients? *Canadian Journal of Counselling and Psychotherapy, 45*(1), 1–16.

Poehnell, G.R., & Amundson, N.E. (2011). *Hope-filled engagement: New possibilities in life/career counselling*. Richmond, BC: Ergon Communications.

Polonijo, A.N., & Hollister, B.A. (2011). Normalcy, boundaries, and heterosexism: An exploration of online lesbian health queries. *Journal of Gay & Lesbian Social Services: The Quarterly Journal of Community & Clinical Practice, 23*(2), 165–187.

Poon, M.K.-L. (2006). The discourse of oppression in contemporary gay Asian diasporal literature: Liberation or limitation? *Sexuality & Culture: An Interdisciplinary Quarterly, 10*(3), 29–58.

Poon, M.K.-L., & Ho, P.T.-T. (2008). Negotiating social stigma among gay Asian men. *Sexualities, 11*(1–2), 245–268.

Poonwassie, A., & Charter, A. (2001). An Aboriginal worldview of helping: Empowering approaches. *Canadian Journal of Counselling, 35*(1), 63–73.

Popadiuk, N.E. (2009). Unaccompanied Asian secondary students in Canada. *International Journal for the Advancement of Counselling, 31*(4), 229–243. doi:10.1007/s10447-009-9080-6

Pope, J.F., & Arthur, N. (2009). Socioeconomic status and class: A challenge for the practice of psychology in Canada. *Canadian Psychology, 50*(2), 55–65. doi:10.1037/a0014222

Pope, M. (2010). Career counseling with diverse adults. In J.G. Ponterotto, J.M. Casas, L.A. Suzuki, & C.M. Alexander (Eds.), *Handbook of multicultural counseling* (3rd ed., pp. 731–743). Thousand Oaks, CA: Sage.

Poushinsky, N., & Tallion-Wasmund, P. (2002). First Nations and mental health. *Foundations for Reform, Section 17.* Champlain District Mental Health Implementation Task Force.

Pride Library at the University of Western Ontario. (n.d.). *History of the gay liberation in Canada, 1970s climate and timeline.* Retrieved 30 August 2011 from http://www.uwo.ca/pridelib/bodypolitic/gaylib/70stimeline.htm

Prilleltensky, I. (1994). Empowerment in mainstream psychology: Legitimacy, obstacles, and possibilities. *Canadian Psychology, 35*(4), 358–374.

Prilleltensky, I., & Nelson, G. (2002). *Doing psychology critically: Making a difference in diverse settings.* New York: Palgrave Macmillan.

Prkachin, K.M., Hughes, E., Schultz, I., Joy, P., & Hunt, D. (2002). Real-time assessment of pain behavior during clinical assessment of low back pain patients. *Pain, 95,* 23–30. doi:10.1016/50304-3959(01)00369-4

Prkachin, K.M., Schultz, I.Z., & Hughes, E. (2007). Pain behavior and the development of pain-related disability: The importance of guarding. *Clinical Journal of Pain, 23,* 270–277. doi:10.1097/AJP.0b013e3180308d28

Pronovost, J. (1995). Facteurs de protection et développement des habiletés personnelles et sociales: un premier pas pour prévenir le suicide.

In Association des centres jeunesse du Québec (Ed.), *Le phénomène du suicide chez les jeunes. La prévention et l'intervention dans les centres jeunesse* (pp. 30–34). Montreal, QC: Association des centres jeunesse du Québec.

Pronovost, J. (1998). Prévenir le suicide chez l'adolescent en misant sur les facteurs de protection. *Revue québécoise de psychologie, 19*(2), 147–165.

Public Health Agency of Canada. (2002). Review of best practices in mental health reform. http://www.phac-aspc.gc.ca/mh-sm/pubs/bp_review/reves1-eng.php

Quartaro, G.K., & Spier, T.E. (2002). We'd like to ask you some questions, but we have to find you first: Internet-based study of lesbian clients in therapy with lesbian feminist therapists. *Journal of Technology in Human Services, 19*(2–3), 109–118.

Rahman, M. (2010). Queer as intersectionality: Theorizing gay Muslim identities. *Sociology, 44*(5), 944–961.

Raj, R. (2007). Transactivism as therapy: A client self-empowerment model linking personal and social agency. *Journal of Gay & Lesbian Psychotherapy, 11*(3–4), 77–98.

Rambukkana, N.P. (2004). Uncomfortable bridges: The bisexual politics of outing polyamory. *Journal of Bisexuality, 4*(3–4), 141–154.

Raphael, D. (2004). Introduction to the social determinants of health. In D. Raphael (Ed.), *Social determinants of health: Canadian perspectives* (pp. 1–18). Toronto: Canadian Scholars.

Rasmi, S., Chuang, S.S., & Safdar, S. (2012). The relationship between perceived parental rejection and adjustment for Arab, Canadian, and Arab Canadian youth. *Journal of Cross-Cultural Psychology, 43*(1), 84–90.

Ratner, P.A., Johnson, J.L., Shoveller, J.A., Chan, K., Martindale, S.L., Schilder, A.J., … Hogg, R.S. (2003). Non-consensual sex experienced by men who have sex with men: Prevalence and association with mental health. *Patient Education and Counseling, 49*(1), 67–74.

Ravel, B., & Rail, G. (2008). From straight to gaie? Quebec sportswomen's discursive constructions of sexuality and destabilization of the linear coming out process. *Journal of Sport & Social Issues, 32*(1), 4–23.

Reese, R.J., Norsworthy, L.A., & Rowlands, S.R. (2009). Does a continuous feedback system improve psychotherapy outcome? *Psychotherapy Theory, Research, Practice, Training, 46*(4), 418–431. doi:10.1037/a0017901

Reese, R.J., Usher, E.L., Bowman, D.C., Norsworthy, L.A., Halstead, J.L., Rowlands, S.R., & Chisholm, R.R. (2009). Using client feedback in psychotherapy training: An analysis of its influence on supervision and counselor self-efficacy. *Training and Education in Professional Psychology, 3*(3), 157–168. doi:10.1037/a0015673

Rehaag, S. (2010). Bisexuals need not apply: A comparative appraisal of refugee law and policy in Canada, the United States, and Australia. In P.C.W. Chan (Ed.), *Protection of sexual minorities since Stonewall: Progress and stalemate in developed and developing countries* (pp. 281–302). New York: Routledge/Taylor & Francis.

Reitz, J.G. (2000). Immigrant success in the knowledge economy: Institutional change and the immigrant experience in Canada, 1970–1995. *Journal of Social Issues, 57,* 579–613. doi:10.1111/0022-4537.00230

Reitz, J.G. (2001). Immigrant skill utilization in the Canadian labour market: Implications of human capital research. *Journal of International Migration and Integration, 2,* 347–378. doi:10.1007/s12134-001-1004-1

Reitz, J.G. (2007). Immigrant employment success in Canada part I: Individual and contextual causes. *International Migration and Integration, 8,* 11–36. doi:10.1007/s12134-0070001-4

Rennie, D.L. (2002). Making a clearing: Qualitative research in Anglophone Canadian psychology. *Canadian Psychology, 43*(3), 139–140.

Rennie, D.L., Watson, K.D., & Monteiro, A.M. (2000). Qualitative research in Canadian psychology. *Forum Qualitative Sozialforschung/ Forum: Qualitative Social Research, 1*(2). http://qualitative-research.net/ fqs-e/2-00inhalt-e.htm

Rennie, D.L., Watson, K.D., & Monteiro, A.M. (2002). The rise of qualitative research in psychology. *Canadian Psychology, 43,* 179–189. doi:10.1037/h0086914

Reynolds, A.L. (2003). Counseling issues for lesbian and bisexual women. In M. Kopala & M.A. Keitel (Eds.), *Handbook of counseling women* (pp. 53–73). Thousand Oaks, CA: Sage.

Reynolds, V. (2010). A supervision of solidarity/Une supervision de solidarité. *Canadian Journal of Counselling and Psychotherapy, 44*(3), 246–257.

Richardson, M.S. (2009a). Intentional and identity processes: A social constructivist investigation using student journals. *Journal of Vocational Behavior, 74,* 63–74. doi:10.1016/j.jvb.2008.10.007

Richardson, M.S. (2009b). Another way to think about the work we do: Counselling for work and relationship. *International Journal for Educational and Vocational Guidance, 9*(2), 75–84. doi:10.1007/ s10775-009-9154-3

Richardson, M.S. (2012). Counselling for work and relationship. *The Counseling Psychologist, 40*(2), 190–242. doi:10.1177/0011000011406452

Rieger, G., Chivers, M.L., & Bailey, J.M. (2005). Sexual arousal patterns of bisexual men. *Psychological Science, 16*(8), 579–584.

Rimm, D.C., & Masters, J.C. (1974). *Behavior therapy: Techniques and empirical findings.* New York: Academic Press.

Ristock, J.L. (2001). Decentering heterosexuality: Responses of feminist counselors to abuse in lesbian relationships. *Women & Therapy, 23*(3), 59–72.

Ristock, J.L. (2002). *No more secrets: Violence in lesbian relationships.* New York: Routledge.

Riverin-Simard, D. (2000). Career development in a changing context of the second part of working life. In A. Collin & R.A. Young (Eds.), *The future of career* (pp. 115–129). Cambridge, UK: Cambridge University Press.

Riverin-Simard, D., & Simard, Y. (2005). *Vers un modèle de participation continue: La place centrale de l'orientation professionnelle.* Quebec: Ministère de l'éducation, Gouvernement du Québec.

Riverin-Simard, D., & Simard, Y. (January/July 2011). L'orientation professionnelle des adultes: une participation sociale toujours renouvelée. In *Revista Educação Skepsis, n. 2 – Formación Profesional. Vol. II. Claves para la formación profesional* (pp. 1012–1065). São Paulo: skepsis.org. http://academiaskepsis.org/revistaEducacao.html

Robertson, L. (2006). The residential school experience: Syndrome or historical trauma. *Pimatisiwin: A Journal of Aboriginal & Indigenous Community Health, 4*(1), 1–28.

Robertson, S.E. (2012, June). Counselling Psychology Section keynote. Keynote speech presented at the meeting of the Canadian Psychological Association, Halifax, NS.

Rohrbaugh, J.B. (2006). Domestic violence in same-gender relationships. *Family Court Review, 44*(2), 287–299.

Ronson, A., & Suprenant, A. (2012). Getting a handle on science policy: Report on the 2011 Canadian science policy conference. *Psynopsis, 34*(1), 52–53.

Rosenberg, R.D. (2008). An analysis of factors that influence matriculation at the masters level. *Dissertation Abstracts International Section A: Humanities and Social Sciences, 69* (4-A), 1298. Dissertation Abstract: 2008-99190-468.

Ross, B.L. (1995). *The house that Jill built: A lesbian nation in formation.* Toronto: University of Toronto Press.

Ross, L.E. (2005). Perinatal mental health in lesbian mothers: A review of potential risk and protective factors. *Women & Health, 41*(3), 113–128.

Ross, L.E., Doctor, F., Dimito, A., Kuehl, D., & Armstrong, M.S. (2007). Can talking about oppression reduce depression? Modified CBT group treatment for LGBT people with depression. *Journal of Gay & Lesbian Social Services: Issues in Practice, Policy & Research, 19*(1), 1–15.

Ross, L., Epstein, R., Goldfinger, C., Steele, L., Anderson, S., & Strike, C. (2008). Lesbian and queer mothers navigating the adoption system: The impacts on mental health. *Health Sociology Review, 17*(3), 254–266.

Ross, L.E., Steele, L., Goldfinger, C., & Strike, C. (2007). Perinatal depressive symptomatology among lesbian and bisexual women. *Archives of Women's Mental Health, 10*(2), 53–59.

Rothman, L. (2007). Oh Canada! Too many children in poverty for too long. *Paediatric Child Health, 12*(8), 661–665.

Rousseau, D.M. (1995). *Psychological contracts in organizations: Understanding written and unwritten agreements.* Newbury Park, CA: Sage.

Royal Commission on Aboriginal Peoples. (1994). *The High Arctic Relocation: A Report on the 1953–55 Relocation.* Ottawa: Minister of Supply and Services.

Rule, N.O. (2011). The influence of target and perceiver race in the categorisation of male sexual orientation. *Perception, 40*(7), 830–839.

Rule, N.O., Ishii, K., Ambady, N., Rosen, K.S., & Hallett, K.C. (2011). Found in translation: Cross-cultural consensus in the accurate categorization of male sexual orientation. *Personality and Social Psychology Bulletin, 37*(11), 1499–1507.

Russell-Mayhew, S. (2007). Preventing a continuum of disordered eating: Going beyond the individual. *Prevention Researcher, 14*(3), 7–10.

Russell-Mayhew, S., Arthur, N., & Ewashen, C. (2007). Targeting students, teachers and parents in a wellness-based prevention program in schools. *Eating Disorders, 15,* 159–181. doi:10.1080/10640260701190709

Saewyc, E.M. (2011). Research on adolescent sexual orientation: Development, health disparities, stigma, and resilience. *Journal of Research on Adolescence, 21*(1), 256–272.

Safren, S.A., Hollander, G., Hart, T.A., & Heimberg, R.G. (2001). Cognitive-behavioral therapy with lesbian, gay, and bisexual youth. *Cognitive and Behavioral Practice, 8,* 215–223.

Sakamoto, I., Ku, J., & Wei, Y. (2009). The deep plunge: Luocha and the experiences of earlier skilled immigrants from mainland China in Toronto. *Qualitative Social Work, 8,* 427–447. doi:10.1177/1473325009346518

Sampson, J.P., Jr. (1999). Internet-based distance guidance with services provided in career centers.*The Career Development Quarterly, 47,* 243–254.

Sanders, G.L. (2000). Men together: Working with gay couples in contemporary times. In P. Papp (Ed.), *Couples on the fault line: New directions for therapists* (pp. 222–256). New York: Guilford Press.

Sanders, G.L., & Kroll, I.T. (2000). Generating stories of resilience: Helping gay and lesbian youth and their families. *Journal of Marital and Family Therapy, 26*(4), 433–442.

Sandhu, J.S. (2005). A Sikh perspective on life-stress: Implications for counselling. *Canadian Journal of Counselling, 39,* 40–51.

Sapin, M., Spini, D., & Widmer E. (2007). *Les parcours de vie: De l'adolescence au grand âge.* Lausanne, Switzerland: Presses polytechniques et universitaires romandes.

Sattler, J.M. (2008). *Assessment of children: Cognitive foundations* (5th ed.). San Diego, CA: Jerome M. Sattler.

Sattler, J.M., & Hoge, R.D. (2006). *Assessment of children: Behavioral, social, and clinical foundations* (5th ed.). San Diego, CA: Jerome M. Sattler.

Savard, R., & Lecomte, C. (2009). Counseling de carrière avec ses enjeux d'orientation, d'réorientation, d'insertion, de réinsertion, d'adaptation et de réadaptation. In R. Savard, course notes, CCO701 Counseling individuel (pp. 81–95). Sherbrooke, QC: Université de Sherbrooke (Département d'orientation professionnelle, Faculté d'éducation).

Savard, R., Michaud, G., Bilodeau, C., & Arseneau, S. (2007). L'effet de l'information sur le marché du travail dans le processus décisionnel relatif au choix de carrière. *Canadian Journal of Counselling, 41,* 158–172.

Savickas, M.L. (2000). Renovating the psychology of careers for the twenty-first century. In A. Collin & R.A. Young (Eds.), *The future of career* (pp. 53–68). Cambridge, UK: Cambridge University Press.

Savickas, M.L. (Ed.). (2001). Envisioning the future of vocational psychology [Special issue]. *Journal of Vocational Behavior, 59*(2), 167–170.

Savickas, M.L. (2005). The theory and practice of career construction. In S.D. Brown & R.W. Lent (Eds.), *Career development and counselling: Putting theory and research to work* (pp. 42–70). Hoboken, NJ: Wiley.

Savickas, M.L., Nota, L., Rossier, J., Dauwalder, J.P., Duarte, M.E., Guichard, J., ... van Vianen, A.E.M. (2009). Life designing: A paradigm for career construction in the 21st century. *Journal of Vocational Behavior, 75,* 239–250. doi:10.1016/j.jvb.2009.04.004

Savin-Williams, R.C. (2005). *The new gay teenager.* Cambridge, M A: Harvard University Press.

Schneider, M.S. (1986). The relationships of cohabiting lesbian and hetero-sexual couples: A comparison. *Psychology of Women Quarterly, 10*(3), 234–239.

Schneider, M. (1989). Sappho was a right-on adolescent: Growing up les-bian. *Journal of Homosexuality, 17*(1–2), 111–130.

Schneider, M.S., Brown, L.S., & Glassgold, J.M. (2002). Implementing the resolution on appropriate therapeutic responses to sexual orientation: A guide for the perplexed. *Professional Psychology: Research and Practice, 33*(3), 265–276.

Schneider, M.S., & Dimito, A. (2010). Factors influencing the career and academic choices of lesbian, gay, bisexual, and transgender people. *Journal of Homosexuality, 57*(10), 1355–1369.

Schroeder, M., Andrews, J.J.W., & Hindes, Y.L. (2009). Cross-racial super-vision: Critical issues in the supervisory relationship. *Canadian Journal of Counselling, 43*(4), 295–310.

Schultz, I.Z., Crook, J.M., Berkowitz, J., Meloche, G.R., Milner, R., Zuberbier, O.A., & Meloche, W. (2002). Biopsychosocial multivariate predictive model of occupational low back disability. *Spine, 27,* 2720–2725. doi:10.1097/00007632-200212010-0002

Schwarz, C. (2008). Cost of living comparison. http://people.stat.sfu.ca/~cschwarz/SFUFA/EBinfo/StatCan/CostLiving.pdf

Seagram, S.,& Daniluk, J. (2002). "It goes with the territory": The meaning and experience of maternal guilt for mothers of preadolescent children. *Women and Therapy, 25,* 61–88. doi:10.1300/J015v25n01_04

Sen, A. (1992). *Inequality re-examined.* Cambridge, M A: Harvard University Press.

Sen, A. (2009). *The idea of justice.* Cambridge, M A: The Belknap Press of Harvard University Press.

Settersten, R.A. & Gannon, L. (2009). Structure, agency, and the space between: On the challenges and contradictions of a blended view of the life course. Reprinted in W.R. Heinz, J.H. Huinink, & A. Weymann (Eds.), *The life course reader: Individuals and societies across time.* Frankfurt, Germany: Campus Verlag.

Sexton, T.L. (1996). The relevance of counseling outcome research: Current trends and practical implications. *Journal of Counseling & Development, 74*, 590–600. doi:10.1002/j.1556-6676.1996.tb02298.x

Sexton, T.L., & Whiston, S.C. (1996). Integrating counseling research and practice. *Journal of Counseling & Development, 74*, 588–589. doi:10.1002/j.1556-6676.1996.tb02297.x

Shain, M. (2010). *Tracking the perfect legal storm: Converging systems create mounting pressure to create the psychologically safe workplace.* Ottawa: Mental Health Commission of Canada. http://www.mentalhealthcommission.ca/SiteCollectionDocuments/workplace/Perfect%20Legal%20Storm%20FINAL%20EN%20wc.pdf

Shariff, A. (2009). Ethnic identity and parenting stress in South Asian families: Implications for culturally sensitive counselling. *Canadian Journal of Counselling, 43*(1), 35–46.

Shepard, B. (2005). Embedded selves: Co-constructing a relationally based career workshop for rural girls. *Canadian Journal of Counselling, 39*, 158–172.

Shepard, B., O'Neill, L., & Guenette, F. (2006). Counselling with First Nations women: Considerations of oppression and renewal. *International Journal for the Advancement of Counselling, 28*(3), 227–240. doi:10.1007/s10447-005-9008-8

Shimokawa, K., Lambert, M.J., & Smart, D.W. (2010). Enhancing treatment outcome of patients at risk of treatment failure: Meta-analytic and mega-analytic review of a psychotherapy quality assurance system. *Journal of Consulting and Clinical Psychology, 78*(3), 298–311. doi:10.1037/a0019247

Simard, G., & Chênevert, D. (2010). Determinants organisationnels et individuels de l'emploi atypique: Le dossier du cumul d'emplois et du travail autonome au Canada. *Canadian Journal of Career Development, 9*, 26–33.

Sinacore, A. (2011a). Canadian counselling psychology coming of age: An overview of the special section. *Canadian Psychology, 52*(4), 245–247. doi:10.1037/a0025549

Sinacore, A. (2011b). A resounding success: The inaugural Canadian counselling psychology conference, *CPA Counsellor:Newsletter of Counselling Psychology Section of the Canadian Psychological Association*, 2–4. http://www.cpa.ca/docs/file/Sections/Counselling/CPA_CounsellingNewsletter_Spring2011.pdf

Sinacore, A.L. (2011c). *Utilizing international, multicultural and social justice perspectives in developing gender equity educational initiatives.*

Conference proceedings from the International Conference on the Comparison and Development of Gender Equity Education, pp. 61–72. Taipei, Taiwan.

Sinacore, A.L., & Boatwright, K. (2005). The feminist classroom: Feminist strategies and student responses. In C.Z. Enns & A.L. Sinacore (Eds.), *Teaching and social justice: Integrating multicultural and feminist theories in the classroom* (pp. 109–124). Washington, D C: American Psychological Association Press.

Sinacore, A., Borgen, B., Daniluk, D., Kassan, A., Long, B.C., & Nicol, J.J. (2011). Canadian counselling psychologists' contributions to applied psychology. *Canadian Psychology, 5*(4), 276–288. doi:10.1037/a0025549

Sinacore, A.L., & Enns, C. (2005a). Multicultural and feminist literatures: Themes, dimensions, and variations. In C. Enns & A.L. Sinacore (Eds.), *Teaching and social justice: Integrating multicultural and feminist theories in the classroom* (pp. 99–107). Washington, D C: American Psychological Association. doi:10.1037/10929-006

Sinacore, A.L., & Enns, C.Z. (2005b). Diversity feminisms: Postmodern, women-of-color, antiracist, lesbian, third-wave, and global perspectives. In C.Z. Enns & A.L. Sinacore (Eds.), *Teaching and social justice: Integrating multicultural and feminist theories in the classroom* (pp. 41–68). Washington, D C: American Psychological Association.

Sinacore, A.L., Healy, P.A., & Justin, M. (2002). A qualitative analysis of the experiences of feminist psychology educators: The classroom. *Feminism and Psychology, 12*(3), 339–362.

Sinacore, A., & Kassan, A. (2011). Utilizing community portfolios in teaching for social justice. *Teaching of Psychology, 38,* 262–264.

Sinacore, A.L., & Lerner, S. (2013). The cultural and educational transitioning of first generation immigrant undergraduate students in Quebec, Canada. *International Journal for Educational and Vocational Guidance, 13,* 67–85. doi:10.1007/s10775-013-9238-y

Sinacore, A.L., Mikhail, A.M., Kassan, A., & Lerner, S. (2009). Cultural transition of Jewish immigrants: Education, employment, and integration. *International Journal for Educational and Vocational Guidance, 9,* 157–176. doi:10.1007/s10775-009-9166-z

Sinacore, A.L., Park-Saltzman, J., Mikhail, A.M., & Wada, K. (2011). Falling through the cracks: Academic and career challenges faced by immigrant graduate students. *Canadian Journal of Counselling and Psychotherapy, 45*(2), 168–187. http://www.cjc-rcc.ucalgary.ca/cjc/index.php/rcc/article/view/963

Sinacore, A.L., Titus, J., & Hofman, S. (2013). The role of relationships in the cultural transitioning of immigrant women. *Women and Therapy*, 36, 235–251.

Sinacore-Guinn, A.L. (1995a). Counselling psychology: A look at the question of identity, roles, and the future. *McGill Journal of Education*, 30(3), 257–295.

Sinacore-Guinn, A.L. (1995b). The diagnostic window: Culture-gender-sensitive diagnosis and training. *Counselor Education and Supervision*, 35(1), 18–31.

Sinclair, C., Simon, N.P., & Pettifor, J.L. (1996). The history of ethical codes and licensure. In L.J. Bass, S.T. DeMers, J.R.P. Ogloff, C. Peterson, J.L. Pettifor, R.P. Reaves, … R.M. Tipton, *Professional conduct and discipline in psychology*. Washington, DC: American Psychological Association & Association of State and Provincial Psychology Boards.

Sinding, C., Barnoff, L., & Grassau, P. (2004). Homophobia and heterosexism in cancer care: The experiences of lesbians. *CJNR: Canadian Journal of Nursing Research*, 36(4), 170–188.

Slijper, F.M.E., Drop, S.L.S., Molenaar, J.C., & de Muinck Keizer-Schrama, S.M.P.F. (2000). Long-term psychological evaluation of intersex children: Reply. *Archives of Sexual Behavior*, 29(1), 119–121.

Slomp, M.K., Bernes, K.B., & Magnussen, K.C. (2011). Evaluating the impact of career development services in Canada: The perceptions of managers and program administrators. *Canadian Journal of Career Development*, 10, 5–12.

Smith, J. (1985). Treatment of ego-dystonic homosexuality: Individual and group psychotherapies. *Journal of the American Academy of Psychoanalysis*, 13(3), 399–412.

Smith, J.D., Cousins, J.B., & Stewart, R. (2005). Antibullying interventions in schools: Ingredients of effective programs. *Canadian Journal of Education*, 28(4), 739–762. doi:10.2307/4126453

Smith, L.T. (1999). *Decolonizing methodologies: Research and Indigenous peoples*. New York: Zed Books.

Smith, L. (2005). Psychotherapy, classism, and the poor: Conspicuous by their absence. *American Psychologist*, 60, 687–696.

Social Sciences and Humanities Research Council (2012). Competition statistics. http://www.sshrc-crsh.gc.ca/results-resultats/stats-statistiques/index-eng.aspx

Sparks, J.A., Kisler, T.S., Adams, J.F., & Blumen, D.G. (2011). Teaching accountability: Using client feedback to train effective family therapists. *Journal of Marital and Family Therapy*, 37, 1–16. doi:10.1111/j.1752-0606.2011.00224.x

Spitzer, R.L. (2003). Can some gay men and lesbians change their sexual orientation? 200 participants reporting a change from homosexual to heterosexual orientation. *Archives of Sexual Behavior, 32*(5), 403–417.

Stanley, J.L., Bartholomew, K., & Oram, D. (2004). Gay and bisexual men's age-discrepant childhood sexual experiences. *Journal of Sex Research, 41*(4), 381–389.

Statistics Canada. (2003a). Ethnic diversity survey: Portrait of a multi-cultural society. http://www.statcan.ca/English/freepub/89-593-XIE/free.htm

Statistics Canada. (2003b). *2001 Census: analysis series. Education in Canada: Raising the standard.* Retrieved on 12 March 2008 from http://www12.statcan.ca/english/census01/Products/Analytic/companion/educ/pdf/96F0030XIE2001012.pdf

Statistics Canada. (2006). *Persons in low income before tax by prevalence in percent (2000–2004)* (Catalogue no. 75-202-X). Ottawa: Author.

Statistics Canada. (2007a). *Ethnic diversity and immigration.* http://www41.statcan.ca/2007/30000/ceb30000_000_e.htm

Statistics Canada. (2007b). *Immigration in Canada: A portrait of the foreign-born population, 2006 census.* (Catalogue No. 97-557-XIE). http://www12.statcan.ca/census-recensement/2006/as-sa/97-557/pdf/97-557XIE2006001.pdf

Statistics Canada. (2008). *Canadian demographics at a glance.* (Catologue no. 91-003-X). http://www.statcan.gc.ca/pub/91-003-x/91-003-x2007001-eng.pdf

Statistics Canada. (2010, March 10). *Study: Projections of the diversity of the Canadian population from 2006–2031: The Statistics Canada Daily.* http://www.statcan.gc.ca/daily-quotidien/100309/dq100309a-eng.htm

Statistics Canada. (2011a). *Population by year, by province and territory.* http://www.statcan.gc.ca/tables-tableaux/sum-som/l01/cst01/demo02a-eng.htm

Statistics Canada. (2011b). *Population growth: Canada, provinces and territories, 2010.* (Catalogue No. 91-209-X). http://www.statcan.gc.ca/pub/91-209x/2011001/article/11508-eng.pdf

Stead, G.B. (2004). Culture and career psychology: A social construction-ist perspective. *Journal of Vocational Behavior, 64*(3), 389–406. doi: 10.1016/j.jvb.2003.12.006

Stead, G.B., Perry, J.C., Munka, L.M., Bonnett, H.R., Shiban, A.P., & Care, E. (2012). Qualitative research in career development: Content analysis from 1990 to 2009. *International Journal of Educational and Vocational Guidance, 12,* 105–122. doi:10.1007/s10775-011-9196-1

Steele, L.S., Ross, L.E., Dobinson, C., Veldhuizen, S., & Tinmouth, J.M. (2009). Women's sexual orientation and health: Results from a Canadian population-based survey. *Women & Health, 49*(5), 353–367.

Steele, L.S., Tinmouth, J.M., & Lu, A. (2006). Regular health care use by lesbians: A path analysis of predictive factors. *Family Practice, 23*(6), 631–636.

Steiner, B.W. (1982). From Sappho to Sand: Historical perspective on crossdressing and cross gender. *The Canadian Journal of Psychiatry/ La Revue canadienne de psychiatrie, 26*(7), 502–506.

Stermac, L., Brazeau, P., & Kelly, T. (2008a). Traumatic stress and mental health among war zone immigrants in Toronto. *International Journal of Health Promotion and Education, 46,* 57–64. http://findarticles.com/p/ articles/mi_6793/is_2_46/ai_n31414729/

Stermac, L., Brazeau, P., & Martin, K. (2008b). Educational experiences and mental health among war-zone immigrants in Toronto. *Education Research and Reviews, 3,* 370–377. http://www.academicjournals.org/ err/PDF/pdf%202008/Dec/Stermac%20et%20al.pdf

Stermac, L., Elgie, S., Clarke, A., & Dunlap, H. (2012). Academic experiences of war-zone students in Canada. *Journal of Youth Studies, 15,* 311–328. doi:10.1080/13676261.2011.643235

Stermac, L., Elgie, S., Dunlap, H., & Kelly, T. (2010). Educational experiences and achievements of war-zone immigrant students in Canada. *Vulnerable Children and Youth Studies, 5*(2), 97–107. doi:10.1080/17450120903440399

Stewart, J.B. (2003). Using portfolios to direct workplace learning. *Canadian Journal of Career Development, 2,* 27–32.

Stewart, J. (2010). Assessment from a contextual perspective. In N. Arthur & S. Collins (Eds.), *Culture-infused counselling: Celebrating the Canadian mosaic* (2nd ed., pp. 189–208). Calgary, AB: Counselling Concepts.

Stewart, M., Reutter, L., Letourneau, N., Makwarimba, E., & Hugler, K. (2010). Supporting homeless youth: Perspectives and preferences, *Journal of Poverty, 14*(2), 145–165.

Stewart, R.E., & Chambless, D.L. (2010). Interesting practitioners in training in empirically supported treatments: Research reviews versus case studies. *Journal of Clinical Psychology, 66*(1), 73–95. doi:10.1002/ Jclp.20630

Stewart, S. (2006). Personal communication with Elise Doctor of Yellowknife Dene First Nation.

Stewart, S.L. (2008). Promoting Indigenous mental health: Cultural perspectives on healing from Native counsellors in Canada. *International*

Journal of Health Promotion & Education, 46(2), 49–56. doi:10.1080/14635240.2008.10708129

Stewart, S. (2009a). Sharing narratives on an Indigenous academic's evolution: A personal experience of cultural mental health stories as research. *First Peoples Child & Family Review, 4*(1), 57–65.

Stewart, S. (2009b). Indigenous family therapy: constructivist perspectives. *First Peoples Child & Family Review, 4*(2), 99–118.

Stewart, S. (2011). Indigenous research methods and healing. *International Journal of Health Promotion and Education, 12*(4), 15–28.

Stewart, S., Riecken, T., Scott, T., Tanaka, M., & Riecken, J. (2008). Expanding health literacy. *Journal of Health Psychology, 13*(2), 180–189. doi:10.1177/1359105307086709

Stone, S.D. (Ed.). (1990). *Lesbians in Canada.* Toronto: Between the Lines Press.

Storm, H. (1972). *Seven arrows. New York:* Harper and Row.

Stricker, G., & Trierweiler, J.J. (1995). The local clinical scientist: A bridge between science and practice. *American Psychologist, 50*, 995–1002. doi:10.1037/0003-066X.50.12.995

Strong, T. (2002). Dialogue in therapy's "borderzone." *Journal of Constructivist Psychology, 15*, 245–262.

Strong, T. (2012). Talking about the D S M-V. *The International Journal of Narrative Therapy and Community Work, 2*, 54–63.

Strong, T., Busch, R., & Couture, S. (2008). Conversational evidence in therapeutic dialogue. *Journal of Marital & Family Therapy, 34*, 388–405. doi:10.1111/j.1752-0606.2008.00079.x

Strong, T., Gaete, J., Sametband, I.N., French, J., & Eeson, J. (2012). Counsellors respond to the D S M-I V-T R. *Canadian Journal of Counselling and Psychotherapy, 46*(2), 85–106.

Strong, T., & Massfeller, H.F. (2010). Negotiating post-consultation homework tasks between counselors and clients. *International Journal for the Advancement of Counselling, 32*, 14–30. doi:10.1007/s10447-009-9085-1

Strong, T., & Zeman, D. (2005). 'Othering' and 'selving' in therapeutic dialogue. *European Journal of Psychotherapy, Counselling and Health, 7*(4), 245–261.

Suarez-Orozco, C., Pimentel, A., & Martin, M. (2009). The significance of relationships: Academic engagement and achievement among newcomer immigrant youth. *Teachers College Record, 111*, 712–749.

Sue, D.W., Arredondo, P., & McDavis, R.J. (1992). Multicultural counseling competencies and standards: A call to the profession. *Journal of Counseling Development, 70*, 477–486.

Sue, D.W., Bernier, J.B., Durran, M., Feinberg, L., Pedersen, P., Smith, E., Vasquez-Nuttall, E. (1982). Cross-cultural counseling competencies. *The Counseling Psychologist, 10*, 45–52. doi:10.1177/0011000082102008

Sue, D.W., Carter, R.T., Casas, J.M., Fouad, N.A., Ivey, A.E., Jensen, M., ... Vasquez-Nuttall, E. (1998). *Multicultural counseling competencies: Individual and organizational development*. Thousand Oaks, CA: Sage.

Sue, D.W., Ivey, A.E., & Pedersen, P.B. (1996). *A theory of multicultural counseling and therapy*. Pacific Grove, CA: Brooks/Cole.

Sue, D.W., & Sue, D. (1990). *Counseling the culturally different*. New York: John Wiley & Sons.

Sue, D. W., & Sue, D. (2008). *Counseling the culturally diverse: Theory and practice* (5th ed.). New York: Wiley.

Sullivan, M., Kessler, L., LeClair, J., Stolee, P., & Whitney, B. (2004). Defining best practices for specialty geriatric mental health outreach services: Lessons for implementing mental health reform. *Canadian Journal of Psychiatry, 49*(7), 458–466.

Sullivan, R., & Harrington, M. (2009). The politics and ethics of same-sex adoption. *Journal of GLBT Family Studies, 5*(3), 235–246.

Sulzer-Azaroff, B., & Mayer, G.R. (1991). *Behavior analysis for lasting change*. Fort Worth, TX: Holt, Rinhart and Winston.

Summers, R.J. (1991). Determinants of the acceptance of co-workers with AIDS. *The Journal of Social Psychology, 131*(4), 577–578.

Sundet, R. (2012). Therapist perspectives on the use of feedback on process and outcome: Patient-focused research in practice. *Canadian Psychology – Psychologie Canadienne, 53*, 122–130. doi:10.1037/a0027776

Sundin, E.C., & Ögren, M.L. (2011). Implications of an individualized admission selection procedure for psychotherapy training in professional programs in psychology. *The Clinical Supervisor, 30*, 36–52. doi:10.1080/07325223.2011.564967

Super, D.E. (1990). A life-span, life-space approach to career development. In D. Brown & L. Brooks (Eds.), *Career choice and development: Applying contemporary theories to practice* (2nd ed., pp. 197–261). San Francisco, CA: Jossey-Bass.

Super, D.E., & Knasel, E.G. (1979). *Development of a model, specifications, and sample items for measuring career adaptability (vocational maturity) in young blue-collar workers*. Cambridge, UK: National Institute for Career Education and Counselling; and Ottawa: Canada Employment and Immigration.

Suto, M. (2009). Compromised careers: The occupational transition of immigration and resettlement. *Work: A Journal of Prevention,*

Assessment and Rehabilitation, 32, 417–429. doi:10.3233/WOR-2009-0853

Swarbrick, M. (2006). A wellness approach. *Psychiatric Rehabilitation Journal, 29,* 311–314. doi:10.2975/29.2006.311.314

Swarbrick, M., & Moosvi, K.V. (2010). Wellness: A practice for our lives and work. *Journal of Psychosocial Nursing & Mental Health Services, 7,* 2–3.

Swift, K.J., & Callahan, M. (2009). *At risk: Social justice in child welfare and other human services.* Toronto: University of Toronto Press.

Szymanski, D. (2005). A feminist approach to working with internalized heterosexism in lesbians. *Journal of College Counseling, 8,* 74–85.

Tardif, C. Y., & Geva, E. (2006). The link between acculturation disparity and conflict among Chinese Canadian immigrant mother-adolescent dyads. *Journal of Cross-Cultural Psychology, 37*(2), 191–211.

Tashakkori, A., & Teddlie, C. (Eds.). (2003). *Handbook of mixed methods in social & behavioral research.* Thousand Oaks, CA: Sage.

Tasker, S. (2003). Acquired brain injury: Meaning-making out of lived trauma. *Illness, Crisis, & Loss, 11,* 337–349. doi:10.1177/1054137303256585

Tatla, S. (2010, 10 March). Diversity will change the face of the workplace. *Financial Post.* http://www.financialpost.com/careers/story.html?id=2697455

Taylor, C., Peter, T., McMinn, T.L., Elliott, T., Beldom, S., Ferry, A., ... Schachter, K. (2011). *Every class in every school: The first national climate survey on homophobia, biphobia, and transphobia in Canadian schools.* Final report. Toronto: Egale Canada Human Rights Trust.

Taylor, J.M., & Niemeyer, G.J. (2009). Graduate school mentoring in clinical, counselling, and experimental academic training programs: An exploratory study. *Counselling Psychology Quarterly, 22,* 257–266. **doi:**10.1080/09515070903157289

Teddlie, C., & Tashakkori, A. (2003). Major issues and controversies in the use of mixed methods in the social and behavioral sciences. In A. Tashakkori & C. Teddlie (Eds.), *Handbook of mixed methods in social & behavioral research* (pp. 3–50). Thousand Oaks, CA: Sage.

Tedeschi, R.G., & Calhoun, L.G. (1996). The posttraumatic growth inventory: Measuring the positive legacy of trauma. *Journal of Traumatic Stress, 9*(3), 455–471.

Tellides-Jaffee, C., Fitzpatrick, M., Drapeau, M., Bracewell, M., Chamodraka, M., & Marini, N. (2012). The manifestation of transference during early psychotherapy sessions: Exploring an alternate data source for therapist narratives in transference research. *Counselling and Psychotherapy Research: Linking Research with Practice, 12,* 1–10. doi: 10.1080/14733145.2011.638081

Tews, L., & Merali, N. (2008). Helping Chinese parents understand and support children with learning disabilities. *Professional Psychology: Research and Practice, 39,* 137–144. doi:10.1037/0735-7028.39.2.137

Thannhauser, J.E. (2009). Grief-peer dynamics: Understanding experiences with pediatric multiple sclerosis. *Qualitative Health Research, 19,* 766–777. doi:10.1177/1049732309334859

Thannhauser, J.E., Mah, J.K., & Metz, L.M. (2009). Adherence of adolescents to multiple sclerosis disease-modifying therapy. *Pediatric Neurology, 41,* 119–123. doi:10.1016/j.pediatrneurol.2009.03.004

Thunderbird, S. (2005). *Medicine wheel teachings.* Retrieved 15 June 2005 from http://www.shannonthunderbird.com/medicine_wheel_teachings.htm

Tieman, G. (2012, April 10). NDP transgender rights proposal returns to Parliament; critics dub it 'bathroom bill.' *National Post.* Retrieved on 17 April 2012 from http://news.nationalpost.com/2012/04/10/ndp-transgender-rights-proposal-returns-to-parliament-critics-dub-it-bathroom-bill/

Toporek, R.L., Gerstein, L., Fouad, N.A., Roysircar, G., & Israel, T. (Eds.). (2006). *Handbook for social justice in counseling psychology: Leadership, vision, & action.* Thousand Oaks, CA: Sage.

Toporek, R.L., & McNally, C.J. (2006). Social justice training in counselling psychology. In R.L. Toporek, L. Gerstein, N.A. Fouad, G. Roysircar, & T. Israel (Eds.), *Handbook for social justice in counseling psychology: Leadership, vision, & action* (pp. 37–43). Thousand Oaks, CA: Sage.

Tremblay, J. (1994a). Dossier: Deux pionniers. *L'Orientation, 7*(2), 17–21.

Tremblay, J. (1994b). Notre histoire: Naissance d'une corporation. *L'Orientation, 7*(3), 21–23.

Trevor-Roberts, E. (2006). Are you sure? The role of uncertainty in career. *Journal of Employment Counseling, 43,* 98–116. doi:10.1002/j.2161-1920.2006.tb00010.x

Trierweiler, S.J., & Stricker, G. (1998). The local clinical scientist. In S.J. Trierweiler & G. Stricker (Eds.), *The scientific practice of professional psychology.* New York: Plenum.

Trierweiler, S.J., Stricker, G., & Peterson, R.L. (2010). The research and evaluation competency: The local clinical scientist – Review, current status, future directions. In M.B. Kenkel & R.L. Peterson (Eds.), *Competency-based education for professional psychology* (pp. 125–141).

Washington, DC: American Psychological Association. doi:10.1037/10103-012

Trimble, J.E., & Thurman, J.P. (2002). Ethnocultural considerations and strategies for providing counselling services to native American Indians. In P. Pedersen, J. Draguns, W. Lonner, and J. Trimble (Eds.), *Counselling across cultures* (5th ed., pp. 53–91). Thousand Oaks, CA: Sage.

Twinn, S. (2003). Status of mixed methods research in nursing. In A. Tashakkori & C. Teddlie (Eds.), *Handbook of mixed methods in social & behavioral research* (pp. 541–556). Thousand Oaks, CA: Sage.

Tyron, G.S., & Winograd, G. (2011). Goal consensus and collaboration. In J.C. Norcross (Ed.), *Psychotherapy relationships that work* (2nd ed., pp. 109–129). New York: Oxford University Press.

Uhlemann, M., Lee, D.Y., & Hiebert, B. (1988). Self-talk of counsellor trainees: A preliminary report. *Canadian Journal of Counselling, 22,* 73–79.

Ungerleider, C.S. (1992). Immigration, multiculturalism, and citizenship: The development of the Canadian social justice infrastructure. *Canadian Ethnic Studies / Etudes ethniques au Canada, 24*(3), 7–22.

Vacha-Haase, T., Davenport, D.S., & Kerewsky, S.D. (2004). Problematic students: gatekeeping practices of academic professional psychology programs. *Professional Psychology: Research and Practice, 35,* 115–122. doi:10.1037/0735-7028.35.2.115

Valetta, R. (2006). The ins and outs of poverty in advanced economies: Poverty dynamics in Canada, Germany, Great Britain, and the United States. *Review of Income and Wealth, 52,* 261–284.

Vandenberghe, C. (2009). Organizational commitments. In H.J. Klein, T.E. Becker, & J.P. Meyer (Eds.), *Commitment in organizations: Accumulated wisdom and new directions* (pp. 99–135). New York: Routledge.

Van Vliet, K.J. (2008). Shame and resilience in adulthood: A grounded theory study. *Journal of Counseling Psychology, 55*(2), 233–245. doi:10.1037/0022-0167.55.2.233

Van Vliet, K.J. (2010). Shame and avoidance in trauma. In E. Martz (Ed.), *Trauma rehabilitation after war and conflict: Community and individual perspectives* (pp. 247–264). New York: Springer.

Van Vliet, K.J., & Kalnins, G.R.C. (2011). A compassion-focused approach to nonsuicidal self-injury. *Journal of Mental Health Counseling, 33*(4), 295–311.

Vasconcellos, D. (2003). Approche clinique aupres d'hommes homosexuels seropositifs au VIH. [Clinical approach with HIV positive homosexual men.] *Revue Quebecoise de Psychologie, 24*(2), 31–42.

Veilleux, A.D. (2008, May). *L'accompagnement et la (re)connaissance de l'autre: le caractère social du counseling par la question de l'hétérocentrisme.* Symposium international, Éducation et Counseling: Confluences et confrontations dans les champs depratiques de formation. M.D. Boivin & J. Descarpentries (Eds.), au Congrès de l'Association francophone pour le savoir (ACFAS), Québec.

Verhoevan, M., Orianne, J.F., & Dupriez, V. (2007). Vers des politiques d'éducation "capacitantes"? *Formation et Emploi. Revue française de sciences sociales, 98,* 93–107.

Vicary, D., & Bishop, B. (2005). Western psychotherapeutic practice: Engaging Aboriginal people in culturally appropriate and respectful ways. *Australian Psychologist, 40,* 8–19.

Vilain, E.J.N. (2008). Genetics of sexual development and differentiation. In D.L. Rowland & L. Incrocci (Eds.), *Handbook of sexual and gender identity disorders* (pp. 329–353). Hoboken, NJ: John Wiley & Sons.

Von Bertalanffy, L. (1968). *General system theory: Foundations, development, applications.* New York: George Braziller.

Vondracek, F.W., & Porfeli, E.J. (2008). Social contexts for career guidance throughout the world. Developmental-contextual perspectives on career across the lifespan. In J.A. Athanasou & R. Van Esbroeck (Eds.), *International handbook of career guidance* (pp. 209–225). New York: Springer.

Vuorinen, R., & Watts, T. (2010). *Lifelong guidance policies: Work in progress.* Jyväskylä, Finland: The European lifelong guidance policy network (ELGPN). http://elgpn.eu

Waldram, J. (2004). *Revenge of the Windigo: The construction of the mind and mental health of North American Aboriginal peoples.* Toronto: University of Toronto Press.

Waldram, J. (2008). The narrative challenge to cognitive behavioral treatment of sexual offenders. *Culture, Medicine and Psychiatry, 32,* 421–439.

Warner, T. (2002). *Never going back: A history of queer activism in Canada.* Toronto: University of Toronto Press.

Waszak, C., & Sines, M.C. (2003). Mixed methods in psychological research. In A. Tashakkori & C. Teddlie (Eds.), *Handbook of mixed methods in social & behavioral research* (pp. 557–576). Thousand Oaks, CA: Sage.

Watkins, C.E., Jr. (1992). Historical influences on the use of assessment methods in counseling psychology. *Counselling Psychology Quarterly, 5*(2), 177–188.

Watson, J.C., McMullen, E.J., Prosser, M.C., & Bedard, D.L. (2011). An examination of the relationships among clients' affect regulation, in-session emotional processing, the working alliance, and outcome. *Psychotherapy Research, 21*, 86–96. doi:10.1080/10503307.2010.518637

Watts, A.G. (2008). Career guidance and public policy. In J.A. Athanasou and R.V. Esbroeck (Eds.), *International Handbook of Career Guidance* (pp. 341–353). New York: Springer.

Watts, A.G., Sultana, R.G., & McCarthy, J. (2010). The involvement of the European Union in career guidance policy: A brief history. *International Journal for Educational and Vocational Guidance, 10*, 89–107.

Waugh, T. (2006). *The romance of transgression in Canada: Queering sexualities, nations, cinemas.* Montreal and Kingston: McGill-Queen's University Press.

Weiss, J.A. (2012). Mental health care for Canadians with developmental disabilities. *Canadian Psychology, 53*(1), 67–69. doi:10.1037/a0026127

Weiss, J.A., Lunsky, Y., & Morin, D. (2010). Psychology graduate student training in developmental disability: A Canadian survey. *Canadian Psychology / Psychologie Canadienne, 51*, 177–184. doi:10.1037/a0019733

Westwood, M.J. (2009). The Veterans' Transition Program: Therapeutic enactment in action. *Educational Insights, 13*(2). http://www.ccfi.educ.ubc.ca/publication/insights/v13no2/articles/westwood/index.html

Westwood, M., & Black, T. (2012). Introduction to the special issue of the Canadian Journal of Counselling and Psychotherapy. *Canadian Journal of Counselling and Psychotherapy, 46*(4), 285–291.

Westwood, M.J., & Ishiyama, F.I. (1991). Challenges in counseling immigrant clients: Understanding intercultural barriers to career adjustment. *Journal of Employment Counseling, 28*, 130–143.

Westwood, M., Kuhl, D., & Shields, D. (2013). Counseling active military clients: Multicultural competence, challenges, and opportunities. In C. Lee (Ed.), *Multicultural issues in counseling: New approaches to diversity* (4th ed., pp. 275–284). Alexandria, VA: American Counseling Association.

Westwood, M.J., Mak, A., Barker, M., & Ishiyama, F.I. (2000). Group procedures and applications for developing sociocultural competencies among immigrants. *International Journal for the Advancement of Counselling, 22*, 317–330. doi:10.1023/A:1005633303702

Westwood, M.J., McLean, H., Cave, D., Borgen, W., & Slakov, P. (2010). Coming home: A group-based approach for assisting military veterans in transition. *Journal for Specialists in Group Work, 35*(1), 44–68. doi:10.1080/01933920903466059

Westwood, M.J.,& Wilensky, P. (2005). *Therapeutic enactment: Restoring vitality through trauma repair in groups*. Vancouver, BC: Group Action.

Whipple, J.L., & Lambert, M.J. (2011). Outcome measures for practice. *Annual Review of Clinical Psychology, 7*, 87–111. doi:10.1146/annurev-clinpsy-040510-143938

Whiston, S.C. (1996). Accountability through action research: Research methods for practitioners. *Journal of Counseling & Development, 74*, 616–623. doi:10.1002/j.1556-6676.1996.tb02301.x

White, J. (2007). Working in the midst of ideological and cultural differences: Critically reflecting on youth suicide prevention in Indigenous communities. *Canadian Journal of Counselling, 41*(4), 213–227.

Wihak, C., & Merali, N. (2003). Culturally sensitive counselling in Nunavut: Implications of Inuit traditional knowledge. *Canadian Journal of Counselling and Psychotherapy, 37*(4), 243–254.

Wihak, C., & Merali, N. (2005). A narrative study of counsellors' understandings of Inuit spirituality. *Canadian Journal of Counselling and Psychotherapy, 39*(4), 245–259.

Williams, C.C. (2001). Increasing access and building equity into mental health services: An examination of the potential for change. *Canadian Journal of Community Mental Health, 20*(1), 37–51.

Wilson, A. (2004). *Living well: Aboriginal women, cultural identity and wellness*. Winnipeg: Centre of Excellence for Prairie Women's Health.

Winter, A., & Daniluk, J. (2004). A gift from the heart: The experiences of women whose egg donations helped their sisters become mothers. *Journal of Counseling & Development, 82*, 483–495. doi:10.1002/j.1556-6678.2004.tb00337.x

Wong, G., & Bell, K. (in press). Reconceiving postpartum depression. In G. Wong (Ed.), *Moms gone mad: Motherhood and madness, oppression and resistance*. Bradford, ON: Demeter.

Wong, G., Bordua, K., Sandhurst, C., & Bell, K. (2012). Postpartum depression: An holistic and sociocultural perspective. In G. Wong (Ed.), *Moms gone mad: Motherhood and madness, oppression and resistance*. Bradford, ON: Demeter.

Wong-Wylie, G. (2007). Barriers and facilitators of reflective practice in counsellor education: Critical incidents from doctoral graduates. *Canadian Journal of Counselling, 41*, 59–76.

Wong-Wylie, G., & Jevne, R.F. (1997). Patient hope: Exploring the interactions between physicians and HIV seropositive individuals. *Qualitative Health Research, 7*(1), 32. doi:10.1177/104973239700700103

Woolsey, L. (1986). The critical incident technique: An innovative method of research. *Canadian Journal of Counselling, 20*(4), 242–254.

World Health Organization. (2012a). Definition of health. https://apps.who.int/aboutwho/en/definition.html

World Health Organization. (2012b). Good health. https://apps.who.int/aboutwho/en/good.htm

World Health Organization. (2012c). Promoting and protecting health. https://apps.who.int/aboutwho/en/promoting/promoting.htm

Wyrostok, N., & Paulson, B. (2007). Traditional healing practices among First Nations students. *Canadian Journal of Counselling and Psychotherapy, 34*(1), 14–24.

Yalnizyan, A. (2005). Canada's commitment to equality: A gender analysis of the last ten budgets, and will community voices shape public choices? *Perception 27*(3/4), 3.

Yamin, S., Rosval, L., Byrne, A., Burr, A., & Aubry, T. (2011). Evaluation of the use of the outcome questionnaire at the centre for psychological services. Ottawa: University of Ottawa.

Yohani, S.C., & Hagen, K.T. (2010). Refugee women survivors of war related sexualised violence: A multicultural framework for service provision in resettlement countries. *Intervention: International Journal of Mental Health, Psychosocial Work & Counselling in Areas of Armed Conflict, 8,* 207–222. doi:10.1097/WTF.0b013e328341665c

Yohani, S.C., & Larsen, D.J. (2009). Hope lives in the heart: Refugee and immigrant children's perceptions of hope and hope-engendering sources during early years of adjustment. *Canadian Journal of Counselling, 43*(4), 246–264.

Yohani, S., & Larsen, D. (2012). The cultivation of hope in trauma-focused counselling. In R.A. McMackin, T.M. Keane, E. Newman, & J.M. Fogler (Eds.), *Toward an integrated approach to trauma focused therapy: Placing evidence-based interventions in an expanded psychological context* (pp.193–210). Washington, DC: American Psychological Association. doi:10.1037/13746-009

Young, R.A. (2002). Counselling psychology in Canada. Paper presented to the Symposium "International Perspectives on Counselling Psychology" at the XXV International Congress of Applied Psychology, Singapore.

Young, R.A., & Collin, A. (2000). Introduction: Framing the future of career. In A. Collin & R.A. Young (Eds.), *The future of career* (pp. 1–17). Cambridge, UK: Cambridge University Press.

Young, R.A., & Domene, J.F. (2012). Creating a research agenda in career counselling: The place of action theory. *British Journal of Guidance and Counselling, 40,* 15–30.

Young, R.A., & Lalande, V. (2011). Canadian counselling psychology: From defining moments to ways forward. *Canadian Psychology, 52,* 248–255. doi:10.1037/a0025165

Young, R.A., Marshall, S.K., & Valach, L. (2007). Making career theories more culturally sensitive: Implications for counseling. *The Career Development Quarterly, 56*(1), 4–18. doi:10.1002/j.2161-0045.2007.tb00016.x

Young, R.A., & Nicol, J.J. (2007). Counselling psychology in Canada: Advancing psychology for all. *Applied Psychology: An International Review, 56,* 20–32. doi:10.1111/j.1464-0597.2007.00273.x

Young, R.A., & Valach, L. (2004). The construction of career through goal directed action. *Journal of Vocational Behavior, 64,* 499–514. doi:16/j.jvb.2003.12.012

Young, R.A., & Valach, L. (2008). Action theory: An integrative paradigm for research and evaluation in career. In J.A. Athanasou & R. Van Esbroeck (Eds.), *International handbook of career guidance* (pp. 643–657). New York: Springer.

Young, R.A.,Valach, L., & Collin, A. (1996). A contextual explanation of career. In I. Brown & L. Brooks (Eds.), *Career choice and development* (3rd ed., pp. 477–512). San Francisco, CA: Jossey-Bass.

Young, R.A., Valach, L., & Collin, A. (2002). A contextual explanation of career. In D. Brown & Associates, *Career choice and development* (4th ed., pp. 206–250). San Francisco, CA: Jossey-Bass.

Young, R.A., Valach, L., & Domene, J.F. (2005). The action-project method in counseling psychology. *Journal of Counseling Psychology, 52,* 215–223. doi:10.1037/0022-0167.52.2.215

Young, T.K. (1988). *Health care and cultural change: The Indian experience in the central sub-arctic.* Toronto: University of Toronto Press.

Zolner, T. (2000). *The impact of culture on psychological assessment.* Unpublished doctoral dissertation. Saskatoon, SK: University of Saskatchewan.

Zolner, T. (2003). Considerations in working with persons of First Nations heritage. *Pimatziwin: A Journal of Aboriginal and Indigenous Community Health, 1,* 41–58.

Zolner, T. (2004). Is nothing sacred? The culture of psychology in a spiritual world. In W. Smythe and A. Baydala (Eds.), *Studies of how the mind publicly enfolds into Being* (pp. 265–302). Lewiston, NY: Mellen Press.

Zuccarini, D., & Karos, L. (2011). Emotionally focused therapy for gay and lesbian couples: Strong identities, strong bonds. In J.L. Furrow,

S.M. Johnson, & B.A. Bradley (Eds.), *The emotionally focused casebook: New directions in treating couples* (pp. 317–342). New York: Routledge/Taylor & Francis.

Zucker, K.J., & Blanchard, R. (1997). Transvestic fetishism: Psychopathology and theory. In D.R. Laws & W.T. O'Donohue (Eds.), *Sexual deviance: Theory, assessment, and treatment* (pp. 253–279). New York: Guilford Press.

Zucker, K.J., & Bradley, S.J. (1999). Gender identity disorder and transvestic fetishism. In S.D. Netherton, D. Holmes, & C.E. Walker (Eds.), *Child and adolescent psychological disorders: A comprehensive textbook* (pp. 367–396). New York: Oxford University Press.

Zumbo, B.D. (2009). Validity as contextualized and pragmatic explanation, and its implications for validation practice. In Robert W. Lissitz (Ed.), *The concept of validity: Revisions, new directions and applications* (pp. 65–82). Charlotte, NC: Information Age.

Zverina, M., Stam, H.J., & Babins-Wagner, R. (2011). Managing victim status in group therapy for men: A discourse analysis. *Journal of Interpersonal Violence, 26*, 2834–2855. doi:10.1177/0886260510390949

Index